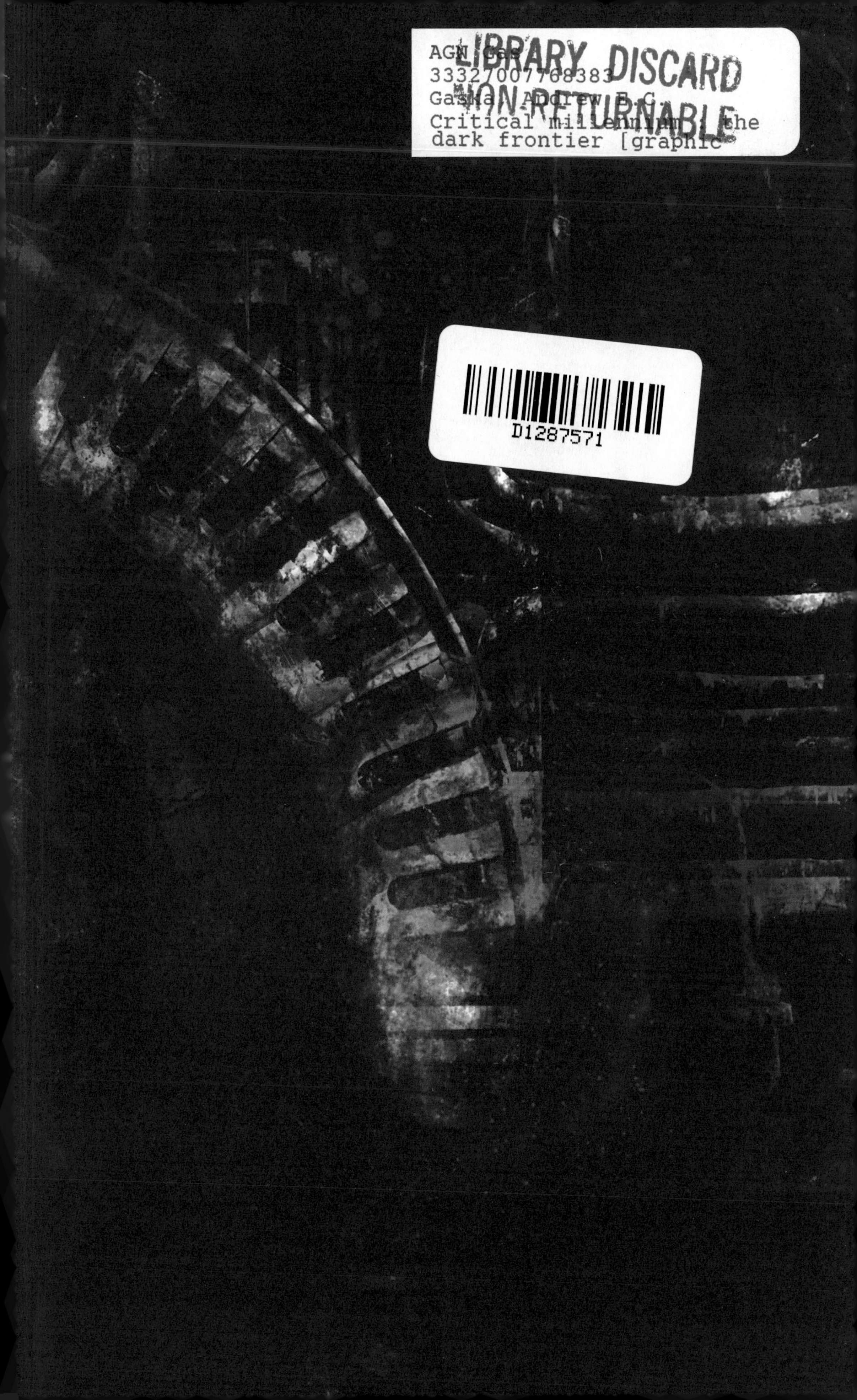

"Five major worldwide extinction events have struck at biodiversity since the origin of complex animal life some 535 million years ago. Global climate change and other causes, probably including collisions with extraterrestrial objects, were responsible for the main extinctions of the past. Right now we are in the sixth extinction, this time caused solely by humanity's transformation of the ecological landscape."

—Engraved in the floor of the Hall of Biodiversity,
Museum of Natural History, New York City

ARCHAIA ENTERTAINMENT LLC
WWW.ARCHAIA.COM

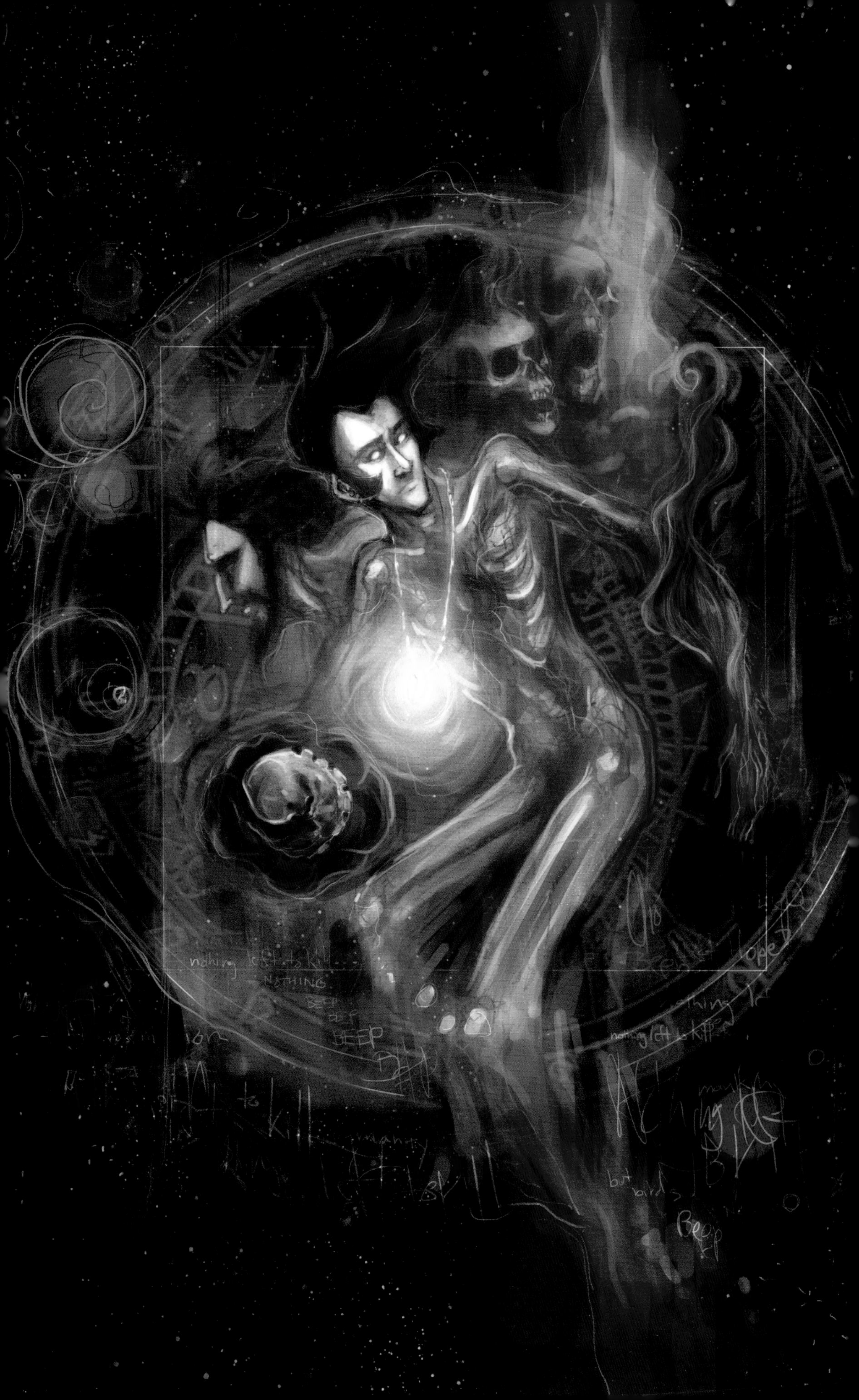
nothing left to kill...
NOTHING
BEEP
BEEP
nothing left to kill
to kill
but birds
Beep

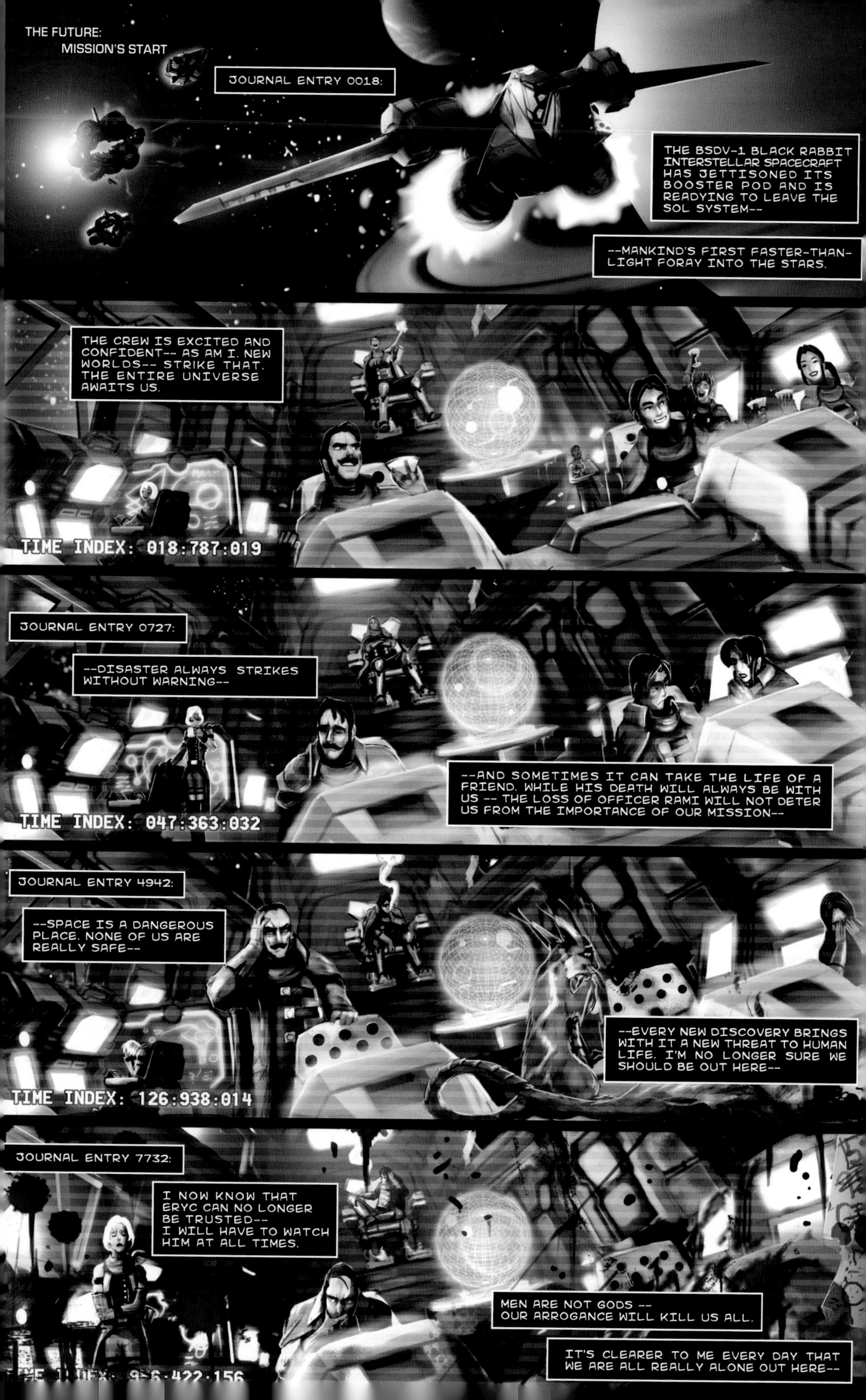
THE FUTURE:
MISSION'S START
JOURNAL ENTRY 0018:
THE BSDV-1 BLACK RABBIT INTERSTELLAR SPACECRAFT HAS JETTISONED ITS BOOSTER POD AND IS READYING TO LEAVE THE SOL SYSTEM--
--MANKIND'S FIRST FASTER-THAN-LIGHT FORAY INTO THE STARS.
THE CREW IS EXCITED AND CONFIDENT-- AS AM I. NEW WORLDS-- STRIKE THAT. THE ENTIRE UNIVERSE AWAITS US.
TIME INDEX: 018:787:019
JOURNAL ENTRY 0727:
--DISASTER ALWAYS STRIKES WITHOUT WARNING--
--AND SOMETIMES IT CAN TAKE THE LIFE OF A FRIEND. WHILE HIS DEATH WILL ALWAYS BE WITH US -- THE LOSS OF OFFICER RAMI WILL NOT DETER US FROM THE IMPORTANCE OF OUR MISSION--
TIME INDEX: 047:363:032
JOURNAL ENTRY 4942:
--SPACE IS A DANGEROUS PLACE. NONE OF US ARE REALLY SAFE--
--EVERY NEW DISCOVERY BRINGS WITH IT A NEW THREAT TO HUMAN LIFE. I'M NO LONGER SURE WE SHOULD BE OUT HERE--
TIME INDEX: 126:938:014
JOURNAL ENTRY 7732:
I NOW KNOW THAT ERYC CAN NO LONGER BE TRUSTED-- I WILL HAVE TO WATCH HIM AT ALL TIMES.
MEN ARE NOT GODS -- OUR ARROGANCE WILL KILL US ALL.
IT'S CLEARER TO ME EVERY DAY THAT WE ARE ALL REALLY ALONE OUT HERE--

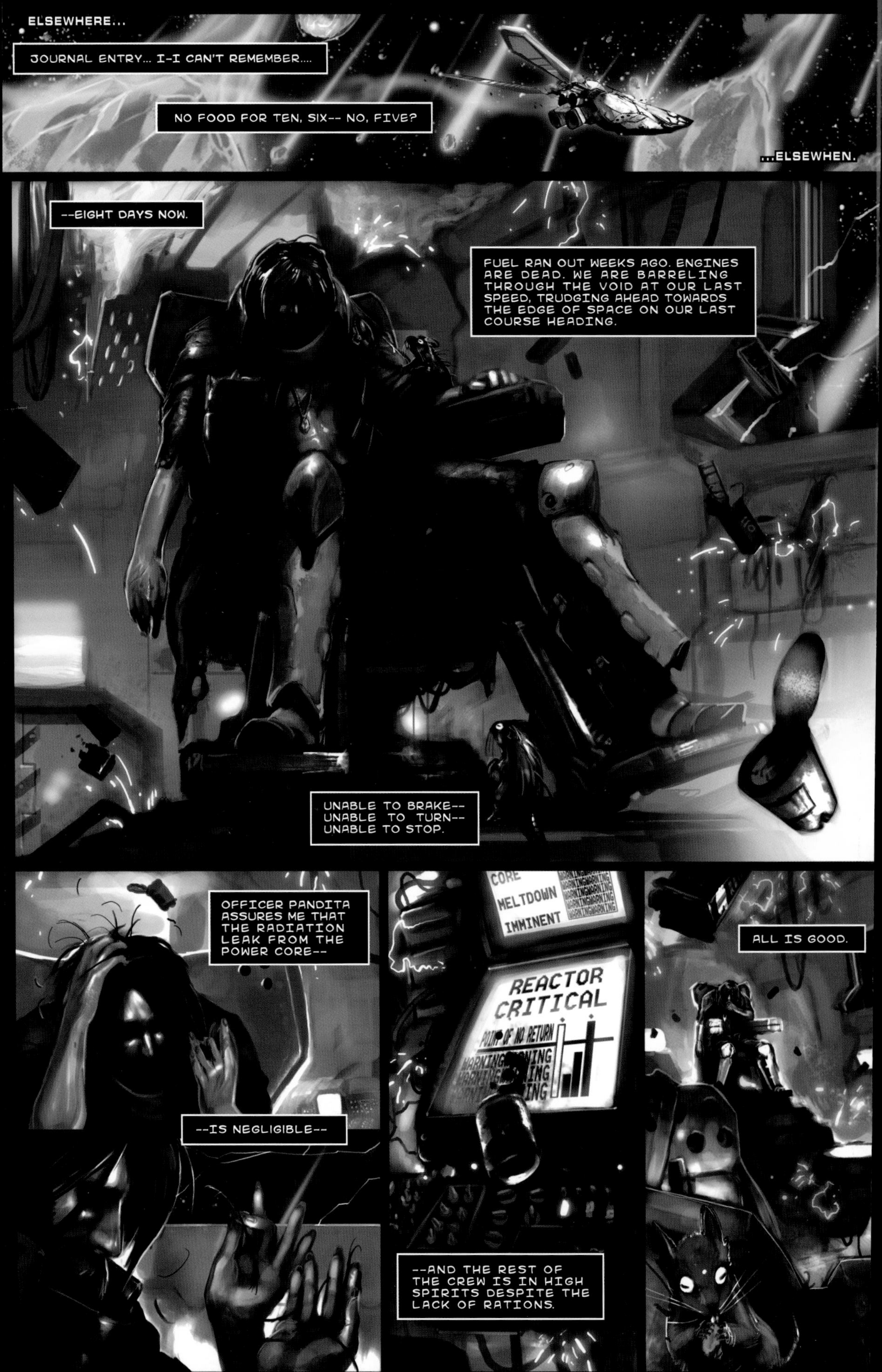
ELSEWHERE...
JOURNAL ENTRY... I-I CAN'T REMEMBER....
NO FOOD FOR TEN, SIX-- NO, FIVE?
...ELSEWHEN.
--EIGHT DAYS NOW.
FUEL RAN OUT WEEKS AGO. ENGINES ARE DEAD. WE ARE BARRELING THROUGH THE VOID AT OUR LAST SPEED, TRUDGING AHEAD TOWARDS THE EDGE OF SPACE ON OUR LAST COURSE HEADING.
UNABLE TO BRAKE-- UNABLE TO TURN-- UNABLE TO STOP.
OFFICER PANDITA ASSURES ME THAT THE RADIATION LEAK FROM THE POWER CORE--
--IS NEGLIGIBLE--
CORE MELTDOWN IMMINENT
REACTOR CRITICAL
POINT OF NO RETURN
--AND THE REST OF THE CREW IS IN HIGH SPIRITS DESPITE THE LACK OF RATIONS.
ALL IS GOOD.

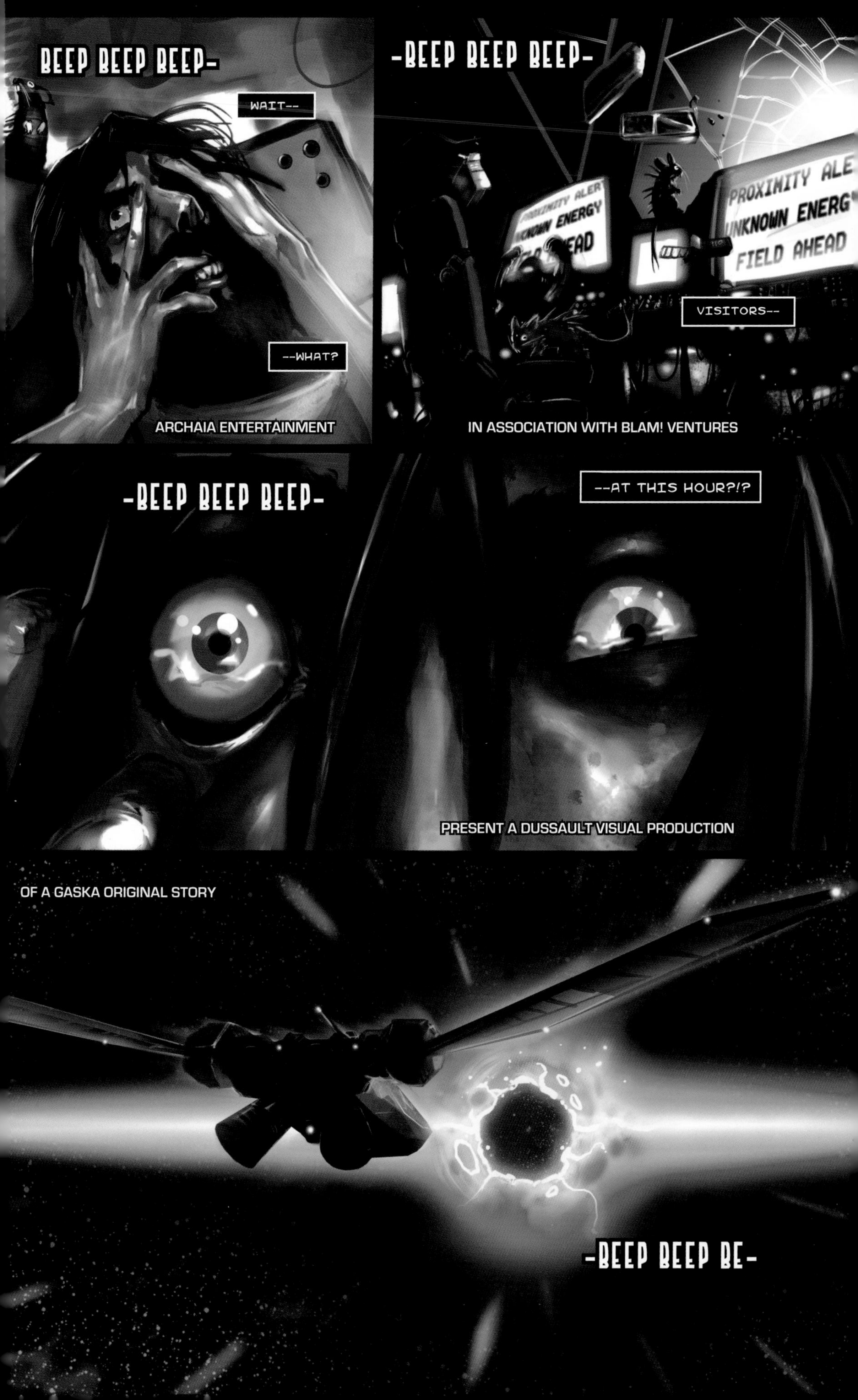
BEEP BEEP BEEP-
WAIT--
--WHAT?
ARCHAIA ENTERTAINMENT
-BEEP BEEP BEEP-
PROXIMITY ALE
UNKNOWN ENERG
FIELD AHEAD
VISITORS--
IN ASSOCIATION WITH BLAM! VENTURES
-BEEP BEEP BEEP-
--AT THIS HOUR?!?
PRESENT A DUSSAULT VISUAL PRODUCTION
OF A GASKA ORIGINAL STORY
-BEEP BEEP BE-

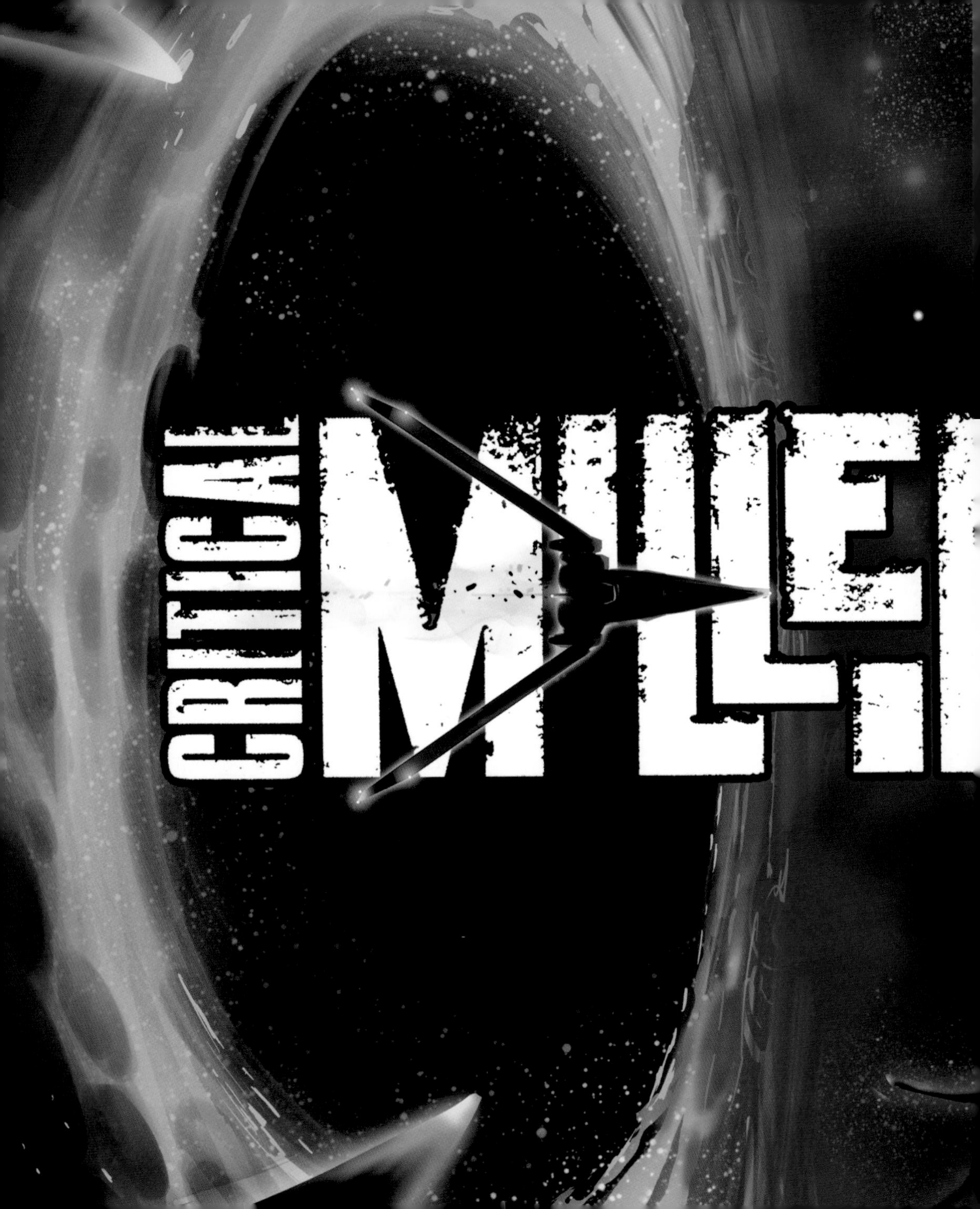
CRITICAL

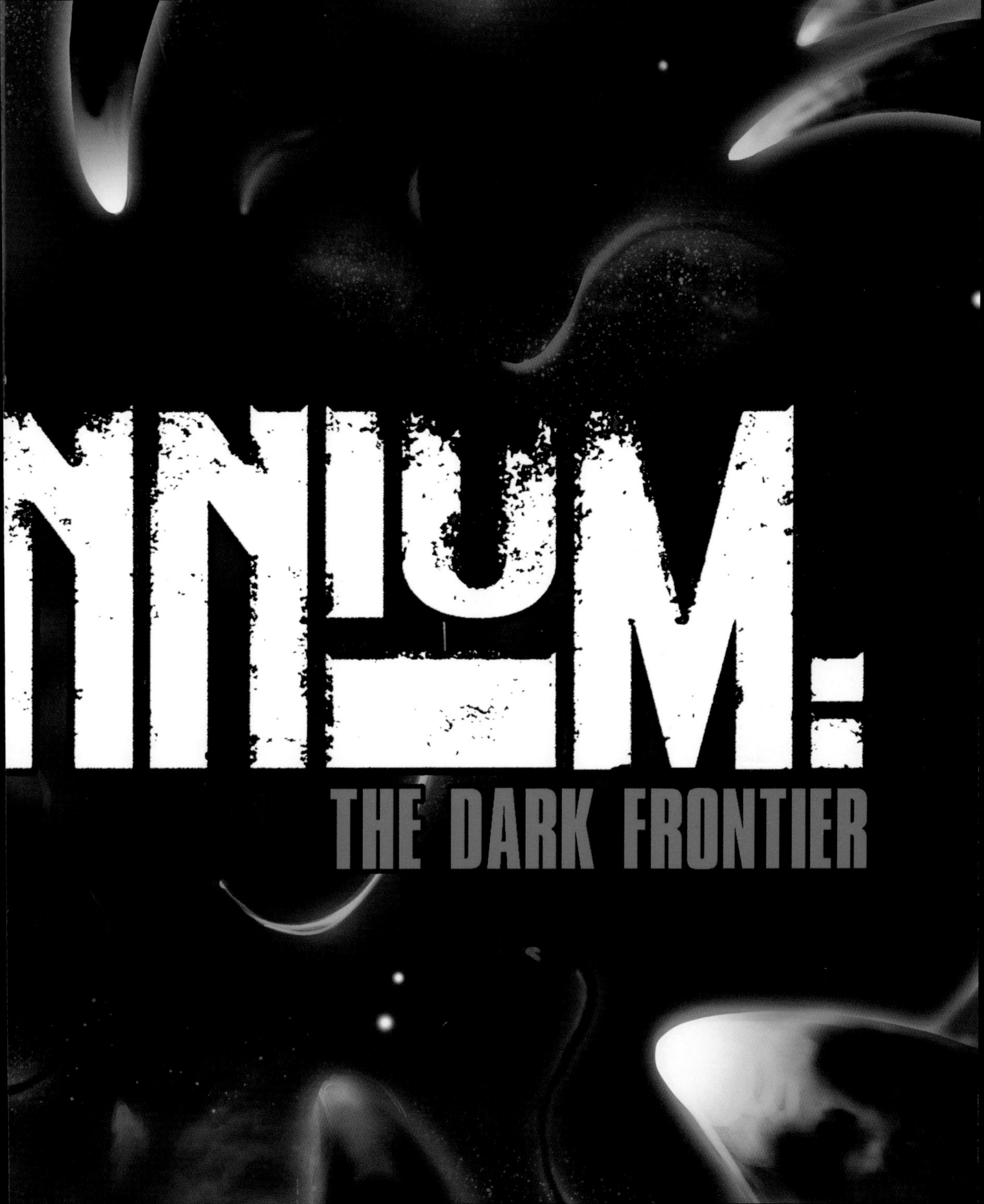
NNIUM:
THE DARK FRONTIER

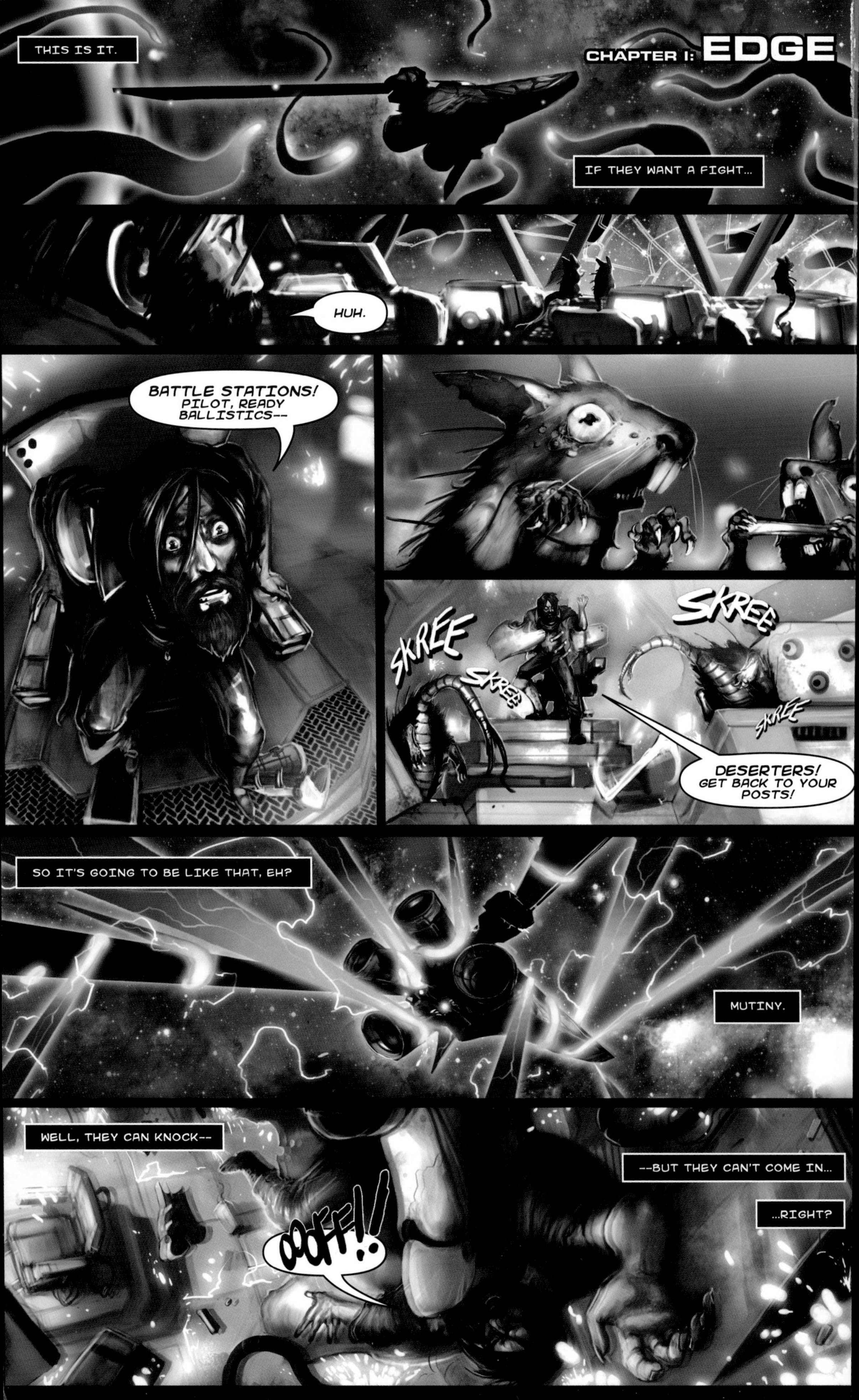

THIS IS IT.
CHAPTER 1: EDGE
IF THEY WANT A FIGHT...
HUH.
BATTLE STATIONS! PILOT, READY BALLISTICS--
SKREE
SKREE
SKREE
SKREE
DESERTERS! GET BACK TO YOUR POSTS!
SO IT'S GOING TO BE LIKE THAT, EH?
MUTINY.
WELL, THEY CAN KNOCK--
--BUT THEY CAN'T COME IN...
...RIGHT?
OOOFF!!

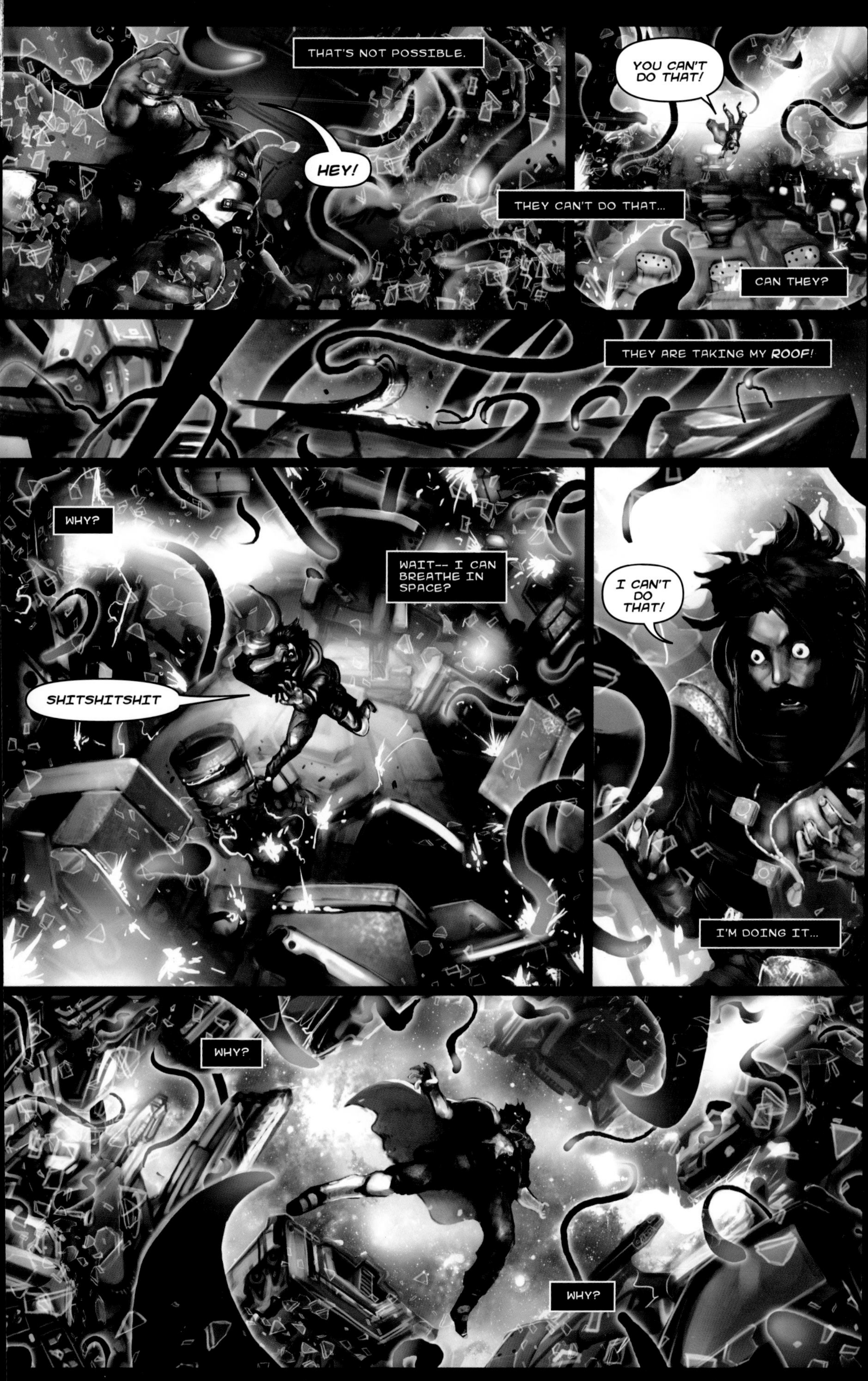
THAT'S NOT POSSIBLE.
HEY!
YOU CAN'T DO THAT!
THEY CAN'T DO THAT...
CAN THEY?
THEY ARE TAKING MY ROOF!
WHY?
WAIT-- I CAN BREATHE IN SPACE?
SHITSHITSHIT
I CAN'T DO THAT!
I'M DOING IT...
WHY?
WHY?

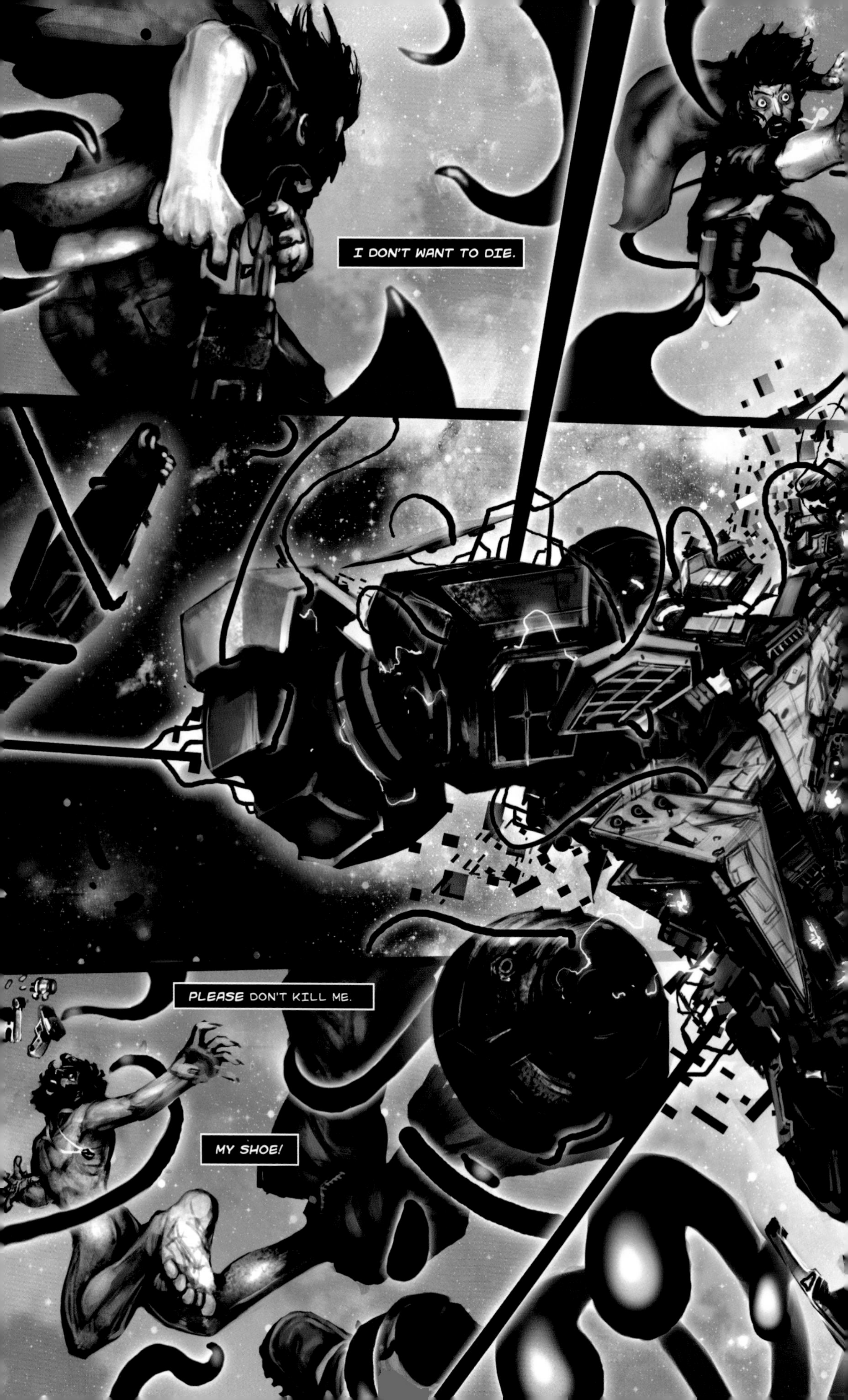
I DON'T WANT TO DIE.
PLEASE DON'T KILL ME.
MY SHOE!

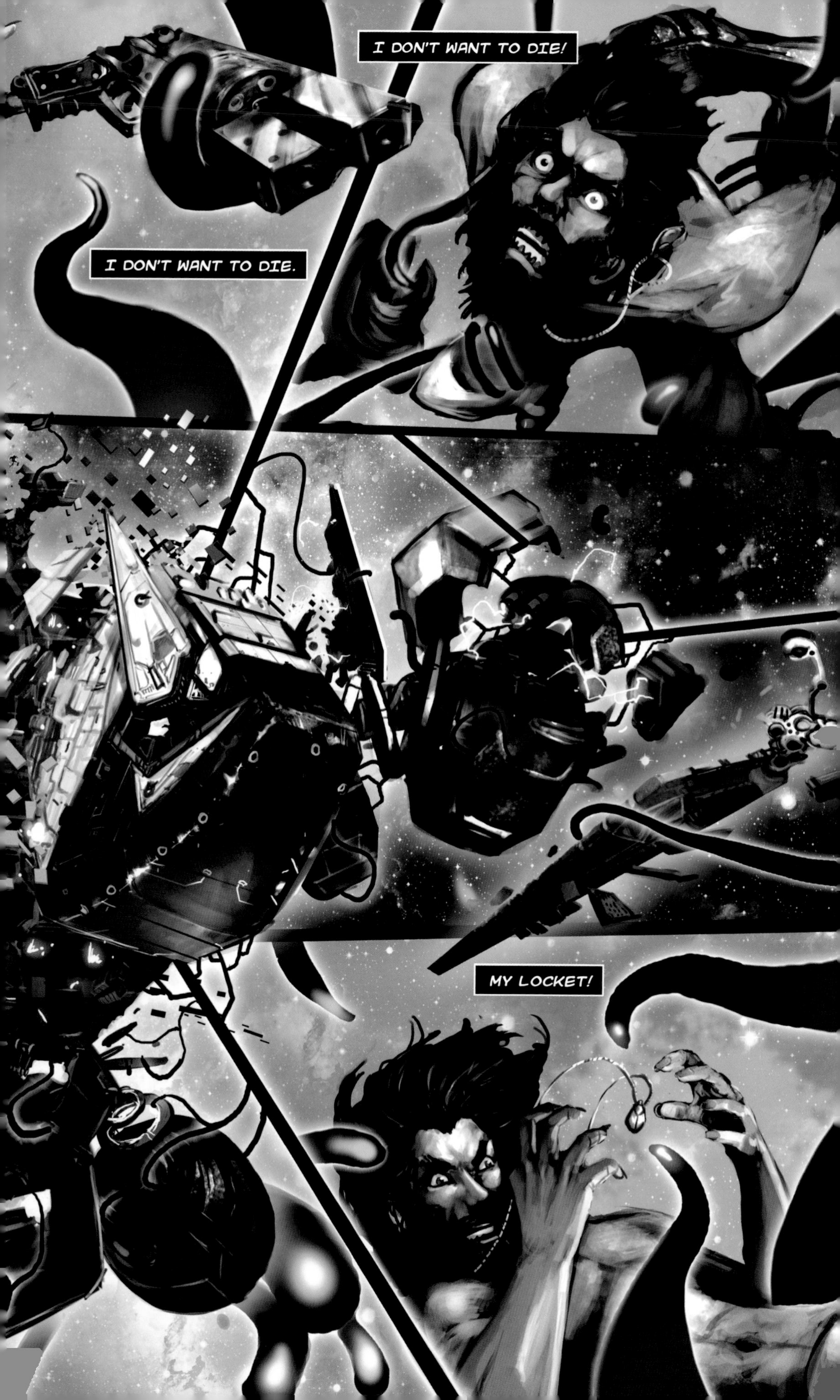
I DON'T WANT TO DIE!
I DON'T WANT TO DIE.
MY LOCKET!

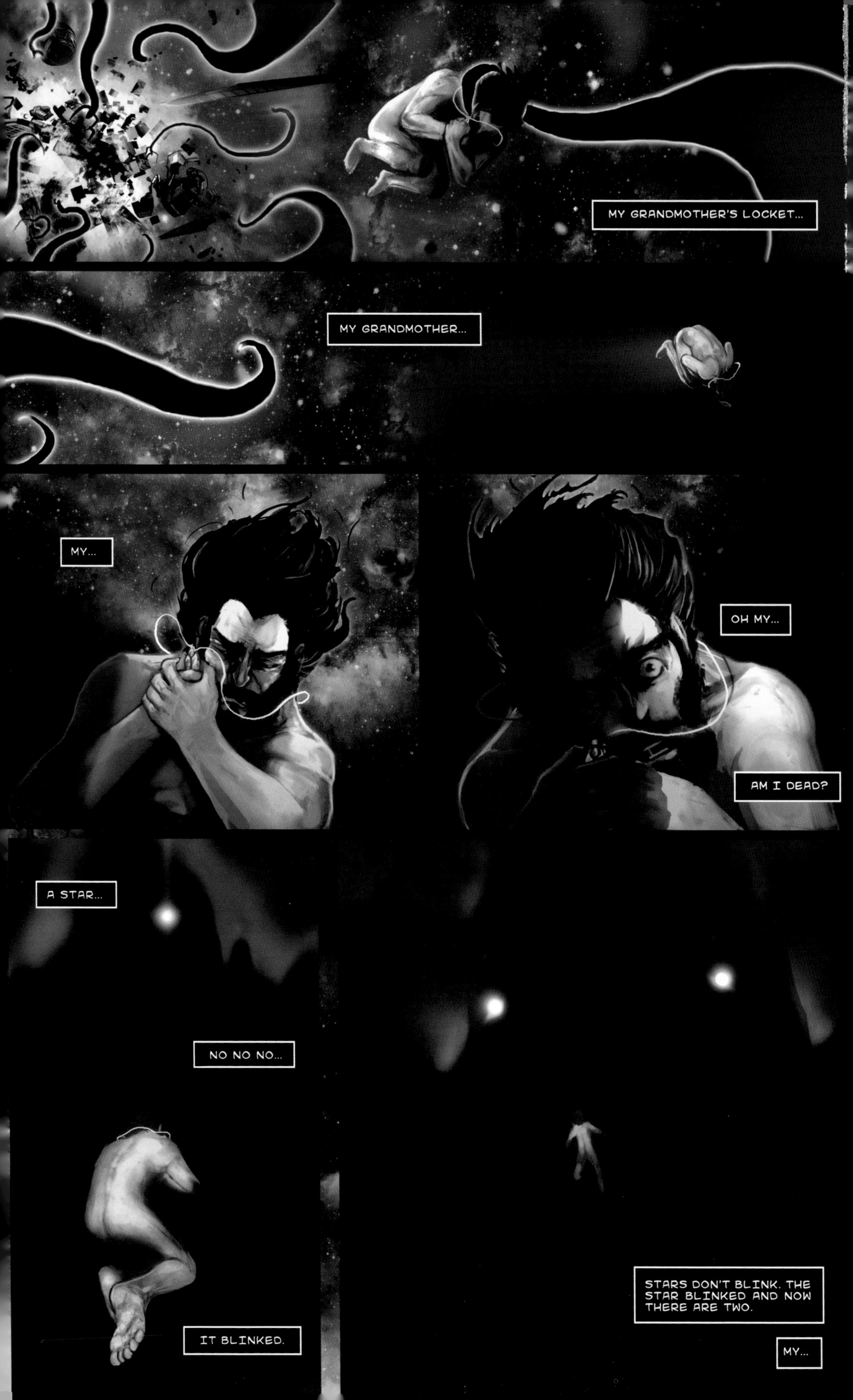
MY GRANDMOTHER'S LOCKET...
MY GRANDMOTHER...
MY...
OH MY...
AM I DEAD?
A STAR...
NO NO NO...
IT BLINKED.
STARS DON'T BLINK. THE STAR BLINKED AND NOW THERE ARE TWO.
MY...

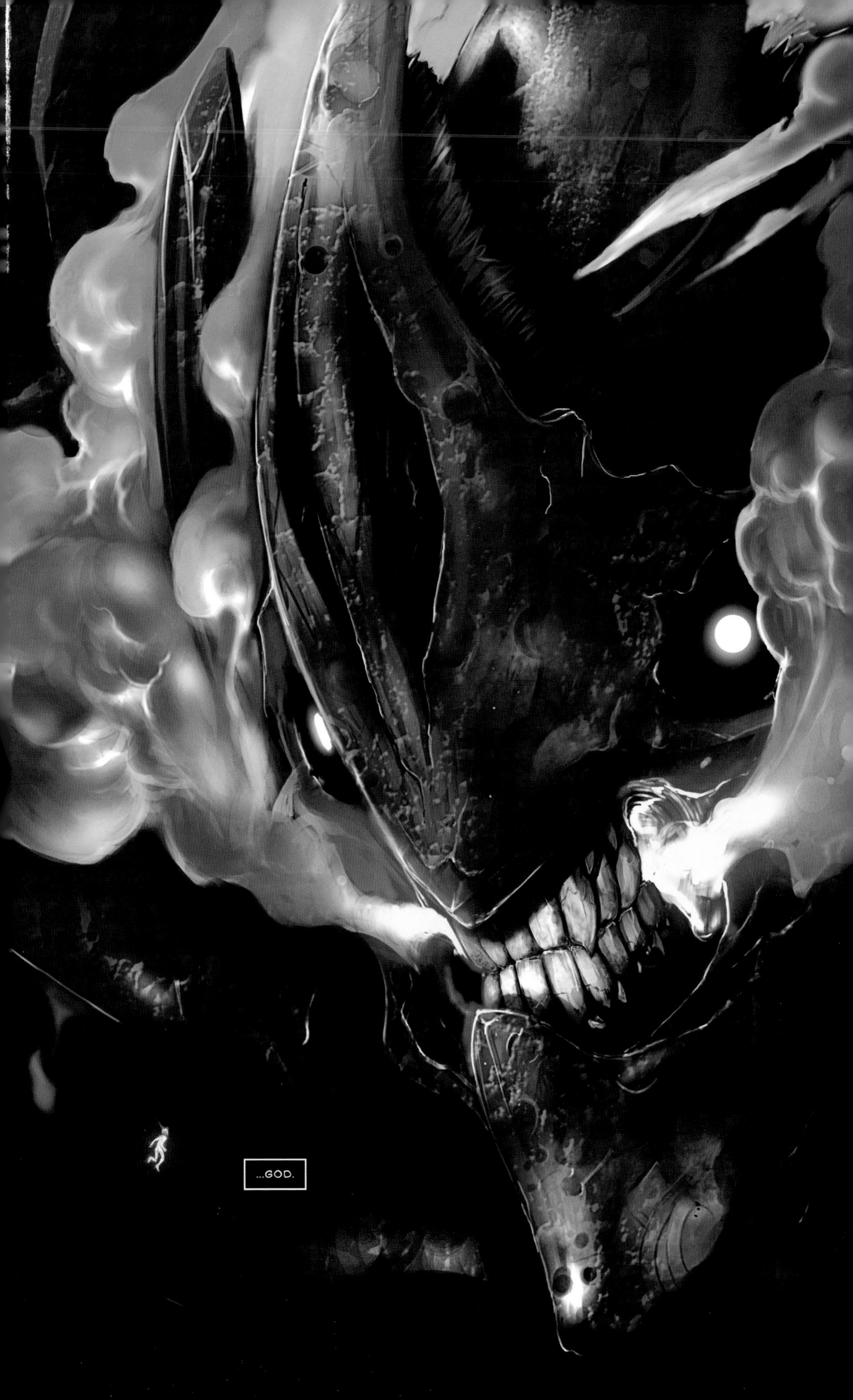
...GOD.

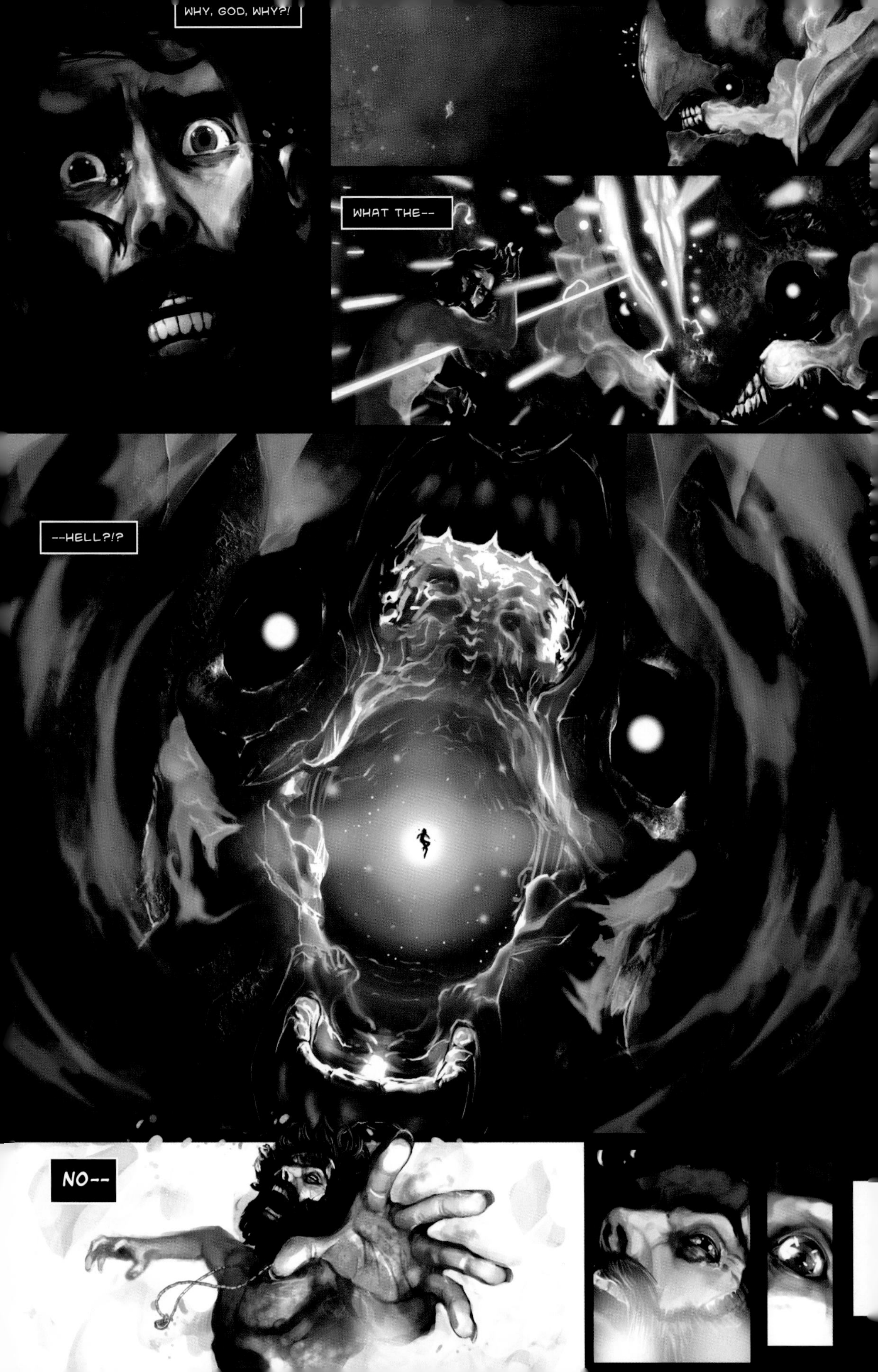
WHY, GOD, WHY?!
WHAT THE--
--HELL?!?
NO--

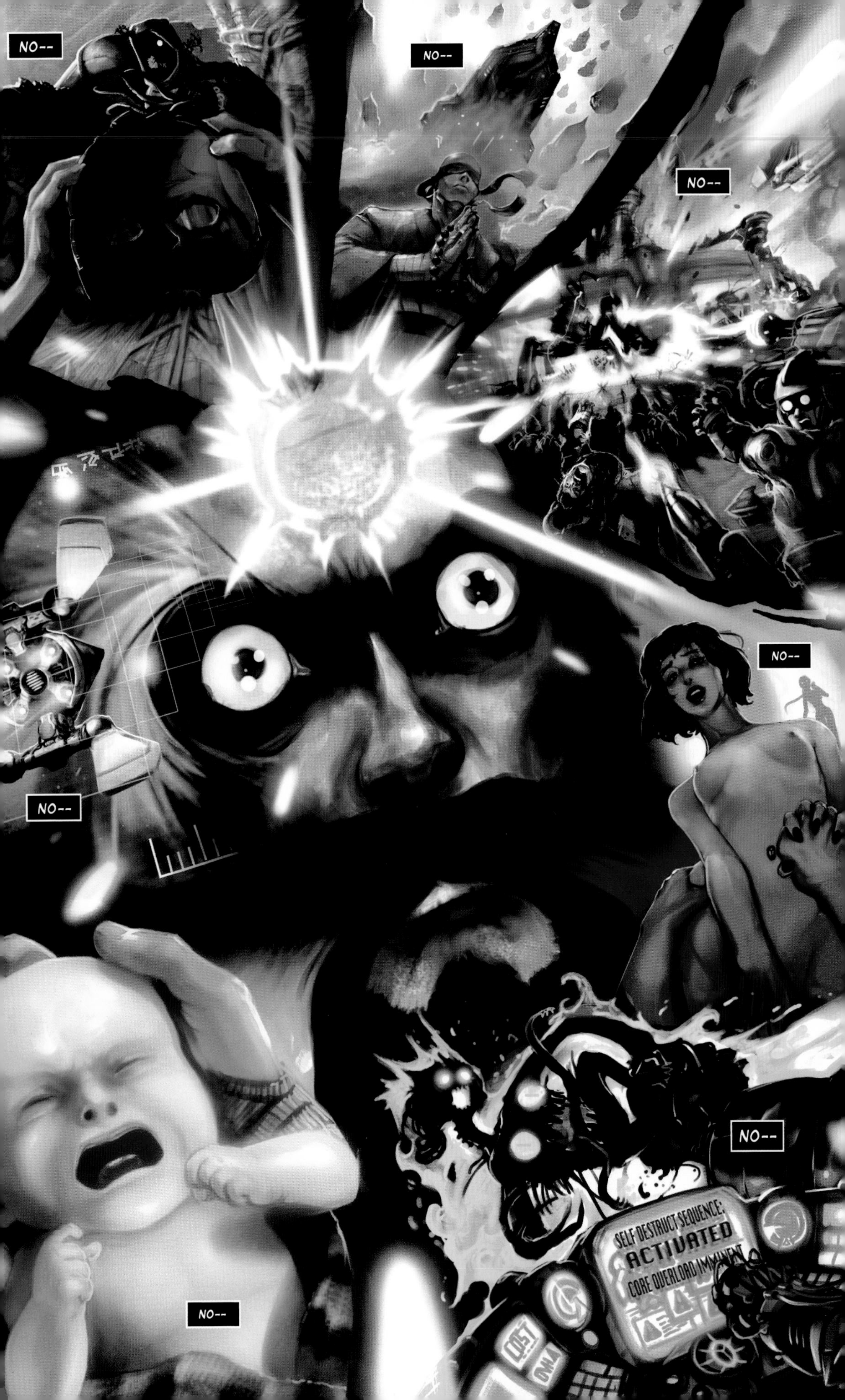
NO--
NO--
NO--
NO--
NO--
NO--
NO--
SELF DESTRUCT SEQUENCE:
ACTIVATED
CORE OVERLOAD IMMINENT

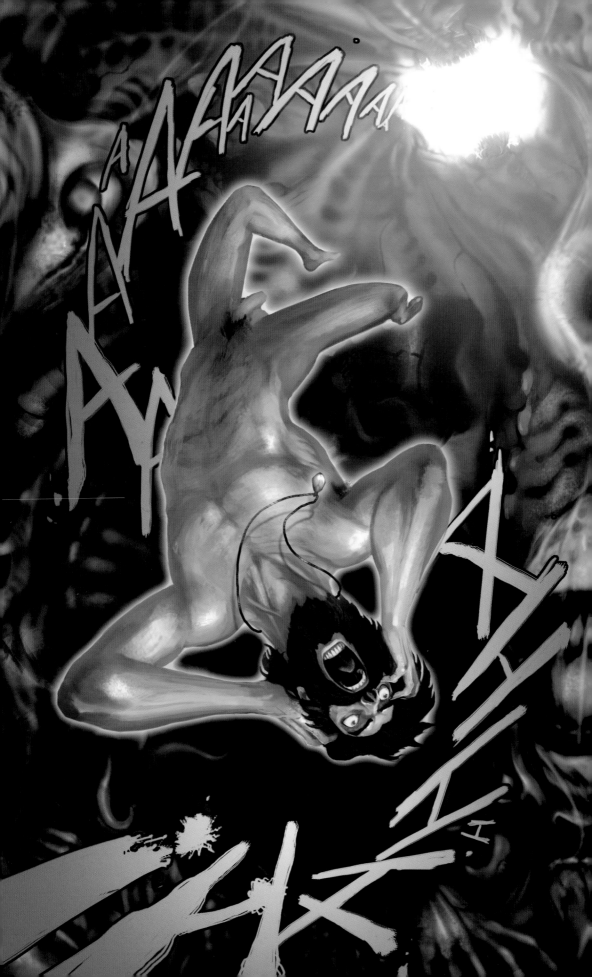

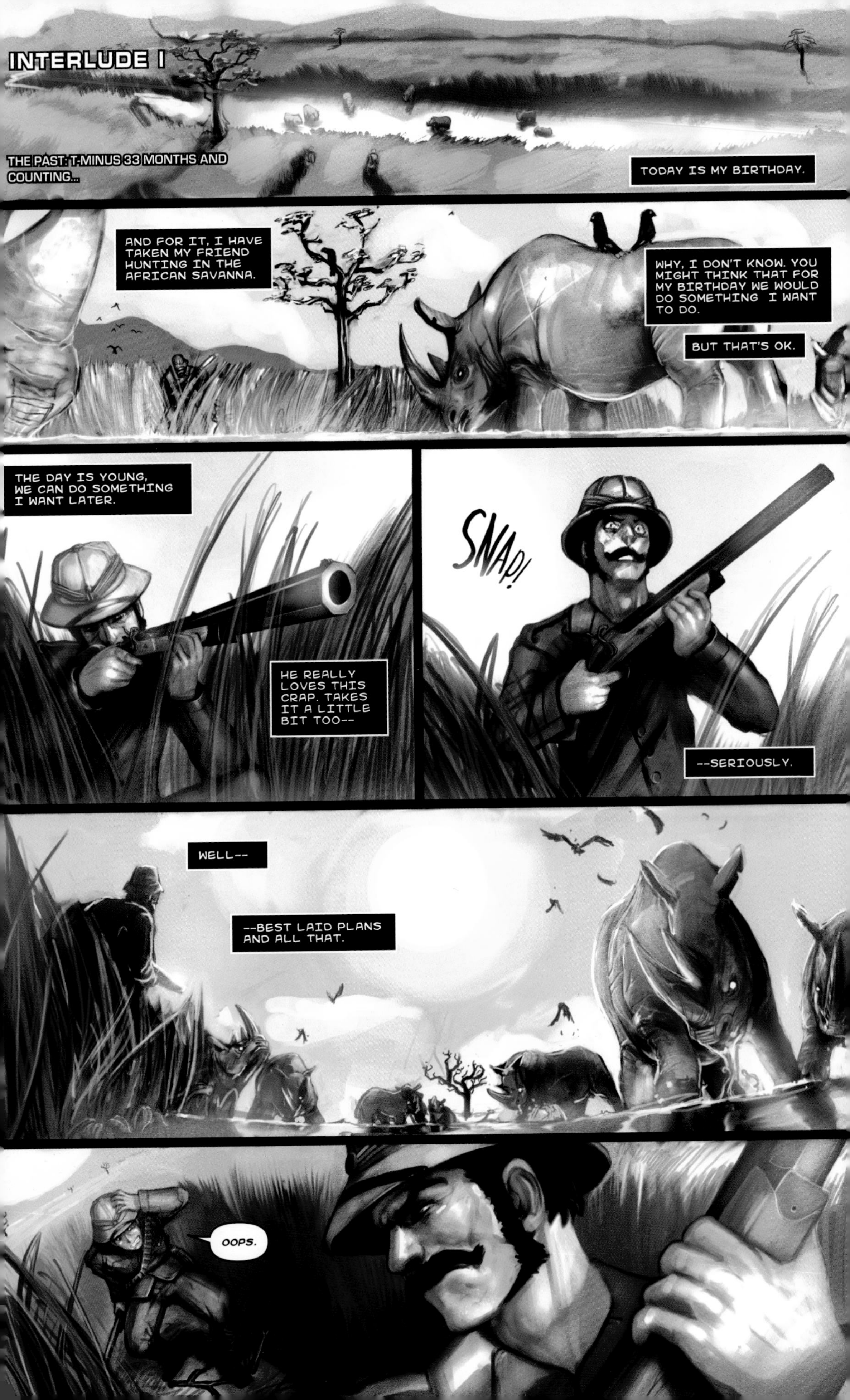
INTERLUDE I
THE PAST: T-MINUS 33 MONTHS AND COUNTING...
TODAY IS MY BIRTHDAY.
AND FOR IT, I HAVE TAKEN MY FRIEND HUNTING IN THE AFRICAN SAVANNA.
WHY, I DON'T KNOW. YOU MIGHT THINK THAT FOR MY BIRTHDAY WE WOULD DO SOMETHING I WANT TO DO.
BUT THAT'S OK.
THE DAY IS YOUNG, WE CAN DO SOMETHING I WANT LATER.
HE REALLY LOVES THIS CRAP. TAKES IT A LITTLE BIT TOO--
SNAP!
--SERIOUSLY.
WELL--
--BEST LAID PLANS AND ALL THAT.
OOPS.

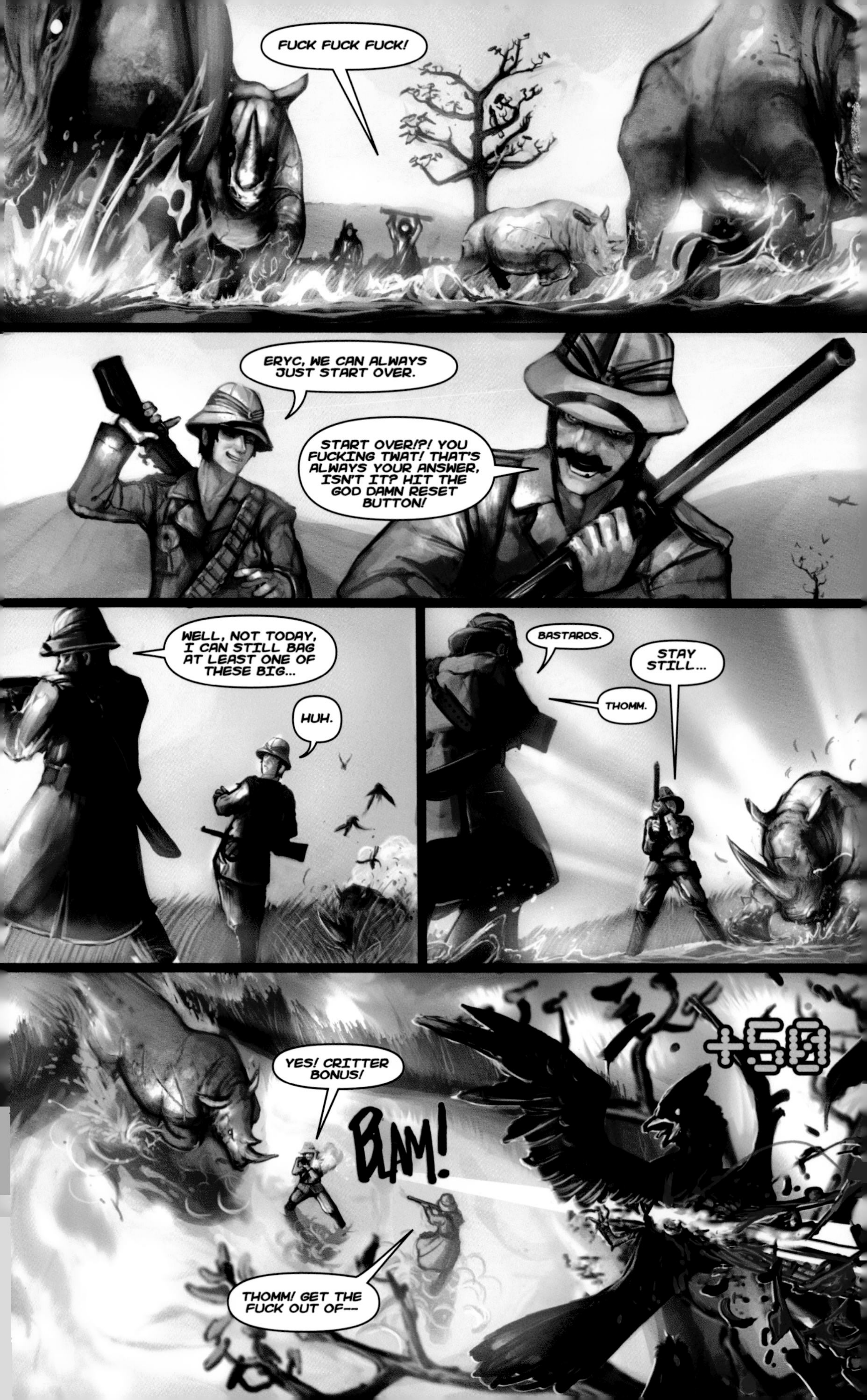
FUCK FUCK FUCK!
ERYC, WE CAN ALWAYS JUST START OVER.
START OVER!?! YOU FUCKING TWAT! THAT'S ALWAYS YOUR ANSWER, ISN'T IT? HIT THE GOD DAMN RESET BUTTON!
WELL, NOT TODAY, I CAN STILL BAG AT LEAST ONE OF THESE BIG...
HUH.
BASTARDS.
THOMM.
STAY STILL...
+50
YES! CRITTER BONUS!
BLAM!
THOMM! GET THE FUCK OUT OF--

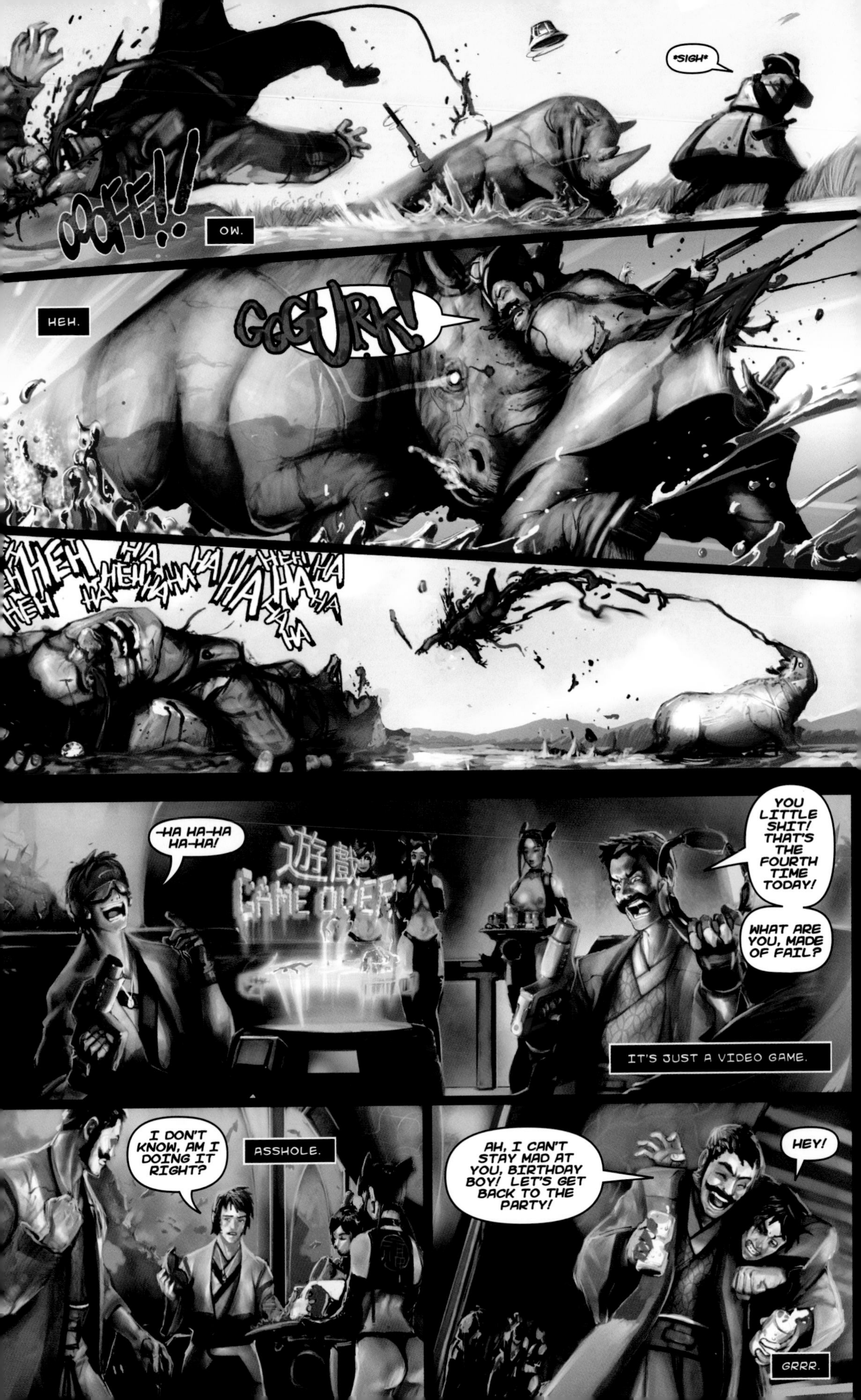
SIGH
OOOFF!!
OW.
HEH.
GGGURK!
HEH HEH HEH HA HEH HA HA HA HA HEH HA HA HA HA HA
-HA HA-HA HA-HA!
遊戲
GAME OVER
YOU LITTLE SHIT! THAT'S THE FOURTH TIME TODAY!
WHAT ARE YOU, MADE OF FAIL?
IT'S JUST A VIDEO GAME.
I DON'T KNOW, AM I DOING IT RIGHT?
ASSHOLE.
AH, I CAN'T STAY MAD AT YOU, BIRTHDAY BOY! LET'S GET BACK TO THE PARTY!
HEY!
GRRR.

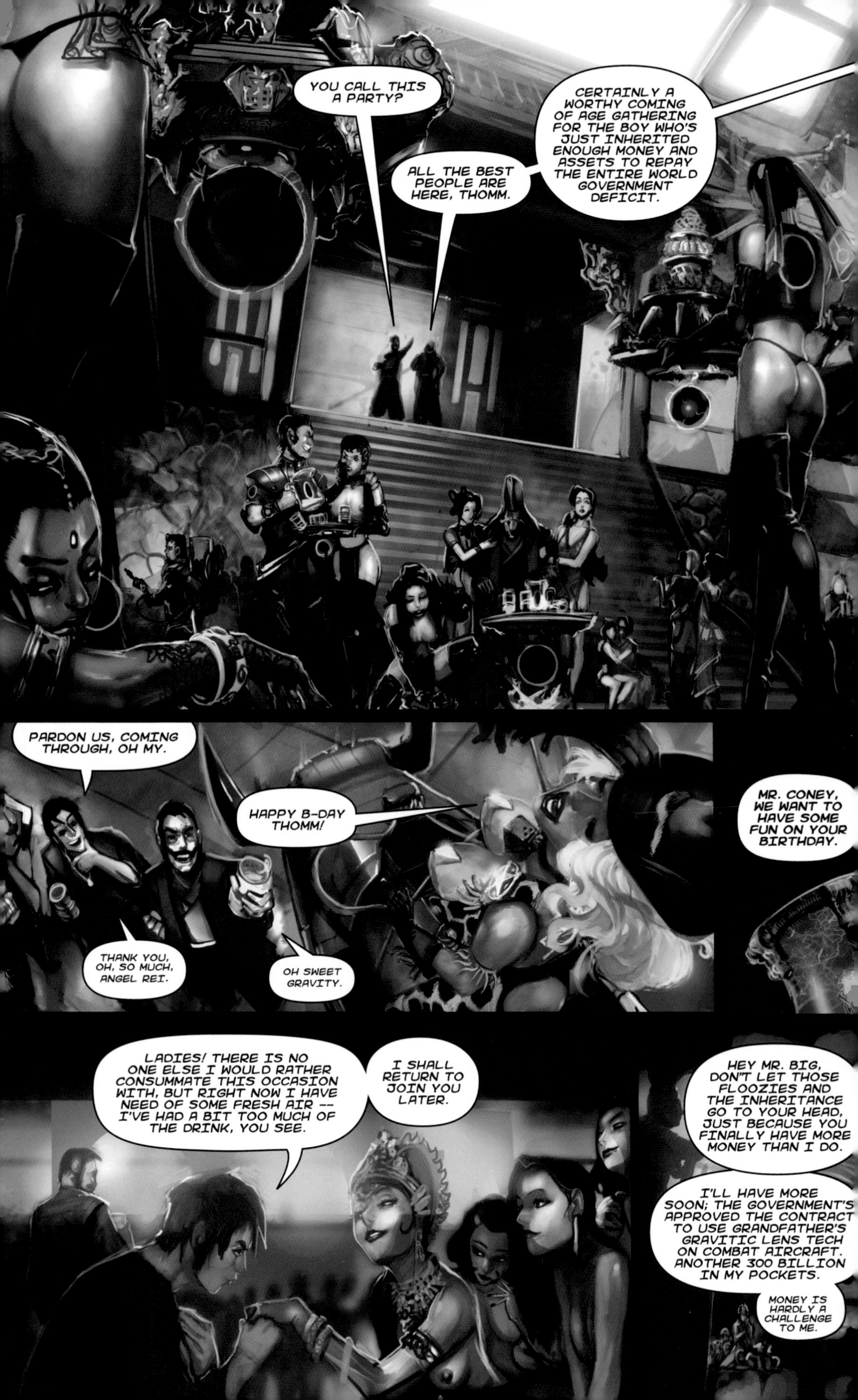
YOU CALL THIS A PARTY?
ALL THE BEST PEOPLE ARE HERE, THOMM.
CERTAINLY A WORTHY COMING OF AGE GATHERING FOR THE BOY WHO'S JUST INHERITED ENOUGH MONEY AND ASSETS TO REPAY THE ENTIRE WORLD GOVERNMENT DEFICIT.
PARDON US, COMING THROUGH, OH MY.
HAPPY B-DAY THOMM!
THANK YOU, OH, SO MUCH, ANGEL REI.
OH SWEET GRAVITY.
MR. CONEY, WE WANT TO HAVE SOME FUN ON YOUR BIRTHDAY.
LADIES! THERE IS NO ONE ELSE I WOULD RATHER CONSUMMATE THIS OCCASION WITH, BUT RIGHT NOW I HAVE NEED OF SOME FRESH AIR -- I'VE HAD A BIT TOO MUCH OF THE DRINK, YOU SEE.
I SHALL RETURN TO JOIN YOU LATER.
HEY MR. BIG, DON'T LET THOSE FLOOZIES AND THE INHERITANCE GO TO YOUR HEAD, JUST BECAUSE YOU FINALLY HAVE MORE MONEY THAN I DO.
I'LL HAVE MORE SOON; THE GOVERNMENT'S APPROVED THE CONTRACT TO USE GRANDFATHER'S GRAVITIC LENS TECH ON COMBAT AIRCRAFT. ANOTHER 300 BILLION IN MY POCKETS.
MONEY IS HARDLY A CHALLENGE TO ME.

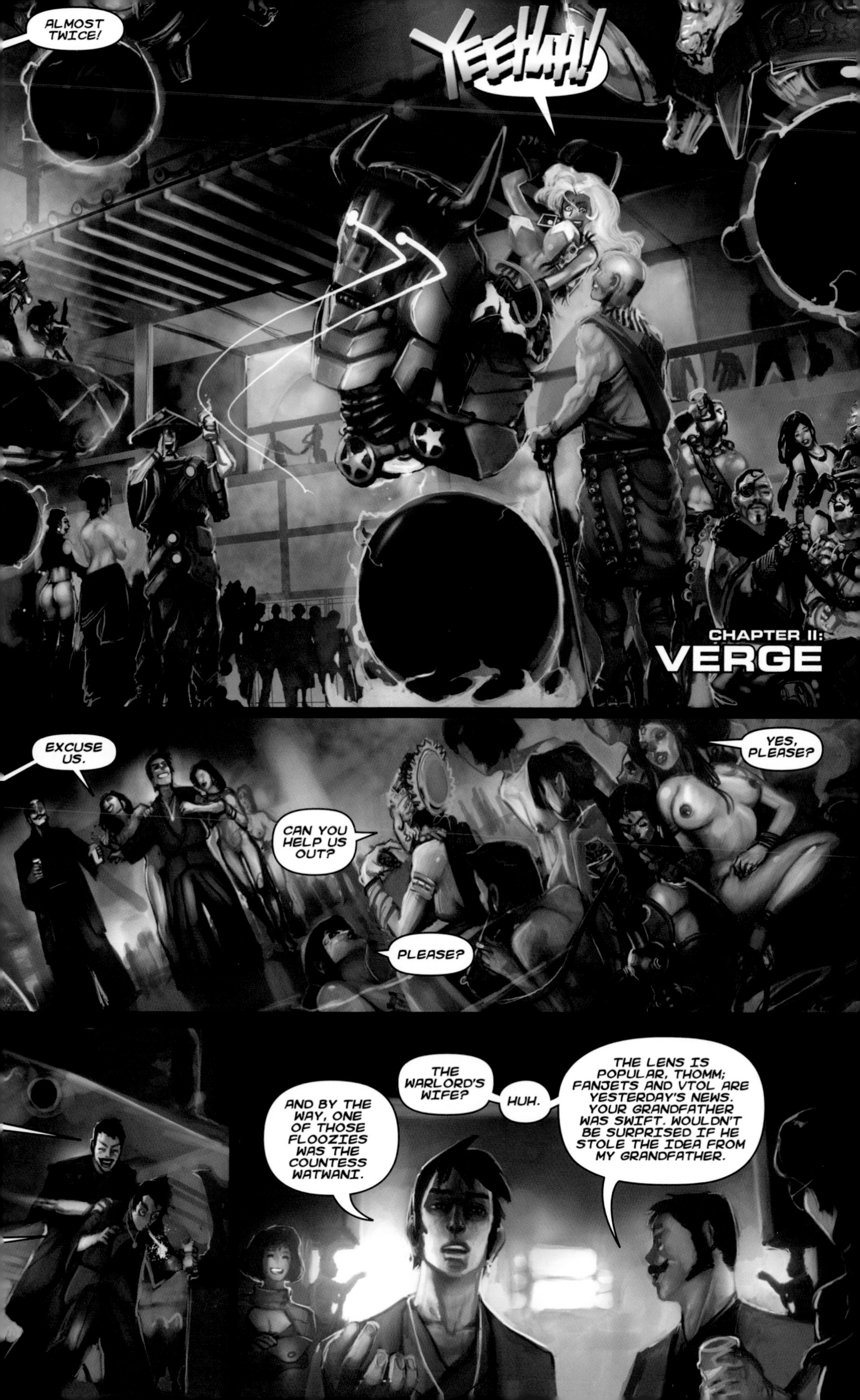
ALMOST TWICE!
YEEHAH!
CHAPTER II:
VERGE
EXCUSE US.
CAN YOU HELP US OUT?
YES, PLEASE?
PLEASE?
AND BY THE WAY, ONE OF THOSE FLOOZIES WAS THE COUNTESS WATWANI.
THE WARLORD'S WIFE?
HUH.
THE LENS IS POPULAR, THOMM; FANJETS AND VTOL ARE YESTERDAY'S NEWS. YOUR GRANDFATHER WAS SWIFT. WOULDN'T BE SURPRISED IF HE STOLE THE IDEA FROM MY GRANDFATHER.

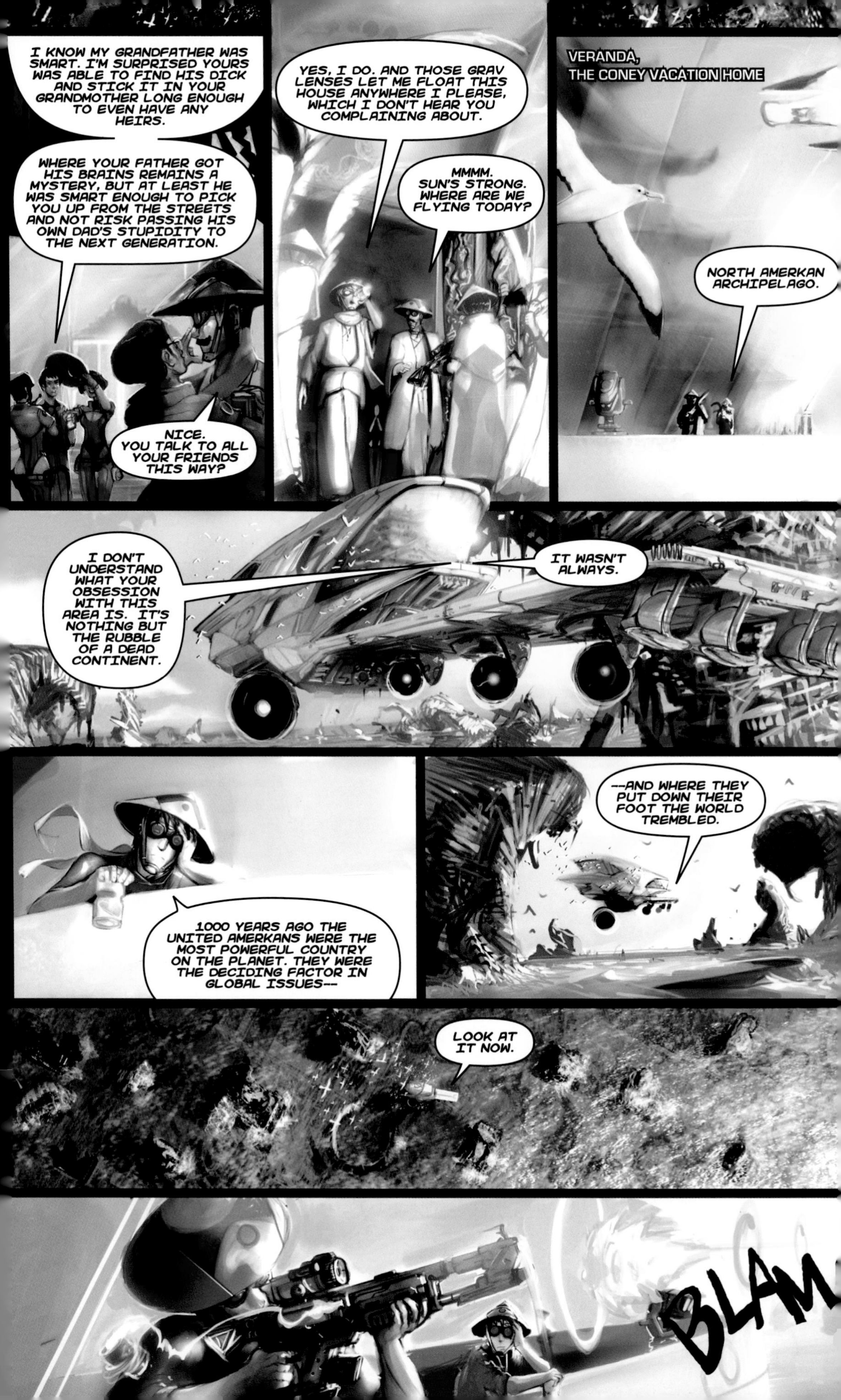

I KNOW MY GRANDFATHER WAS SMART. I'M SURPRISED YOURS WAS ABLE TO FIND HIS DICK AND STICK IT IN YOUR GRANDMOTHER LONG ENOUGH TO EVEN HAVE ANY HEIRS.
WHERE YOUR FATHER GOT HIS BRAINS REMAINS A MYSTERY, BUT AT LEAST HE WAS SMART ENOUGH TO PICK YOU UP FROM THE STREETS AND NOT RISK PASSING HIS OWN DAD'S STUPIDITY TO THE NEXT GENERATION.
NICE. YOU TALK TO ALL YOUR FRIENDS THIS WAY?
YES, I DO. AND THOSE GRAV LENSES LET ME FLOAT THIS HOUSE ANYWHERE I PLEASE, WHICH I DON'T HEAR YOU COMPLAINING ABOUT.
MMMM. SUN'S STRONG. WHERE ARE WE FLYING TODAY?
VERANDA, THE CONEY VACATION HOME
NORTH AMERKAN ARCHIPELAGO.
I DON'T UNDERSTAND WHAT YOUR OBSESSION WITH THIS AREA IS. IT'S NOTHING BUT THE RUBBLE OF A DEAD CONTINENT.
IT WASN'T ALWAYS.
1000 YEARS AGO THE UNITED AMERKANS WERE THE MOST POWERFUL COUNTRY ON THE PLANET. THEY WERE THE DECIDING FACTOR IN GLOBAL ISSUES--
--AND WHERE THEY PUT DOWN THEIR FOOT THE WORLD TREMBLED.
LOOK AT IT NOW.
BLAM

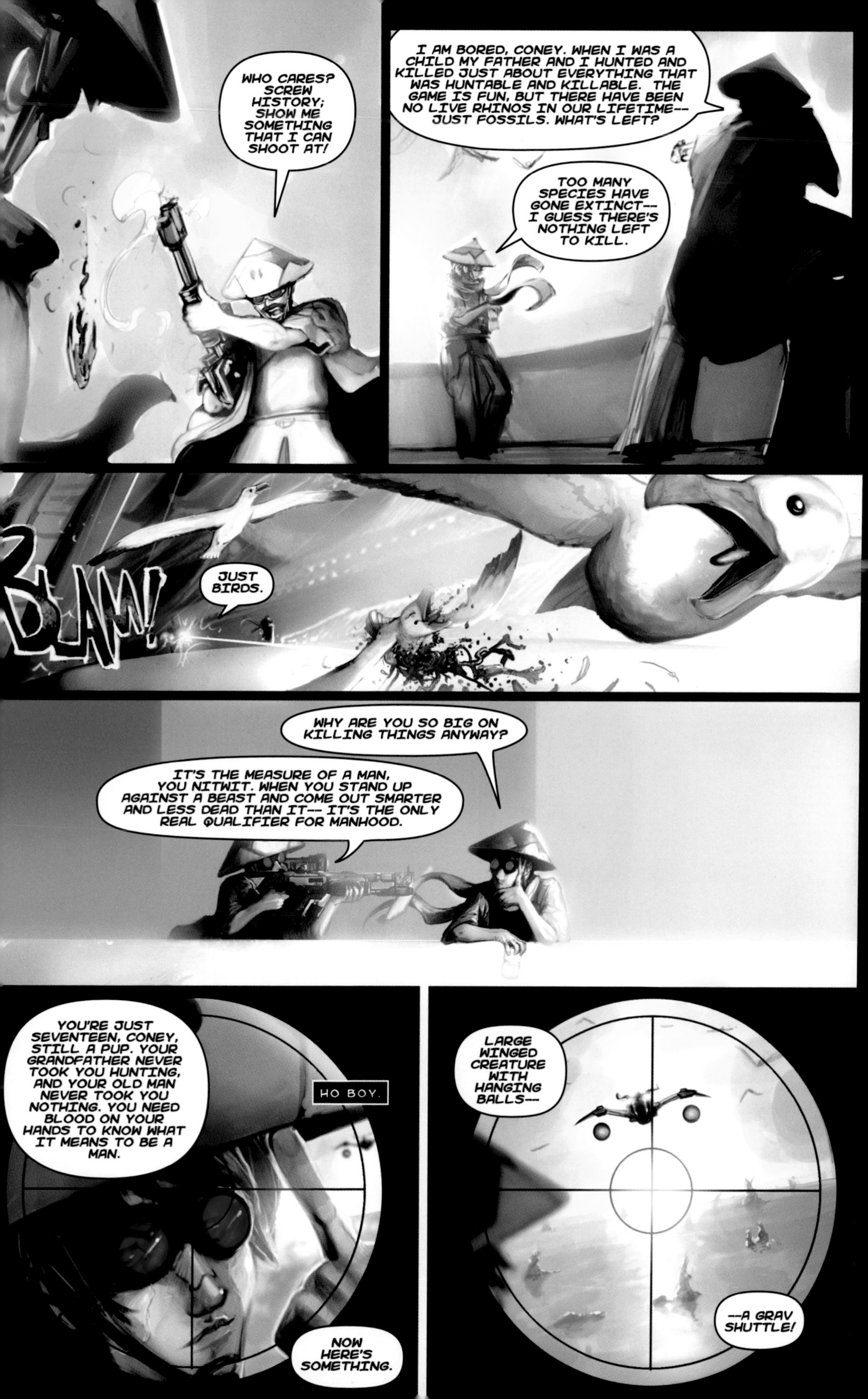
WHO CARES? SCREW HISTORY; SHOW ME SOMETHING THAT I CAN SHOOT AT!
I AM BORED, CONEY. WHEN I WAS A CHILD MY FATHER AND I HUNTED AND KILLED JUST ABOUT EVERYTHING THAT WAS HUNTABLE AND KILLABLE. THE GAME IS FUN, BUT THERE HAVE BEEN NO LIVE RHINOS IN OUR LIFETIME--JUST FOSSILS. WHAT'S LEFT?
TOO MANY SPECIES HAVE GONE EXTINCT--I GUESS THERE'S NOTHING LEFT TO KILL.
BLAM!
JUST BIRDS.
WHY ARE YOU SO BIG ON KILLING THINGS ANYWAY?
IT'S THE MEASURE OF A MAN, YOU NITWIT. WHEN YOU STAND UP AGAINST A BEAST AND COME OUT SMARTER AND LESS DEAD THAN IT-- IT'S THE ONLY REAL QUALIFIER FOR MANHOOD.
YOU'RE JUST SEVENTEEN, CONEY, STILL A PUP. YOUR GRANDFATHER NEVER TOOK YOU HUNTING, AND YOUR OLD MAN NEVER TOOK YOU NOTHING. YOU NEED BLOOD ON YOUR HANDS TO KNOW WHAT IT MEANS TO BE A MAN.
HO BOY.
NOW HERE'S SOMETHING.
LARGE WINGED CREATURE WITH HANGING BALLS---
--A GRAV SHUTTLE!

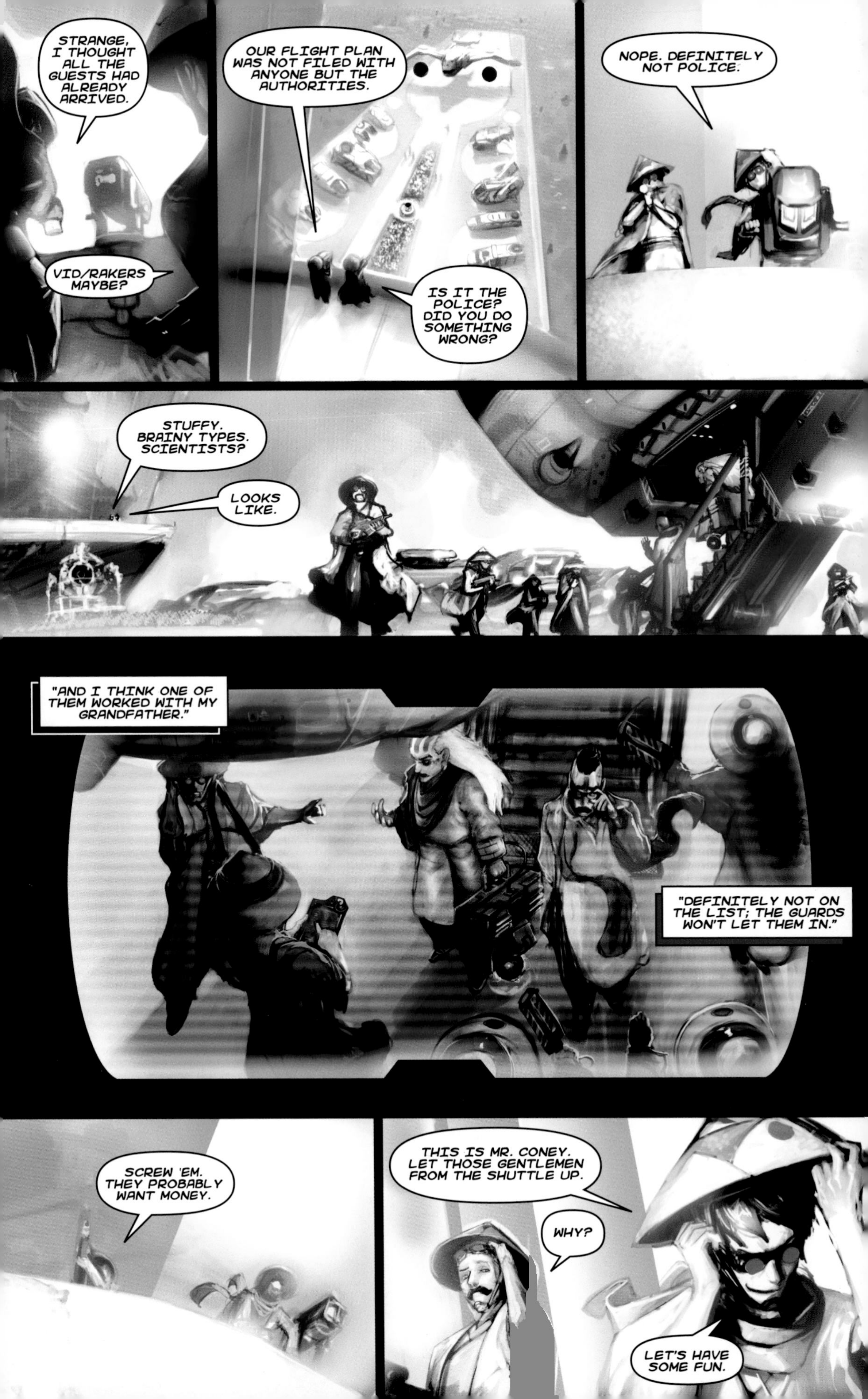
STRANGE, I THOUGHT ALL THE GUESTS HAD ALREADY ARRIVED.
VID/RAKERS MAYBE?
OUR FLIGHT PLAN WAS NOT FILED WITH ANYONE BUT THE AUTHORITIES.
IS IT THE POLICE? DID YOU DO SOMETHING WRONG?
NOPE. DEFINITELY NOT POLICE.
STUFFY. BRAINY TYPES. SCIENTISTS?
LOOKS LIKE.
"AND I THINK ONE OF THEM WORKED WITH MY GRANDFATHER."
"DEFINITELY NOT ON THE LIST; THE GUARDS WON'T LET THEM IN."
SCREW 'EM. THEY PROBABLY WANT MONEY.
THIS IS MR. CONEY. LET THOSE GENTLEMEN FROM THE SHUTTLE UP.
WHY?
LET'S HAVE SOME FUN.

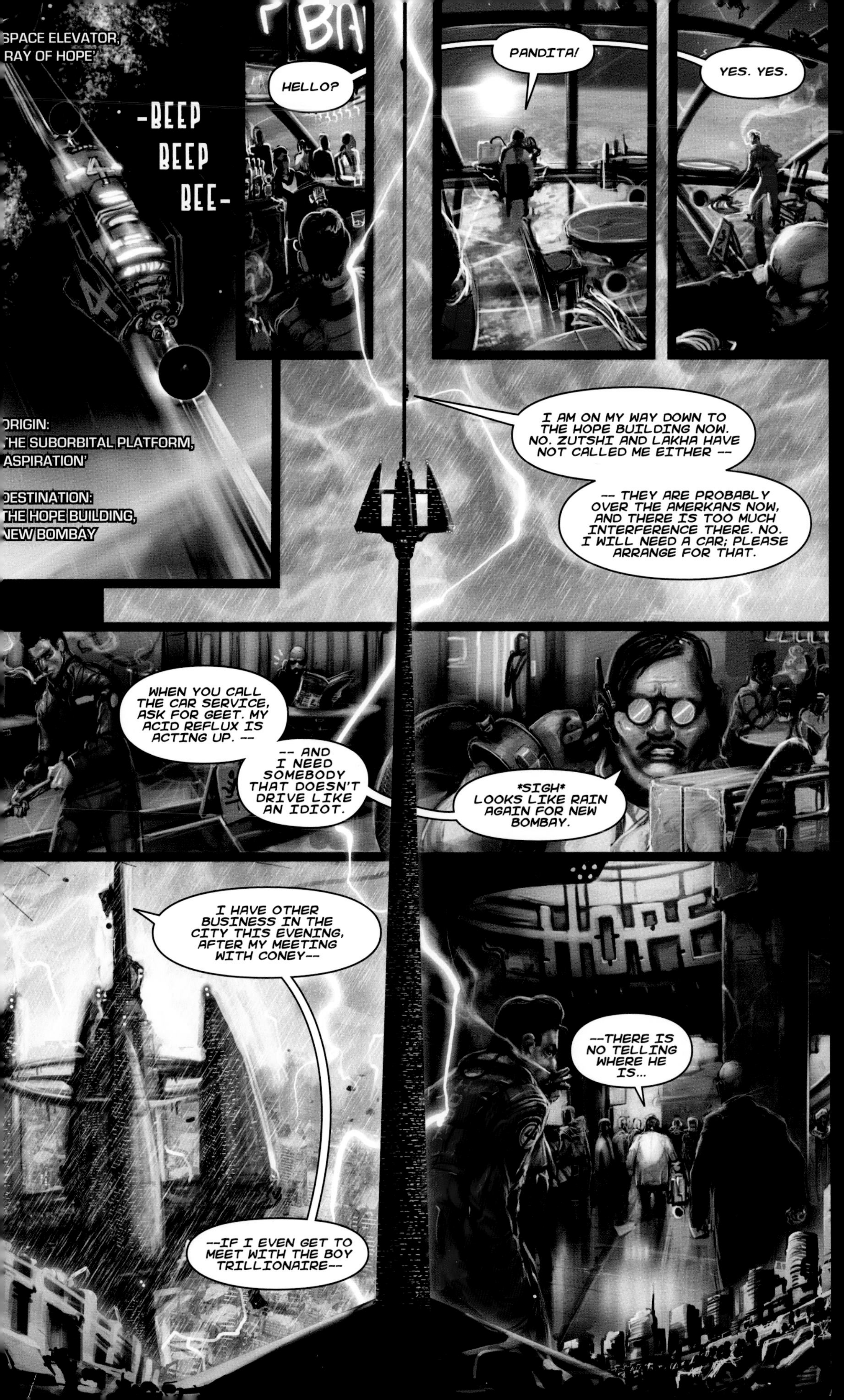
SPACE ELEVATOR, 'RAY OF HOPE'
-BEEP
BEEP
BEE-
HELLO?
PANDITA!
YES. YES.
ORIGIN: THE SUBORBITAL PLATFORM, 'ASPIRATION'
DESTINATION: THE HOPE BUILDING, NEW BOMBAY
I AM ON MY WAY DOWN TO THE HOPE BUILDING NOW. NO. ZUTSHI AND LAKHA HAVE NOT CALLED ME EITHER --
-- THEY ARE PROBABLY OVER THE AMERKANS NOW, AND THERE IS TOO MUCH INTERFERENCE THERE. NO. I WILL NEED A CAR; PLEASE ARRANGE FOR THAT.
WHEN YOU CALL THE CAR SERVICE, ASK FOR GEET. MY ACID REFLUX IS ACTING UP. --
-- AND I NEED SOMEBODY THAT DOESN'T DRIVE LIKE AN IDIOT.
SIGH LOOKS LIKE RAIN AGAIN FOR NEW BOMBAY.
I HAVE OTHER BUSINESS IN THE CITY THIS EVENING, AFTER MY MEETING WITH CONEY--
--IF I EVEN GET TO MEET WITH THE BOY TRILLIONAIRE--
--THERE IS NO TELLING WHERE HE IS...

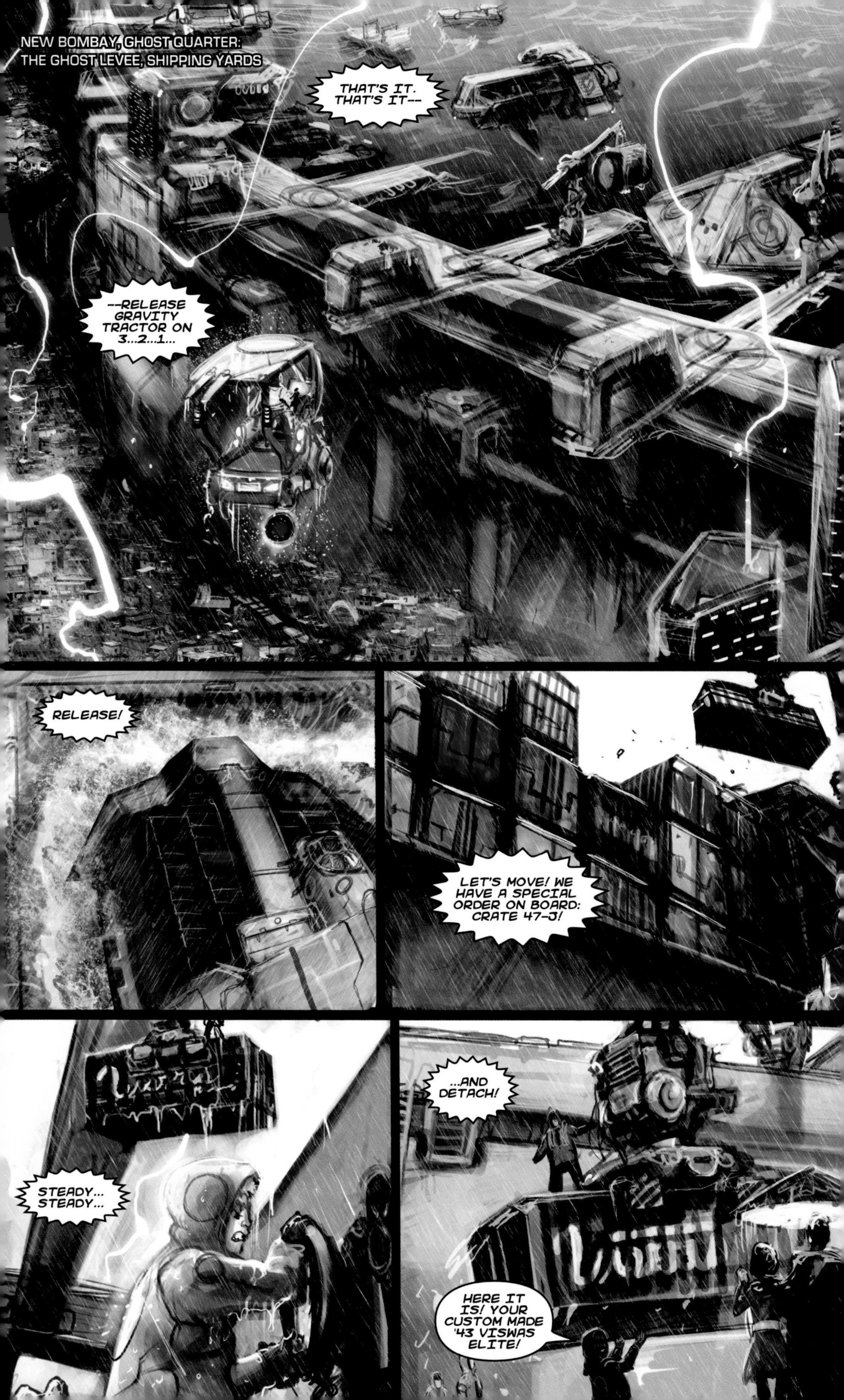
NEW BOMBAY, GHOST QUARTER:
THE GHOST LEVEE, SHIPPING YARDS
THAT'S IT. THAT'S IT--
--RELEASE GRAVITY TRACTOR ON 3...2...1...
RELEASE!
LET'S MOVE! WE HAVE A SPECIAL ORDER ON BOARD: CRATE 47-J!
STEADY... STEADY...
...AND DETACH!
HERE IT IS! YOUR CUSTOM MADE '43 VISWAS ELITE!

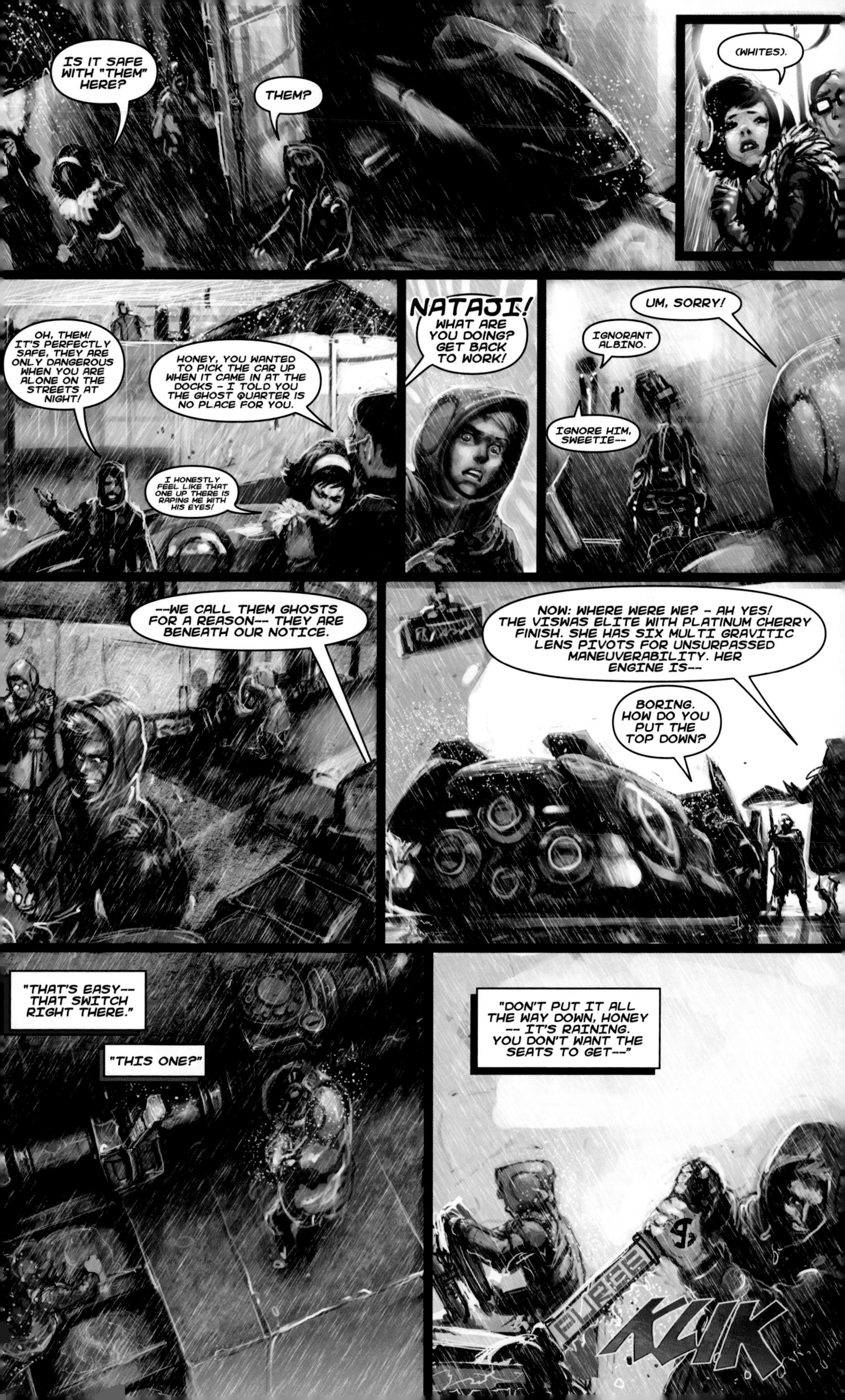
IS IT SAFE WITH "THEM" HERE?
THEM?
(WHITES).
OH, THEM! IT'S PERFECTLY SAFE, THEY ARE ONLY DANGEROUS WHEN YOU ARE ALONE ON THE STREETS AT NIGHT!
HONEY, YOU WANTED TO PICK THE CAR UP WHEN IT CAME IN AT THE DOCKS - I TOLD YOU THE GHOST QUARTER IS NO PLACE FOR YOU.
I HONESTLY FEEL LIKE THAT ONE UP THERE IS RAPING ME WITH HIS EYES!
NATAJI!
WHAT ARE YOU DOING? GET BACK TO WORK!
UM, SORRY!
IGNORANT ALBINO.
IGNORE HIM, SWEETIE--
--WE CALL THEM GHOSTS FOR A REASON-- THEY ARE BENEATH OUR NOTICE.
NOW: WHERE WERE WE? - AH YES! THE VISWAS ELITE WITH PLATINUM CHERRY FINISH. SHE HAS SIX MULTI GRAVITIC LENS PIVOTS FOR UNSURPASSED MANEUVERABILITY. HER ENGINE IS--
BORING. HOW DO YOU PUT THE TOP DOWN?
"THAT'S EASY-- THAT SWITCH RIGHT THERE."
"THIS ONE?"
"DON'T PUT IT ALL THE WAY DOWN, HONEY -- IT'S RAINING. YOU DON'T WANT THE SEATS TO GET--"
KLIK

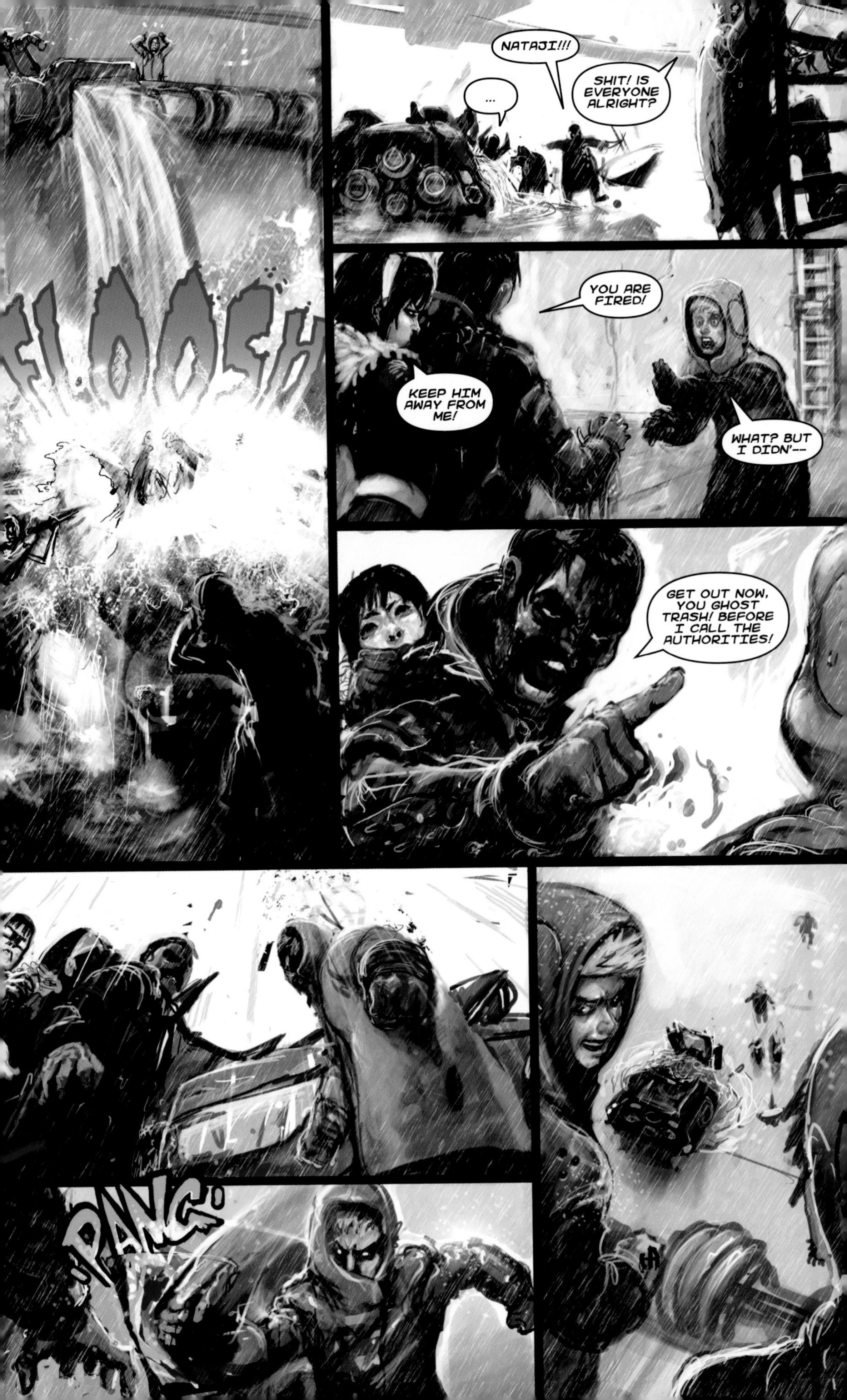
FLOOSH
...
NATAJI!!!
SHIT! IS EVERYONE ALRIGHT?
YOU ARE FIRED!
KEEP HIM AWAY FROM ME!
WHAT? BUT I DIDN'--
GET OUT NOW, YOU GHOST TRASH! BEFORE I CALL THE AUTHORITIES!
PANG!

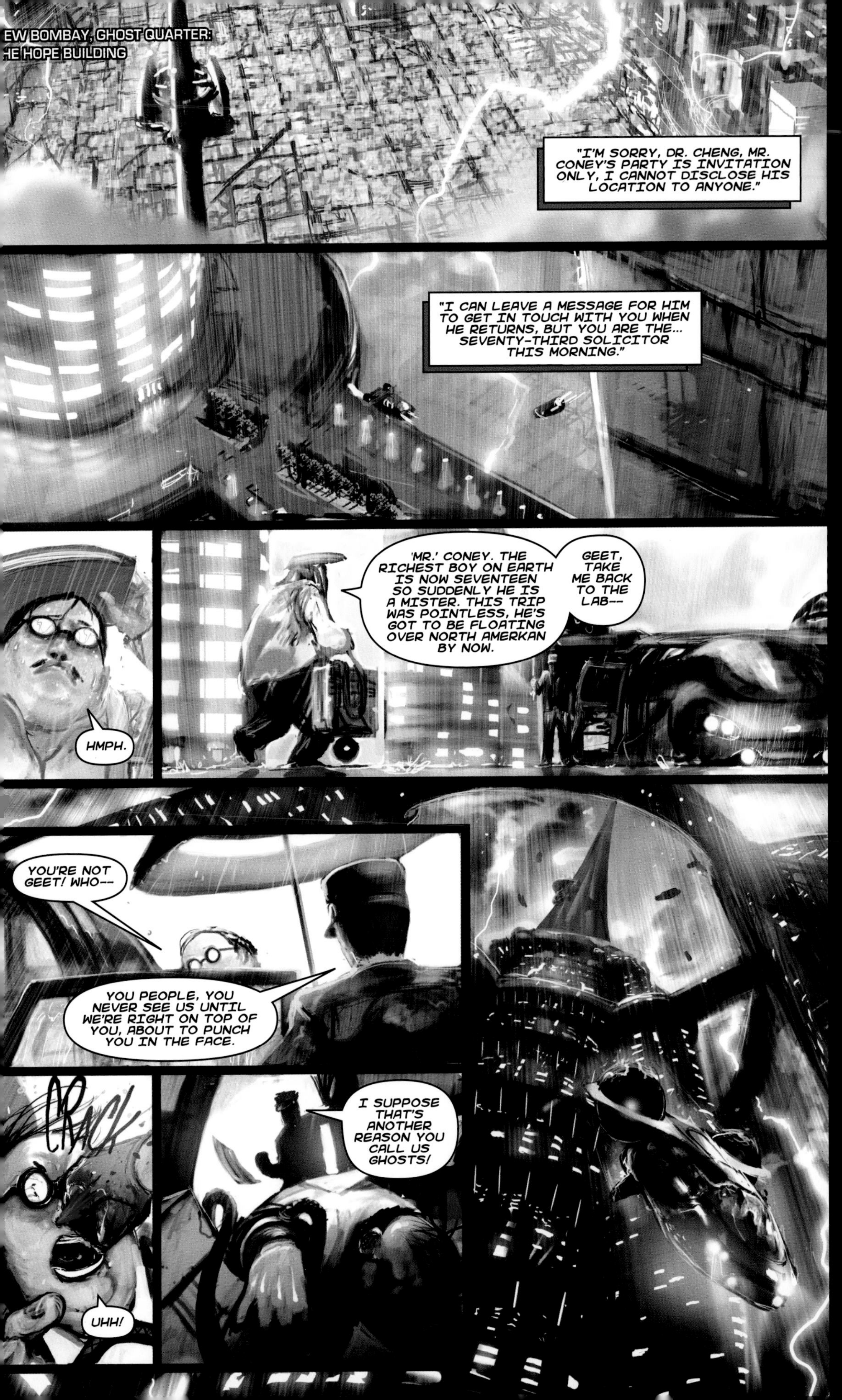
EW BOMBAY, GHOST QUARTER:
HE HOPE BUILDING
"I'M SORRY, DR. CHENG, MR. CONEY'S PARTY IS INVITATION ONLY, I CANNOT DISCLOSE HIS LOCATION TO ANYONE."
"I CAN LEAVE A MESSAGE FOR HIM TO GET IN TOUCH WITH YOU WHEN HE RETURNS, BUT YOU ARE THE... SEVENTY-THIRD SOLICITOR THIS MORNING."
HMPH.
'MR.' CONEY. THE RICHEST BOY ON EARTH IS NOW SEVENTEEN SO SUDDENLY HE IS A MISTER. THIS TRIP WAS POINTLESS, HE'S GOT TO BE FLOATING OVER NORTH AMERKAN BY NOW.
GEET, TAKE ME BACK TO THE LAB--
YOU'RE NOT GEET! WHO--
YOU PEOPLE, YOU NEVER SEE US UNTIL WE'RE RIGHT ON TOP OF YOU, ABOUT TO PUNCH YOU IN THE FACE.
CRACK
UHH!
I SUPPOSE THAT'S ANOTHER REASON YOU CALL US GHOSTS!

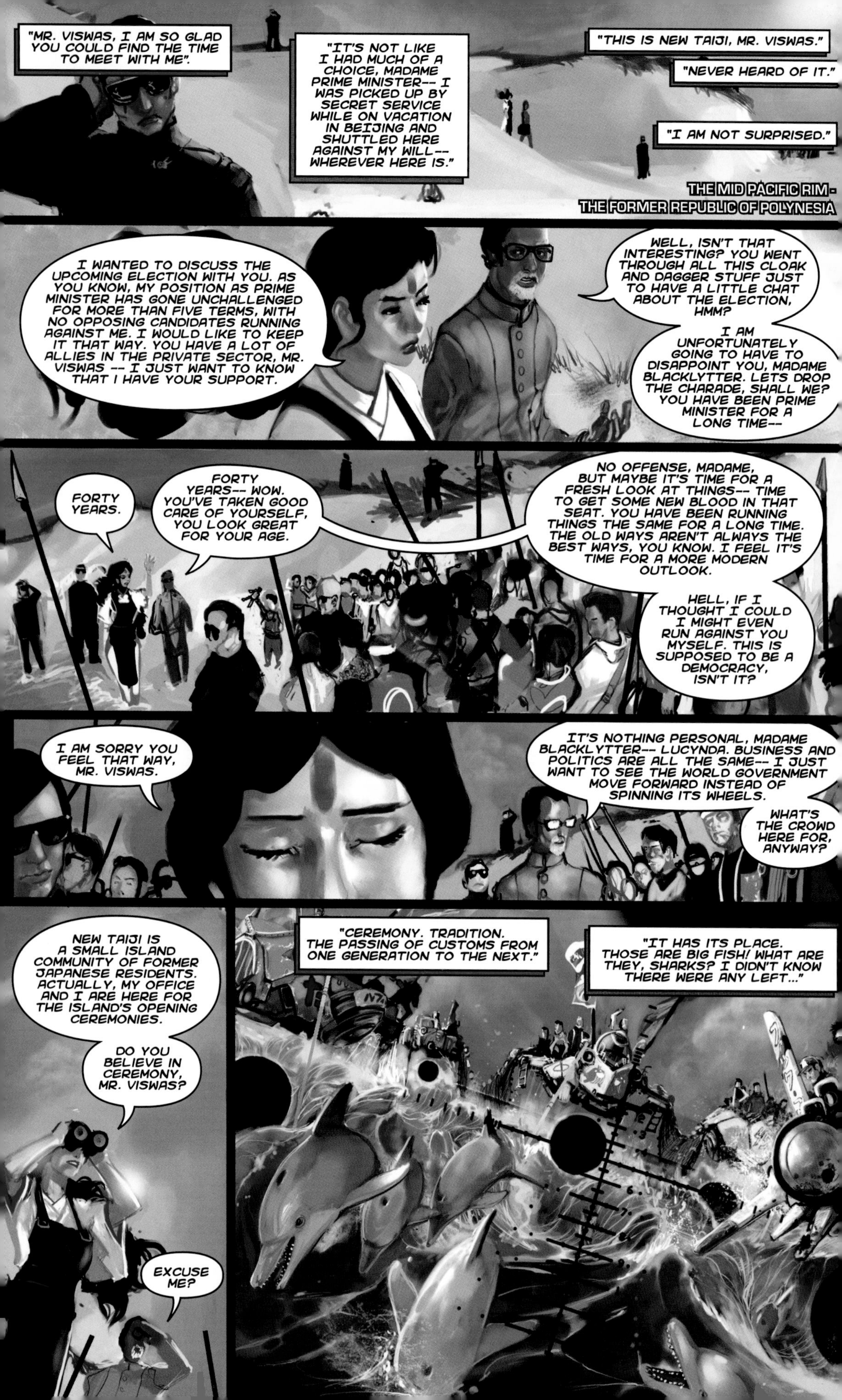
"MR. VISWAS, I AM SO GLAD YOU COULD FIND THE TIME TO MEET WITH ME".
"IT'S NOT LIKE I HAD MUCH OF A CHOICE, MADAME PRIME MINISTER-- I WAS PICKED UP BY SECRET SERVICE WHILE ON VACATION IN BEIJING AND SHUTTLED HERE AGAINST MY WILL-- WHEREVER HERE IS."
"THIS IS NEW TAIJI, MR. VISWAS."
"NEVER HEARD OF IT."
"I AM NOT SURPRISED."
THE MID PACIFIC RIM - THE FORMER REPUBLIC OF POLYNESIA
I WANTED TO DISCUSS THE UPCOMING ELECTION WITH YOU. AS YOU KNOW, MY POSITION AS PRIME MINISTER HAS GONE UNCHALLENGED FOR MORE THAN FIVE TERMS, WITH NO OPPOSING CANDIDATES RUNNING AGAINST ME. I WOULD LIKE TO KEEP IT THAT WAY. YOU HAVE A LOT OF ALLIES IN THE PRIVATE SECTOR, MR. VISWAS -- I JUST WANT TO KNOW THAT I HAVE YOUR SUPPORT.
WELL, ISN'T THAT INTERESTING? YOU WENT THROUGH ALL THIS CLOAK AND DAGGER STUFF JUST TO HAVE A LITTLE CHAT ABOUT THE ELECTION, HMM?
I AM UNFORTUNATELY GOING TO HAVE TO DISAPPOINT YOU, MADAME BLACKLYTTER. LETS DROP THE CHARADE, SHALL WE? YOU HAVE BEEN PRIME MINISTER FOR A LONG TIME--
FORTY YEARS.
FORTY YEARS-- WOW. YOU'VE TAKEN GOOD CARE OF YOURSELF, YOU LOOK GREAT FOR YOUR AGE.
NO OFFENSE, MADAME, BUT MAYBE IT'S TIME FOR A FRESH LOOK AT THINGS-- TIME TO GET SOME NEW BLOOD IN THAT SEAT. YOU HAVE BEEN RUNNING THINGS THE SAME FOR A LONG TIME. THE OLD WAYS AREN'T ALWAYS THE BEST WAYS, YOU KNOW. I FEEL IT'S TIME FOR A MORE MODERN OUTLOOK.
HELL, IF I THOUGHT I COULD I MIGHT EVEN RUN AGAINST YOU MYSELF. THIS IS SUPPOSED TO BE A DEMOCRACY, ISN'T IT?
I AM SORRY YOU FEEL THAT WAY, MR. VISWAS.
IT'S NOTHING PERSONAL, MADAME BLACKLYTTER-- LUCYNDA. BUSINESS AND POLITICS ARE ALL THE SAME-- I JUST WANT TO SEE THE WORLD GOVERNMENT MOVE FORWARD INSTEAD OF SPINNING ITS WHEELS.
WHAT'S THE CROWD HERE FOR, ANYWAY?
NEW TAIJI IS A SMALL ISLAND COMMUNITY OF FORMER JAPANESE RESIDENTS. ACTUALLY, MY OFFICE AND I ARE HERE FOR THE ISLAND'S OPENING CEREMONIES.
DO YOU BELIEVE IN CEREMONY, MR. VISWAS?
EXCUSE ME?
"CEREMONY. TRADITION. THE PASSING OF CUSTOMS FROM ONE GENERATION TO THE NEXT."
"IT HAS ITS PLACE. THOSE ARE BIG FISH! WHAT ARE THEY, SHARKS? I DIDN'T KNOW THERE WERE ANY LEFT..."

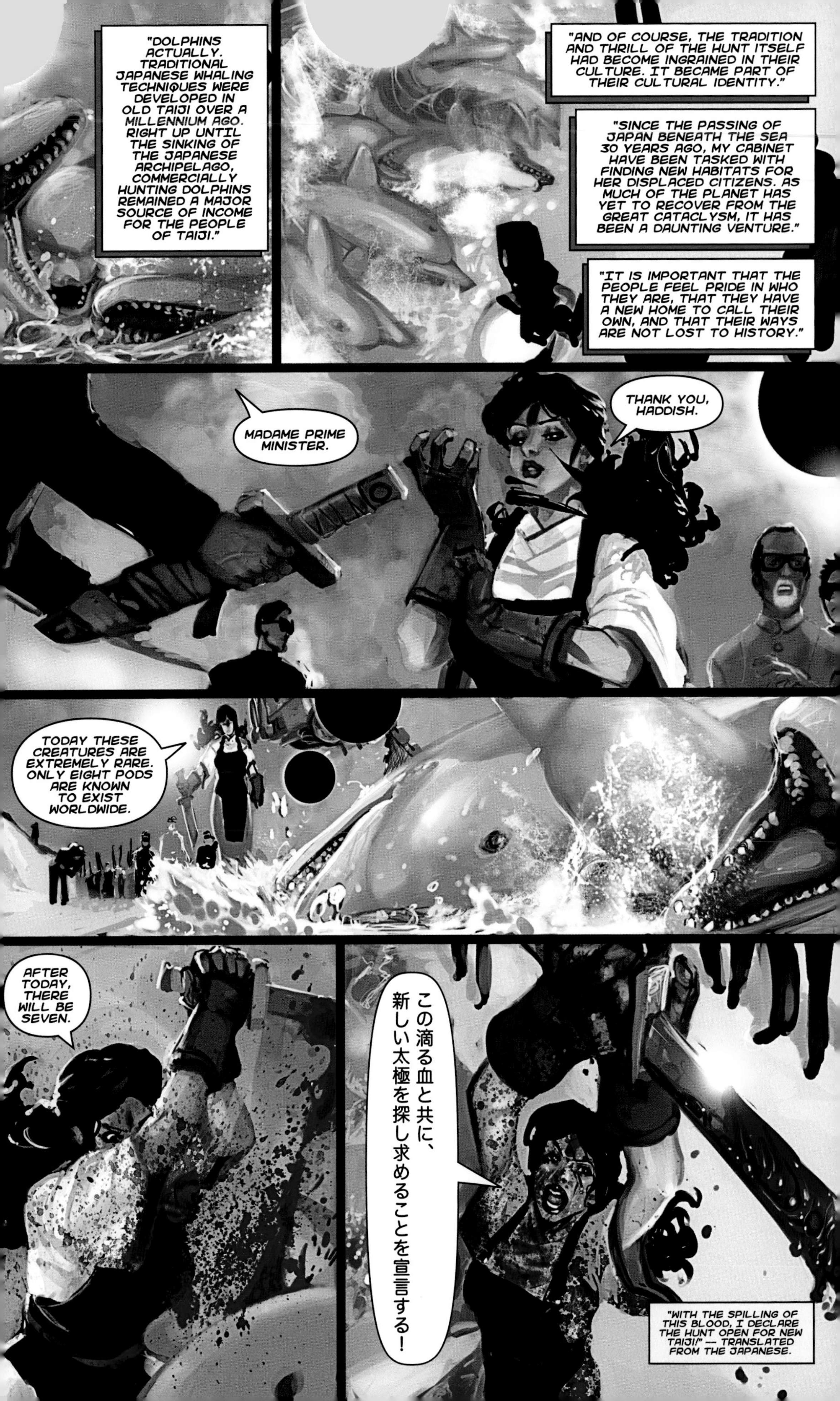
"DOLPHINS ACTUALLY. TRADITIONAL JAPANESE WHALING TECHNIQUES WERE DEVELOPED IN OLD TAIJI OVER A MILLENNIUM AGO. RIGHT UP UNTIL THE SINKING OF THE JAPANESE ARCHIPELAGO, COMMERCIALLY HUNTING DOLPHINS REMAINED A MAJOR SOURCE OF INCOME FOR THE PEOPLE OF TAIJI."
"AND OF COURSE, THE TRADITION AND THRILL OF THE HUNT ITSELF HAD BECOME INGRAINED IN THEIR CULTURE. IT BECAME PART OF THEIR CULTURAL IDENTITY."
"SINCE THE PASSING OF JAPAN BENEATH THE SEA 30 YEARS AGO, MY CABINET HAVE BEEN TASKED WITH FINDING NEW HABITATS FOR HER DISPLACED CITIZENS. AS MUCH OF THE PLANET HAS YET TO RECOVER FROM THE GREAT CATACLYSM, IT HAS BEEN A DAUNTING VENTURE."
"IT IS IMPORTANT THAT THE PEOPLE FEEL PRIDE IN WHO THEY ARE, THAT THEY HAVE A NEW HOME TO CALL THEIR OWN, AND THAT THEIR WAYS ARE NOT LOST TO HISTORY."
MADAME PRIME MINISTER.
THANK YOU, HADDISH.
TODAY THESE CREATURES ARE EXTREMELY RARE. ONLY EIGHT PODS ARE KNOWN TO EXIST WORLDWIDE.
AFTER TODAY, THERE WILL BE SEVEN.
この滴る血と共に、新しい太極を探し求めることを宣言する！
"WITH THE SPILLING OF THIS BLOOD, I DECLARE THE HUNT OPEN FOR NEW TAIJI!" -- TRANSLATED FROM THE JAPANESE.

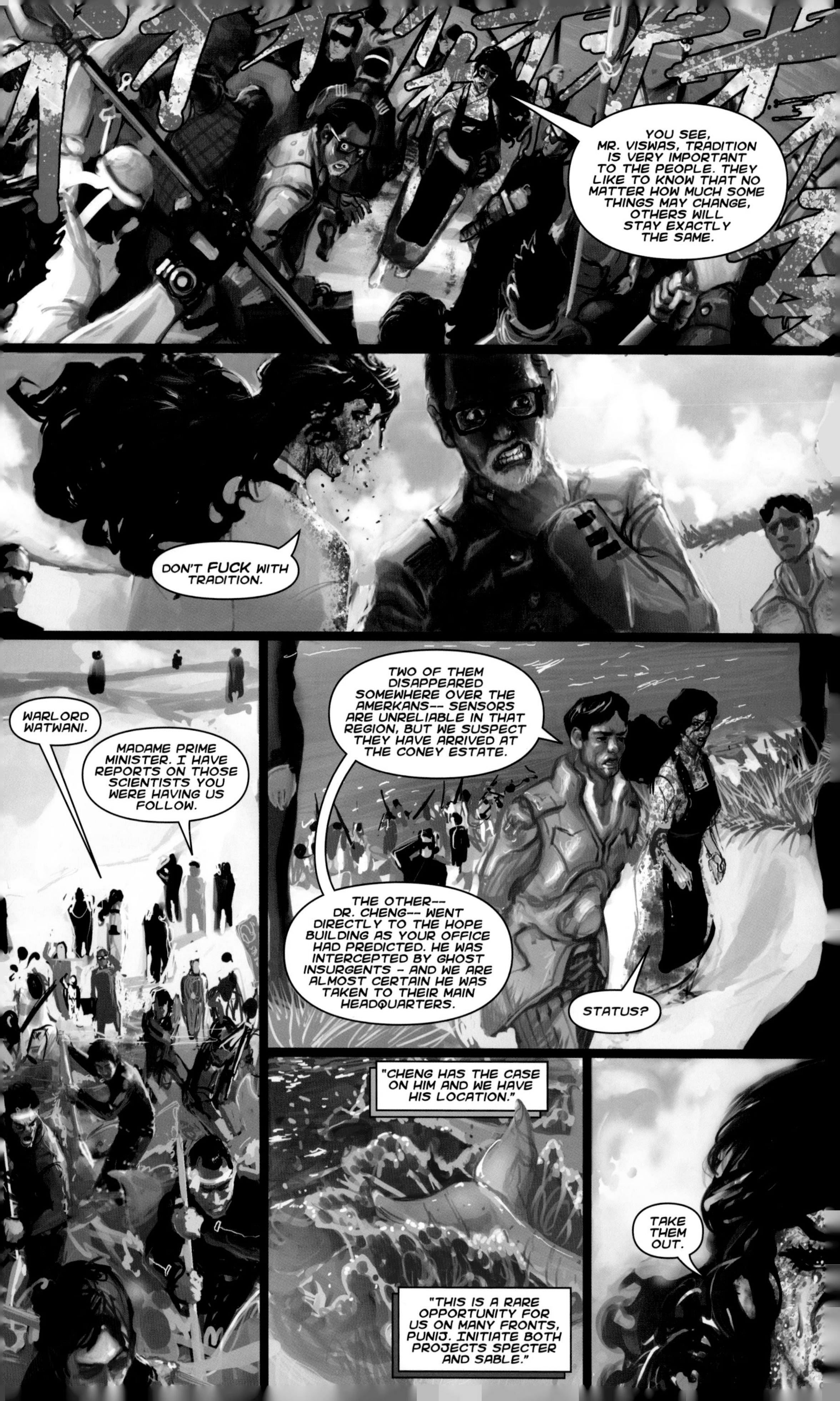
YOU SEE, MR. VISWAS, TRADITION IS VERY IMPORTANT TO THE PEOPLE. THEY LIKE TO KNOW THAT NO MATTER HOW MUCH SOME THINGS MAY CHANGE, OTHERS WILL STAY EXACTLY THE SAME.
DON'T FUCK WITH TRADITION.
WARLORD WATWANI.
MADAME PRIME MINISTER. I HAVE REPORTS ON THOSE SCIENTISTS YOU WERE HAVING US FOLLOW.
STATUS?
TWO OF THEM DISAPPEARED SOMEWHERE OVER THE AMERKANS-- SENSORS ARE UNRELIABLE IN THAT REGION, BUT WE SUSPECT THEY HAVE ARRIVED AT THE CONEY ESTATE.
THE OTHER-- DR. CHENG-- WENT DIRECTLY TO THE HOPE BUILDING AS YOUR OFFICE HAD PREDICTED. HE WAS INTERCEPTED BY GHOST INSURGENTS - AND WE ARE ALMOST CERTAIN HE WAS TAKEN TO THEIR MAIN HEADQUARTERS.
"CHENG HAS THE CASE ON HIM AND WE HAVE HIS LOCATION."
"THIS IS A RARE OPPORTUNITY FOR US ON MANY FRONTS, PUNIJ. INITIATE BOTH PROJECTS SPECTER AND SABLE."
TAKE THEM OUT.

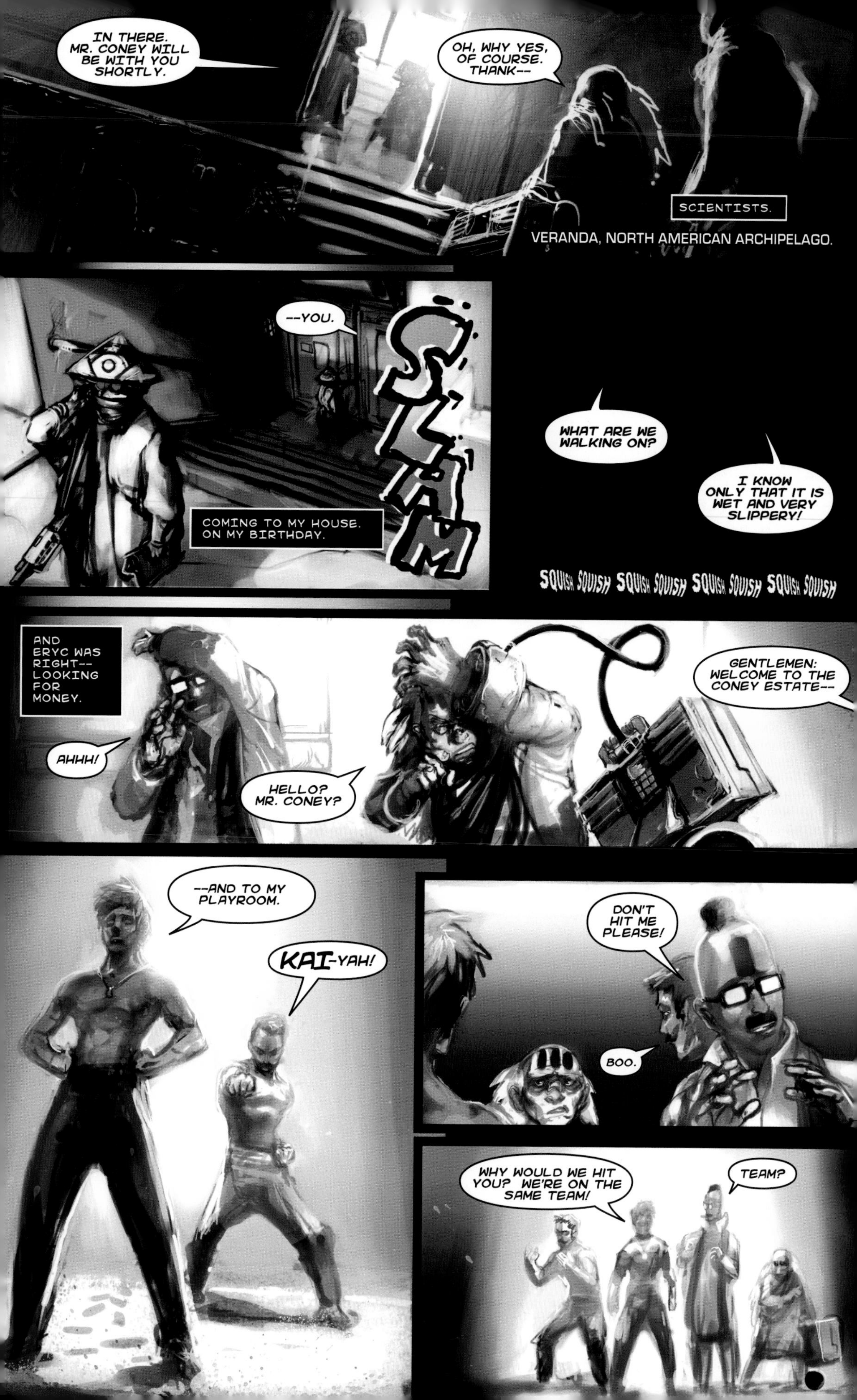

IN THERE. MR. CONEY WILL BE WITH YOU SHORTLY.
OH, WHY YES, OF COURSE. THANK--
SCIENTISTS.
VERANDA, NORTH AMERICAN ARCHIPELAGO.
--YOU.
SLAM
COMING TO MY HOUSE. ON MY BIRTHDAY.
WHAT ARE WE WALKING ON?
I KNOW ONLY THAT IT IS WET AND VERY SLIPPERY!
SQUISH SQUISH SQUISH SQUISH SQUISH SQUISH SQUISH SQUISH
AND ERYC WAS RIGHT-- LOOKING FOR MONEY.
AHHH!
HELLO? MR. CONEY?
GENTLEMEN: WELCOME TO THE CONEY ESTATE--
--AND TO MY PLAYROOM.
KAI-YAH!
DON'T HIT ME PLEASE!
BOO.
WHY WOULD WE HIT YOU? WE'RE ON THE SAME TEAM!
TEAM?

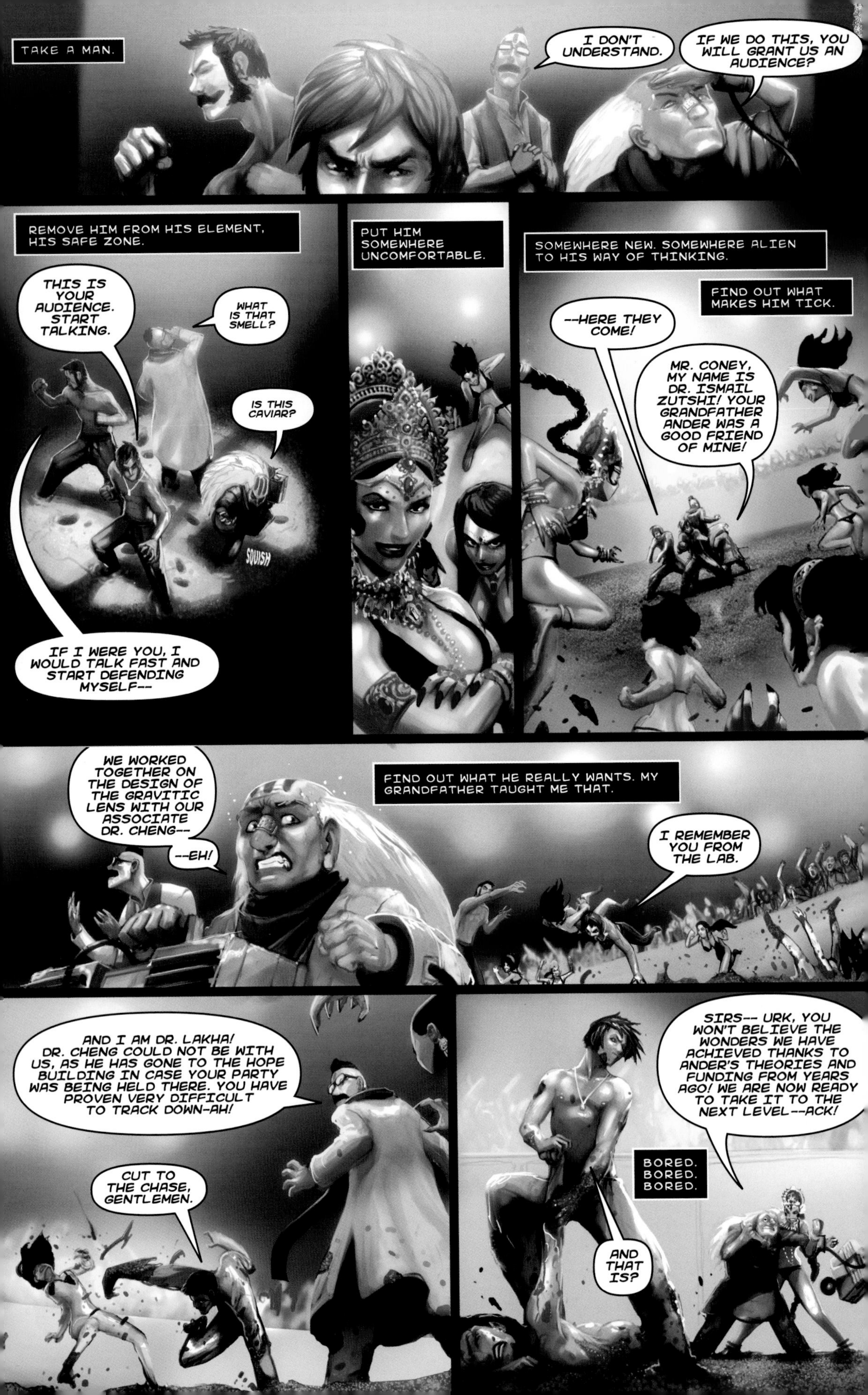
TAKE A MAN.
I DON'T UNDERSTAND.
IF WE DO THIS, YOU WILL GRANT US AN AUDIENCE?
REMOVE HIM FROM HIS ELEMENT, HIS SAFE ZONE.
THIS IS YOUR AUDIENCE. START TALKING.
WHAT IS THAT SMELL?
IS THIS CAVIAR?
SQUISH
IF I WERE YOU, I WOULD TALK FAST AND START DEFENDING MYSELF--
PUT HIM SOMEWHERE UNCOMFORTABLE.
SOMEWHERE NEW. SOMEWHERE ALIEN TO HIS WAY OF THINKING.
FIND OUT WHAT MAKES HIM TICK.
--HERE THEY COME!
MR. CONEY, MY NAME IS DR. ISMAIL ZUTSHI! YOUR GRANDFATHER ANDER WAS A GOOD FRIEND OF MINE!
WE WORKED TOGETHER ON THE DESIGN OF THE GRAVITIC LENS WITH OUR ASSOCIATE DR. CHENG--
--EH!
FIND OUT WHAT HE REALLY WANTS. MY GRANDFATHER TAUGHT ME THAT.
I REMEMBER YOU FROM THE LAB.
AND I AM DR. LAKHA! DR. CHENG COULD NOT BE WITH US, AS HE HAS GONE TO THE HOPE BUILDING IN CASE YOUR PARTY WAS BEING HELD THERE. YOU HAVE PROVEN VERY DIFFICULT TO TRACK DOWN-AH!
CUT TO THE CHASE, GENTLEMEN.
SIRS-- URK, YOU WON'T BELIEVE THE WONDERS WE HAVE ACHIEVED THANKS TO ANDER'S THEORIES AND FUNDING FROM YEARS AGO! WE ARE NOW READY TO TAKE IT TO THE NEXT LEVEL--ACK!
BORED. BORED. BORED.
AND THAT IS?

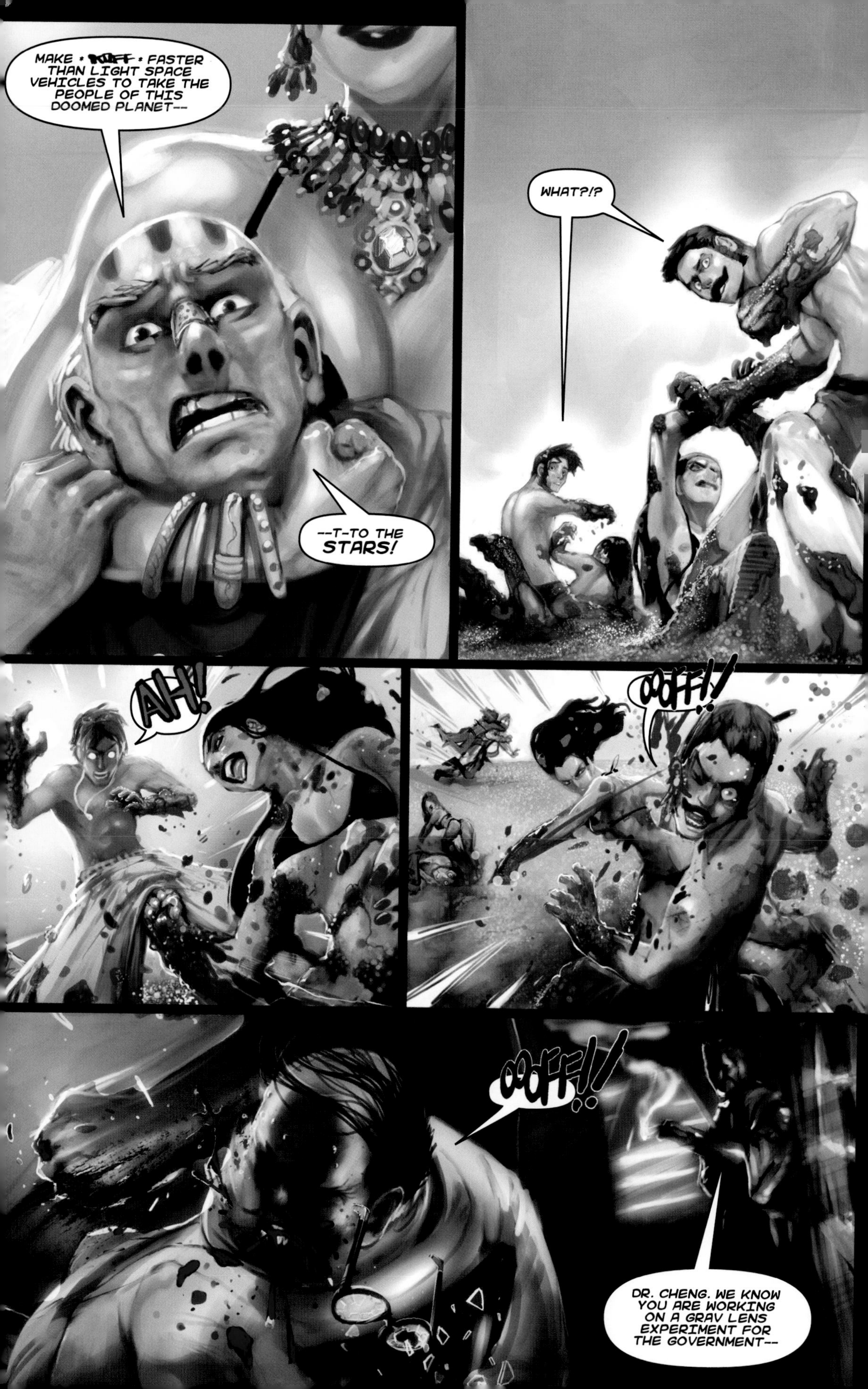
MAKE *[redacted]* FASTER THAN LIGHT SPACE VEHICLES TO TAKE THE PEOPLE OF THIS DOOMED PLANET--
--T-TO THE STARS!
WHAT?!?
AH!
OOOFF!!
OOOFF!!
DR. CHENG. WE KNOW YOU ARE WORKING ON A GRAV LENS EXPERIMENT FOR THE GOVERNMENT--

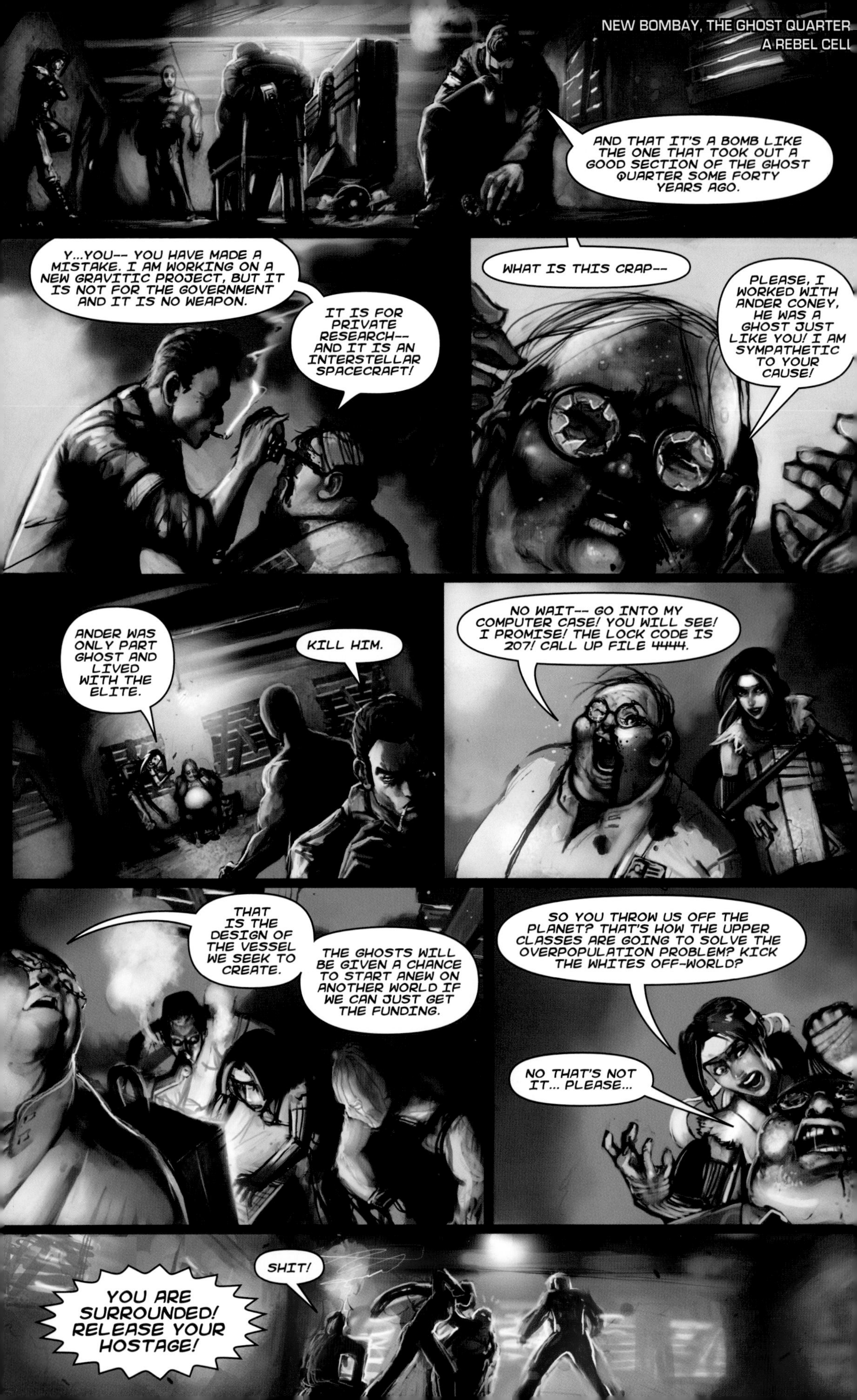
NEW BOMBAY, THE GHOST QUARTER
A REBEL CELL
AND THAT IT'S A BOMB LIKE THE ONE THAT TOOK OUT A GOOD SECTION OF THE GHOST QUARTER SOME FORTY YEARS AGO.
Y...YOU-- YOU HAVE MADE A MISTAKE. I AM WORKING ON A NEW GRAVITIC PROJECT, BUT IT IS NOT FOR THE GOVERNMENT AND IT IS NO WEAPON.
IT IS FOR PRIVATE RESEARCH-- AND IT IS AN INTERSTELLAR SPACECRAFT!
WHAT IS THIS CRAP--
PLEASE, I WORKED WITH ANDER CONEY, HE WAS A GHOST JUST LIKE YOU! I AM SYMPATHETIC TO YOUR CAUSE!
ANDER WAS ONLY PART GHOST AND LIVED WITH THE ELITE.
KILL HIM.
NO WAIT-- GO INTO MY COMPUTER CASE! YOU WILL SEE! I PROMISE! THE LOCK CODE IS 207! CALL UP FILE 4444.
THAT IS THE DESIGN OF THE VESSEL WE SEEK TO CREATE.
THE GHOSTS WILL BE GIVEN A CHANCE TO START ANEW ON ANOTHER WORLD IF WE CAN JUST GET THE FUNDING.
SO YOU THROW US OFF THE PLANET? THAT'S HOW THE UPPER CLASSES ARE GOING TO SOLVE THE OVERPOPULATION PROBLEM? KICK THE WHITES OFF-WORLD?
NO THAT'S NOT IT... PLEASE...
SHIT!
YOU ARE SURROUNDED! RELEASE YOUR HOSTAGE!

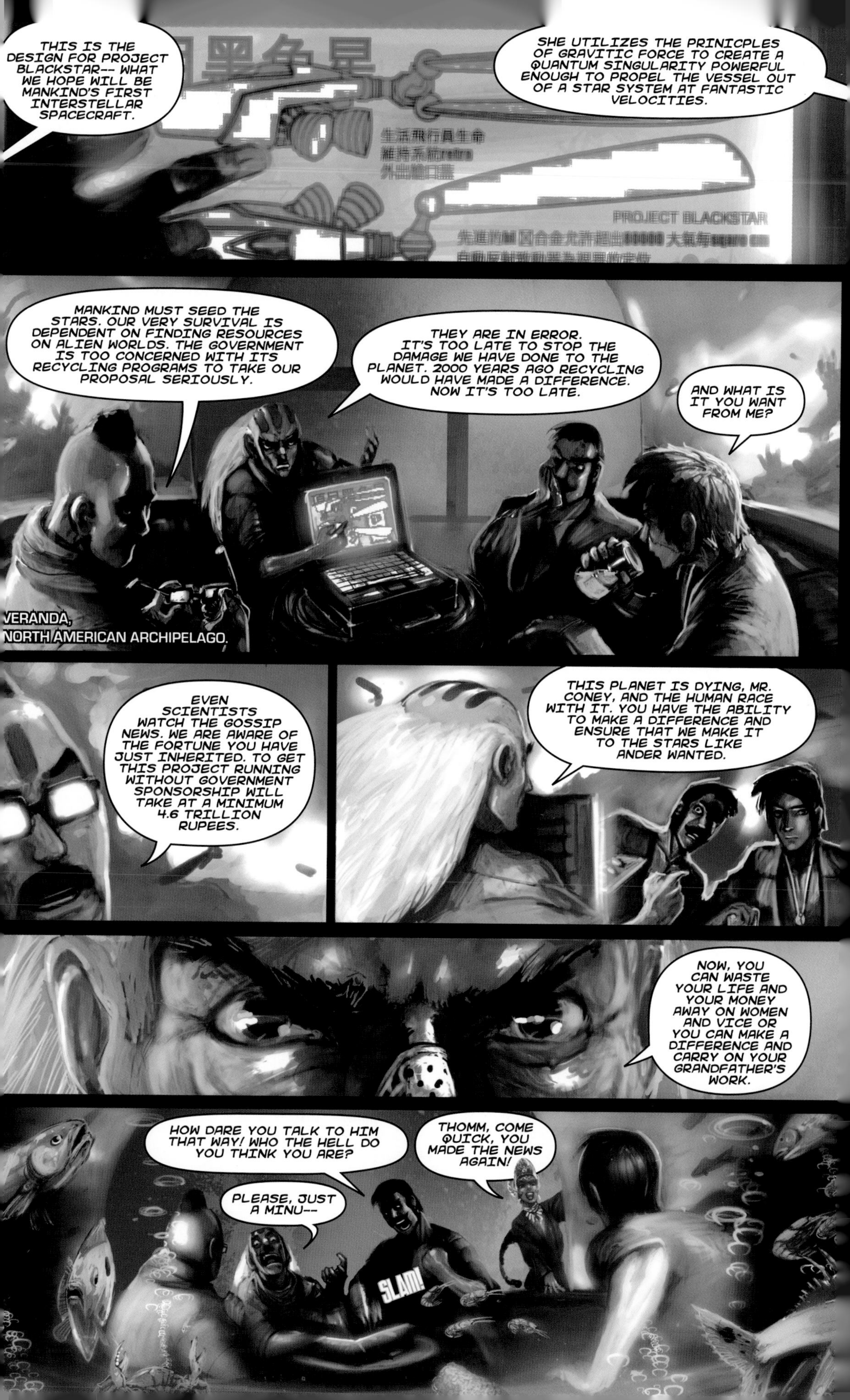
THIS IS THE DESIGN FOR PROJECT BLACKSTAR-- WHAT WE HOPE WILL BE MANKIND'S FIRST INTERSTELLAR SPACECRAFT.
SHE UTILIZES THE PRINICPLES OF GRAVITIC FORCE TO CREATE A QUANTUM SINGULARITY POWERFUL ENOUGH TO PROPEL THE VESSEL OUT OF A STAR SYSTEM AT FANTASTIC VELOCITIES.
PROJECT BLACKSTAR
VERANDA, NORTH AMERICAN ARCHIPELAGO.
MANKIND MUST SEED THE STARS. OUR VERY SURVIVAL IS DEPENDENT ON FINDING RESOURCES ON ALIEN WORLDS. THE GOVERNMENT IS TOO CONCERNED WITH ITS RECYCLING PROGRAMS TO TAKE OUR PROPOSAL SERIOUSLY.
THEY ARE IN ERROR. IT'S TOO LATE TO STOP THE DAMAGE WE HAVE DONE TO THE PLANET. 2000 YEARS AGO RECYCLING WOULD HAVE MADE A DIFFERENCE. NOW IT'S TOO LATE.
AND WHAT IS IT YOU WANT FROM ME?
EVEN SCIENTISTS WATCH THE GOSSIP NEWS. WE ARE AWARE OF THE FORTUNE YOU HAVE JUST INHERITED. TO GET THIS PROJECT RUNNING WITHOUT GOVERNMENT SPONSORSHIP WILL TAKE AT A MINIMUM 4.6 TRILLION RUPEES.
THIS PLANET IS DYING, MR. CONEY, AND THE HUMAN RACE WITH IT. YOU HAVE THE ABILITY TO MAKE A DIFFERENCE AND ENSURE THAT WE MAKE IT TO THE STARS LIKE ANDER WANTED.
NOW, YOU CAN WASTE YOUR LIFE AND YOUR MONEY AWAY ON WOMEN AND VICE OR YOU CAN MAKE A DIFFERENCE AND CARRY ON YOUR GRANDFATHER'S WORK.
HOW DARE YOU TALK TO HIM THAT WAY! WHO THE HELL DO YOU THINK YOU ARE?
PLEASE, JUST A MINU--
THOMM, COME QUICK, YOU MADE THE NEWS AGAIN!
SLAM!

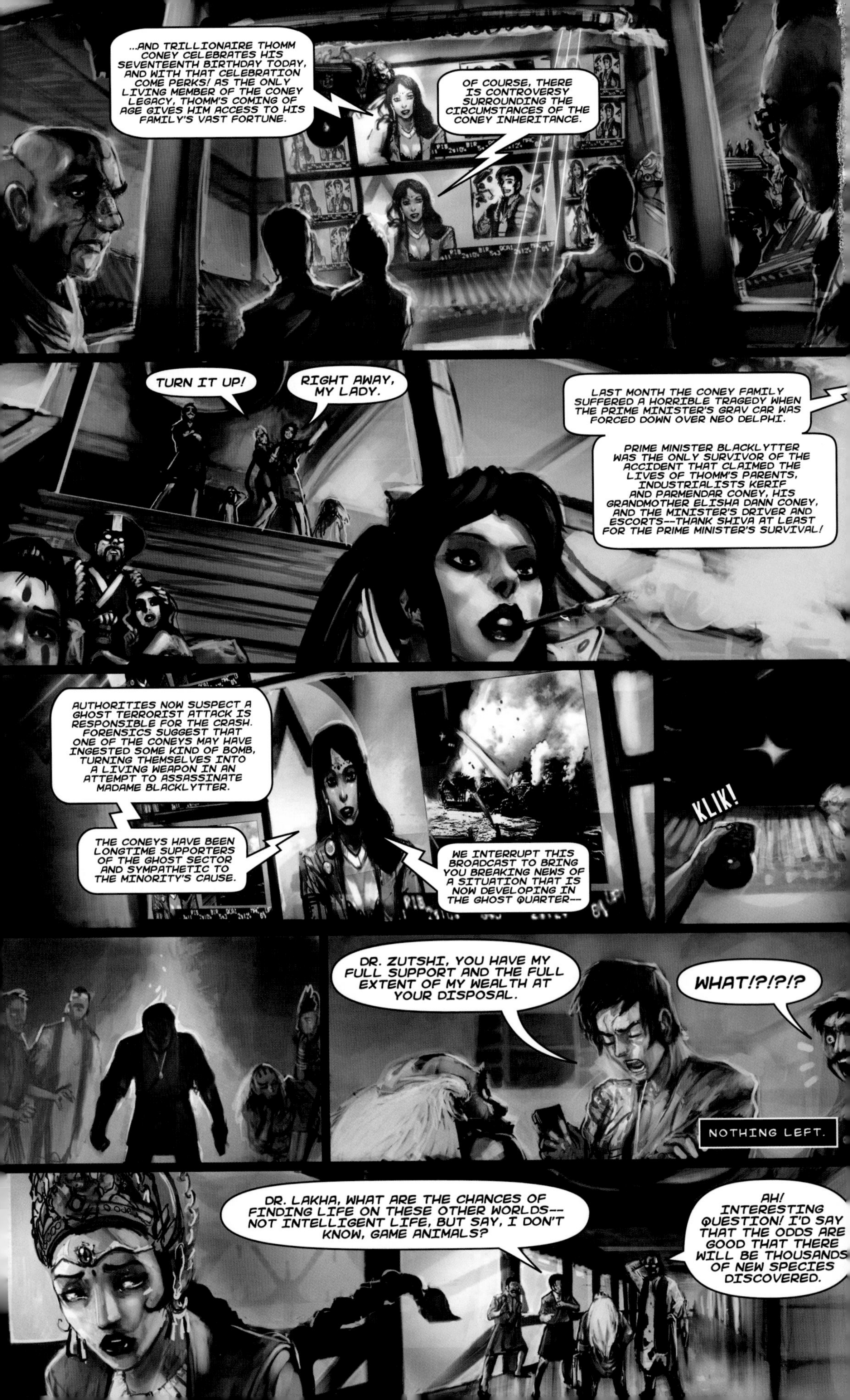
...AND TRILLIONAIRE THOMM CONEY CELEBRATES HIS SEVENTEENTH BIRTHDAY TODAY, AND WITH THAT CELEBRATION COME PERKS! AS THE ONLY LIVING MEMBER OF THE CONEY LEGACY, THOMM'S COMING OF AGE GIVES HIM ACCESS TO HIS FAMILY'S VAST FORTUNE.
OF COURSE, THERE IS CONTROVERSY SURROUNDING THE CIRCUMSTANCES OF THE CONEY INHERITANCE.
TURN IT UP!
RIGHT AWAY, MY LADY.
LAST MONTH THE CONEY FAMILY SUFFERED A HORRIBLE TRAGEDY WHEN THE PRIME MINISTER'S GRAV CAR WAS FORCED DOWN OVER NEO DELPHI.
PRIME MINISTER BLACKLYTTER WAS THE ONLY SURVIVOR OF THE ACCIDENT THAT CLAIMED THE LIVES OF THOMM'S PARENTS, INDUSTRIALISTS KERIF AND PARMENDAR CONEY, HIS GRANDMOTHER ELISHA DANN CONEY, AND THE MINISTER'S DRIVER AND ESCORTS--THANK SHIVA AT LEAST FOR THE PRIME MINISTER'S SURVIVAL!
AUTHORITIES NOW SUSPECT A GHOST TERRORIST ATTACK IS RESPONSIBLE FOR THE CRASH. FORENSICS SUGGEST THAT ONE OF THE CONEYS MAY HAVE INGESTED SOME KIND OF BOMB, TURNING THEMSELVES INTO A LIVING WEAPON IN AN ATTEMPT TO ASSASSINATE MADAME BLACKLYTTER.
THE CONEYS HAVE BEEN LONGTIME SUPPORTERS OF THE GHOST SECTOR AND SYMPATHETIC TO THE MINORITY'S CAUSE.
WE INTERRUPT THIS BROADCAST TO BRING YOU BREAKING NEWS OF A SITUATION THAT IS NOW DEVELOPING IN THE GHOST QUARTER--
KLIK!
DR. ZUTSHI, YOU HAVE MY FULL SUPPORT AND THE FULL EXTENT OF MY WEALTH AT YOUR DISPOSAL.
WHAT!?!?!?
NOTHING LEFT.
DR. LAKHA, WHAT ARE THE CHANCES OF FINDING LIFE ON THESE OTHER WORLDS-- NOT INTELLIGENT LIFE, BUT SAY, I DON'T KNOW, GAME ANIMALS?
AH! INTERESTING QUESTION! I'D SAY THAT THE ODDS ARE GOOD THAT THERE WILL BE THOUSANDS OF NEW SPECIES DISCOVERED.

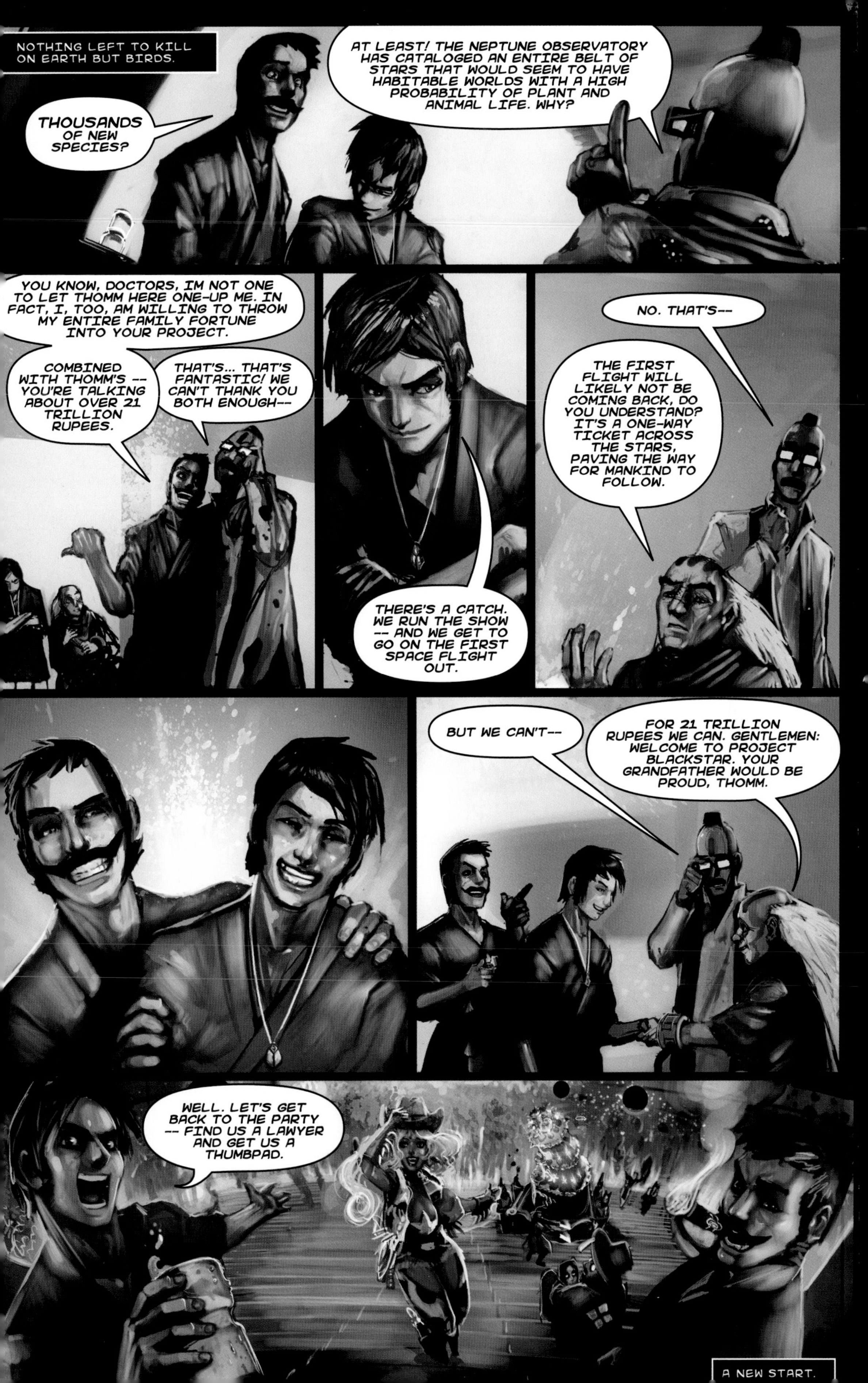
NOTHING LEFT TO KILL ON EARTH BUT BIRDS.
THOUSANDS OF NEW SPECIES?
AT LEAST! THE NEPTUNE OBSERVATORY HAS CATALOGED AN ENTIRE BELT OF STARS THAT WOULD SEEM TO HAVE HABITABLE WORLDS WITH A HIGH PROBABILITY OF PLANT AND ANIMAL LIFE. WHY?
YOU KNOW, DOCTORS, IM NOT ONE TO LET THOMM HERE ONE-UP ME. IN FACT, I, TOO, AM WILLING TO THROW MY ENTIRE FAMILY FORTUNE INTO YOUR PROJECT.
COMBINED WITH THOMM'S -- YOU'RE TALKING ABOUT OVER 21 TRILLION RUPEES.
THAT'S... THAT'S FANTASTIC! WE CAN'T THANK YOU BOTH ENOUGH--
THERE'S A CATCH. WE RUN THE SHOW -- AND WE GET TO GO ON THE FIRST SPACE FLIGHT OUT.
NO. THAT'S--
THE FIRST FLIGHT WILL LIKELY NOT BE COMING BACK, DO YOU UNDERSTAND? IT'S A ONE-WAY TICKET ACROSS THE STARS, PAVING THE WAY FOR MANKIND TO FOLLOW.
BUT WE CAN'T--
FOR 21 TRILLION RUPEES WE CAN. GENTLEMEN: WELCOME TO PROJECT BLACKSTAR. YOUR GRANDFATHER WOULD BE PROUD, THOMM.
WELL. LET'S GET BACK TO THE PARTY -- FIND US A LAWYER AND GET US A THUMBPAD.
A NEW START.

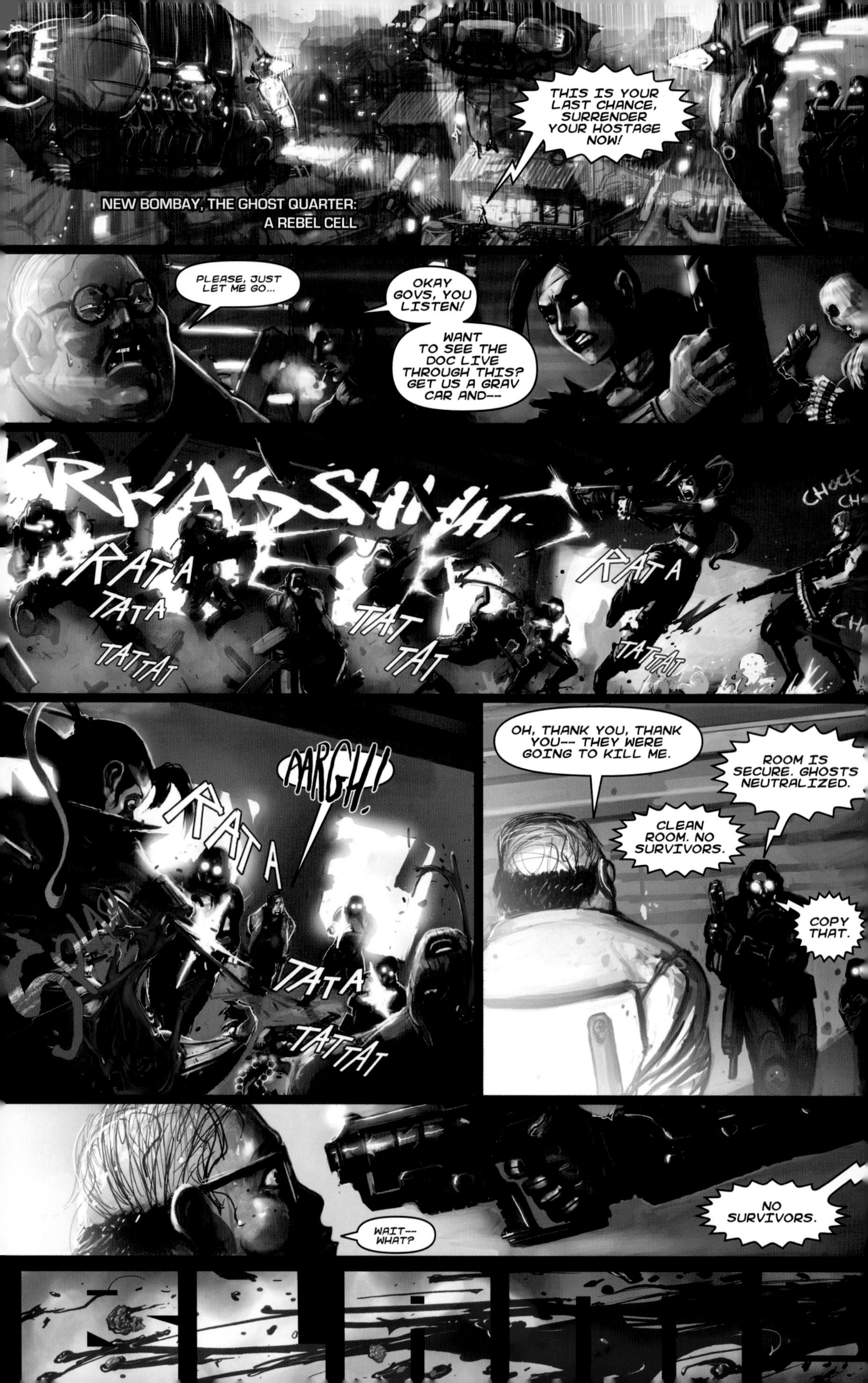
THIS IS YOUR LAST CHANCE, SURRENDER YOUR HOSTAGE NOW!
NEW BOMBAY, THE GHOST QUARTER: A REBEL CELL
PLEASE, JUST LET ME GO...
OKAY GOVS, YOU LISTEN!
WANT TO SEE THE DOC LIVE THROUGH THIS? GET US A GRAV CAR AND--
KRKASSHHH
RATA TATA TATTAT
TAT TAT
RATA TATTAT
CHOCK CH
AARGH!
RATA
TATA TATTAT
OH, THANK YOU, THANK YOU-- THEY WERE GOING TO KILL ME.
ROOM IS SECURE. GHOSTS NEUTRALIZED.
CLEAN ROOM. NO SURVIVORS.
COPY THAT.
WAIT-- WHAT?
NO SURVIVORS.

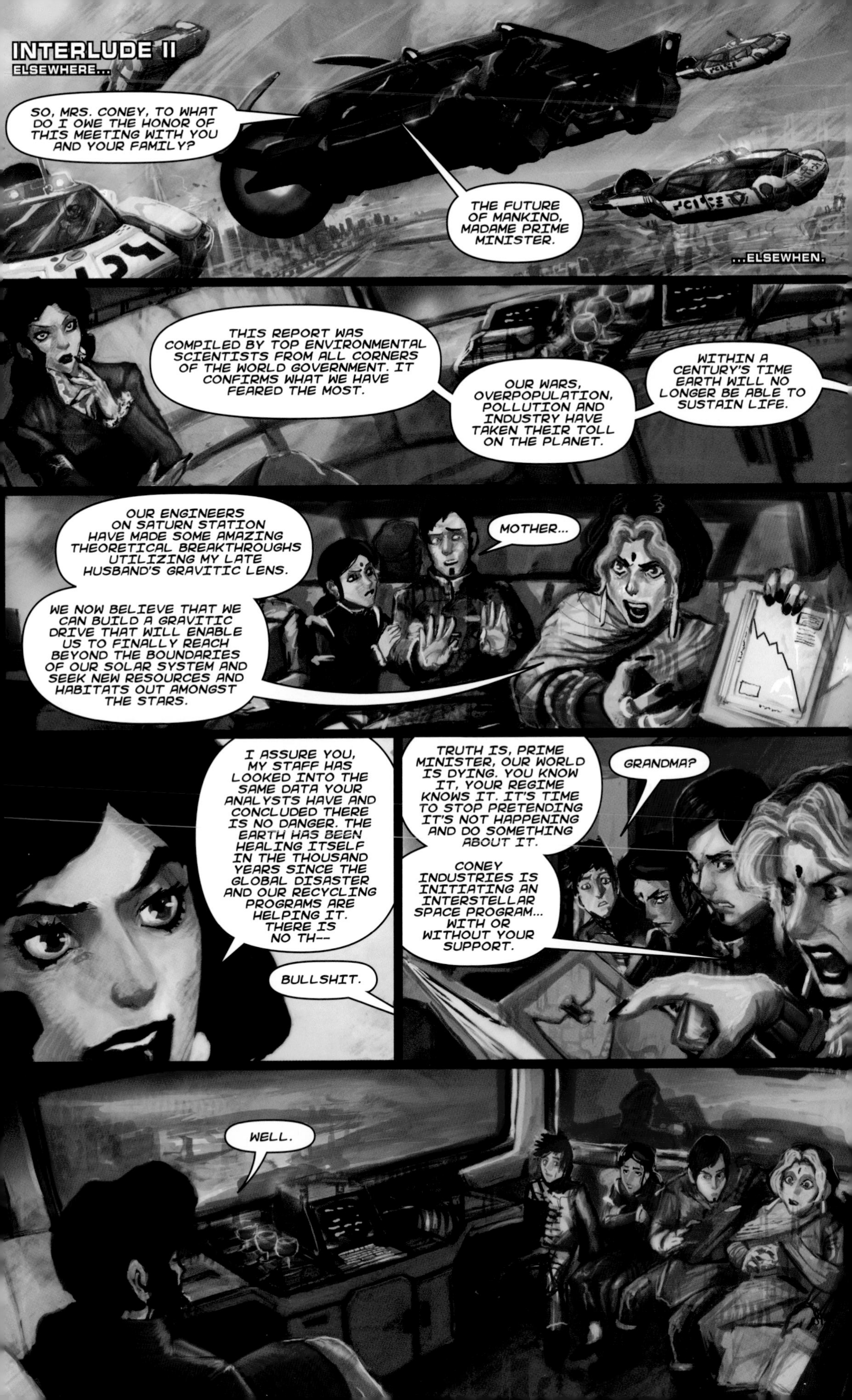
INTERLUDE II
ELSEWHERE...
SO, MRS. CONEY, TO WHAT DO I OWE THE HONOR OF THIS MEETING WITH YOU AND YOUR FAMILY?
THE FUTURE OF MANKIND, MADAME PRIME MINISTER.
...ELSEWHEN.
THIS REPORT WAS COMPILED BY TOP ENVIRONMENTAL SCIENTISTS FROM ALL CORNERS OF THE WORLD GOVERNMENT. IT CONFIRMS WHAT WE HAVE FEARED THE MOST.
OUR WARS, OVERPOPULATION, POLLUTION AND INDUSTRY HAVE TAKEN THEIR TOLL ON THE PLANET.
WITHIN A CENTURY'S TIME EARTH WILL NO LONGER BE ABLE TO SUSTAIN LIFE.
OUR ENGINEERS ON SATURN STATION HAVE MADE SOME AMAZING THEORETICAL BREAKTHROUGHS UTILIZING MY LATE HUSBAND'S GRAVITIC LENS.
MOTHER...
WE NOW BELIEVE THAT WE CAN BUILD A GRAVITIC DRIVE THAT WILL ENABLE US TO FINALLY REACH BEYOND THE BOUNDARIES OF OUR SOLAR SYSTEM AND SEEK NEW RESOURCES AND HABITATS OUT AMONGST THE STARS.
I ASSURE YOU, MY STAFF HAS LOOKED INTO THE SAME DATA YOUR ANALYSTS HAVE AND CONCLUDED THERE IS NO DANGER. THE EARTH HAS BEEN HEALING ITSELF IN THE THOUSAND YEARS SINCE THE GLOBAL DISASTER AND OUR RECYCLING PROGRAMS ARE HELPING IT. THERE IS NO TH--
BULLSHIT.
TRUTH IS, PRIME MINISTER, OUR WORLD IS DYING. YOU KNOW IT, YOUR REGIME KNOWS IT. IT'S TIME TO STOP PRETENDING IT'S NOT HAPPENING AND DO SOMETHING ABOUT IT.
GRANDMA?
CONEY INDUSTRIES IS INITIATING AN INTERSTELLAR SPACE PROGRAM... WITH OR WITHOUT YOUR SUPPORT.
WELL.

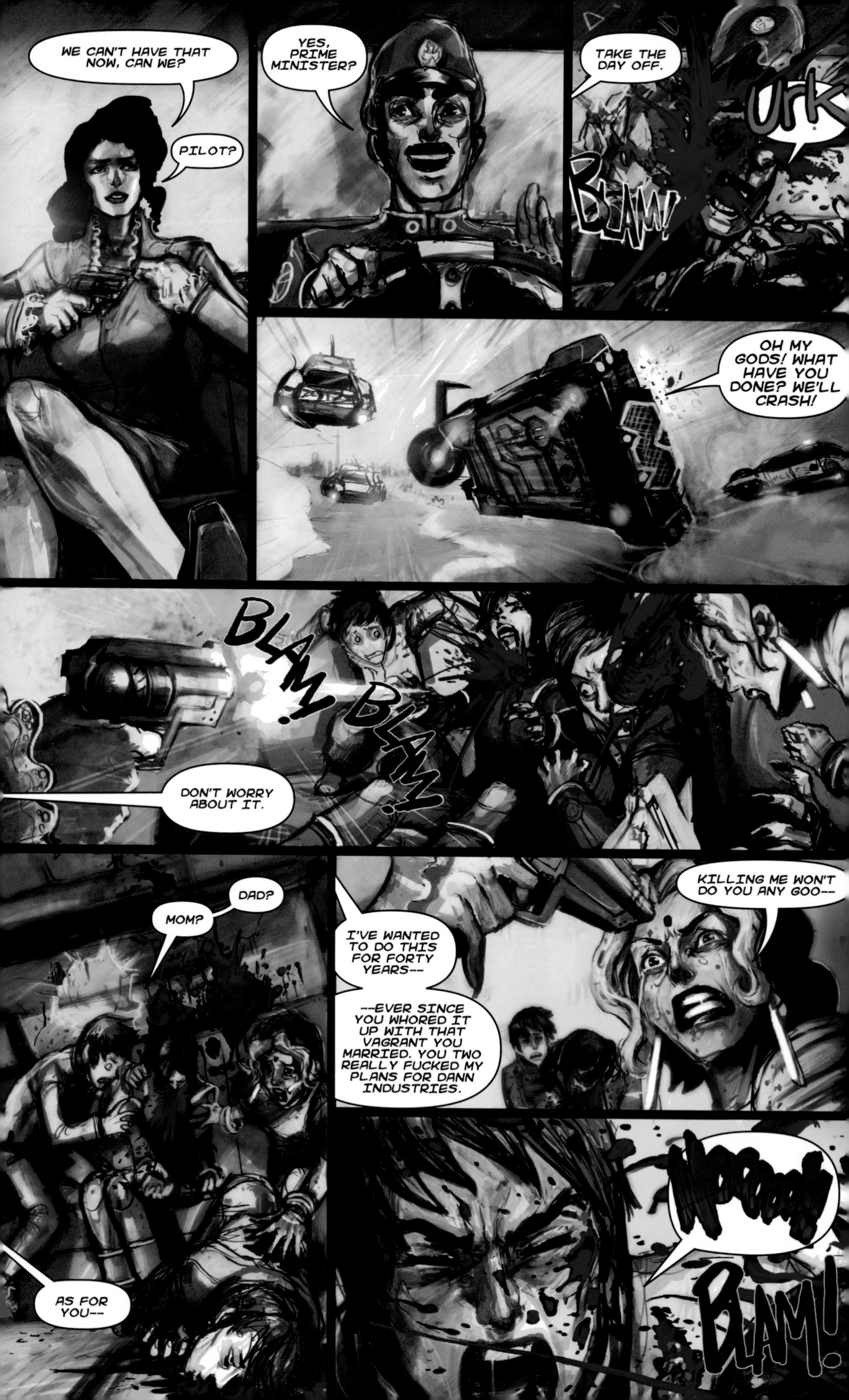
WE CAN'T HAVE THAT NOW, CAN WE?
PILOT?
YES, PRIME MINISTER?
TAKE THE DAY OFF.
URK
BLAM!
OH MY GODS! WHAT HAVE YOU DONE? WE'LL CRASH!
BLAM! BLAM! BLAM!
DON'T WORRY ABOUT IT.
DAD?
MOM?
AS FOR YOU--
I'VE WANTED TO DO THIS FOR FORTY YEARS--
--EVER SINCE YOU WHORED IT UP WITH THAT VAGRANT YOU MARRIED. YOU TWO REALLY FUCKED MY PLANS FOR DANN INDUSTRIES.
KILLING ME WON'T DO YOU ANY GOO--
BLAM!

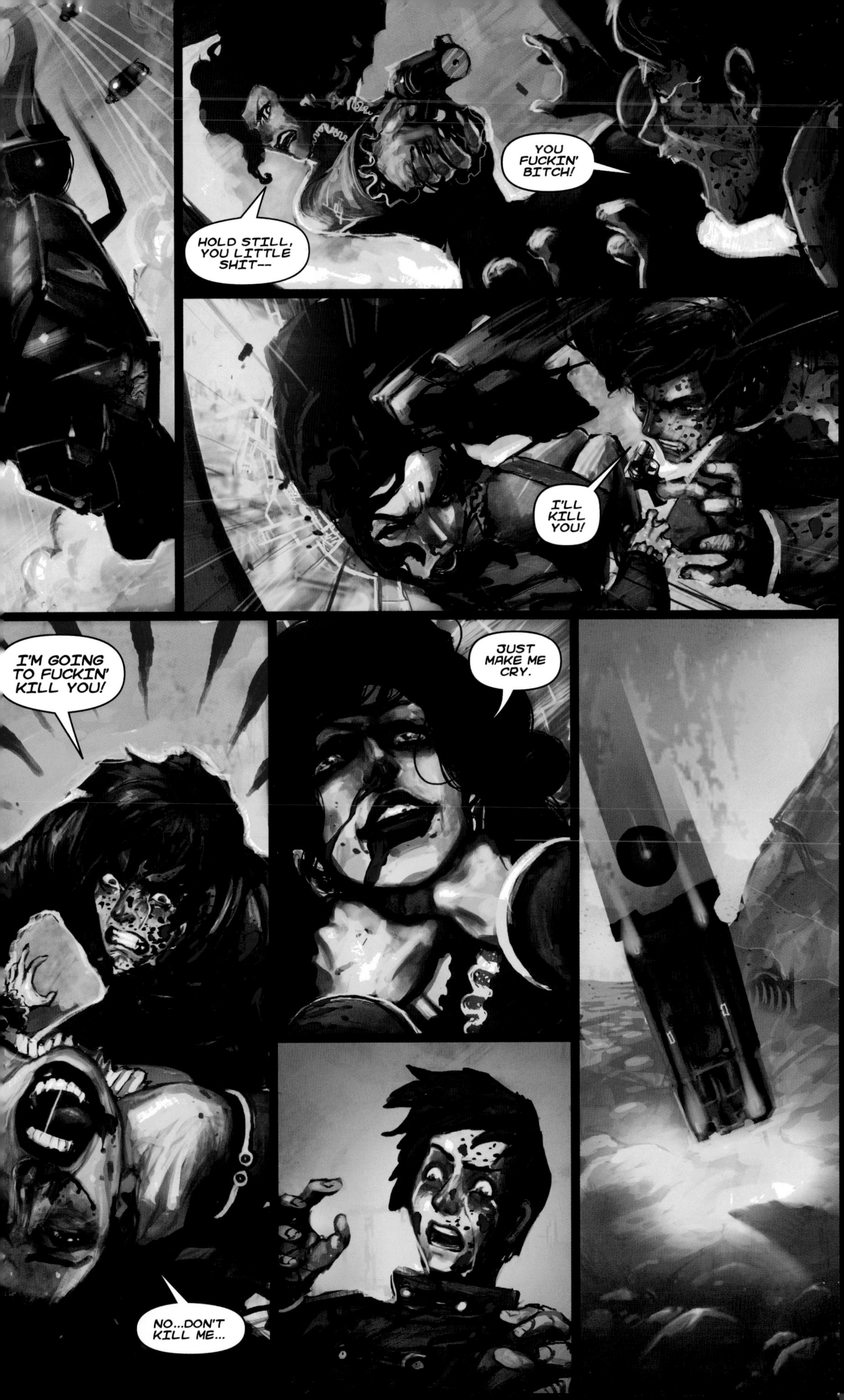
HOLD STILL, YOU LITTLE SHIT--
YOU FUCKIN' BITCH!
I'LL KILL YOU!
I'M GOING TO FUCKIN' KILL YOU!
JUST MAKE ME CRY.
NO...DON'T KILL ME...

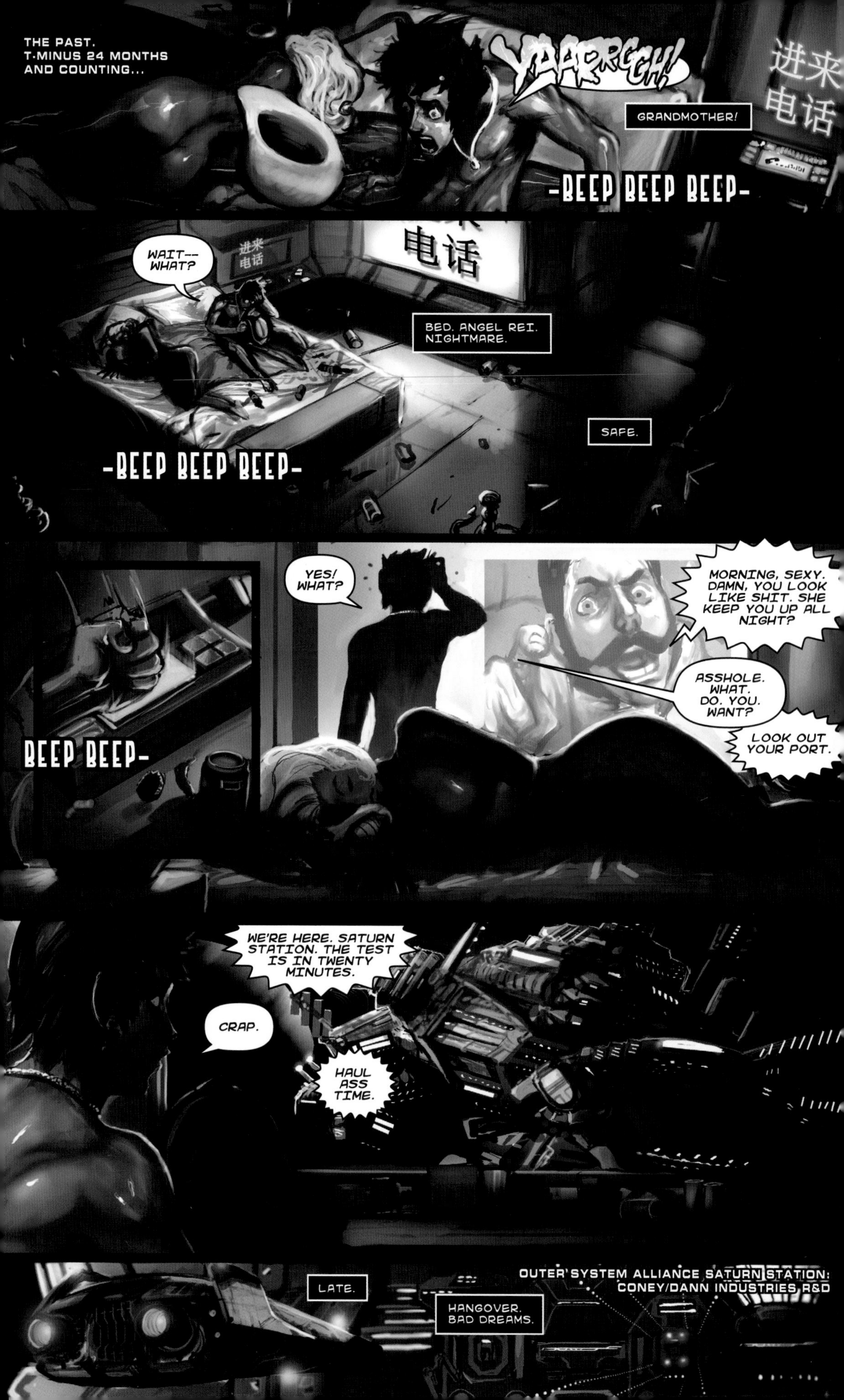
THE PAST.
T-MINUS 24 MONTHS
AND COUNTING...
YAARRGGH!
GRANDMOTHER!
进来
电话
-BEEP BEEP BEEP-
WAIT--
WHAT?
进来
电话
BED. ANGEL REI.
NIGHTMARE.
SAFE.
-BEEP BEEP BEEP-
BEEP BEEP-
YES!
WHAT?
MORNING, SEXY. DAMN, YOU LOOK LIKE SHIT. SHE KEEP YOU UP ALL NIGHT?
ASSHOLE. WHAT. DO. YOU. WANT?
LOOK OUT YOUR PORT.
WE'RE HERE. SATURN STATION. THE TEST IS IN TWENTY MINUTES.
CRAP.
HAUL ASS TIME.
OUTER SYSTEM ALLIANCE SATURN STATION:
CONEY/DANN INDUSTRIES R&D
LATE.
HANGOVER.
BAD DREAMS.

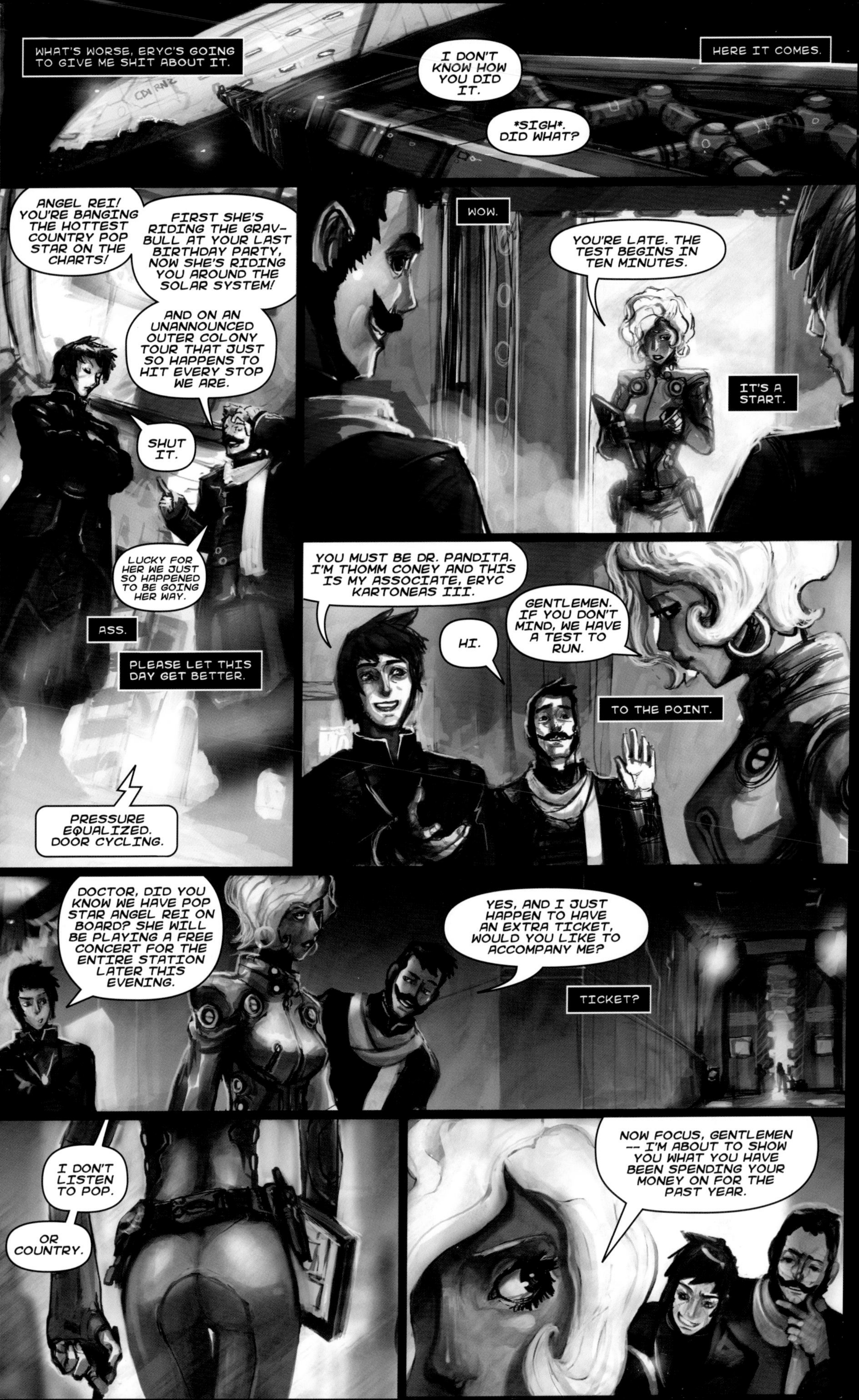

WHAT'S WORSE, ERYC'S GOING TO GIVE ME SHIT ABOUT IT.
I DON'T KNOW HOW YOU DID IT.
SIGH. DID WHAT?
HERE IT COMES.
ANGEL REI! YOU'RE BANGING THE HOTTEST COUNTRY POP STAR ON THE CHARTS!
FIRST SHE'S RIDING THE GRAV-BULL AT YOUR LAST BIRTHDAY PARTY, NOW SHE'S RIDING YOU AROUND THE SOLAR SYSTEM!
AND ON AN UNANNOUNCED OUTER COLONY TOUR THAT JUST SO HAPPENS TO HIT EVERY STOP WE ARE.
SHUT IT.
LUCKY FOR HER WE JUST SO HAPPENED TO BE GOING HER WAY.
ASS.
PLEASE LET THIS DAY GET BETTER.
PRESSURE EQUALIZED. DOOR CYCLING.
WOW.
YOU'RE LATE. THE TEST BEGINS IN TEN MINUTES.
IT'S A START.
YOU MUST BE DR. PANDITA. I'M THOMM CONEY AND THIS IS MY ASSOCIATE, ERYC KARTONEAS III.
HI.
GENTLEMEN. IF YOU DON'T MIND, WE HAVE A TEST TO RUN.
TO THE POINT.
DOCTOR, DID YOU KNOW WE HAVE POP STAR ANGEL REI ON BOARD? SHE WILL BE PLAYING A FREE CONCERT FOR THE ENTIRE STATION LATER THIS EVENING.
YES, AND I JUST HAPPEN TO HAVE AN EXTRA TICKET, WOULD YOU LIKE TO ACCOMPANY ME?
TICKET?
I DON'T LISTEN TO POP.
OR COUNTRY.
NOW FOCUS, GENTLEMEN -- I'M ABOUT TO SHOW YOU WHAT YOU HAVE BEEN SPENDING YOUR MONEY ON FOR THE PAST YEAR.

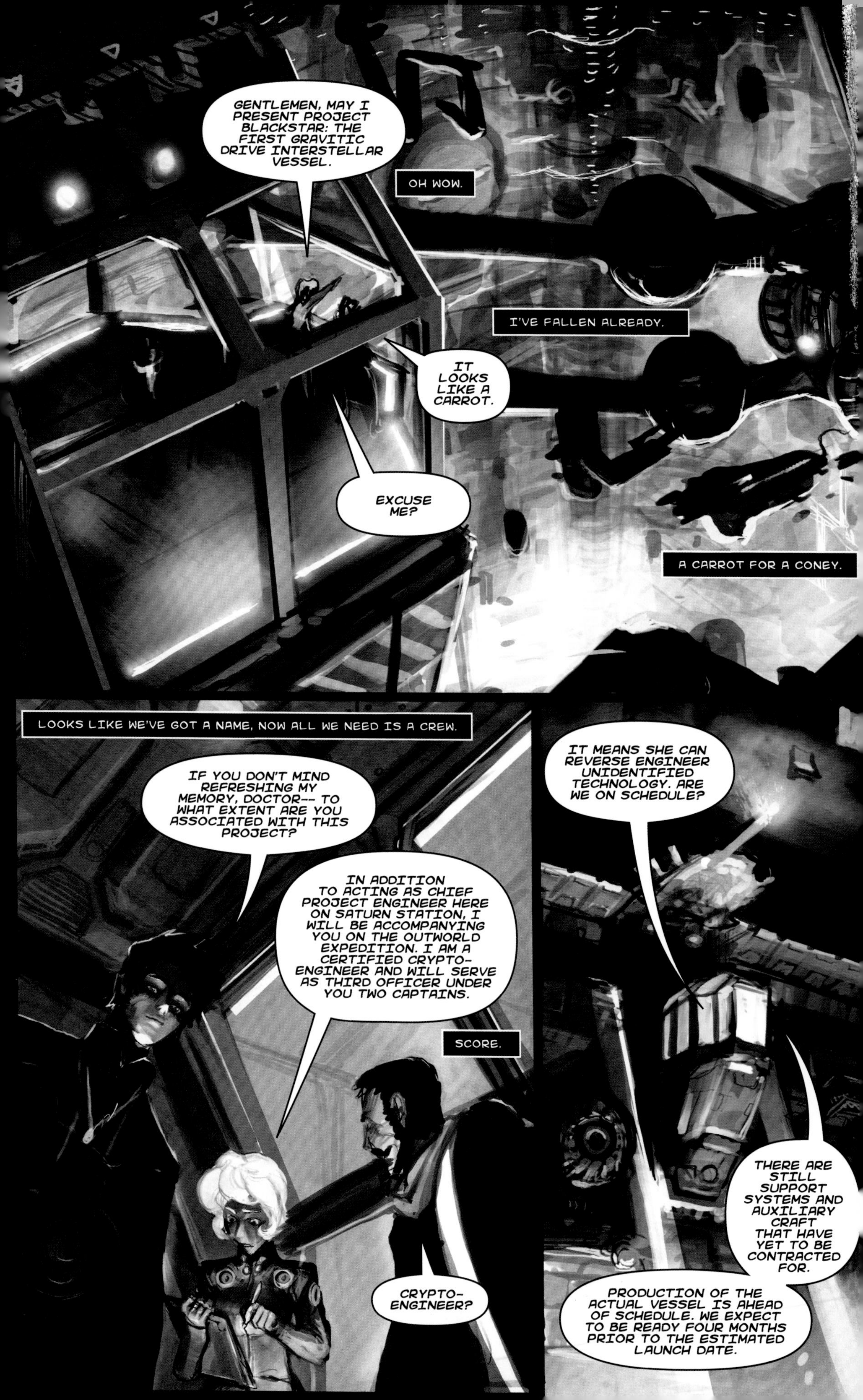
GENTLEMEN, MAY I PRESENT PROJECT BLACKSTAR: THE FIRST GRAVITIC DRIVE INTERSTELLAR VESSEL.
OH WOW.
I'VE FALLEN ALREADY.
IT LOOKS LIKE A CARROT.
EXCUSE ME?
A CARROT FOR A CONEY.
LOOKS LIKE WE'VE GOT A NAME, NOW ALL WE NEED IS A CREW.
IF YOU DON'T MIND REFRESHING MY MEMORY, DOCTOR-- TO WHAT EXTENT ARE YOU ASSOCIATED WITH THIS PROJECT?
IN ADDITION TO ACTING AS CHIEF PROJECT ENGINEER HERE ON SATURN STATION, I WILL BE ACCOMPANYING YOU ON THE OUTWORLD EXPEDITION. I AM A CERTIFIED CRYPTO-ENGINEER AND WILL SERVE AS THIRD OFFICER UNDER YOU TWO CAPTAINS.
SCORE.
CRYPTO-ENGINEER?
IT MEANS SHE CAN REVERSE ENGINEER UNIDENTIFIED TECHNOLOGY. ARE WE ON SCHEDULE?
PRODUCTION OF THE ACTUAL VESSEL IS AHEAD OF SCHEDULE. WE EXPECT TO BE READY FOUR MONTHS PRIOR TO THE ESTIMATED LAUNCH DATE.
THERE ARE STILL SUPPORT SYSTEMS AND AUXILIARY CRAFT THAT HAVE YET TO BE CONTRACTED FOR.

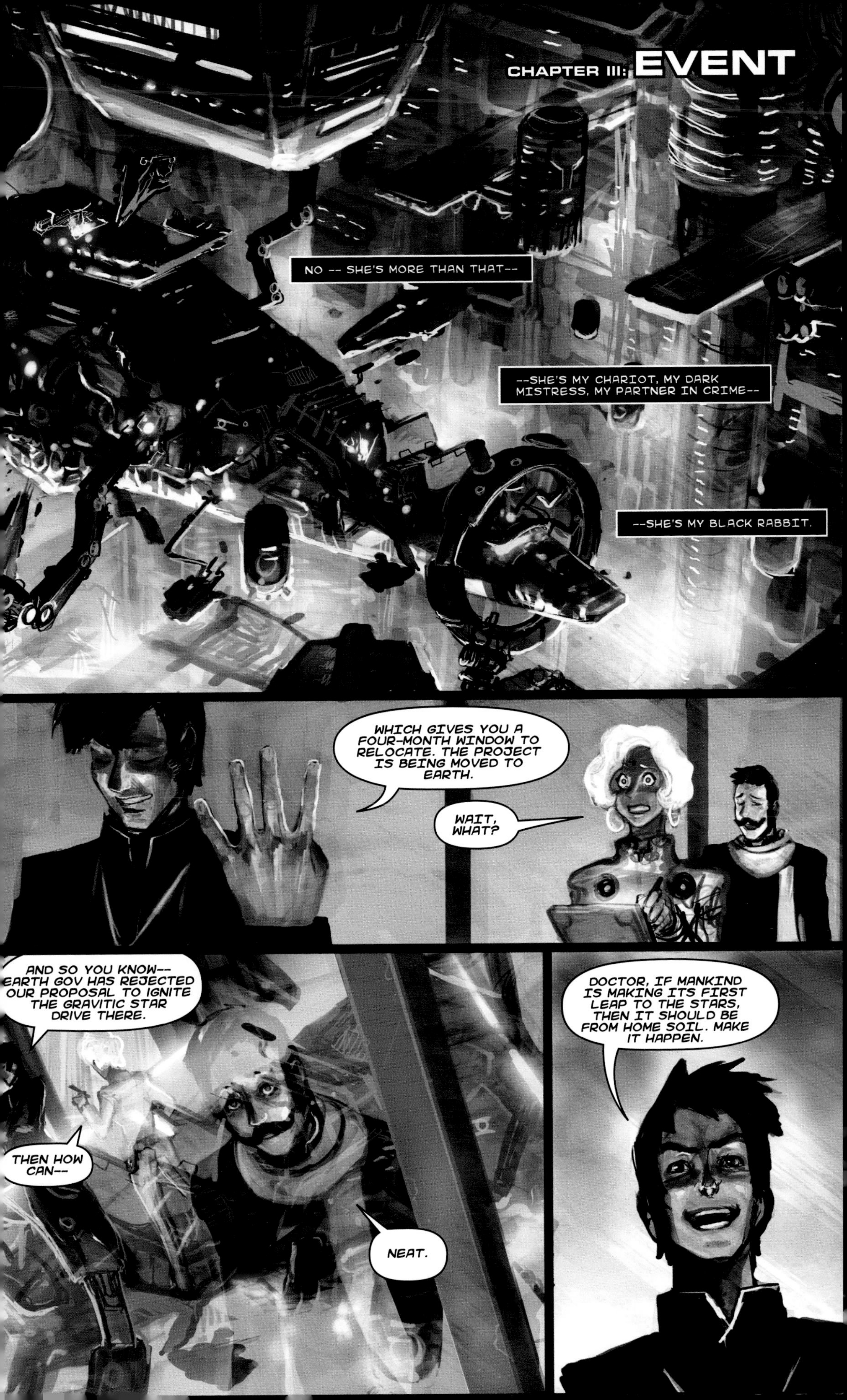
CHAPTER III: EVENT
NO -- SHE'S MORE THAN THAT--
--SHE'S MY CHARIOT, MY DARK MISTRESS, MY PARTNER IN CRIME--
--SHE'S MY BLACK RABBIT.
WHICH GIVES YOU A FOUR-MONTH WINDOW TO RELOCATE. THE PROJECT IS BEING MOVED TO EARTH.
WAIT, WHAT?
AND SO YOU KNOW-- EARTH GOV HAS REJECTED OUR PROPOSAL TO IGNITE THE GRAVITIC STAR DRIVE THERE.
THEN HOW CAN--
NEAT.
DOCTOR, IF MANKIND IS MAKING ITS FIRST LEAP TO THE STARS, THEN IT SHOULD BE FROM HOME SOIL. MAKE IT HAPPEN.

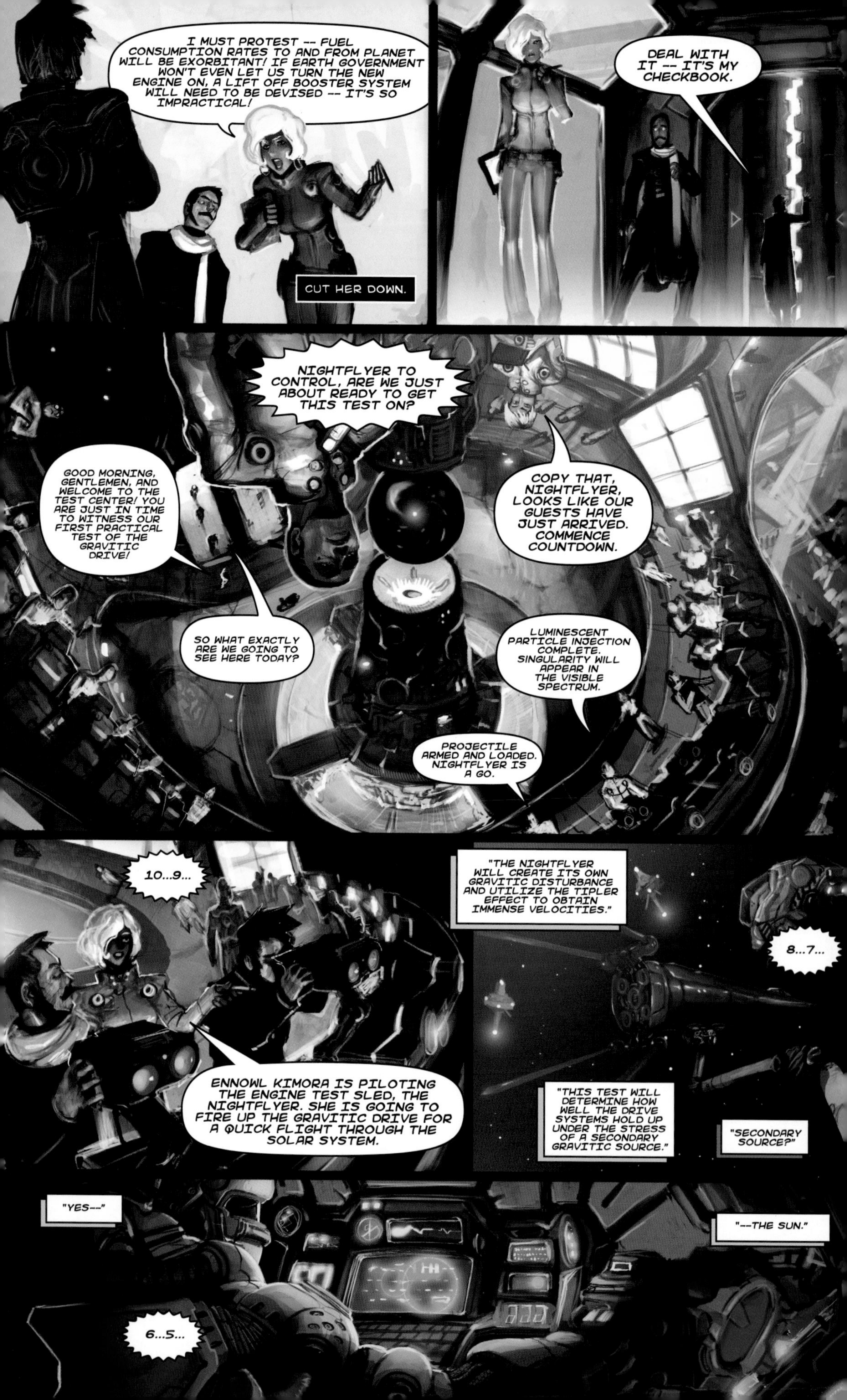
I MUST PROTEST -- FUEL CONSUMPTION RATES TO AND FROM PLANET WILL BE EXORBITANT! IF EARTH GOVERNMENT WON'T EVEN LET US TURN THE NEW ENGINE ON, A LIFT OFF BOOSTER SYSTEM WILL NEED TO BE DEVISED -- IT'S SO IMPRACTICAL!
CUT HER DOWN.
DEAL WITH IT -- IT'S MY CHECKBOOK.
NIGHTFLYER TO CONTROL, ARE WE JUST ABOUT READY TO GET THIS TEST ON?
COPY THAT, NIGHTFLYER, LOOKS LIKE OUR GUESTS HAVE JUST ARRIVED. COMMENCE COUNTDOWN.
GOOD MORNING, GENTLEMEN, AND WELCOME TO THE TEST CENTER! YOU ARE JUST IN TIME TO WITNESS OUR FIRST PRACTICAL TEST OF THE GRAVITIC DRIVE!
SO WHAT EXACTLY ARE WE GOING TO SEE HERE TODAY?
LUMINESCENT PARTICLE INJECTION COMPLETE. SINGULARITY WILL APPEAR IN THE VISIBLE SPECTRUM.
PROJECTILE ARMED AND LOADED. NIGHTFLYER IS A GO.
10...9...
ENNOWL KIMORA IS PILOTING THE ENGINE TEST SLED, THE NIGHTFLYER. SHE IS GOING TO FIRE UP THE GRAVITIC DRIVE FOR A QUICK FLIGHT THROUGH THE SOLAR SYSTEM.
"THE NIGHTFLYER WILL CREATE ITS OWN GRAVITIC DISTURBANCE AND UTILIZE THE TIPLER EFFECT TO OBTAIN IMMENSE VELOCITIES."
8...7...
"THIS TEST WILL DETERMINE HOW WELL THE DRIVE SYSTEMS HOLD UP UNDER THE STRESS OF A SECONDARY GRAVITIC SOURCE."
"SECONDARY SOURCE?"
"YES--"
"--THE SUN."
6...5...

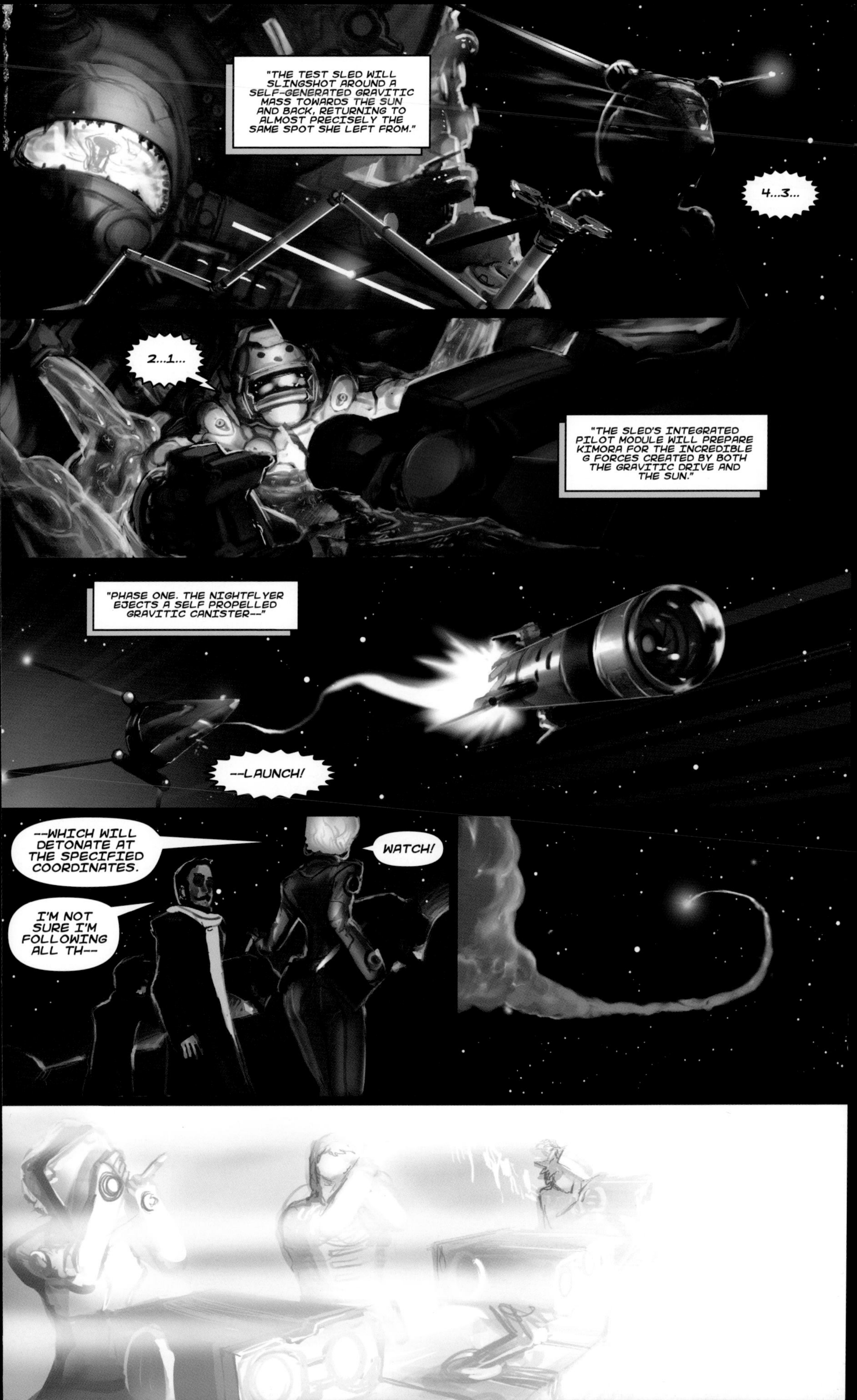
"THE TEST SLED WILL SLINGSHOT AROUND A SELF-GENERATED GRAVITIC MASS TOWARDS THE SUN AND BACK, RETURNING TO ALMOST PRECISELY THE SAME SPOT SHE LEFT FROM."
4...3...
2...1...
"THE SLED'S INTEGRATED PILOT MODULE WILL PREPARE KIMORA FOR THE INCREDIBLE G FORCES CREATED BY BOTH THE GRAVITIC DRIVE AND THE SUN."
"PHASE ONE. THE NIGHTFLYER EJECTS A SELF PROPELLED GRAVITIC CANISTER--"
--LAUNCH!
--WHICH WILL DETONATE AT THE SPECIFIED COORDINATES.
WATCH!
I'M NOT SURE I'M FOLLOWING ALL TH--

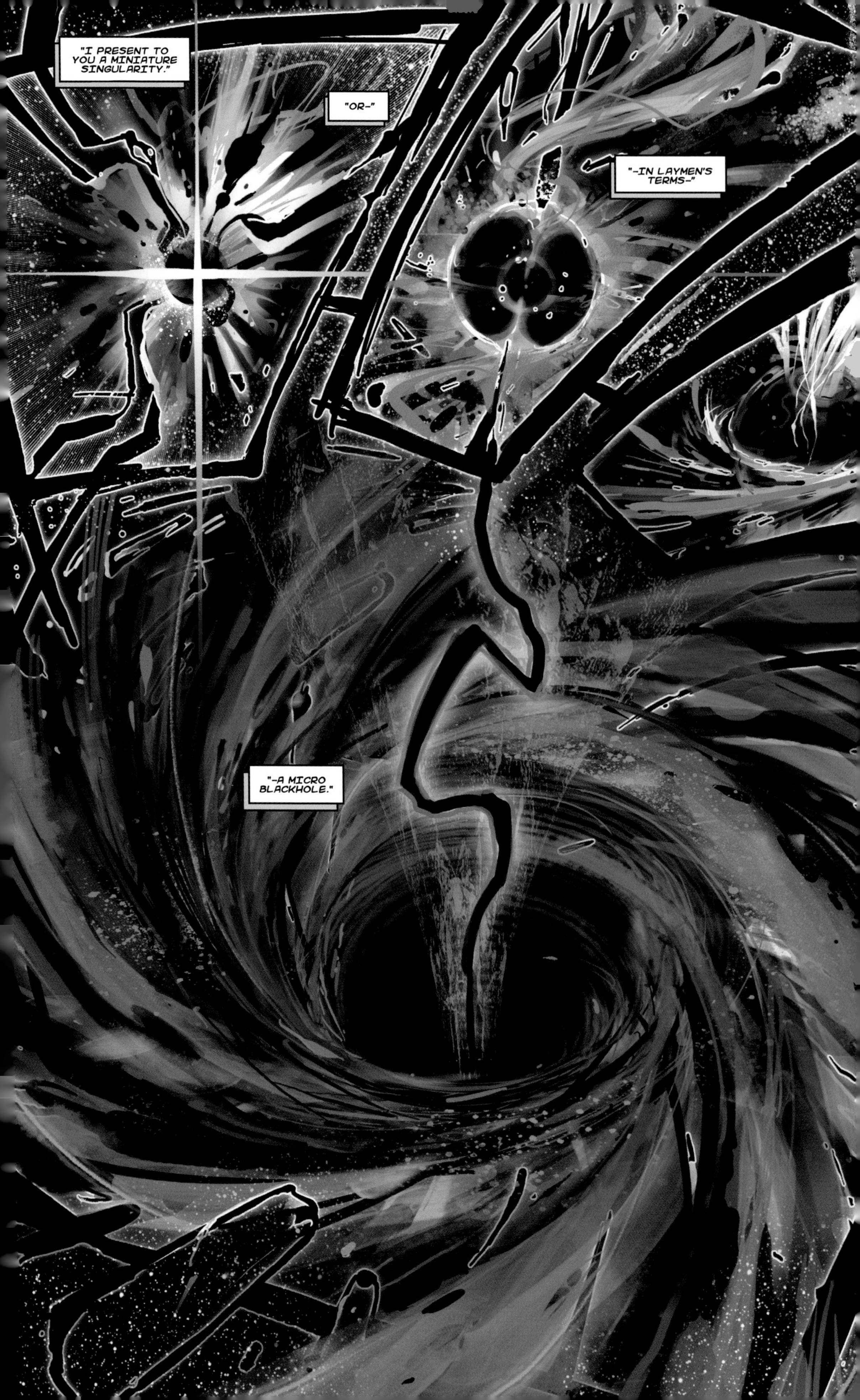
"I PRESENT TO YOU A MINIATURE SINGULARITY."
"OR-"
"-IN LAYMEN'S TERMS-"
"-A MICRO BLACKHOLE."

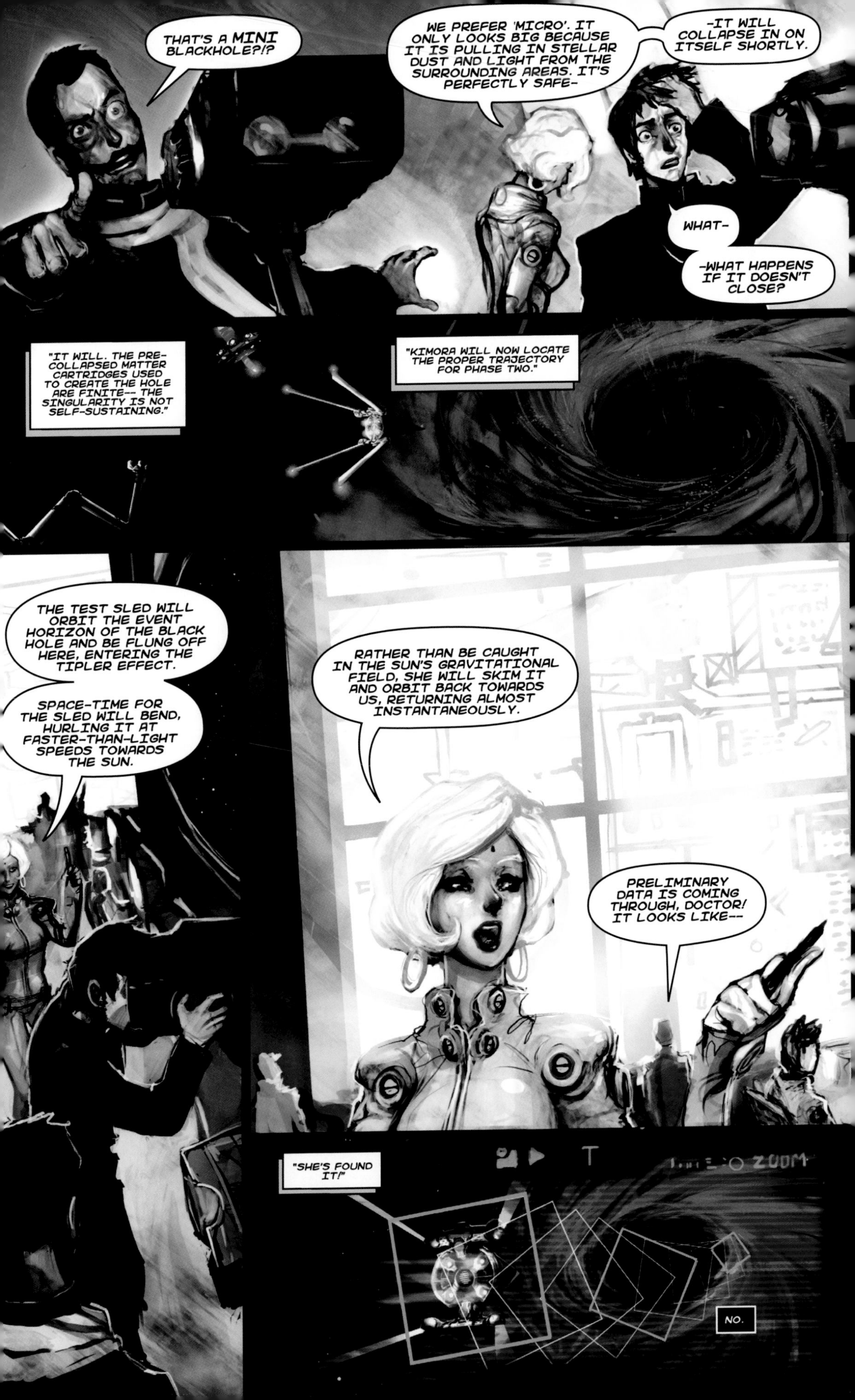
THAT'S A MINI BLACKHOLE?!?
WE PREFER 'MICRO'. IT ONLY LOOKS BIG BECAUSE IT IS PULLING IN STELLAR DUST AND LIGHT FROM THE SURROUNDING AREAS. IT'S PERFECTLY SAFE-
-IT WILL COLLAPSE IN ON ITSELF SHORTLY.
WHAT-
-WHAT HAPPENS IF IT DOESN'T CLOSE?
"IT WILL. THE PRE-COLLAPSED MATTER CARTRIDGES USED TO CREATE THE HOLE ARE FINITE-- THE SINGULARITY IS NOT SELF-SUSTAINING."
"KIMORA WILL NOW LOCATE THE PROPER TRAJECTORY FOR PHASE TWO."
THE TEST SLED WILL ORBIT THE EVENT HORIZON OF THE BLACK HOLE AND BE FLUNG OFF HERE, ENTERING THE TIPLER EFFECT.
SPACE-TIME FOR THE SLED WILL BEND, HURLING IT AT FASTER-THAN-LIGHT SPEEDS TOWARDS THE SUN.
RATHER THAN BE CAUGHT IN THE SUN'S GRAVITATIONAL FIELD, SHE WILL SKIM IT AND ORBIT BACK TOWARDS US, RETURNING ALMOST INSTANTANEOUSLY.
PRELIMINARY DATA IS COMING THROUGH, DOCTOR! IT LOOKS LIKE--
"SHE'S FOUND IT!"
ZOOM
NO.

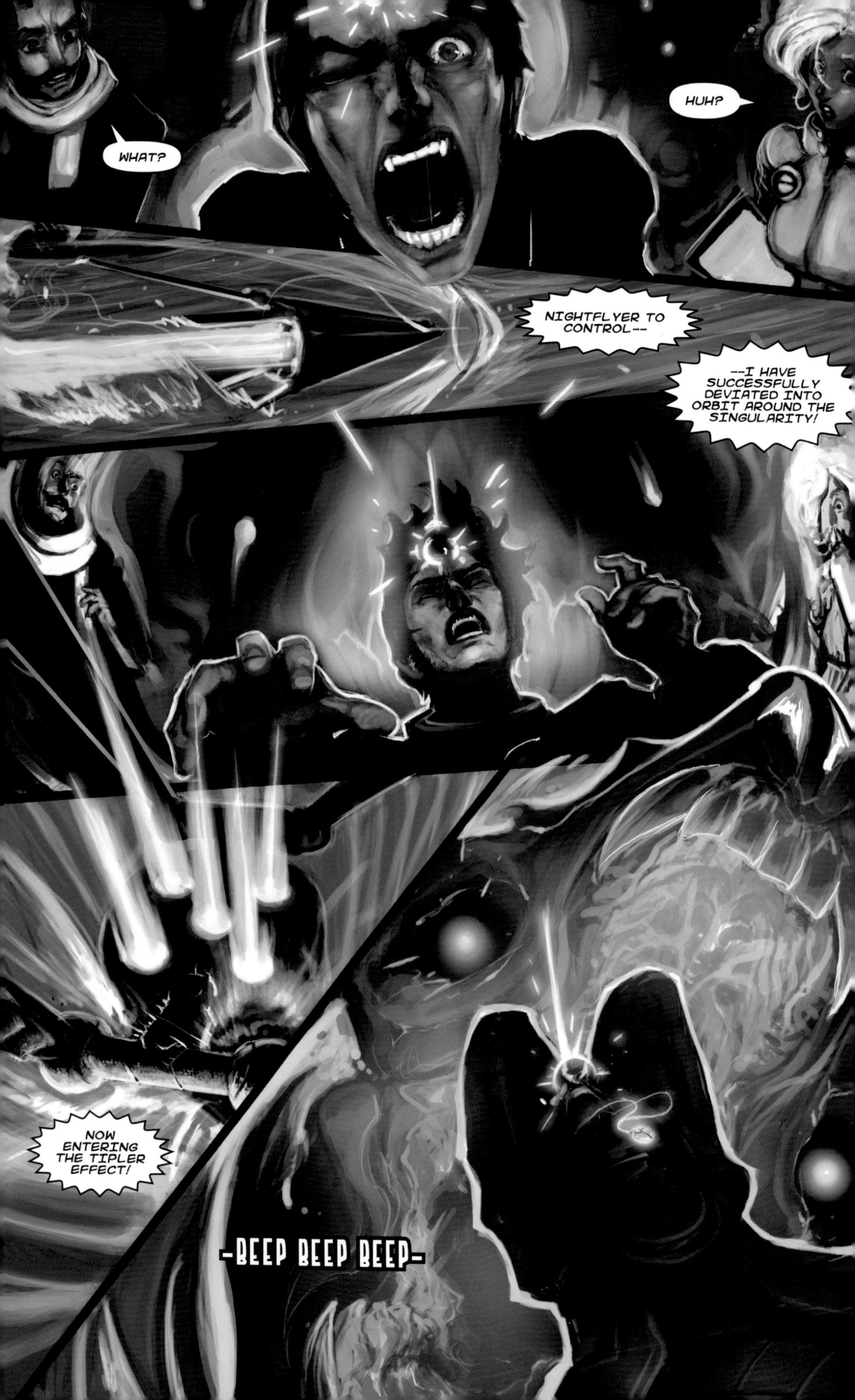
WHAT?
HUH?
NIGHTFLYER TO CONTROL--
--I HAVE SUCCESSFULLY DEVIATED INTO ORBIT AROUND THE SINGULARITY!
NOW ENTERING THE TIPLER EFFECT!
-BEEP BEEP BEEP-

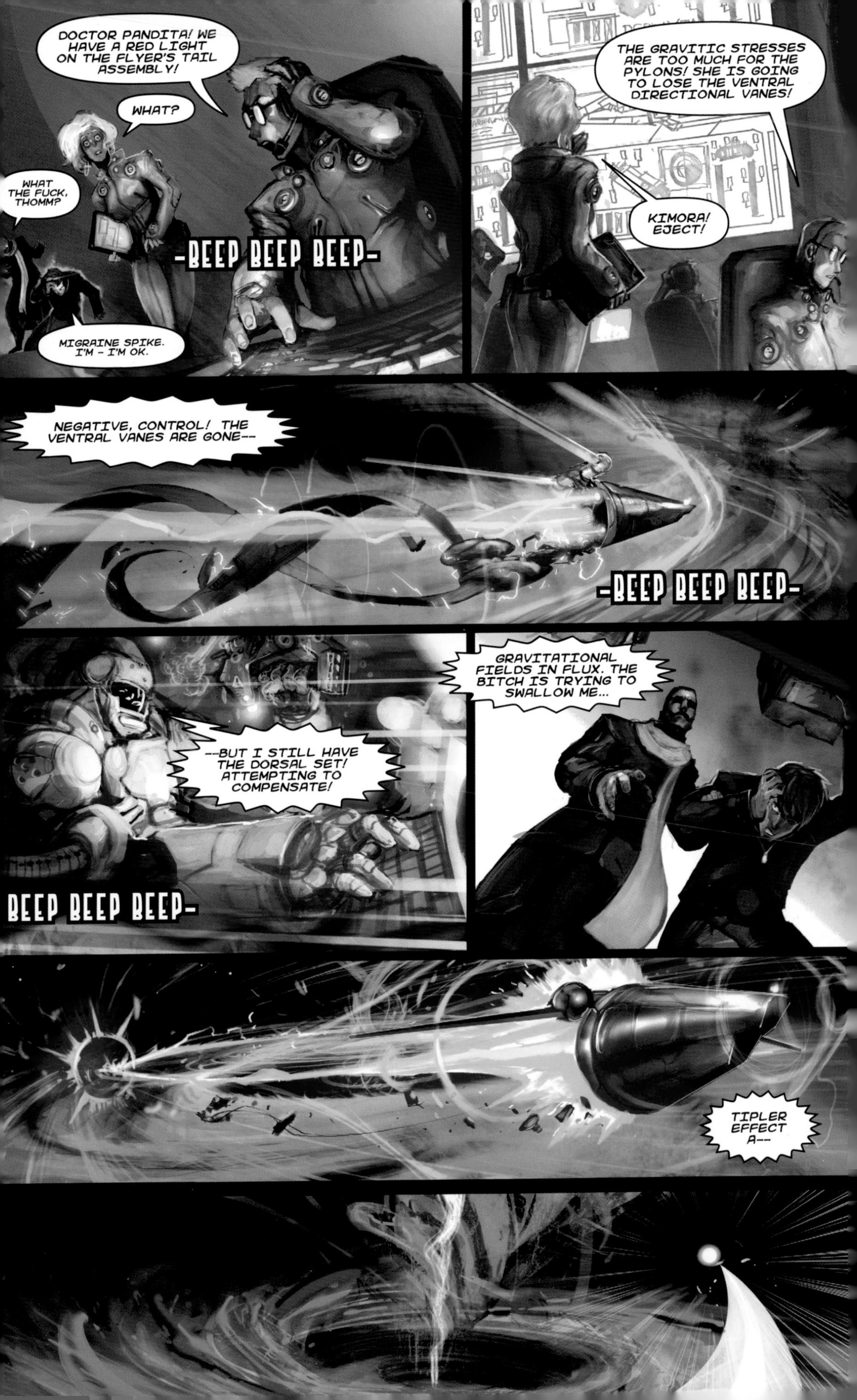
DOCTOR PANDITA! WE HAVE A RED LIGHT ON THE FLYER'S TAIL ASSEMBLY!
WHAT?
WHAT THE FUCK, THOMM?
-BEEP BEEP BEEP-
MIGRAINE SPIKE. I'M - I'M OK.
THE GRAVITIC STRESSES ARE TOO MUCH FOR THE PYLONS! SHE IS GOING TO LOSE THE VENTRAL DIRECTIONAL VANES!
KIMORA! EJECT!
NEGATIVE, CONTROL! THE VENTRAL VANES ARE GONE--
-BEEP BEEP BEEP-
--BUT I STILL HAVE THE DORSAL SET! ATTEMPTING TO COMPENSATE!
BEEP BEEP BEEP-
GRAVITATIONAL FIELDS IN FLUX. THE BITCH IS TRYING TO SWALLOW ME...
TIPLER EFFECT A--

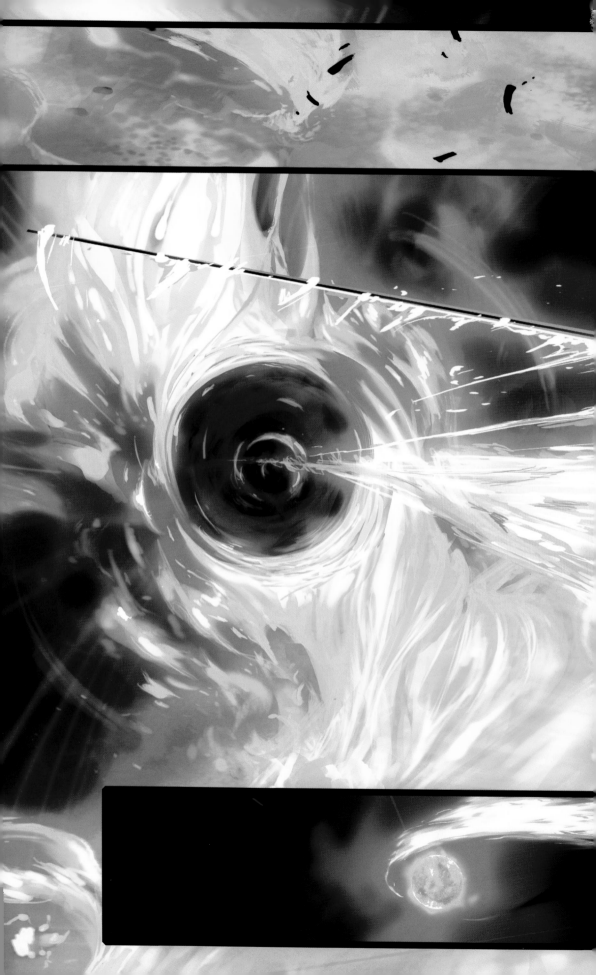

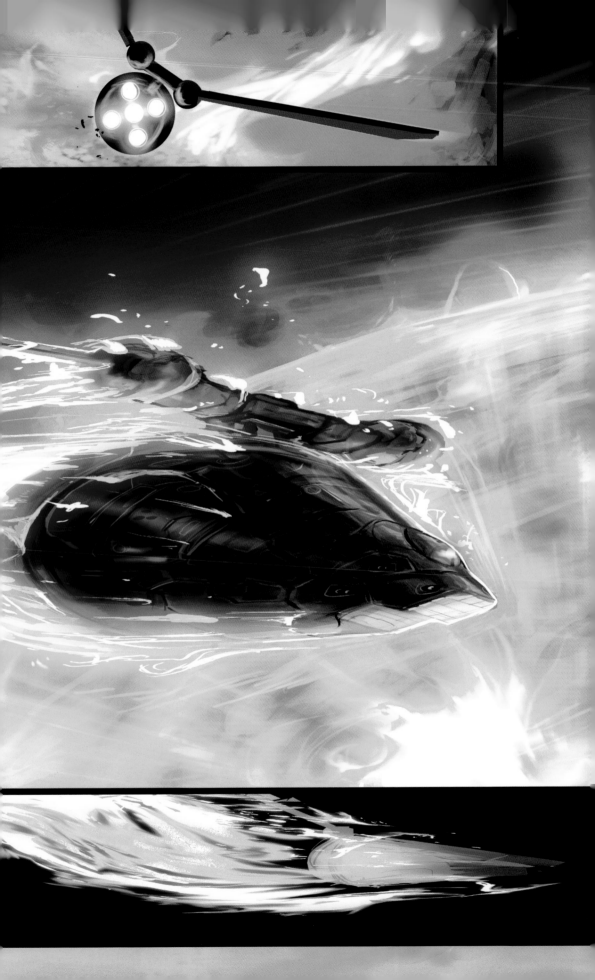

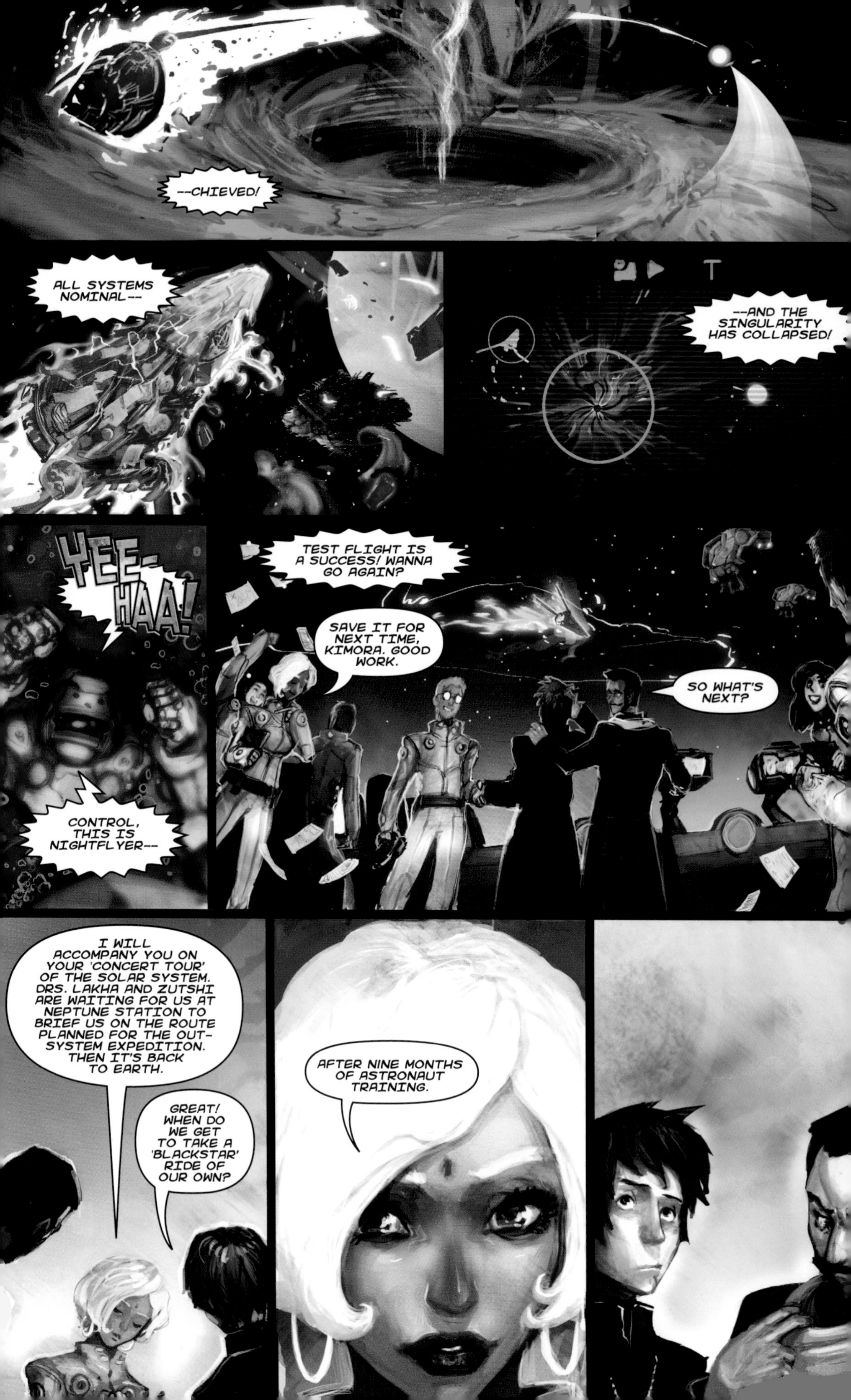
--CHIEVED!
ALL SYSTEMS NOMINAL--
--AND THE SINGULARITY HAS COLLAPSED!
YEE-HAA!
CONTROL, THIS IS NIGHTFLYER--
TEST FLIGHT IS A SUCCESS! WANNA GO AGAIN?
SAVE IT FOR NEXT TIME, KIMORA. GOOD WORK.
SO WHAT'S NEXT?
I WILL ACCOMPANY YOU ON YOUR 'CONCERT TOUR' OF THE SOLAR SYSTEM. DRS. LAKHA AND ZUTSHI ARE WAITING FOR US AT NEPTUNE STATION TO BRIEF US ON THE ROUTE PLANNED FOR THE OUT-SYSTEM EXPEDITION. THEN IT'S BACK TO EARTH.
GREAT! WHEN DO WE GET TO TAKE A 'BLACKSTAR' RIDE OF OUR OWN?
AFTER NINE MONTHS OF ASTRONAUT TRAINING.

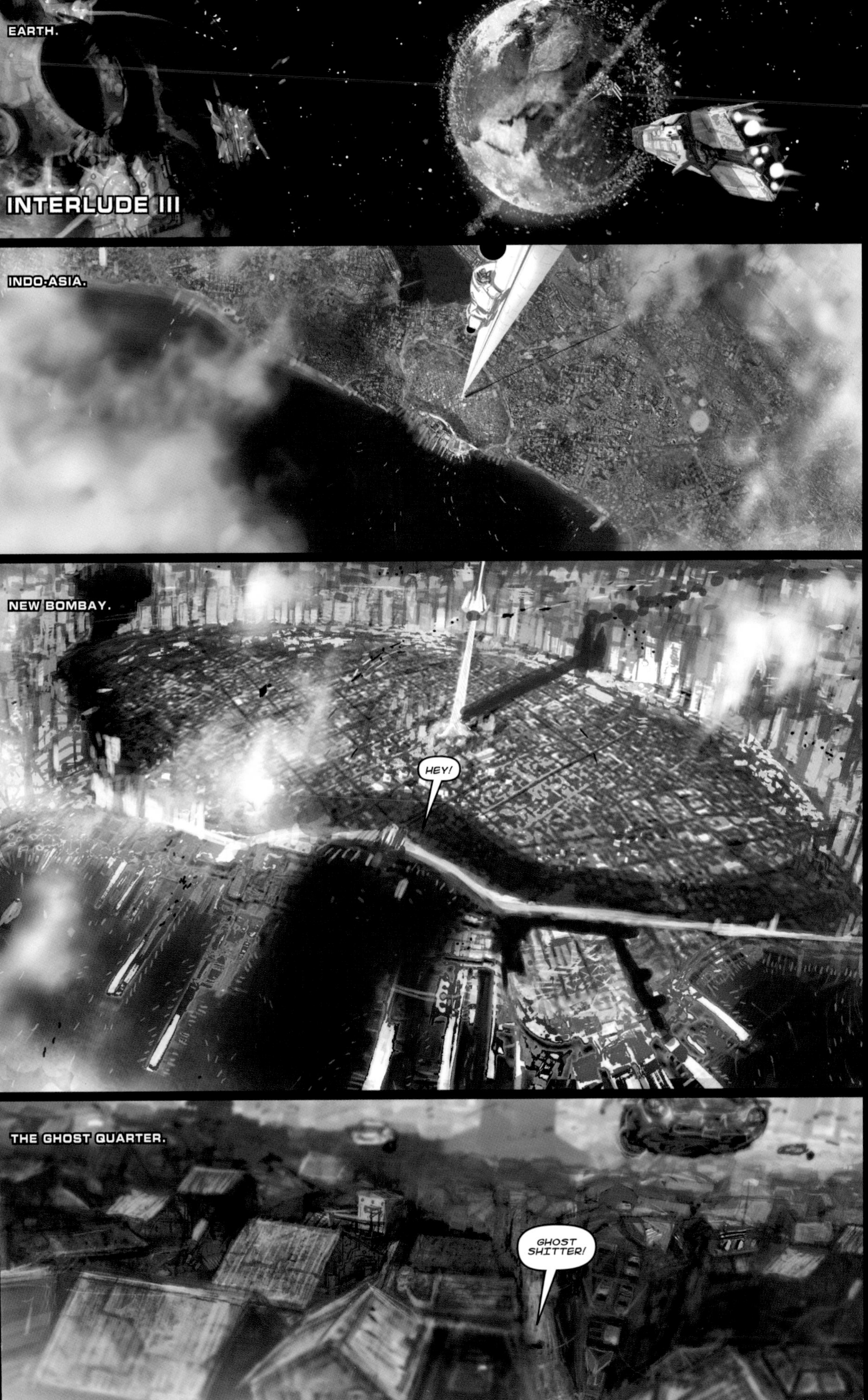
EARTH.
INTERLUDE III
INDO-ASIA.
NEW BOMBAY.
HEY!
THE GHOST QUARTER.
GHOST SHITTER!

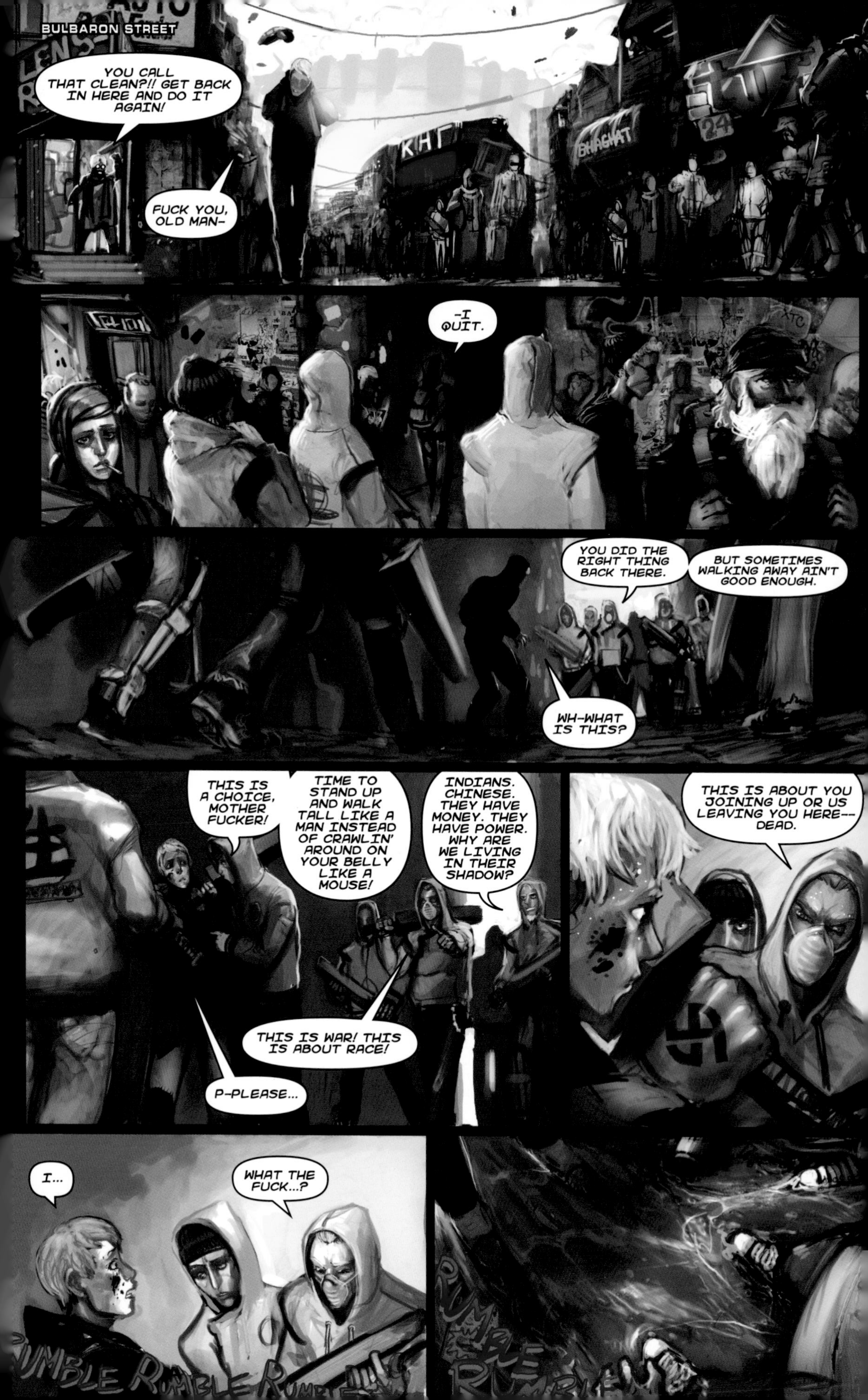
BULBARON STREET
YOU CALL THAT CLEAN?!! GET BACK IN HERE AND DO IT AGAIN!
FUCK YOU, OLD MAN-
KHT
BHAGWAT
24
-I QUIT.
XTC
YOU DID THE RIGHT THING BACK THERE.
BUT SOMETIMES WALKING AWAY AIN'T GOOD ENOUGH.
WH-WHAT IS THIS?
THIS IS A CHOICE, MOTHER FUCKER!
TIME TO STAND UP AND WALK TALL LIKE A MAN INSTEAD OF CRAWLIN' AROUND ON YOUR BELLY LIKE A MOUSE!
INDIANS. CHINESE. THEY HAVE MONEY. THEY HAVE POWER. WHY ARE WE LIVING IN THEIR SHADOW?
THIS IS WAR! THIS IS ABOUT RACE!
P-PLEASE...
THIS IS ABOUT YOU JOINING UP OR US LEAVING YOU HERE--DEAD.
I...
WHAT THE FUCK...?
RUMBLE RUMBLE
RUMBLE RUMBLE

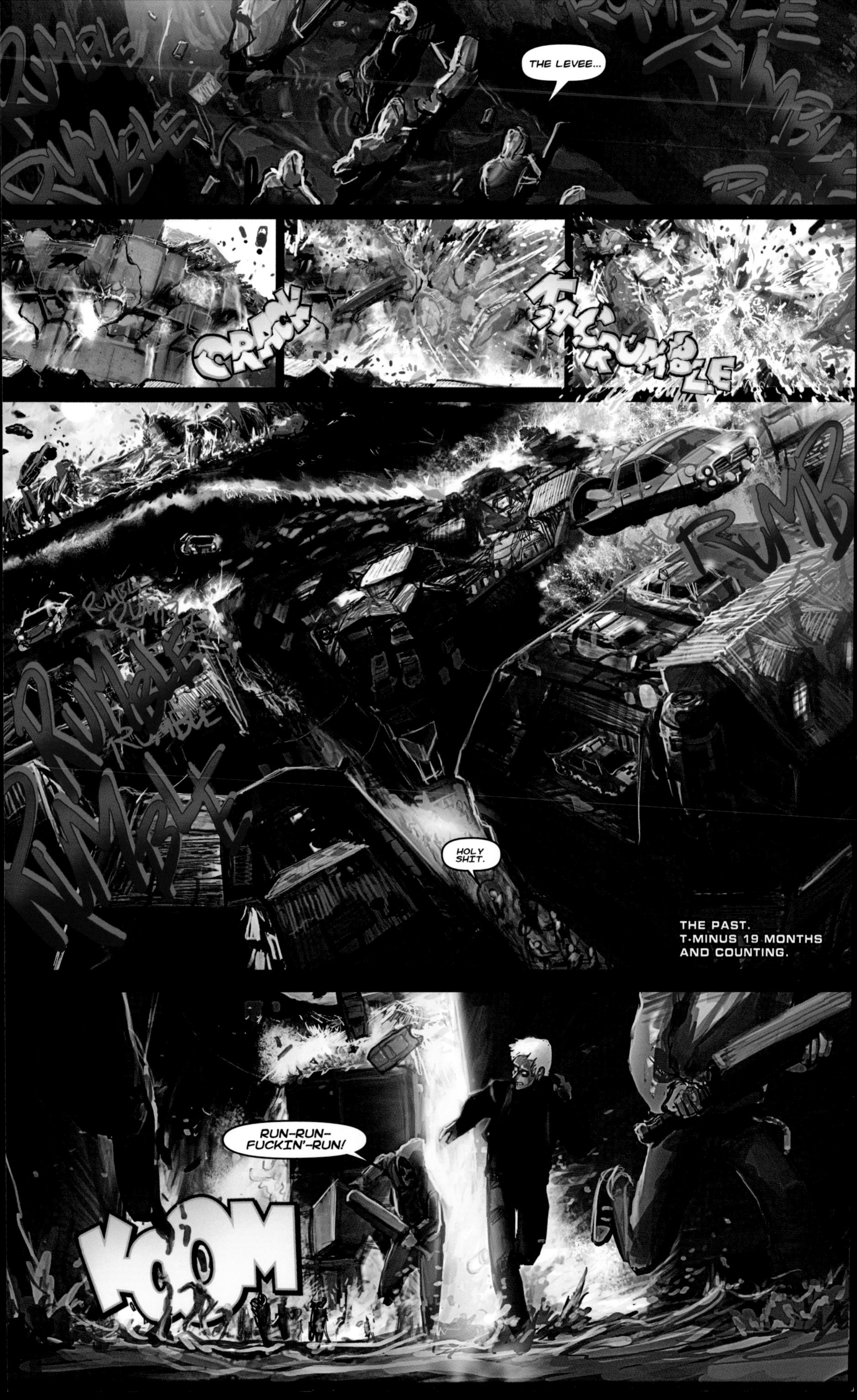
RUMBLE
THE LEVEE...
CRACK
RUMBLE
HOLY SHIT.
THE PAST.
T-MINUS 19 MONTHS
AND COUNTING.
RUN-RUN-
FUCKIN'-RUN!
KOOM

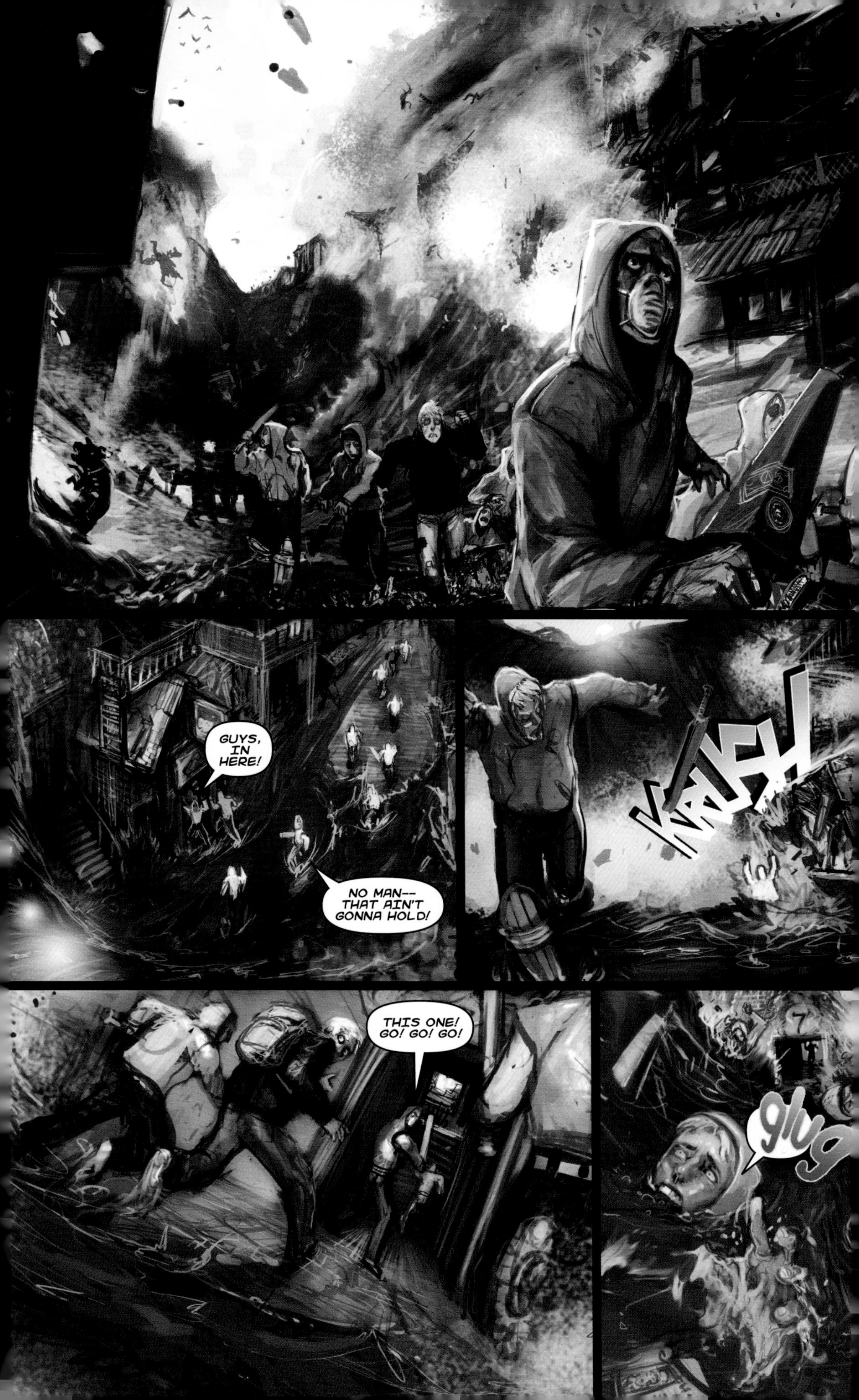
GUYS, IN HERE!
NO MAN-- THAT AIN'T GONNA HOLD!
THIS ONE! GO! GO! GO!
glug

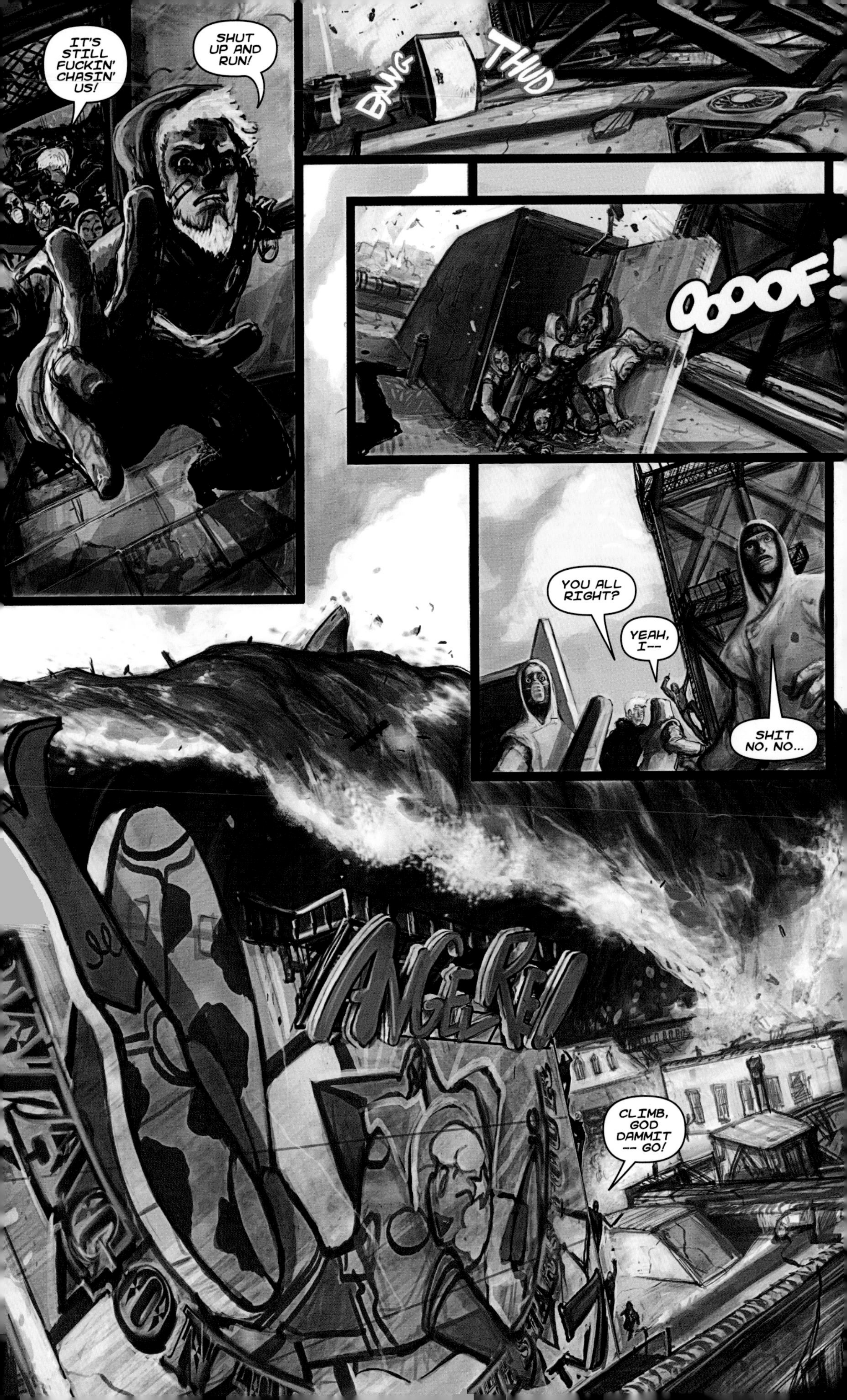
IT'S STILL FUCKIN' CHASIN' US!
SHUT UP AND RUN!
BANG
THUD
OOOF!
YOU ALL RIGHT?
YEAH, I--
SHIT NO, NO...
ANGEREI
CLIMB, GOD DAMMIT -- GO!

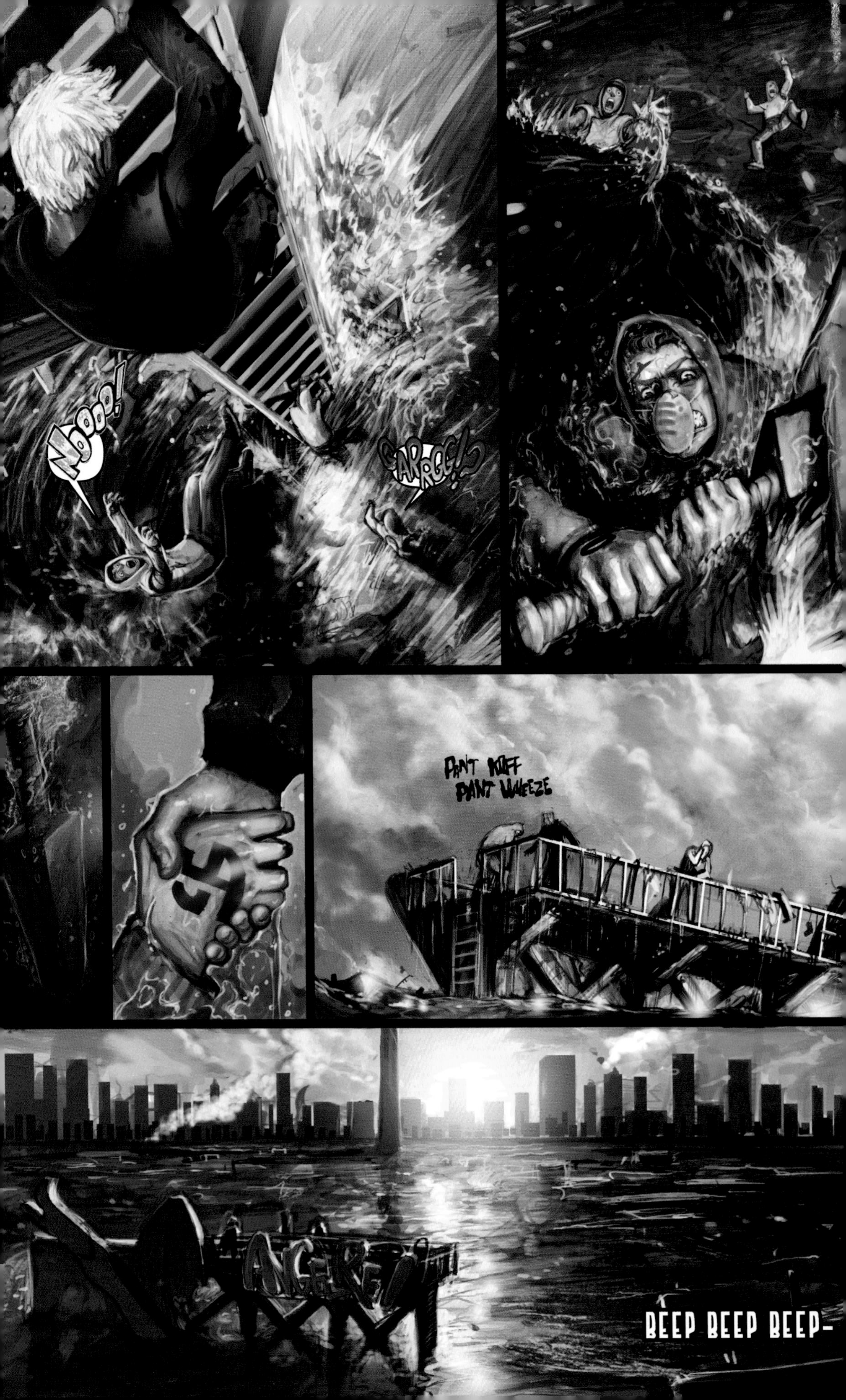
NOOOO!
GARRGG!?
PANT KOFF
PANT WHEEZE
BEEP BEEP BEEP-

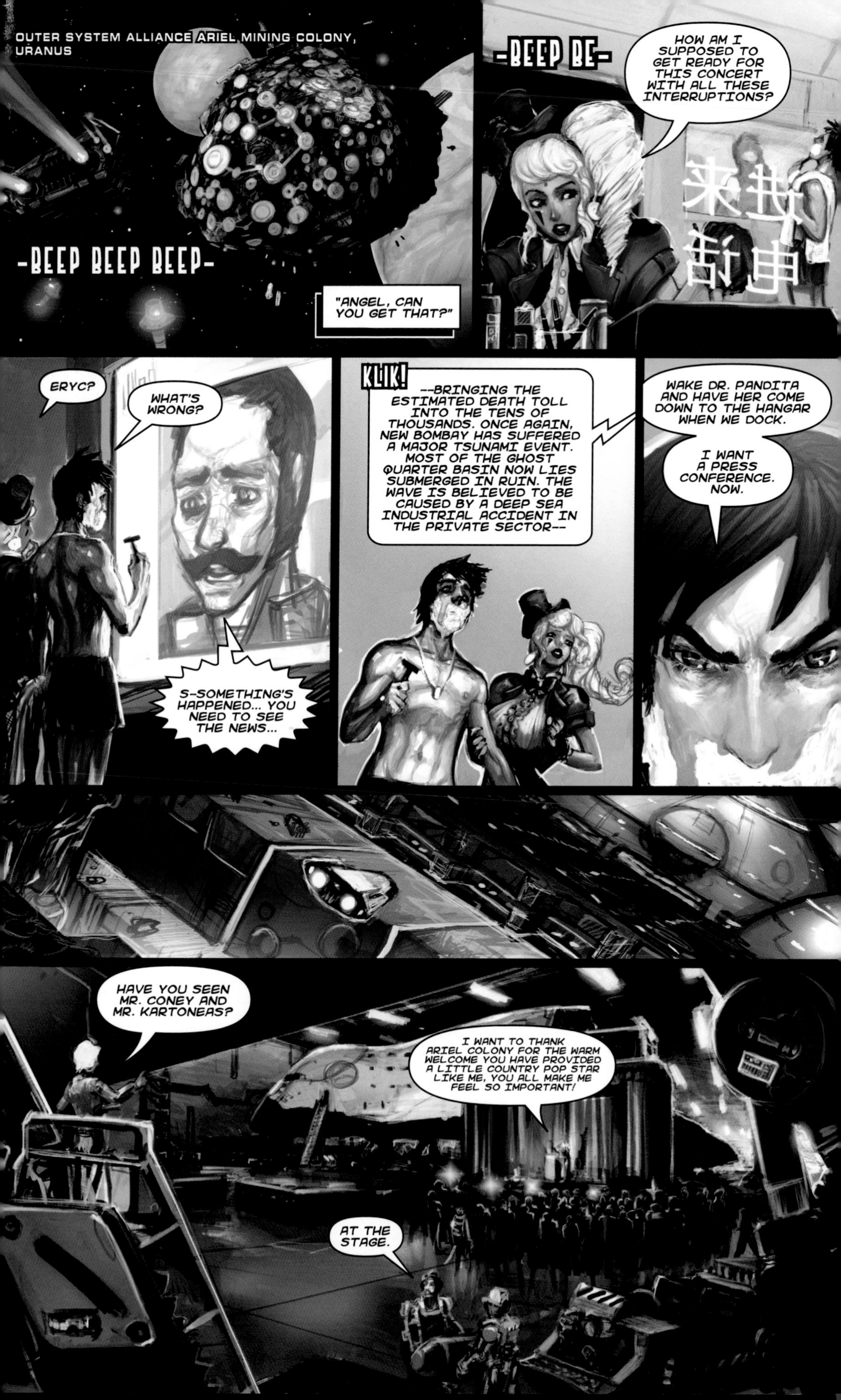
OUTER SYSTEM ALLIANCE ARIEL MINING COLONY, URANUS
-BEEP BEEP BEEP-
"ANGEL, CAN YOU GET THAT?"
-BEEP BE-
HOW AM I SUPPOSED TO GET READY FOR THIS CONCERT WITH ALL THESE INTERRUPTIONS?
ERYC?
WHAT'S WRONG?
S-SOMETHING'S HAPPENED... YOU NEED TO SEE THE NEWS...
KLIK!
--BRINGING THE ESTIMATED DEATH TOLL INTO THE TENS OF THOUSANDS. ONCE AGAIN, NEW BOMBAY HAS SUFFERED A MAJOR TSUNAMI EVENT. MOST OF THE GHOST QUARTER BASIN NOW LIES SUBMERGED IN RUIN. THE WAVE IS BELIEVED TO BE CAUSED BY A DEEP SEA INDUSTRIAL ACCIDENT IN THE PRIVATE SECTOR--
WAKE DR. PANDITA AND HAVE HER COME DOWN TO THE HANGAR WHEN WE DOCK.
I WANT A PRESS CONFERENCE. NOW.
HAVE YOU SEEN MR. CONEY AND MR. KARTONEAS?
I WANT TO THANK ARIEL COLONY FOR THE WARM WELCOME YOU HAVE PROVIDED A LITTLE COUNTRY POP STAR LIKE ME, YOU ALL MAKE ME FEEL SO IMPORTANT!
AT THE STAGE.

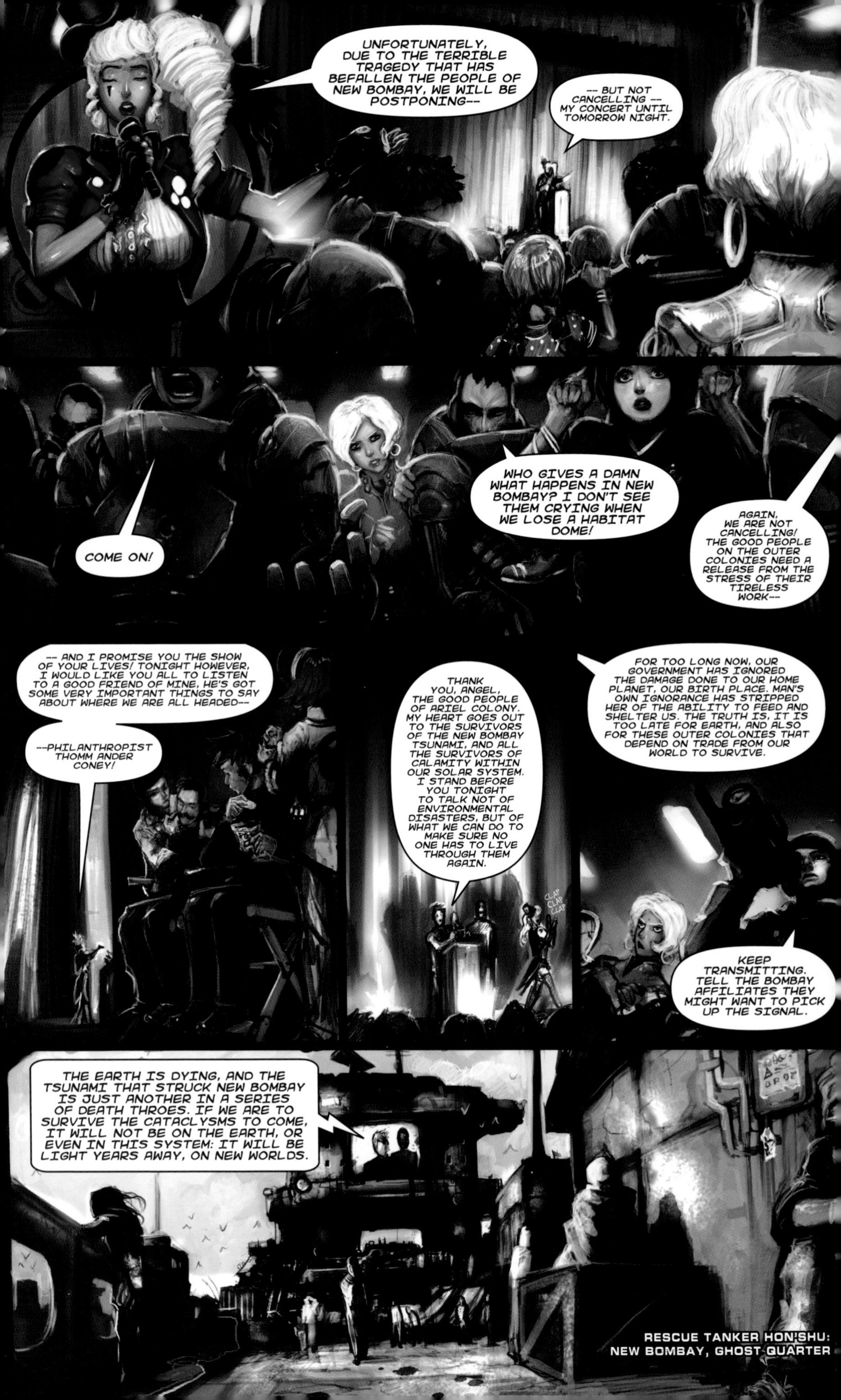
UNFORTUNATELY, DUE TO THE TERRIBLE TRAGEDY THAT HAS BEFALLEN THE PEOPLE OF NEW BOMBAY, WE WILL BE POSTPONING--
-- BUT NOT CANCELLING -- MY CONCERT UNTIL TOMORROW NIGHT.
COME ON!
WHO GIVES A DAMN WHAT HAPPENS IN NEW BOMBAY? I DON'T SEE THEM CRYING WHEN WE LOSE A HABITAT DOME!
AGAIN, WE ARE NOT CANCELLING! THE GOOD PEOPLE ON THE OUTER COLONIES NEED A RELEASE FROM THE STRESS OF THEIR TIRELESS WORK--
-- AND I PROMISE YOU THE SHOW OF YOUR LIVES! TONIGHT HOWEVER, I WOULD LIKE YOU ALL TO LISTEN TO A GOOD FRIEND OF MINE, HE'S GOT SOME VERY IMPORTANT THINGS TO SAY ABOUT WHERE WE ARE ALL HEADED--
--PHILANTHROPIST THOMM ANDER CONEY!
THANK YOU, ANGEL, THE GOOD PEOPLE OF ARIEL COLONY. MY HEART GOES OUT TO THE SURVIVORS OF THE NEW BOMBAY TSUNAMI, AND ALL THE SURVIVORS OF CALAMITY WITHIN OUR SOLAR SYSTEM. I STAND BEFORE YOU TONIGHT TO TALK NOT OF ENVIRONMENTAL DISASTERS, BUT OF WHAT WE CAN DO TO MAKE SURE NO ONE HAS TO LIVE THROUGH THEM AGAIN.
CLAP CLAP CLAP
FOR TOO LONG NOW, OUR GOVERNMENT HAS IGNORED THE DAMAGE DONE TO OUR HOME PLANET, OUR BIRTH PLACE. MAN'S OWN IGNORANCE HAS STRIPPED HER OF THE ABILITY TO FEED AND SHELTER US. THE TRUTH IS, IT IS TOO LATE FOR EARTH, AND ALSO FOR THESE OUTER COLONIES THAT DEPEND ON TRADE FROM OUR WORLD TO SURVIVE.
KEEP TRANSMITTING. TELL THE BOMBAY AFFILIATES THEY MIGHT WANT TO PICK UP THE SIGNAL.
THE EARTH IS DYING, AND THE TSUNAMI THAT STRUCK NEW BOMBAY IS JUST ANOTHER IN A SERIES OF DEATH THROES. IF WE ARE TO SURVIVE THE CATACLYSMS TO COME, IT WILL NOT BE ON THE EARTH, OR EVEN IN THIS SYSTEM: IT WILL BE LIGHT YEARS AWAY, ON NEW WORLDS.
RESCUE TANKER HON'SHU: NEW BOMBAY, GHOST QUARTER

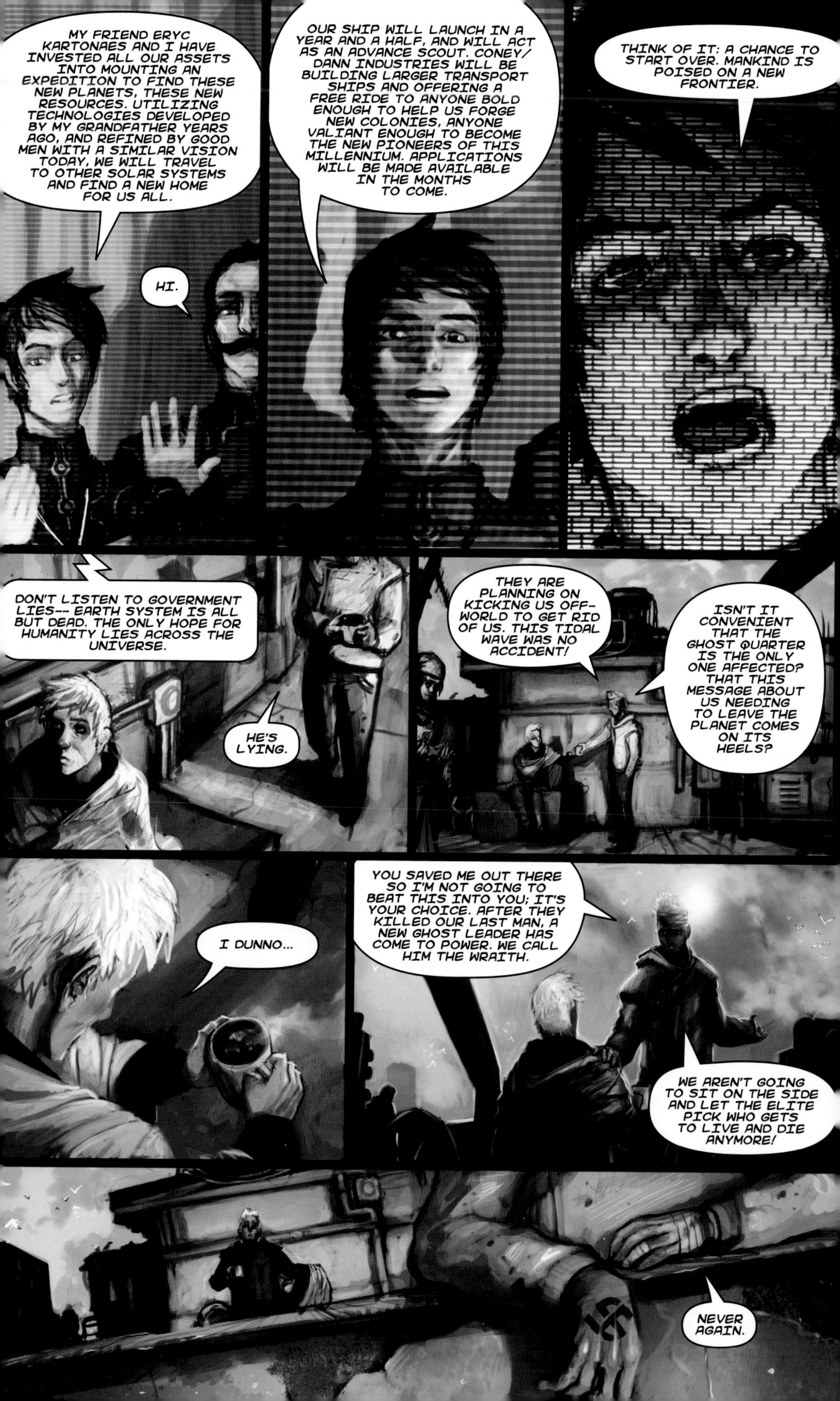
MY FRIEND ERYC KARTONAES AND I HAVE INVESTED ALL OUR ASSETS INTO MOUNTING AN EXPEDITION TO FIND THESE NEW PLANETS, THESE NEW RESOURCES. UTILIZING TECHNOLOGIES DEVELOPED BY MY GRANDFATHER YEARS AGO, AND REFINED BY GOOD MEN WITH A SIMILAR VISION TODAY, WE WILL TRAVEL TO OTHER SOLAR SYSTEMS AND FIND A NEW HOME FOR US ALL.
HI.
OUR SHIP WILL LAUNCH IN A YEAR AND A HALF, AND WILL ACT AS AN ADVANCE SCOUT. CONEY/ DANN INDUSTRIES WILL BE BUILDING LARGER TRANSPORT SHIPS AND OFFERING A FREE RIDE TO ANYONE BOLD ENOUGH TO HELP US FORGE NEW COLONIES, ANYONE VALIANT ENOUGH TO BECOME THE NEW PIONEERS OF THIS MILLENNIUM. APPLICATIONS WILL BE MADE AVAILABLE IN THE MONTHS TO COME.
THINK OF IT: A CHANCE TO START OVER. MANKIND IS POISED ON A NEW FRONTIER.
DON'T LISTEN TO GOVERNMENT LIES-- EARTH SYSTEM IS ALL BUT DEAD. THE ONLY HOPE FOR HUMANITY LIES ACROSS THE UNIVERSE.
HE'S LYING.
THEY ARE PLANNING ON KICKING US OFF-WORLD TO GET RID OF US. THIS TIDAL WAVE WAS NO ACCIDENT!
ISN'T IT CONVENIENT THAT THE GHOST QUARTER IS THE ONLY ONE AFFECTED? THAT THIS MESSAGE ABOUT US NEEDING TO LEAVE THE PLANET COMES ON ITS HEELS?
I DUNNO...
YOU SAVED ME OUT THERE SO I'M NOT GOING TO BEAT THIS INTO YOU; IT'S YOUR CHOICE. AFTER THEY KILLED OUR LAST MAN, A NEW GHOST LEADER HAS COME TO POWER. WE CALL HIM THE WRAITH.
WE AREN'T GOING TO SIT ON THE SIDE AND LET THE ELITE PICK WHO GETS TO LIVE AND DIE ANYMORE!
NEVER AGAIN.

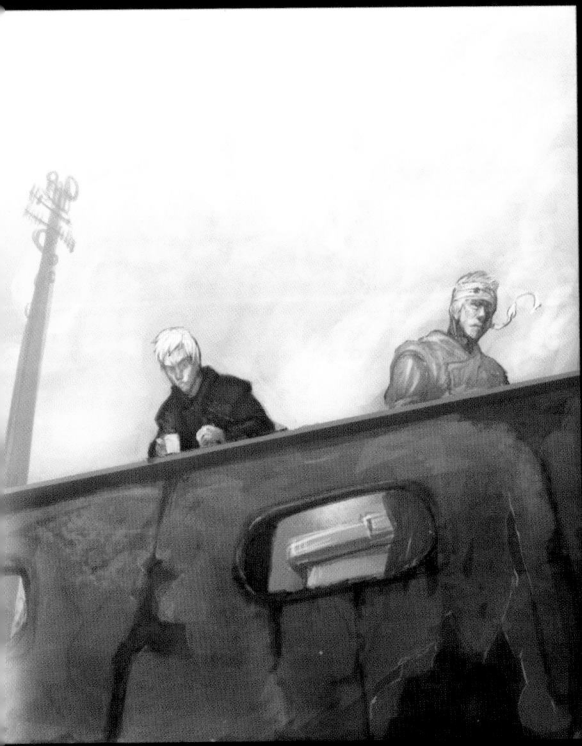
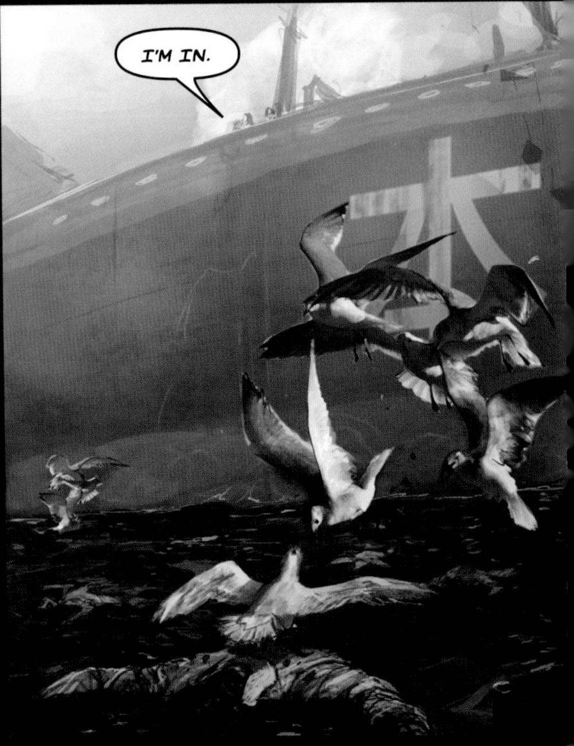
I'M IN.
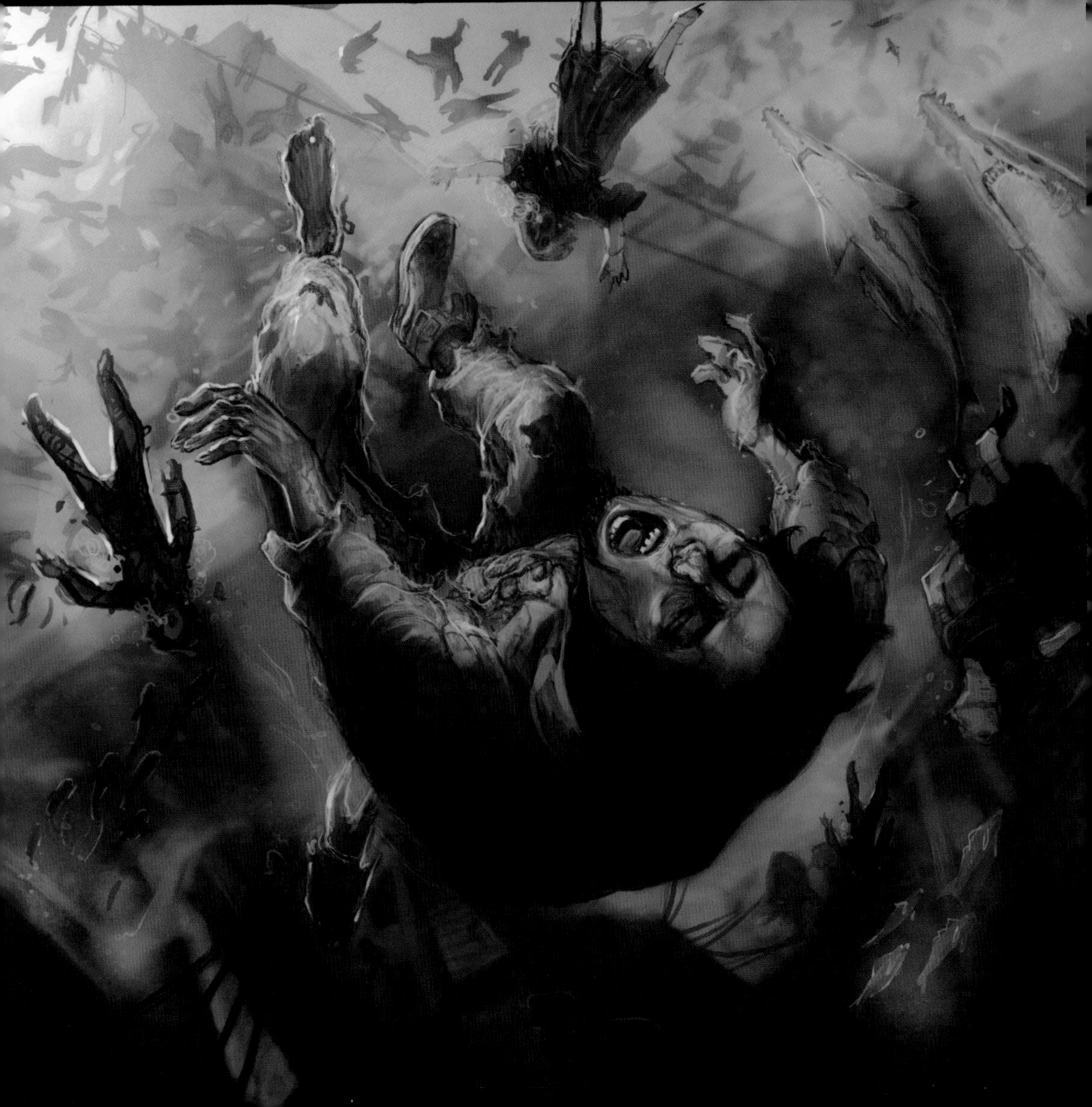

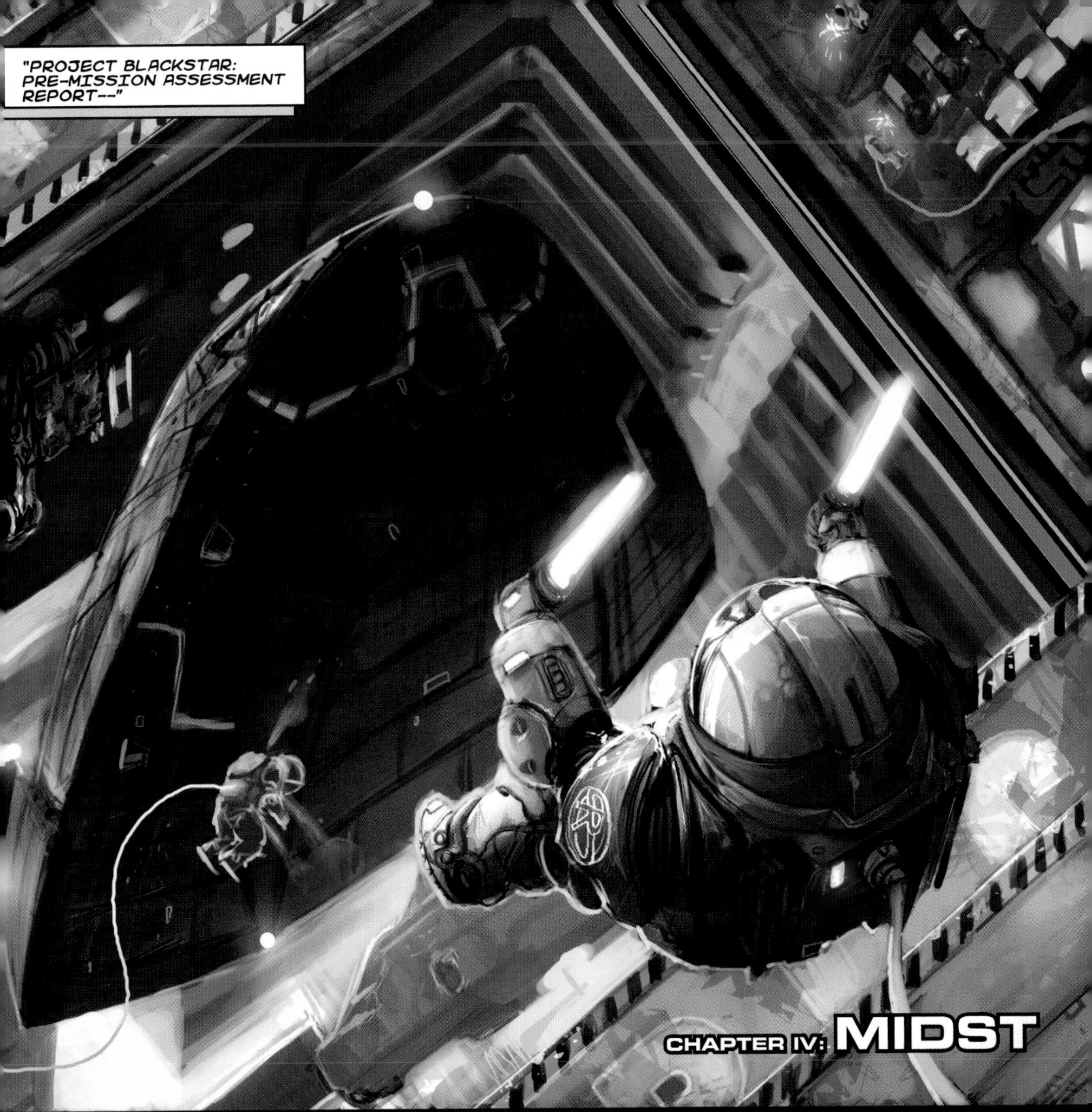
"PROJECT BLACKSTAR: PRE-MISSION ASSESSMENT REPORT--"
CHAPTER IV: MIDST

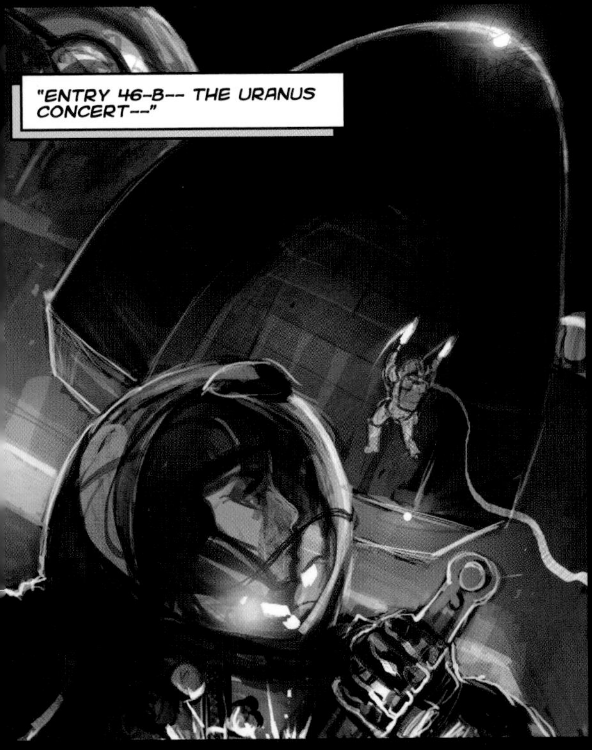
"ENTRY 46-B-- THE URANUS CONCERT--"

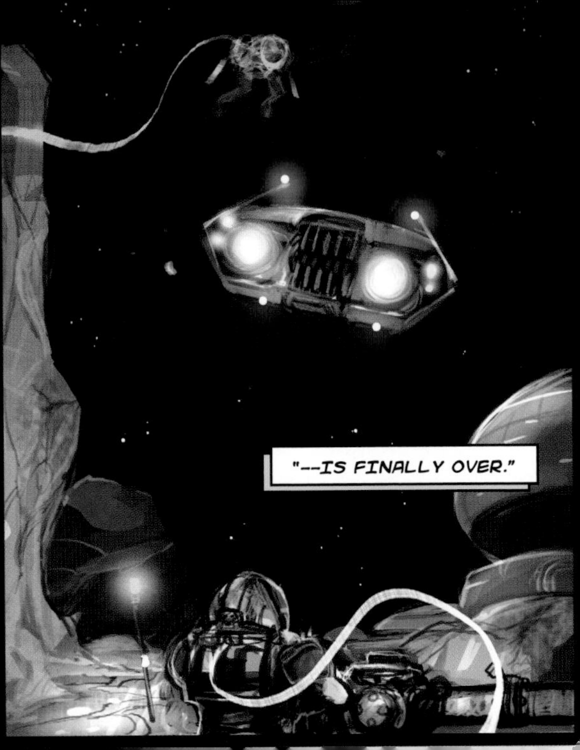
"--IS FINALLY OVER."

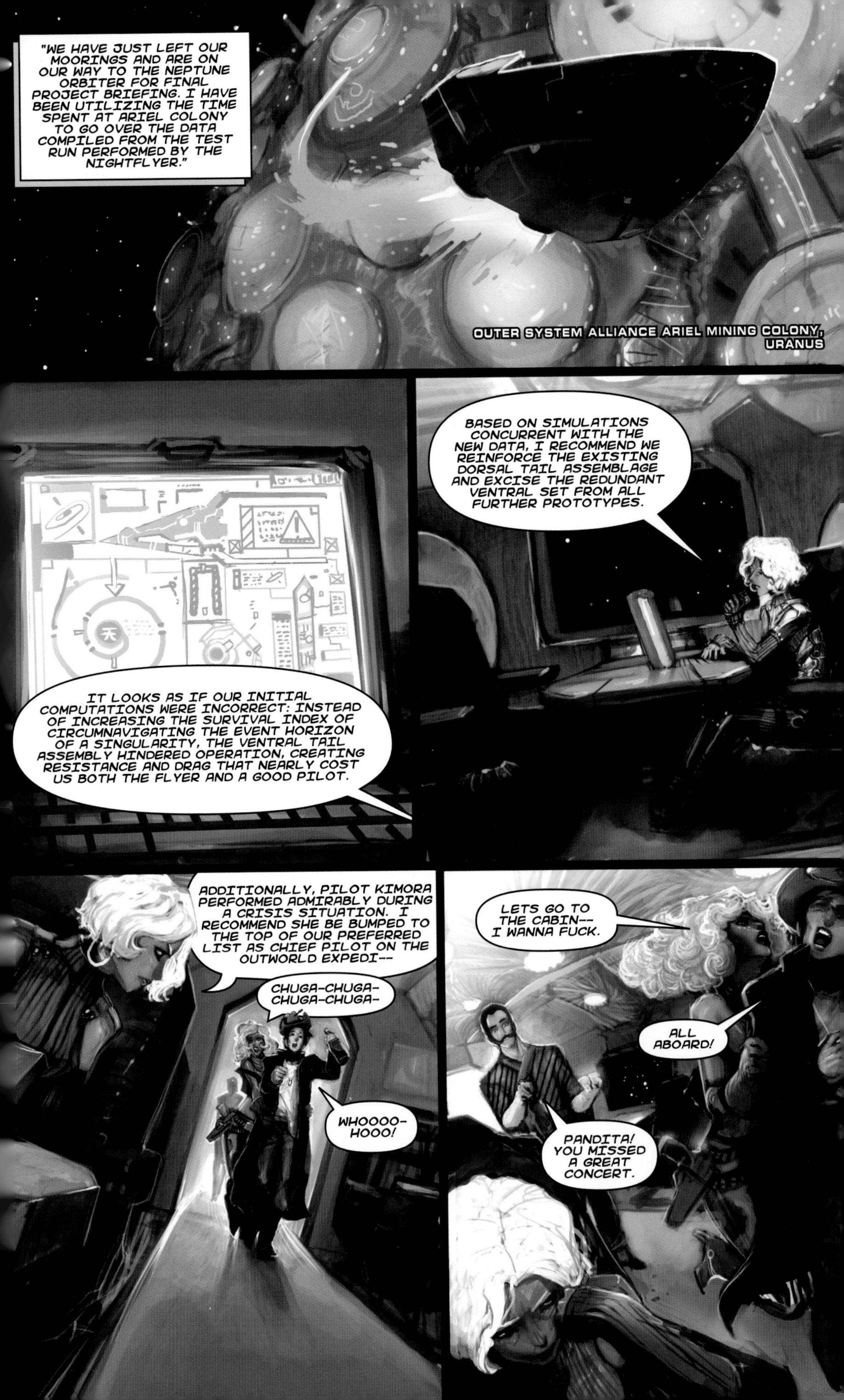
"WE HAVE JUST LEFT OUR MOORINGS AND ARE ON OUR WAY TO THE NEPTUNE ORBITER FOR FINAL PROJECT BRIEFING. I HAVE BEEN UTILIZING THE TIME SPENT AT ARIEL COLONY TO GO OVER THE DATA COMPILED FROM THE TEST RUN PERFORMED BY THE NIGHTFLYER."
OUTER SYSTEM ALLIANCE ARIEL MINING COLONY, URANUS
IT LOOKS AS IF OUR INITIAL COMPUTATIONS WERE INCORRECT: INSTEAD OF INCREASING THE SURVIVAL INDEX OF CIRCUMNAVIGATING THE EVENT HORIZON OF A SINGULARITY, THE VENTRAL TAIL ASSEMBLY HINDERED OPERATION, CREATING RESISTANCE AND DRAG THAT NEARLY COST US BOTH THE FLYER AND A GOOD PILOT.
BASED ON SIMULATIONS CONCURRENT WITH THE NEW DATA, I RECOMMEND WE REINFORCE THE EXISTING DORSAL TAIL ASSEMBLAGE AND EXCISE THE REDUNDANT VENTRAL SET FROM ALL FURTHER PROTOTYPES.
ADDITIONALLY, PILOT KIMORA PERFORMED ADMIRABLY DURING A CRISIS SITUATION. I RECOMMEND SHE BE BUMPED TO THE TOP OF OUR PREFERRED LIST AS CHIEF PILOT ON THE OUTWORLD EXPEDI--
CHUGA-CHUGA-CHUGA-CHUGA-
WHOOOO-HOOO!
LETS GO TO THE CABIN-- I WANNA FUCK.
ALL ABOARD!
PANDITA! YOU MISSED A GREAT CONCERT.

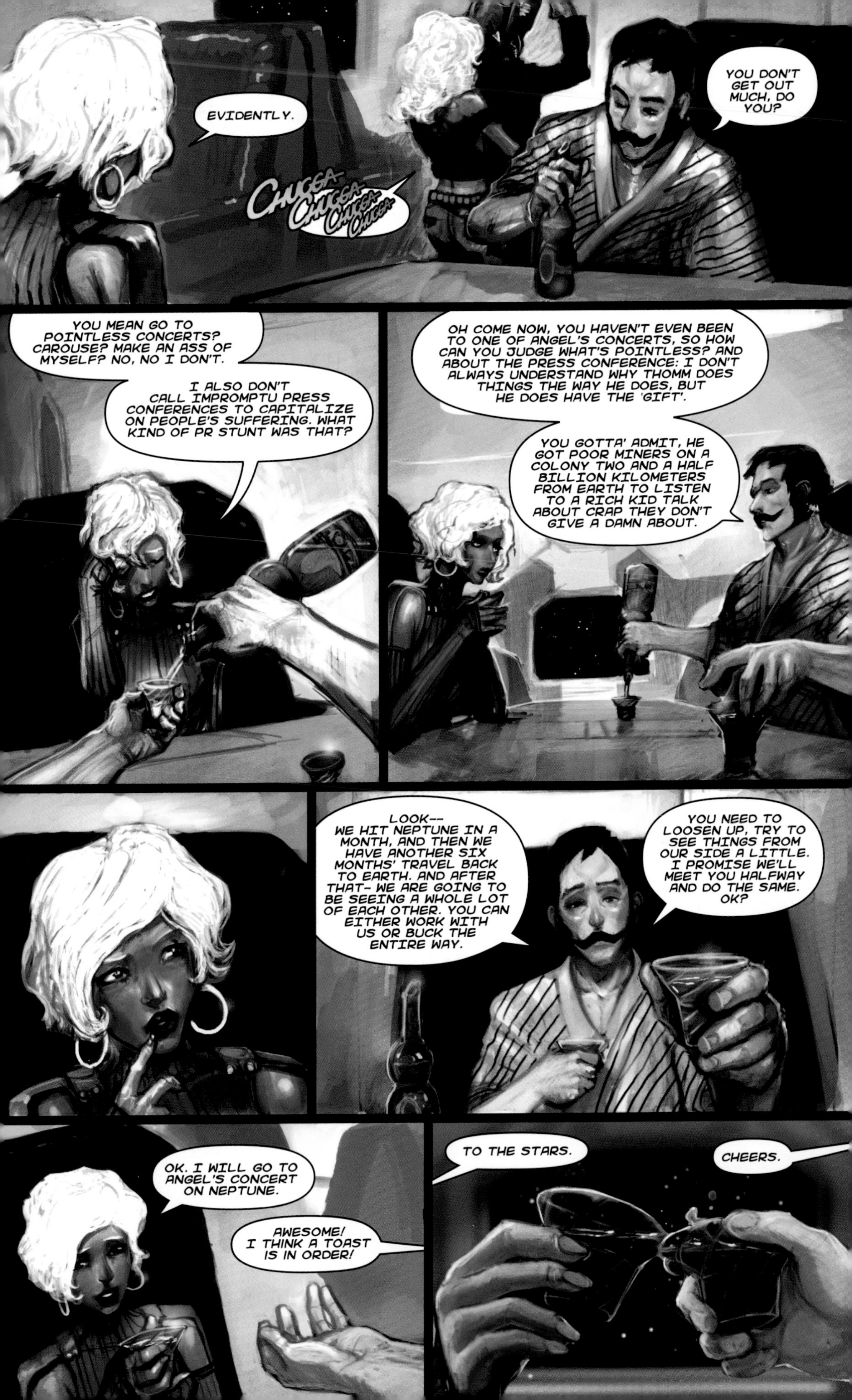
EVIDENTLY.
YOU DON'T GET OUT MUCH, DO YOU?
CHUGGA CHUGGA CHUGGA CHUGGA
YOU MEAN GO TO POINTLESS CONCERTS? CAROUSE? MAKE AN ASS OF MYSELF? NO, NO I DON'T.
I ALSO DON'T CALL IMPROMPTU PRESS CONFERENCES TO CAPITALIZE ON PEOPLE'S SUFFERING. WHAT KIND OF PR STUNT WAS THAT?
OH COME NOW, YOU HAVEN'T EVEN BEEN TO ONE OF ANGEL'S CONCERTS, SO HOW CAN YOU JUDGE WHAT'S POINTLESS? AND ABOUT THE PRESS CONFERENCE: I DON'T ALWAYS UNDERSTAND WHY THOMM DOES THINGS THE WAY HE DOES, BUT HE DOES HAVE THE 'GIFT'.
YOU GOTTA' ADMIT, HE GOT POOR MINERS ON A COLONY TWO AND A HALF BILLION KILOMETERS FROM EARTH TO LISTEN TO A RICH KID TALK ABOUT CRAP THEY DON'T GIVE A DAMN ABOUT.
LOOK-- WE HIT NEPTUNE IN A MONTH, AND THEN WE HAVE ANOTHER SIX MONTHS' TRAVEL BACK TO EARTH. AND AFTER THAT- WE ARE GOING TO BE SEEING A WHOLE LOT OF EACH OTHER. YOU CAN EITHER WORK WITH US OR BUCK THE ENTIRE WAY.
YOU NEED TO LOOSEN UP, TRY TO SEE THINGS FROM OUR SIDE A LITTLE. I PROMISE WE'LL MEET YOU HALFWAY AND DO THE SAME. OK?
OK. I WILL GO TO ANGEL'S CONCERT ON NEPTUNE.
AWESOME! I THINK A TOAST IS IN ORDER!
TO THE STARS.
CHEERS.

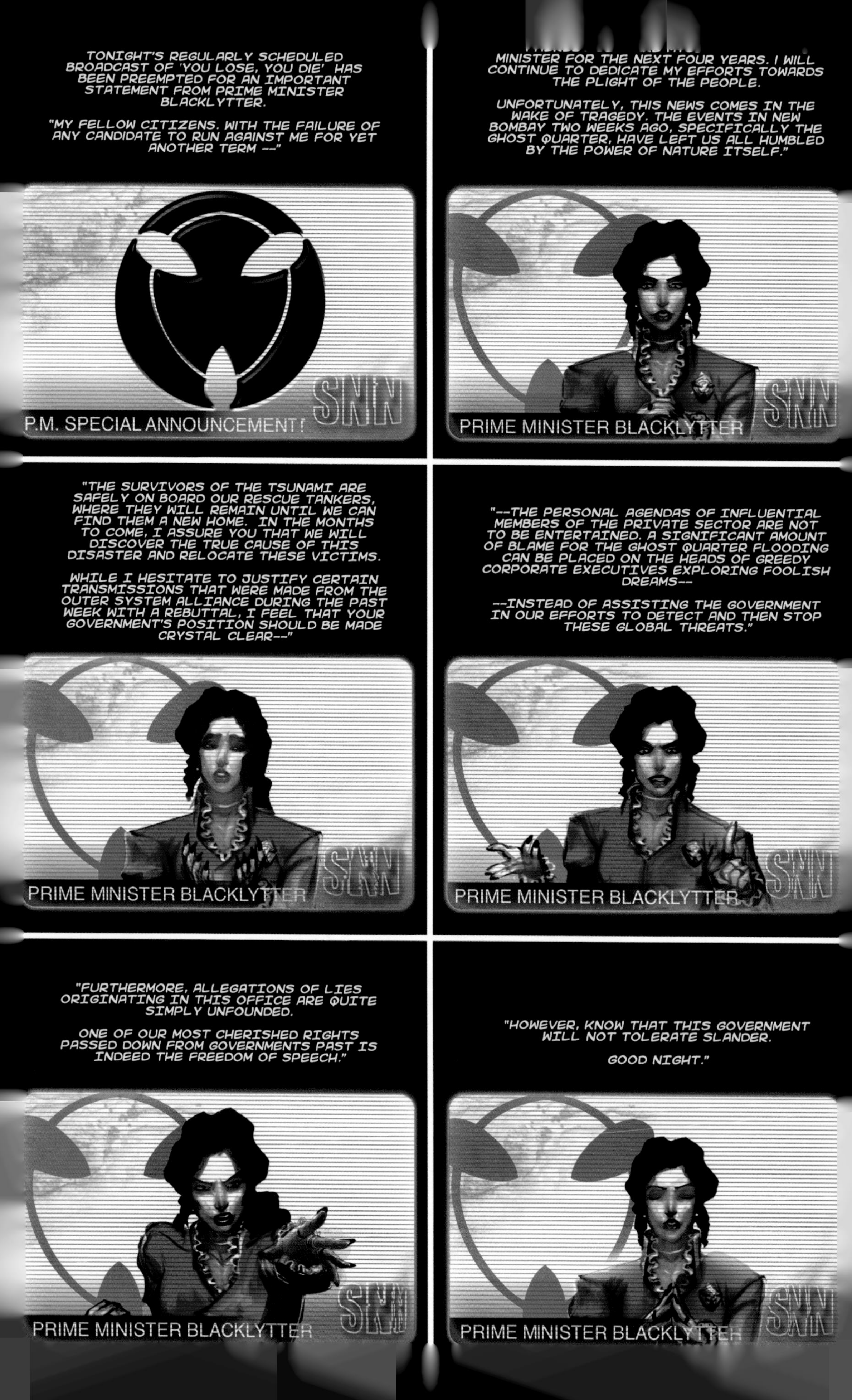
TONIGHT'S REGULARLY SCHEDULED BROADCAST OF 'YOU LOSE, YOU DIE' HAS BEEN PREEMPTED FOR AN IMPORTANT STATEMENT FROM PRIME MINISTER BLACKLYTTER.
"MY FELLOW CITIZENS. WITH THE FAILURE OF ANY CANDIDATE TO RUN AGAINST ME FOR YET ANOTHER TERM --"
P.M. SPECIAL ANNOUNCEMENT!
SNN
MINISTER FOR THE NEXT FOUR YEARS. I WILL CONTINUE TO DEDICATE MY EFFORTS TOWARDS THE PLIGHT OF THE PEOPLE.
UNFORTUNATELY, THIS NEWS COMES IN THE WAKE OF TRAGEDY. THE EVENTS IN NEW BOMBAY TWO WEEKS AGO, SPECIFICALLY THE GHOST QUARTER, HAVE LEFT US ALL HUMBLED BY THE POWER OF NATURE ITSELF."
PRIME MINISTER BLACKLYTTER
SNN
"THE SURVIVORS OF THE TSUNAMI ARE SAFELY ON BOARD OUR RESCUE TANKERS, WHERE THEY WILL REMAIN UNTIL WE CAN FIND THEM A NEW HOME. IN THE MONTHS TO COME, I ASSURE YOU THAT WE WILL DISCOVER THE TRUE CAUSE OF THIS DISASTER AND RELOCATE THESE VICTIMS.
WHILE I HESITATE TO JUSTIFY CERTAIN TRANSMISSIONS THAT WERE MADE FROM THE OUTER SYSTEM ALLIANCE DURING THE PAST WEEK WITH A REBUTTAL, I FEEL THAT YOUR GOVERNMENT'S POSITION SHOULD BE MADE CRYSTAL CLEAR--"
PRIME MINISTER BLACKLYTTER
SNN
"--THE PERSONAL AGENDAS OF INFLUENTIAL MEMBERS OF THE PRIVATE SECTOR ARE NOT TO BE ENTERTAINED. A SIGNIFICANT AMOUNT OF BLAME FOR THE GHOST QUARTER FLOODING CAN BE PLACED ON THE HEADS OF GREEDY CORPORATE EXECUTIVES EXPLORING FOOLISH DREAMS--
--INSTEAD OF ASSISTING THE GOVERNMENT IN OUR EFFORTS TO DETECT AND THEN STOP THESE GLOBAL THREATS."
PRIME MINISTER BLACKLYTTER
SNN
"FURTHERMORE, ALLEGATIONS OF LIES ORIGINATING IN THIS OFFICE ARE QUITE SIMPLY UNFOUNDED.
ONE OF OUR MOST CHERISHED RIGHTS PASSED DOWN FROM GOVERNMENTS PAST IS INDEED THE FREEDOM OF SPEECH."
PRIME MINISTER BLACKLYTTER
SNN
"HOWEVER, KNOW THAT THIS GOVERNMENT WILL NOT TOLERATE SLANDER.
GOOD NIGHT."
PRIME MINISTER BLACKLYTTER
SNN

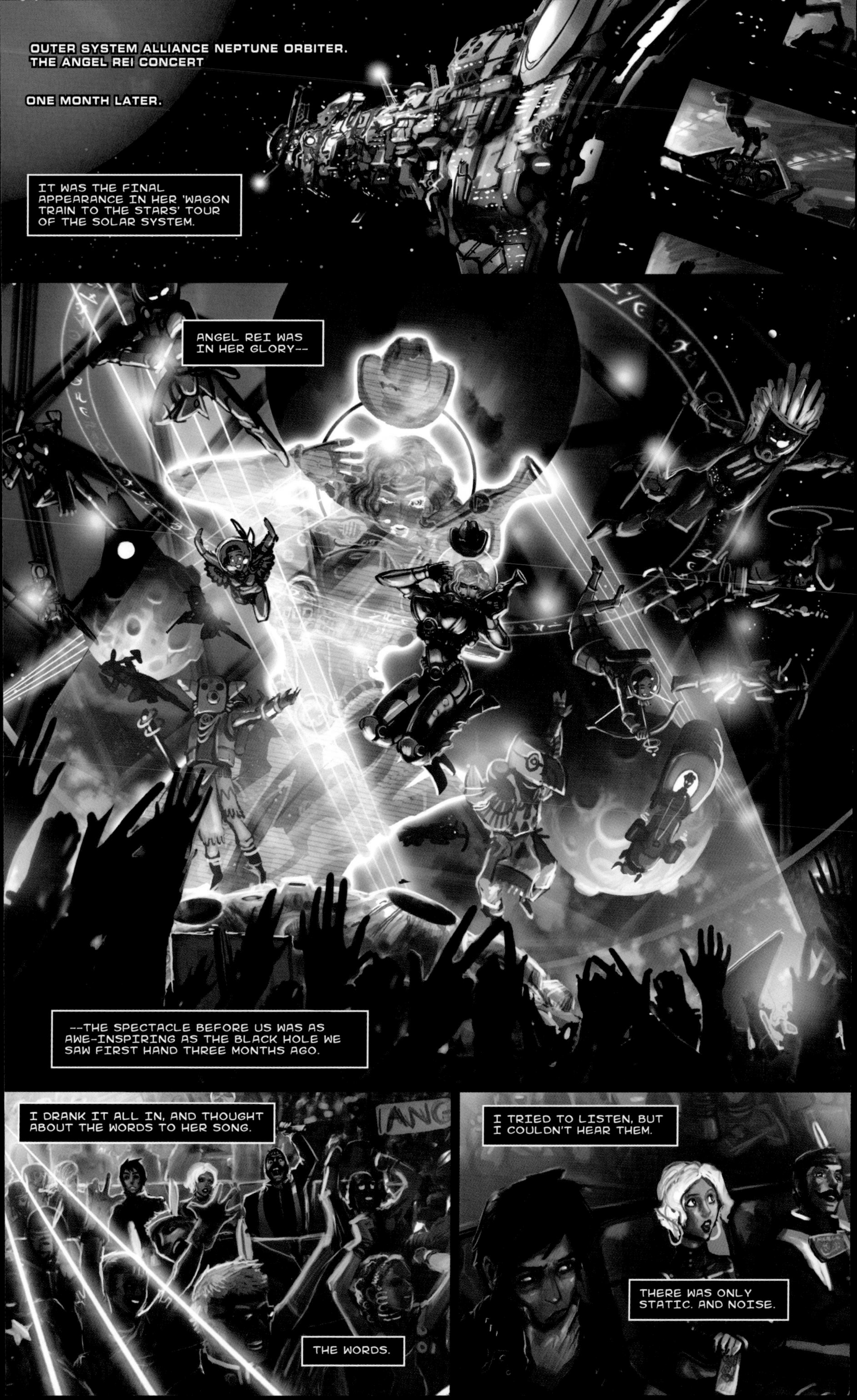
OUTER SYSTEM ALLIANCE NEPTUNE ORBITER.
THE ANGEL REI CONCERT
ONE MONTH LATER.
IT WAS THE FINAL APPEARANCE IN HER 'WAGON TRAIN TO THE STARS' TOUR OF THE SOLAR SYSTEM.
ANGEL REI WAS IN HER GLORY--
--THE SPECTACLE BEFORE US WAS AS AWE-INSPIRING AS THE BLACK HOLE WE SAW FIRST HAND THREE MONTHS AGO.
I DRANK IT ALL IN, AND THOUGHT ABOUT THE WORDS TO HER SONG.
THE WORDS.
I TRIED TO LISTEN, BUT I COULDN'T HEAR THEM.
THERE WAS ONLY STATIC. AND NOISE.

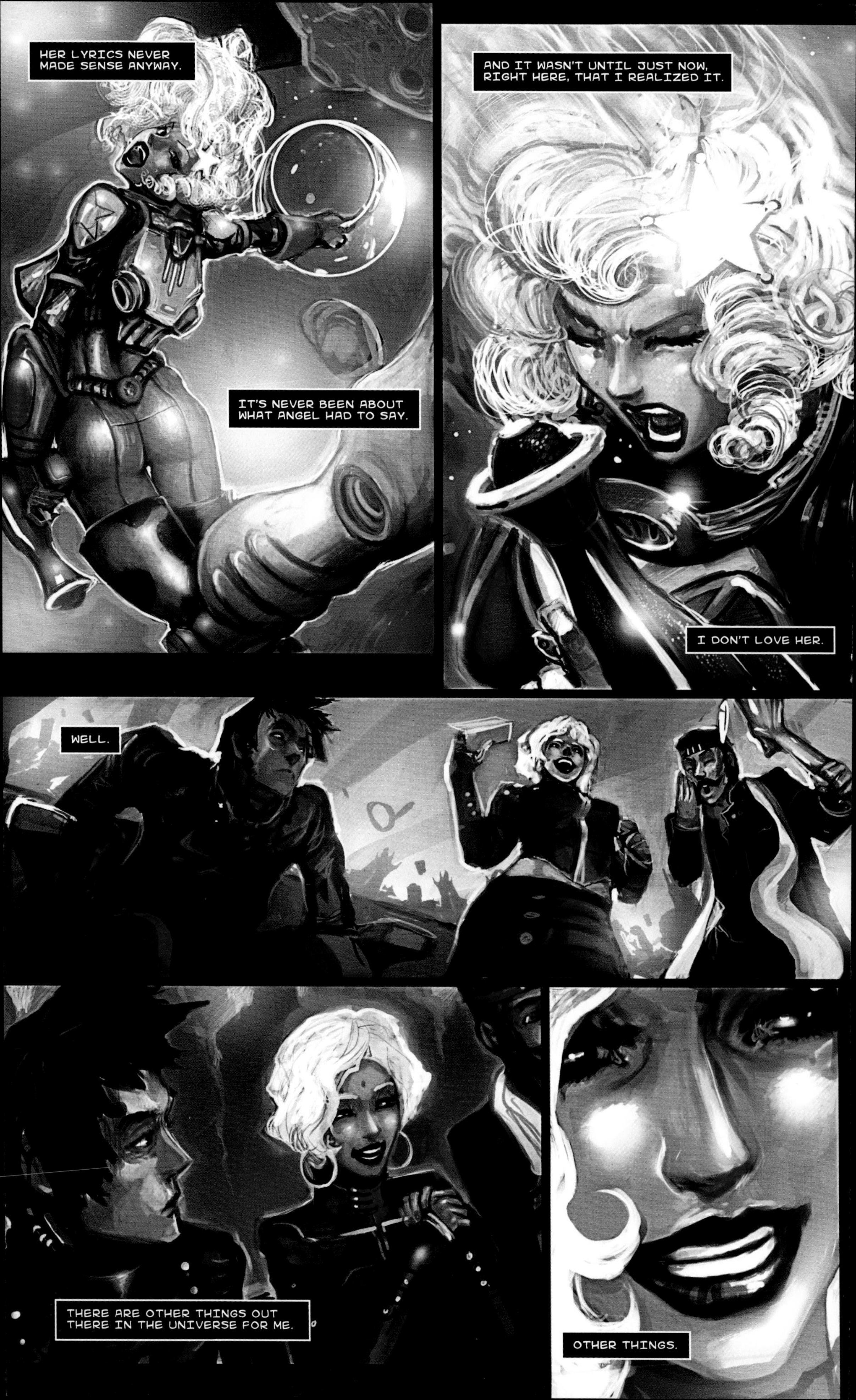
HER LYRICS NEVER MADE SENSE ANYWAY.
IT'S NEVER BEEN ABOUT WHAT ANGEL HAD TO SAY.
AND IT WASN'T UNTIL JUST NOW, RIGHT HERE, THAT I REALIZED IT.
I DON'T LOVE HER.
WELL.
THERE ARE OTHER THINGS OUT THERE IN THE UNIVERSE FOR ME.
OTHER THINGS.

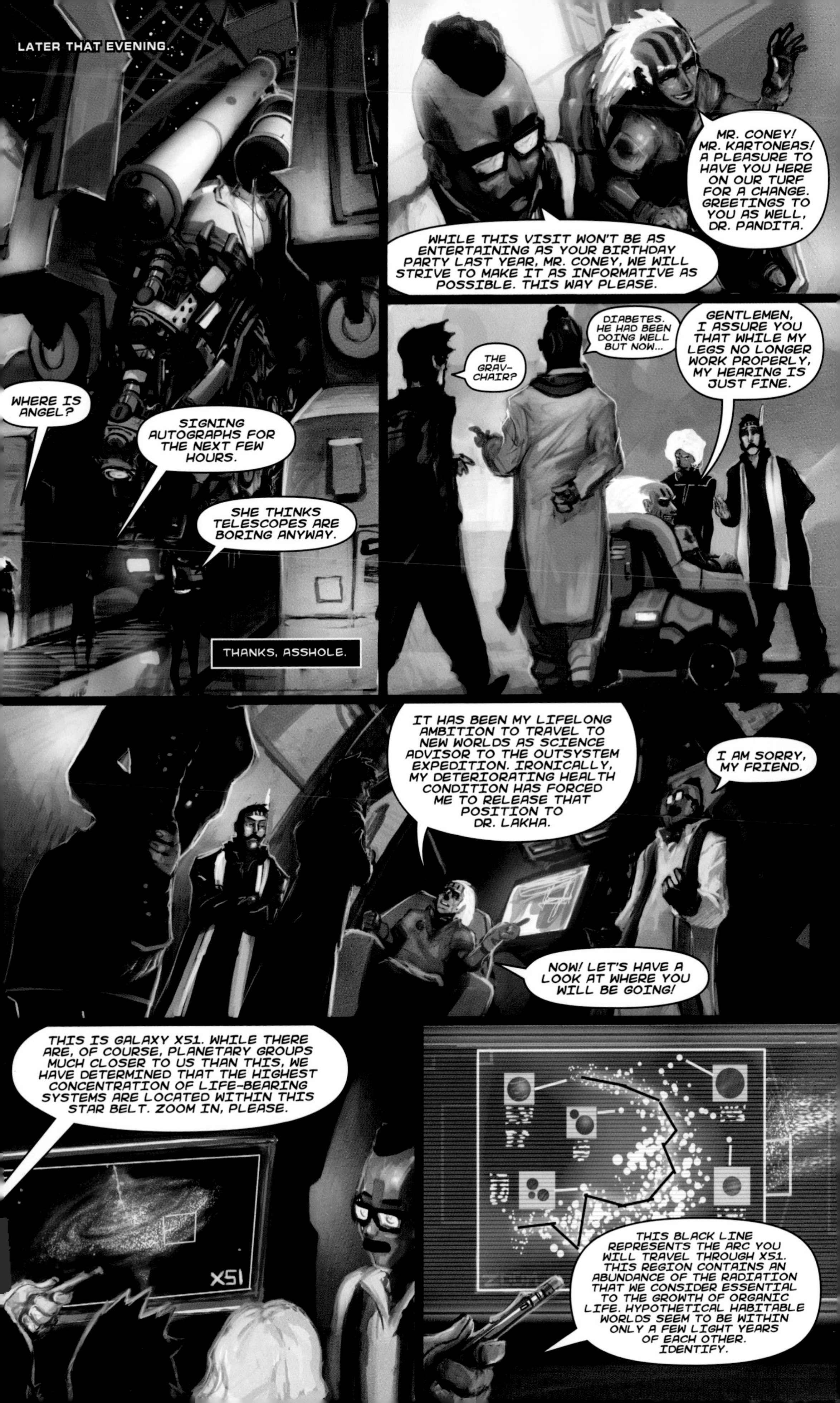
LATER THAT EVENING.
WHERE IS ANGEL?
SIGNING AUTOGRAPHS FOR THE NEXT FEW HOURS.
SHE THINKS TELESCOPES ARE BORING ANYWAY.
THANKS, ASSHOLE.
MR. CONEY! MR. KARTONEAS! A PLEASURE TO HAVE YOU HERE ON OUR TURF FOR A CHANGE. GREETINGS TO YOU AS WELL, DR. PANDITA.
WHILE THIS VISIT WON'T BE AS ENTERTAINING AS YOUR BIRTHDAY PARTY LAST YEAR, MR. CONEY, WE WILL STRIVE TO MAKE IT AS INFORMATIVE AS POSSIBLE. THIS WAY PLEASE.
THE GRAV-CHAIR?
DIABETES. HE HAD BEEN DOING WELL BUT NOW...
GENTLEMEN, I ASSURE YOU THAT WHILE MY LEGS NO LONGER WORK PROPERLY, MY HEARING IS JUST FINE.
IT HAS BEEN MY LIFELONG AMBITION TO TRAVEL TO NEW WORLDS AS SCIENCE ADVISOR TO THE OUTSYSTEM EXPEDITION. IRONICALLY, MY DETERIORATING HEALTH CONDITION HAS FORCED ME TO RELEASE THAT POSITION TO DR. LAKHA.
I AM SORRY, MY FRIEND.
NOW! LET'S HAVE A LOOK AT WHERE YOU WILL BE GOING!
THIS IS GALAXY X51. WHILE THERE ARE, OF COURSE, PLANETARY GROUPS MUCH CLOSER TO US THAN THIS, WE HAVE DETERMINED THAT THE HIGHEST CONCENTRATION OF LIFE-BEARING SYSTEMS ARE LOCATED WITHIN THIS STAR BELT. ZOOM IN, PLEASE.
X51
THIS BLACK LINE REPRESENTS THE ARC YOU WILL TRAVEL THROUGH X51. THIS REGION CONTAINS AN ABUNDANCE OF THE RADIATION THAT WE CONSIDER ESSENTIAL TO THE GROWTH OF ORGANIC LIFE. HYPOTHETICAL HABITABLE WORLDS SEEM TO BE WITHIN ONLY A FEW LIGHT YEARS OF EACH OTHER. IDENTIFY.

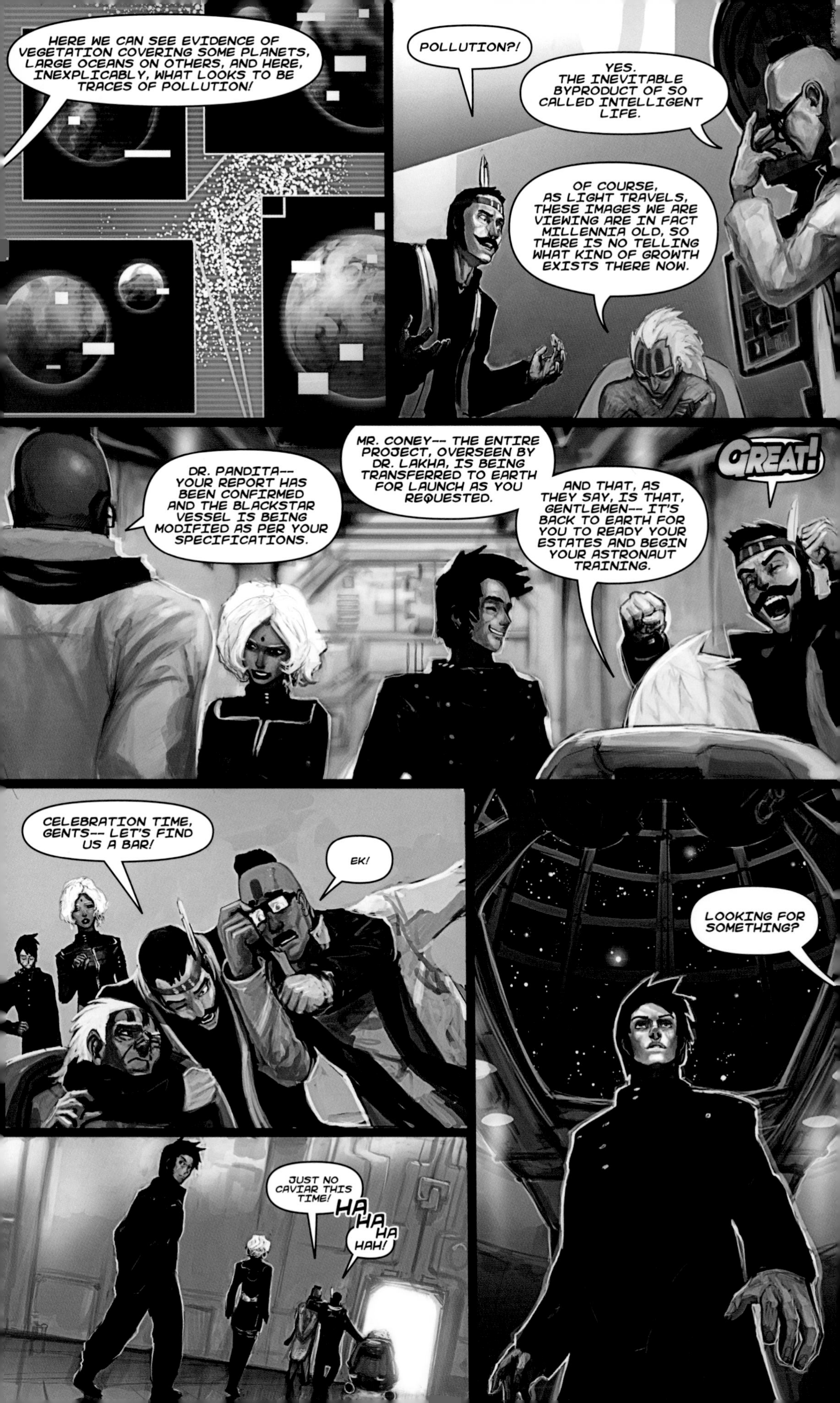

HERE WE CAN SEE EVIDENCE OF VEGETATION COVERING SOME PLANETS, LARGE OCEANS ON OTHERS, AND HERE, INEXPLICABLY, WHAT LOOKS TO BE TRACES OF POLLUTION!
POLLUTION?!
YES. THE INEVITABLE BYPRODUCT OF SO CALLED INTELLIGENT LIFE.
OF COURSE, AS LIGHT TRAVELS, THESE IMAGES WE ARE VIEWING ARE IN FACT MILLENNIA OLD, SO THERE IS NO TELLING WHAT KIND OF GROWTH EXISTS THERE NOW.
DR. PANDITA-- YOUR REPORT HAS BEEN CONFIRMED AND THE BLACKSTAR VESSEL IS BEING MODIFIED AS PER YOUR SPECIFICATIONS.
MR. CONEY-- THE ENTIRE PROJECT, OVERSEEN BY DR. LAKHA, IS BEING TRANSFERRED TO EARTH FOR LAUNCH AS YOU REQUESTED.
AND THAT, AS THEY SAY, IS THAT, GENTLEMEN-- IT'S BACK TO EARTH FOR YOU TO READY YOUR ESTATES AND BEGIN YOUR ASTRONAUT TRAINING.
GREAT!
CELEBRATION TIME, GENTS-- LET'S FIND US A BAR!
EK!
JUST NO CAVIAR THIS TIME!
HA HA HA HAH!
LOOKING FOR SOMETHING?

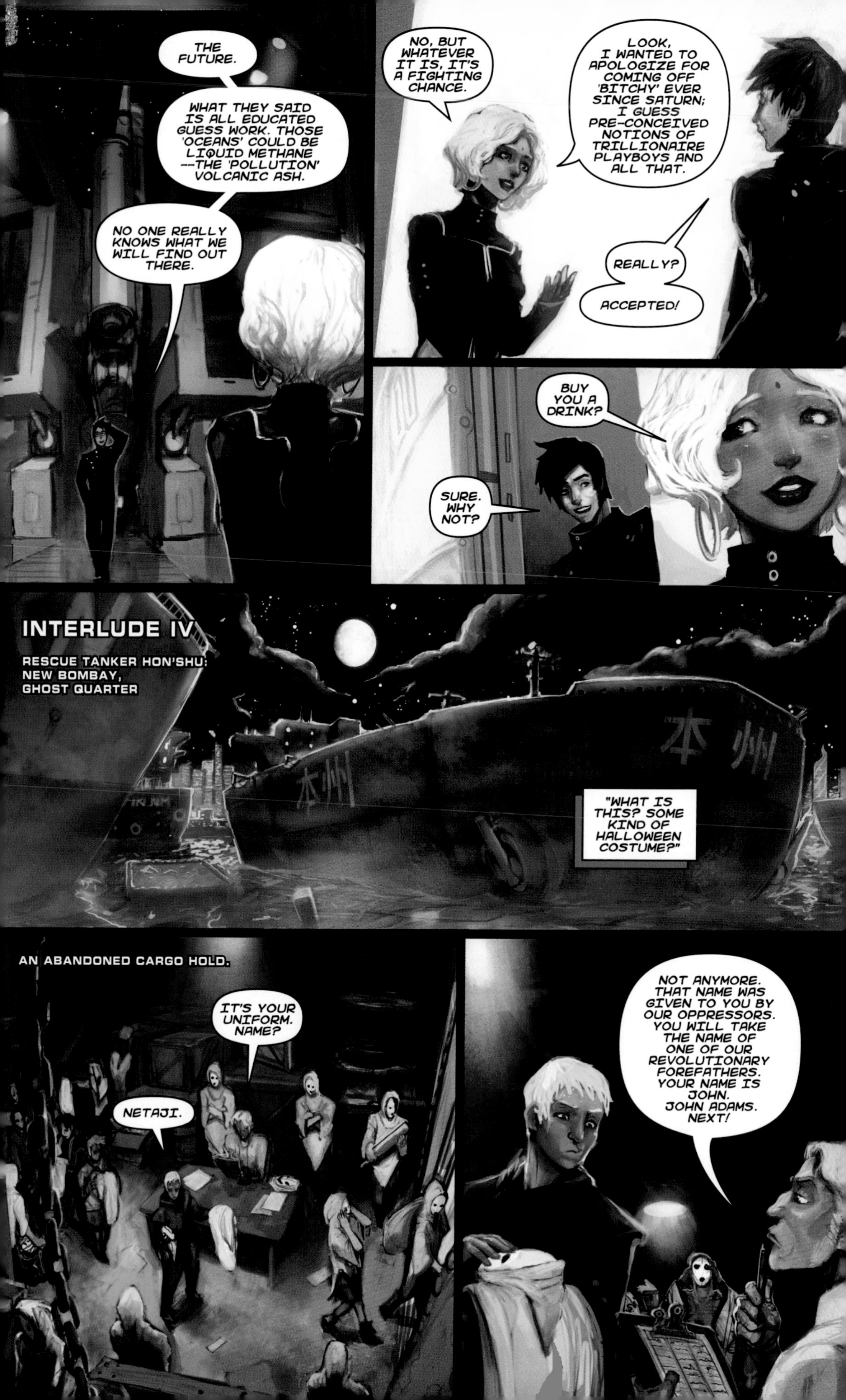
THE FUTURE.
WHAT THEY SAID IS ALL EDUCATED GUESS WORK. THOSE 'OCEANS' COULD BE LIQUID METHANE --THE 'POLLUTION' VOLCANIC ASH.
NO ONE REALLY KNOWS WHAT WE WILL FIND OUT THERE.
NO, BUT WHATEVER IT IS, IT'S A FIGHTING CHANCE.
LOOK, I WANTED TO APOLOGIZE FOR COMING OFF 'BITCHY' EVER SINCE SATURN; I GUESS PRE-CONCEIVED NOTIONS OF TRILLIONAIRE PLAYBOYS AND ALL THAT.
REALLY?
ACCEPTED!
BUY YOU A DRINK?
SURE. WHY NOT?
INTERLUDE IV
RESCUE TANKER HON'SHU: NEW BOMBAY, GHOST QUARTER
本州
"WHAT IS THIS? SOME KIND OF HALLOWEEN COSTUME?"
AN ABANDONED CARGO HOLD.
IT'S YOUR UNIFORM. NAME?
NETAJI.
NOT ANYMORE. THAT NAME WAS GIVEN TO YOU BY OUR OPPRESSORS. YOU WILL TAKE THE NAME OF ONE OF OUR REVOLUTIONARY FOREFATHERS. YOUR NAME IS JOHN. JOHN ADAMS. NEXT!

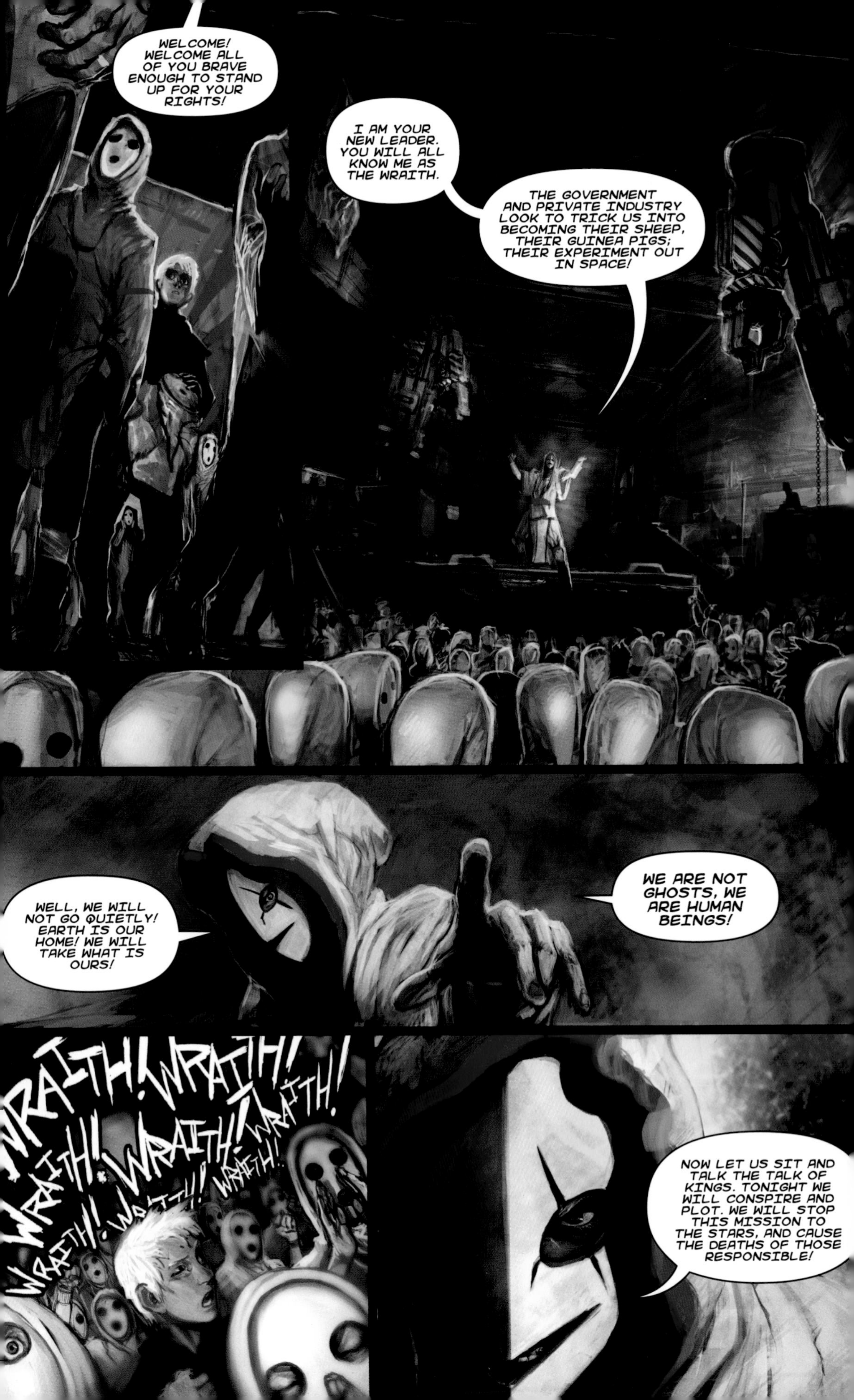
WELCOME! WELCOME ALL OF YOU BRAVE ENOUGH TO STAND UP FOR YOUR RIGHTS!
I AM YOUR NEW LEADER. YOU WILL ALL KNOW ME AS THE WRAITH.
THE GOVERNMENT AND PRIVATE INDUSTRY LOOK TO TRICK US INTO BECOMING THEIR SHEEP, THEIR GUINEA PIGS; THEIR EXPERIMENT OUT IN SPACE!
WELL, WE WILL NOT GO QUIETLY! EARTH IS OUR HOME! WE WILL TAKE WHAT IS OURS!
WE ARE NOT GHOSTS, WE ARE HUMAN BEINGS!
WRAITH! WRAITH! WRAITH! WRAITH! WRAITH! WRAITH! WRAITH!
NOW LET US SIT AND TALK THE TALK OF KINGS. TONIGHT WE WILL CONSPIRE AND PLOT. WE WILL STOP THIS MISSION TO THE STARS, AND CAUSE THE DEATHS OF THOSE RESPONSIBLE!

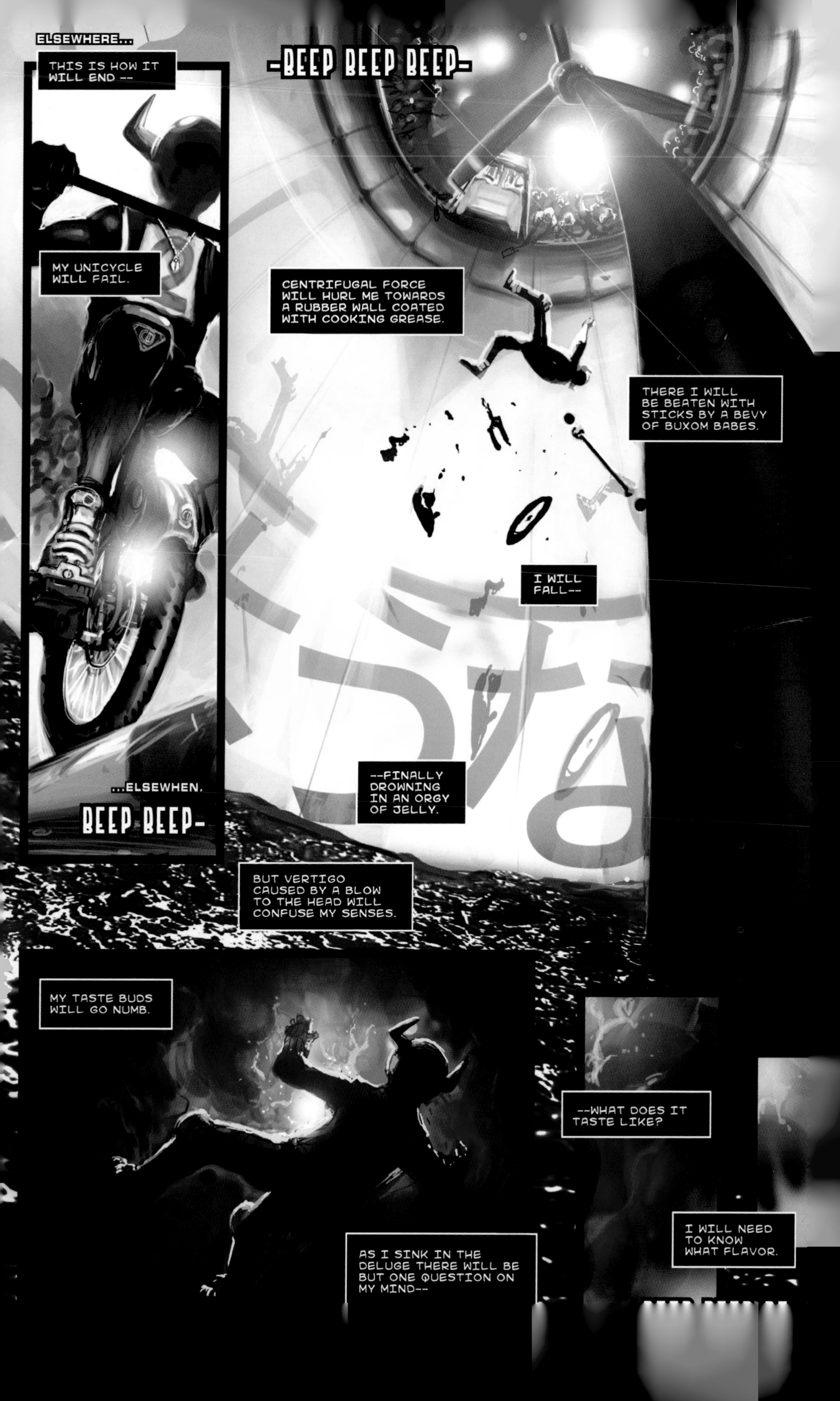
ELSEWHERE...
THIS IS HOW IT WILL END --
-BEEP BEEP BEEP-
MY UNICYCLE WILL FAIL.
CENTRIFUGAL FORCE WILL HURL ME TOWARDS A RUBBER WALL COATED WITH COOKING GREASE.
THERE I WILL BE BEATEN WITH STICKS BY A BEVY OF BUXOM BABES.
I WILL FALL--
--FINALLY DROWNING IN AN ORGY OF JELLY.
...ELSEWHEN.
BEEP BEEP-
BUT VERTIGO CAUSED BY A BLOW TO THE HEAD WILL CONFUSE MY SENSES.
MY TASTE BUDS WILL GO NUMB.
--WHAT DOES IT TASTE LIKE?
AS I SINK IN THE DELUGE THERE WILL BE BUT ONE QUESTION ON MY MIND--
I WILL NEED TO KNOW WHAT FLAVOR.

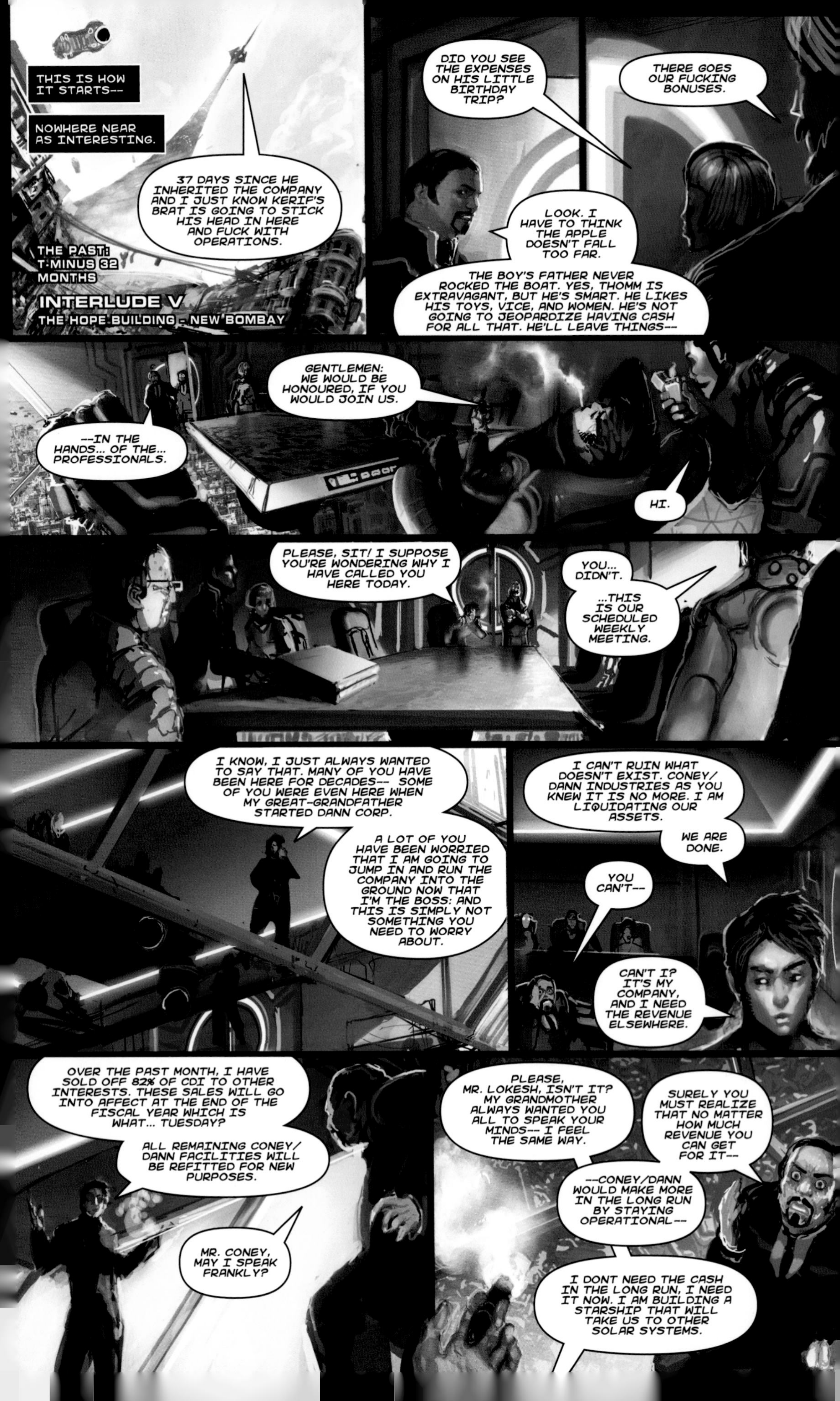
THIS IS HOW IT STARTS--
NOWHERE NEAR AS INTERESTING.
37 DAYS SINCE HE INHERITED THE COMPANY AND I JUST KNOW KERIF'S BRAT IS GOING TO STICK HIS HEAD IN HERE AND FUCK WITH OPERATIONS.
THE PAST: T-MINUS 32 MONTHS
INTERLUDE V
THE HOPE BUILDING - NEW BOMBAY
DID YOU SEE THE EXPENSES ON HIS LITTLE BIRTHDAY TRIP?
THERE GOES OUR FUCKING BONUSES.
LOOK. I HAVE TO THINK THE APPLE DOESN'T FALL TOO FAR.
THE BOY'S FATHER NEVER ROCKED THE BOAT. YES, THOMM IS EXTRAVAGANT, BUT HE'S SMART. HE LIKES HIS TOYS, VICE, AND WOMEN. HE'S NOT GOING TO JEOPARDIZE HAVING CASH FOR ALL THAT. HE'LL LEAVE THINGS--
--IN THE HANDS... OF THE... PROFESSIONALS.
GENTLEMEN: WE WOULD BE HONOURED, IF YOU WOULD JOIN US.
HI.
PLEASE, SIT! I SUPPOSE YOU'RE WONDERING WHY I HAVE CALLED YOU HERE TODAY.
YOU... DIDN'T.
...THIS IS OUR SCHEDULED WEEKLY MEETING.
I KNOW, I JUST ALWAYS WANTED TO SAY THAT. MANY OF YOU HAVE BEEN HERE FOR DECADES-- SOME OF YOU WERE EVEN HERE WHEN MY GREAT-GRANDFATHER STARTED DANN CORP.
A LOT OF YOU HAVE BEEN WORRIED THAT I AM GOING TO JUMP IN AND RUN THE COMPANY INTO THE GROUND NOW THAT I'M THE BOSS: AND THIS IS SIMPLY NOT SOMETHING YOU NEED TO WORRY ABOUT.
I CAN'T RUIN WHAT DOESN'T EXIST. CONEY/DANN INDUSTRIES AS YOU KNEW IT IS NO MORE. I AM LIQUIDATING OUR ASSETS.
WE ARE DONE.
YOU CAN'T--
CAN'T I? IT'S MY COMPANY, AND I NEED THE REVENUE ELSEWHERE.
OVER THE PAST MONTH, I HAVE SOLD OFF 82% OF CDI TO OTHER INTERESTS. THESE SALES WILL GO INTO AFFECT AT THE END OF THE FISCAL YEAR WHICH IS WHAT... TUESDAY?
ALL REMAINING CONEY/DANN FACILITIES WILL BE REFITTED FOR NEW PURPOSES.
MR. CONEY, MAY I SPEAK FRANKLY?
PLEASE, MR. LOKESH, ISN'T IT? MY GRANDMOTHER ALWAYS WANTED YOU ALL TO SPEAK YOUR MINDS-- I FEEL THE SAME WAY.
SURELY YOU MUST REALIZE THAT NO MATTER HOW MUCH REVENUE YOU CAN GET FOR IT--
--CONEY/DANN WOULD MAKE MORE IN THE LONG RUN BY STAYING OPERATIONAL--
I DONT NEED THE CASH IN THE LONG RUN, I NEED IT NOW. I AM BUILDING A STARSHIP THAT WILL TAKE US TO OTHER SOLAR SYSTEMS.

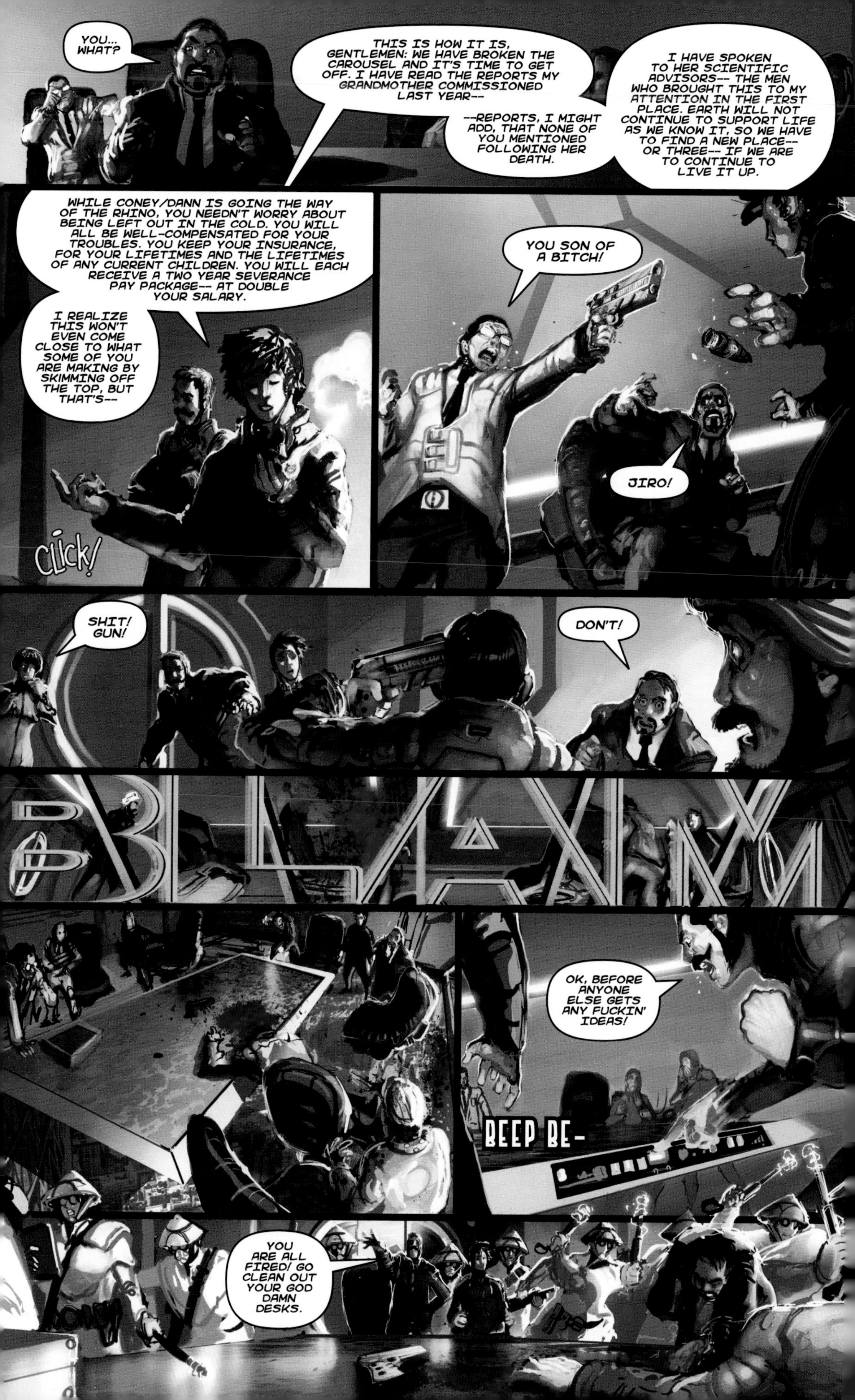

YOU... WHAT?
THIS IS HOW IT IS, GENTLEMEN: WE HAVE BROKEN THE CAROUSEL AND IT'S TIME TO GET OFF. I HAVE READ THE REPORTS MY GRANDMOTHER COMMISSIONED LAST YEAR--
--REPORTS, I MIGHT ADD, THAT NONE OF YOU MENTIONED FOLLOWING HER DEATH.
I HAVE SPOKEN TO HER SCIENTIFIC ADVISORS-- THE MEN WHO BROUGHT THIS TO MY ATTENTION IN THE FIRST PLACE. EARTH WILL NOT CONTINUE TO SUPPORT LIFE AS WE KNOW IT, SO WE HAVE TO FIND A NEW PLACE-- OR THREE-- IF WE ARE TO CONTINUE TO LIVE IT UP.
WHILE CONEY/DANN IS GOING THE WAY OF THE RHINO, YOU NEEDN'T WORRY ABOUT BEING LEFT OUT IN THE COLD. YOU WILL ALL BE WELL-COMPENSATED FOR YOUR TROUBLES. YOU KEEP YOUR INSURANCE, FOR YOUR LIFETIMES AND THE LIFETIMES OF ANY CURRENT CHILDREN. YOU WILL EACH RECEIVE A TWO YEAR SEVERANCE PAY PACKAGE-- AT DOUBLE YOUR SALARY.
I REALIZE THIS WON'T EVEN COME CLOSE TO WHAT SOME OF YOU ARE MAKING BY SKIMMING OFF THE TOP, BUT THAT'S--
CLICK!
YOU SON OF A BITCH!
JIRO!
SHIT! GUN!
DON'T!
BLAAM
OK, BEFORE ANYONE ELSE GETS ANY FUCKIN' IDEAS!
BEEP BE-
YOU ARE ALL FIRED! GO CLEAN OUT YOUR GOD DAMN DESKS.

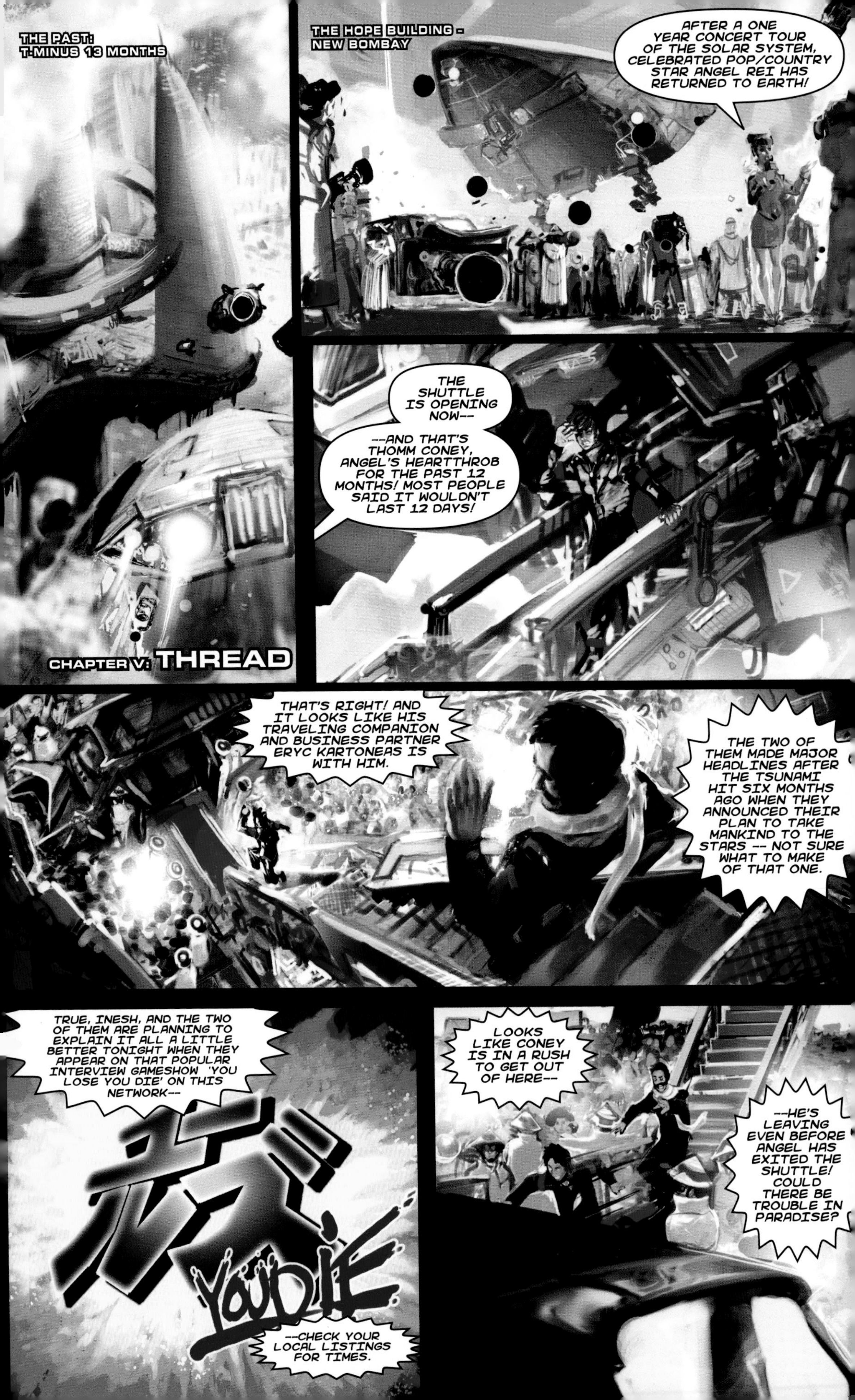
THE PAST:
T-MINUS 13 MONTHS
CHAPTER V: THREAD
THE HOPE BUILDING - NEW BOMBAY
AFTER A ONE YEAR CONCERT TOUR OF THE SOLAR SYSTEM, CELEBRATED POP/COUNTRY STAR ANGEL REI HAS RETURNED TO EARTH!
THE SHUTTLE IS OPENING NOW--
--AND THAT'S THOMM CONEY, ANGEL'S HEARTTHROB FOR THE PAST 12 MONTHS! MOST PEOPLE SAID IT WOULDN'T LAST 12 DAYS!
THAT'S RIGHT! AND IT LOOKS LIKE HIS TRAVELING COMPANION AND BUSINESS PARTNER ERYC KARTONEAS IS WITH HIM.
THE TWO OF THEM MADE MAJOR HEADLINES AFTER THE TSUNAMI HIT SIX MONTHS AGO WHEN THEY ANNOUNCED THEIR PLAN TO TAKE MANKIND TO THE STARS -- NOT SURE WHAT TO MAKE OF THAT ONE.
TRUE, INESH, AND THE TWO OF THEM ARE PLANNING TO EXPLAIN IT ALL A LITTLE BETTER TONIGHT WHEN THEY APPEAR ON THAT POPULAR INTERVIEW GAMESHOW 'YOU LOSE YOU DIE' ON THIS NETWORK--
ユーズ
YOU DIE
--CHECK YOUR LOCAL LISTINGS FOR TIMES.
LOOKS LIKE CONEY IS IN A RUSH TO GET OUT OF HERE--
--HE'S LEAVING EVEN BEFORE ANGEL HAS EXITED THE SHUTTLE! COULD THERE BE TROUBLE IN PARADISE?

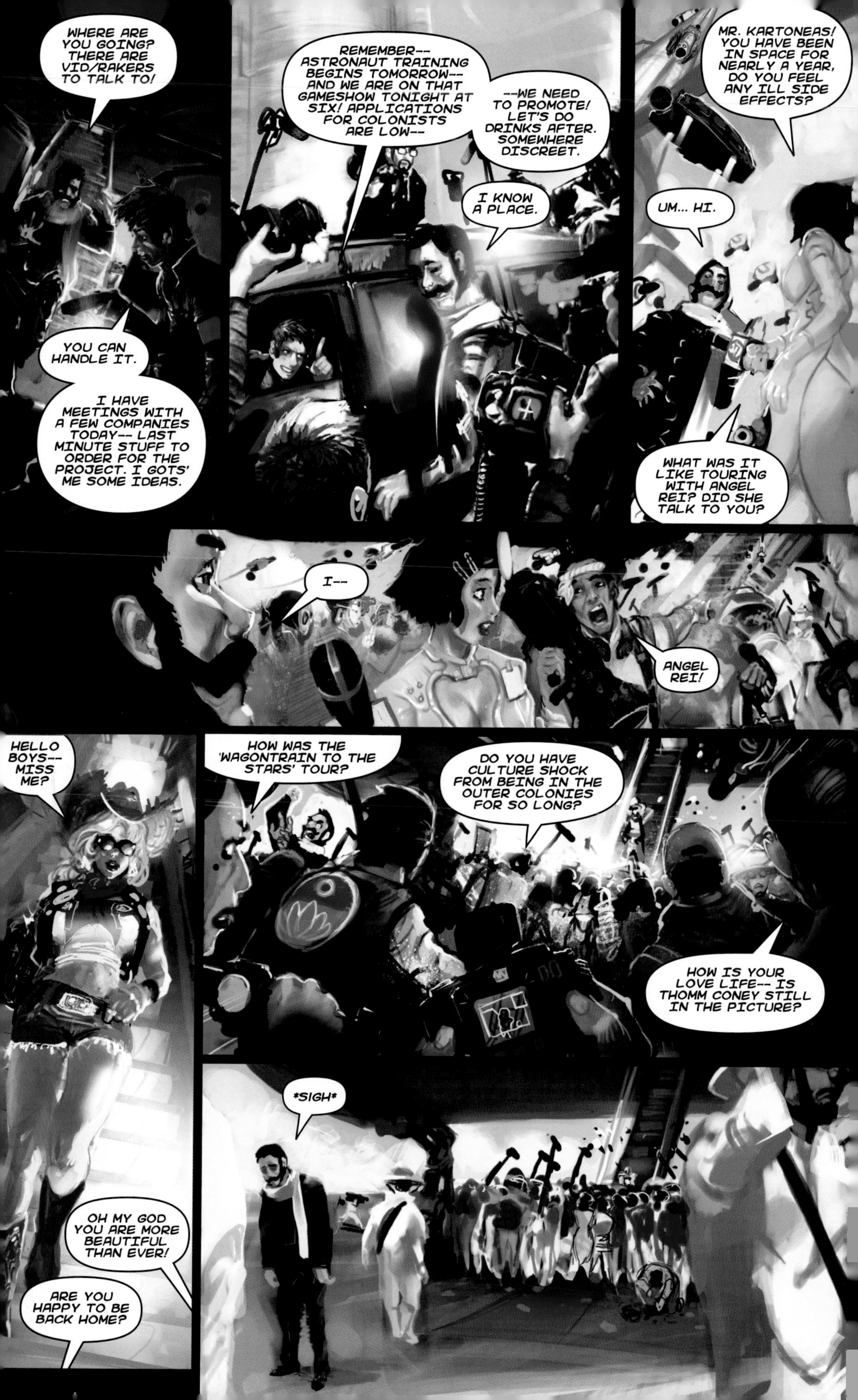
WHERE ARE YOU GOING? THERE ARE VID/RAKERS TO TALK TO!
YOU CAN HANDLE IT.
I HAVE MEETINGS WITH A FEW COMPANIES TODAY-- LAST MINUTE STUFF TO ORDER FOR THE PROJECT. I GOTS' ME SOME IDEAS.
REMEMBER-- ASTRONAUT TRAINING BEGINS TOMORROW-- AND WE ARE ON THAT GAMESHOW TONIGHT AT SIX! APPLICATIONS FOR COLONISTS ARE LOW--
--WE NEED TO PROMOTE! LET'S DO DRINKS AFTER. SOMEWHERE DISCREET.
I KNOW A PLACE.
MR. KARTONEAS! YOU HAVE BEEN IN SPACE FOR NEARLY A YEAR, DO YOU FEEL ANY ILL SIDE EFFECTS?
UM... HI.
WHAT WAS IT LIKE TOURING WITH ANGEL REI? DID SHE TALK TO YOU?
I--
ANGEL REI!
HELLO BOYS-- MISS ME?
OH MY GOD YOU ARE MORE BEAUTIFUL THAN EVER!
ARE YOU HAPPY TO BE BACK HOME?
HOW WAS THE 'WAGONTRAIN TO THE STARS' TOUR?
DO YOU HAVE CULTURE SHOCK FROM BEING IN THE OUTER COLONIES FOR SO LONG?
HOW IS YOUR LOVE LIFE-- IS THOMM CONEY STILL IN THE PICTURE?
SIGH

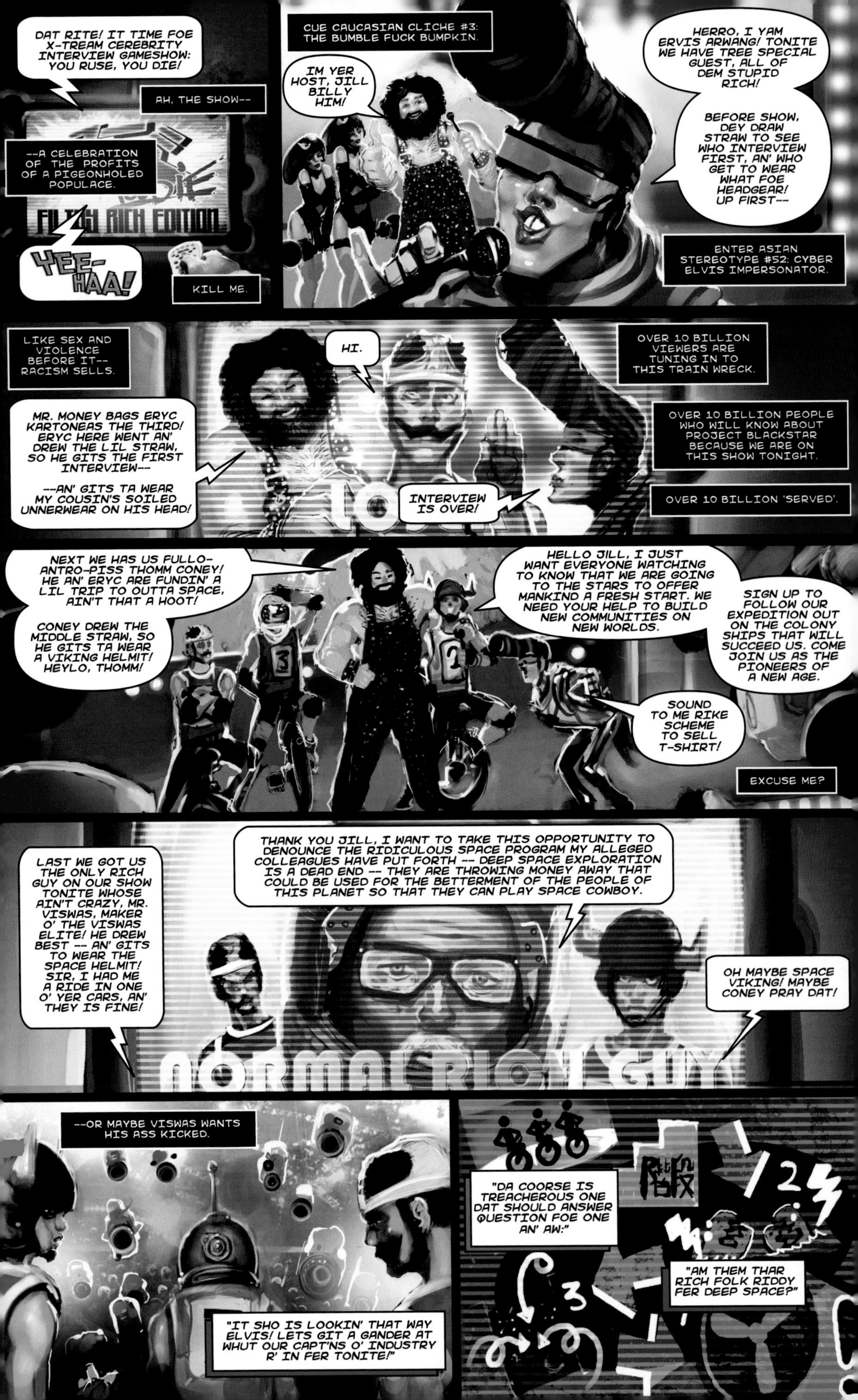
DAT RITE! IT TIME FOE X-TREAM CEREBRITY INTERVIEW GAMESHOW: YOU RUSE, YOU DIE!
AH, THE SHOW--
--A CELEBRATION OF THE PROFITS OF A PIGEONHOLED POPULACE.
YEE-HAA!
KILL ME.
CUE CAUCASIAN CLICHE #3: THE BUMBLE FUCK BUMPKIN.
IM YER HOST, JILL BILLY HIM!
HERRO, I YAM ERVIS ARWANG! TONITE WE HAVE TREE SPECIAL GUEST, ALL OF DEM STUPID RICH!
BEFORE SHOW, DEY DRAW STRAW TO SEE WHO INTERVIEW FIRST, AN' WHO GET TO WEAR WHAT FOE HEADGEAR! UP FIRST--
ENTER ASIAN STEREOTYPE #52: CYBER ELVIS IMPERSONATOR.
LIKE SEX AND VIOLENCE BEFORE IT-- RACISM SELLS.
MR. MONEY BAGS ERYC KARTONEAS THE THIRD! ERYC HERE WENT AN' DREW THE LIL STRAW, SO HE GITS THE FIRST INTERVIEW--
--AN' GITS TA WEAR MY COUSIN'S SOILED UNNERWEAR ON HIS HEAD!
HI.
INTERVIEW IS OVER!
OVER 10 BILLION VIEWERS ARE TUNING IN TO THIS TRAIN WRECK.
OVER 10 BILLION PEOPLE WHO WILL KNOW ABOUT PROJECT BLACKSTAR BECAUSE WE ARE ON THIS SHOW TONIGHT.
OVER 10 BILLION 'SERVED'.
NEXT WE HAS US FULLO-ANTRO-PISS THOMM CONEY! HE AN' ERYC ARE FUNDIN' A LIL TRIP TO OUTTA SPACE, AIN'T THAT A HOOT!
CONEY DREW THE MIDDLE STRAW, SO HE GITS TA WEAR A VIKING HELMIT! HEYLO, THOMM!
HELLO JILL, I JUST WANT EVERYONE WATCHING TO KNOW THAT WE ARE GOING TO THE STARS TO OFFER MANKIND A FRESH START. WE NEED YOUR HELP TO BUILD NEW COMMUNITIES ON NEW WORLDS.
SIGN UP TO FOLLOW OUR EXPEDITION OUT ON THE COLONY SHIPS THAT WILL SUCCEED US. COME JOIN US AS THE PIONEERS OF A NEW AGE.
SOUND TO ME RIKE SCHEME TO SELL T-SHIRT!
EXCUSE ME?
LAST WE GOT US THE ONLY RICH GUY ON OUR SHOW TONITE WHOSE AIN'T CRAZY, MR. VISWAS, MAKER O' THE VISWAS ELITE! HE DREW BEST -- AN' GITS TO WEAR THE SPACE HELMIT! SIR, I HAD ME A RIDE IN ONE O' YER CARS, AN' THEY IS FINE!
THANK YOU JILL, I WANT TO TAKE THIS OPPORTUNITY TO DENOUNCE THE RIDICULOUS SPACE PROGRAM MY ALLEGED COLLEAGUES HAVE PUT FORTH -- DEEP SPACE EXPLORATION IS A DEAD END -- THEY ARE THROWING MONEY AWAY THAT COULD BE USED FOR THE BETTERMENT OF THE PEOPLE OF THIS PLANET SO THAT THEY CAN PLAY SPACE COWBOY.
OH MAYBE SPACE VIKING! MAYBE CONEY PRAY DAT!
NORMAL RICH GUY
--OR MAYBE VISWAS WANTS HIS ASS KICKED.
"IT SHO IS LOOKIN' THAT WAY ELVIS! LETS GIT A GANDER AT WHUT OUR CAPT'NS O' INDUSTRY R' IN FER TONITE!"
"DA COORSE IS TREACHEROUS ONE DAT SHOULD ANSWER QUESTION FOE ONE AN' AW:"
"AM THEM THAR RICH FOLK RIDDY FER DEEP SPACE?"

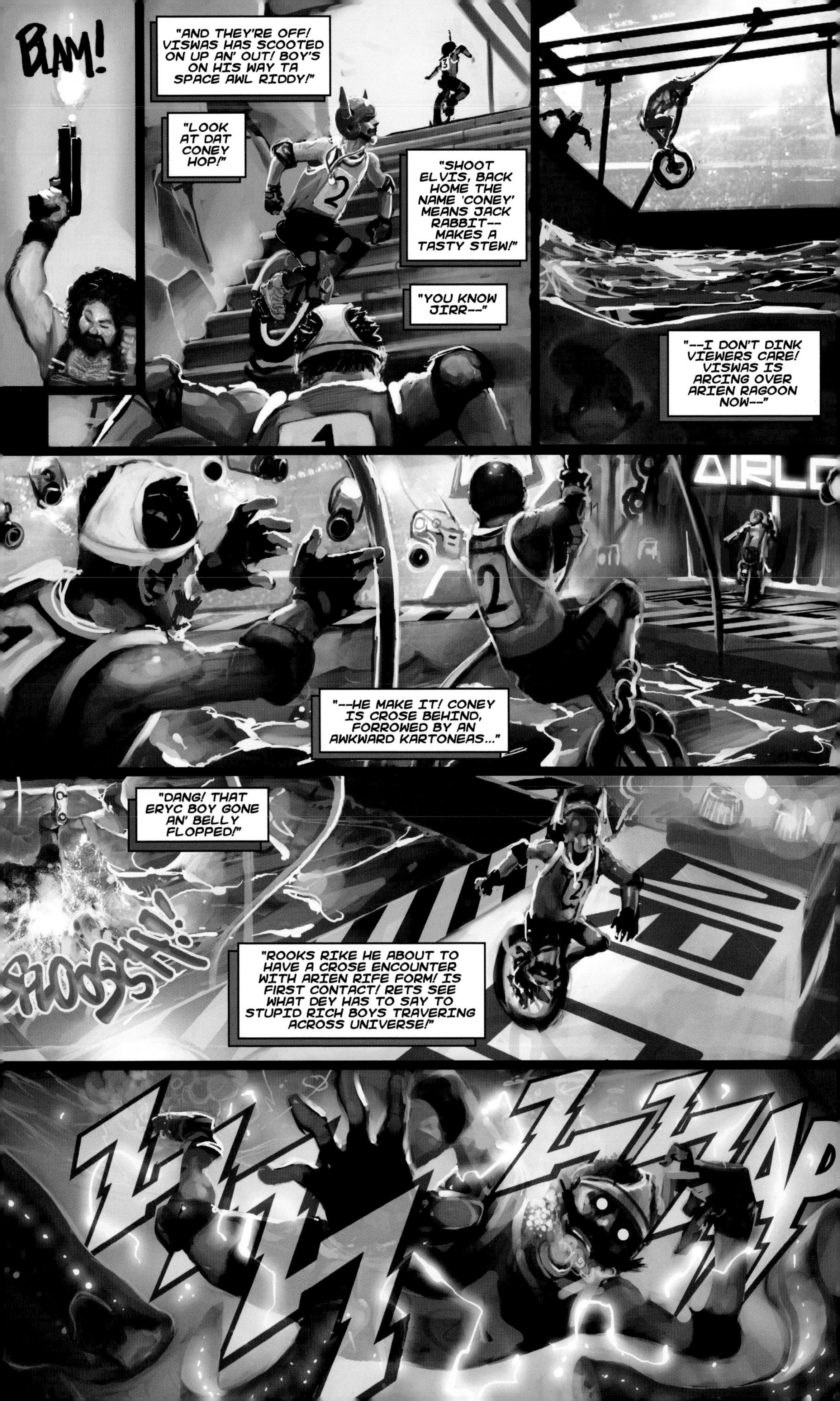
BLAM!
"AND THEY'RE OFF! VISWAS HAS SCOOTED ON UP AN' OUT! BOY'S ON HIS WAY TA SPACE AWL RIDDY!"
"LOOK AT DAT CONEY HOP!"
"SHOOT ELVIS, BACK HOME THE NAME 'CONEY' MEANS JACK RABBIT-- MAKES A TASTY STEW!"
"YOU KNOW JIRR--"
"--I DON'T DINK VIEWERS CARE! VISWAS IS ARCING OVER ARIEN RAGOON NOW--"
"--HE MAKE IT! CONEY IS CROSE BEHIND, FORROWED BY AN AWKWARD KARTONEAS..."
"DANG! THAT ERYC BOY GONE AN' BELLY FLOPPED!"
SPLOOSH!!
"ROOKS RIKE HE ABOUT TO HAVE A CROSE ENCOUNTER WITH ARIEN RIFE FORM! IS FIRST CONTACT! RETS SEE WHAT DEY HAS TO SAY TO STUPID RICH BOYS TRAVERING ACROSS UNIVERSE!"
ZZZZAP

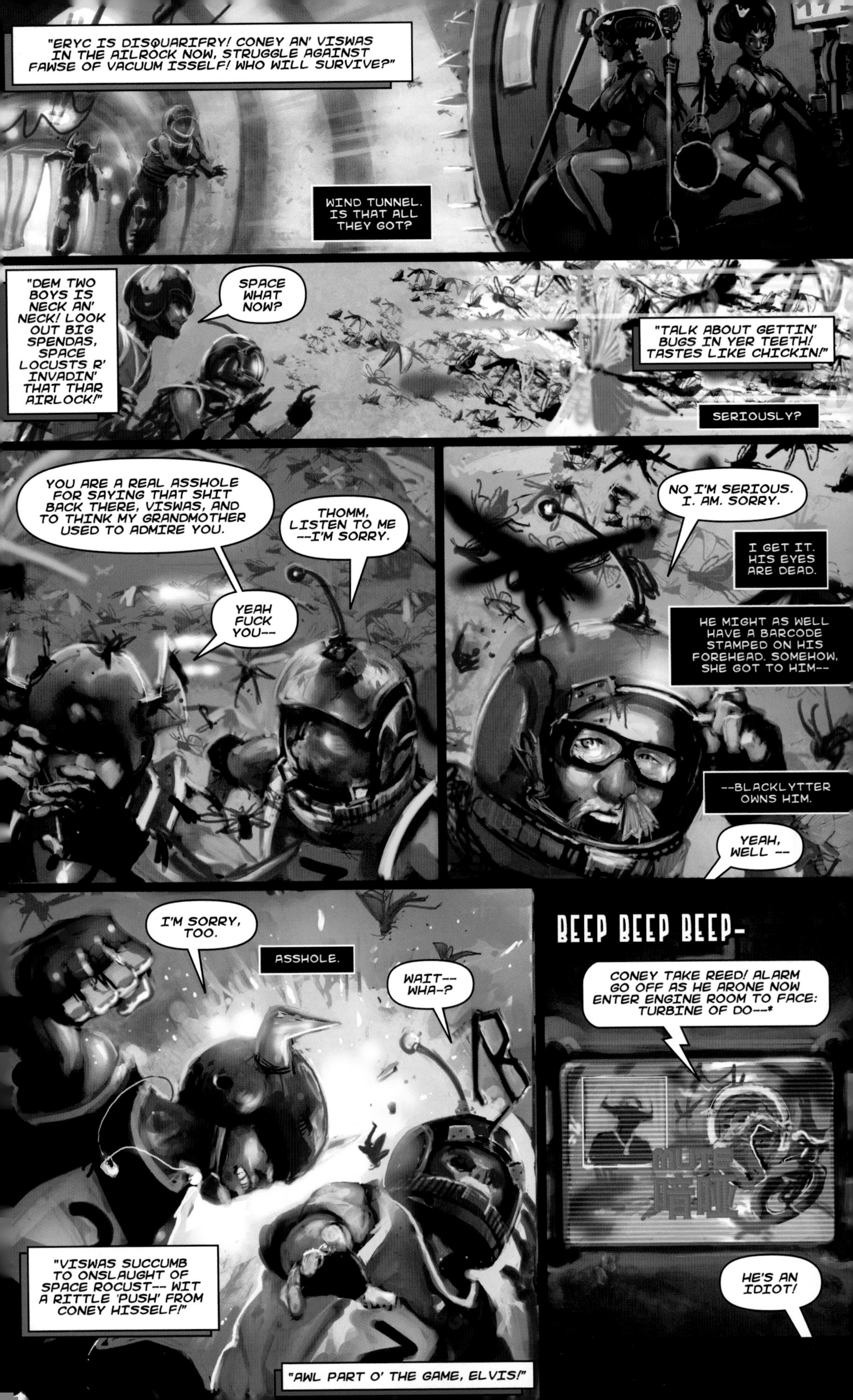
"ERYC IS DISQUARIFRY! CONEY AN' VISWAS IN THE AIRLOCK NOW, STRUGGLE AGAINST FAWSE OF VACUUM ISSELF! WHO WILL SURVIVE?"
WIND TUNNEL. IS THAT ALL THEY GOT?
"DEM TWO BOYS IS NECK AN' NECK! LOOK OUT BIG SPENDAS, SPACE LOCUSTS R' INVADIN' THAT THAR AIRLOCK!"
SPACE WHAT NOW?
"TALK ABOUT GETTIN' BUGS IN YER TEETH! TASTES LIKE CHICKIN!"
SERIOUSLY?
YOU ARE A REAL ASSHOLE FOR SAYING THAT SHIT BACK THERE, VISWAS, AND TO THINK MY GRANDMOTHER USED TO ADMIRE YOU.
THOMM, LISTEN TO ME --I'M SORRY.
YEAH FUCK YOU--
NO I'M SERIOUS. I. AM. SORRY.
I GET IT. HIS EYES ARE DEAD.
HE MIGHT AS WELL HAVE A BARCODE STAMPED ON HIS FOREHEAD. SOMEHOW, SHE GOT TO HIM--
--BLACKLYTTER OWNS HIM.
YEAH, WELL --
I'M SORRY, TOO.
ASSHOLE.
WAIT-- WHA-?
"VISWAS SUCCUMB TO ONSLAUGHT OF SPACE ROCUST-- WIT A RITTLE 'PUSH' FROM CONEY HISSELF!"
"AWL PART O' THE GAME, ELVIS!"
BEEP BEEP BEEP-
CONEY TAKE REED! ALARM GO OFF AS HE ARONE NOW ENTER ENGINE ROOM TO FACE: TURBINE OF DO--*
HE'S AN IDIOT!

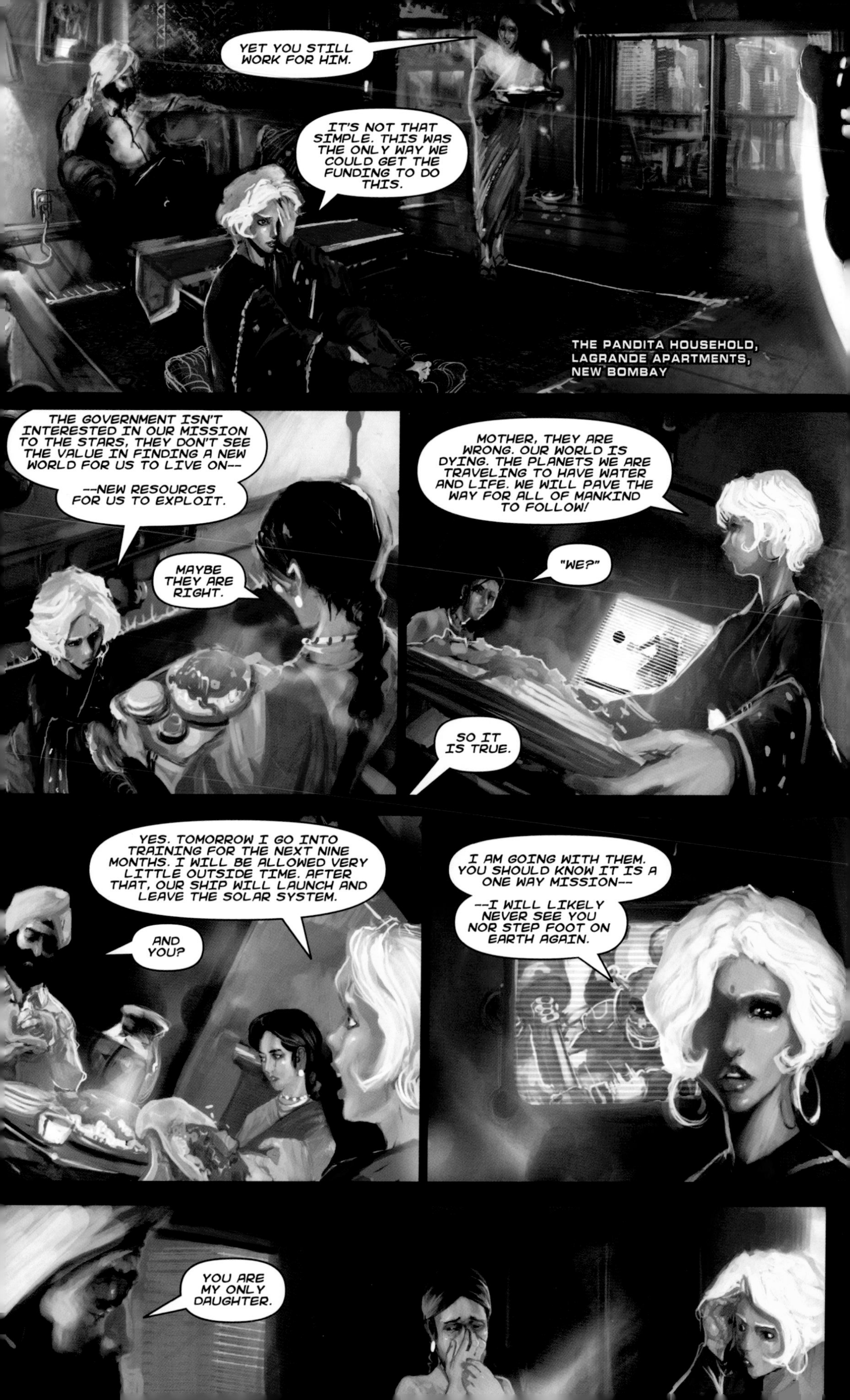
YET YOU STILL WORK FOR HIM.
IT'S NOT THAT SIMPLE. THIS WAS THE ONLY WAY WE COULD GET THE FUNDING TO DO THIS.
THE PANDITA HOUSEHOLD, LAGRANDE APARTMENTS, NEW BOMBAY
THE GOVERNMENT ISN'T INTERESTED IN OUR MISSION TO THE STARS, THEY DON'T SEE THE VALUE IN FINDING A NEW WORLD FOR US TO LIVE ON--
--NEW RESOURCES FOR US TO EXPLOIT.
MAYBE THEY ARE RIGHT.
MOTHER, THEY ARE WRONG. OUR WORLD IS DYING. THE PLANETS WE ARE TRAVELING TO HAVE WATER AND LIFE. WE WILL PAVE THE WAY FOR ALL OF MANKIND TO FOLLOW!
"WE?"
SO IT IS TRUE.
YES. TOMORROW I GO INTO TRAINING FOR THE NEXT NINE MONTHS. I WILL BE ALLOWED VERY LITTLE OUTSIDE TIME. AFTER THAT, OUR SHIP WILL LAUNCH AND LEAVE THE SOLAR SYSTEM.
AND YOU?
I AM GOING WITH THEM. YOU SHOULD KNOW IT IS A ONE WAY MISSION--
--I WILL LIKELY NEVER SEE YOU NOR STEP FOOT ON EARTH AGAIN.
YOU ARE MY ONLY DAUGHTER.

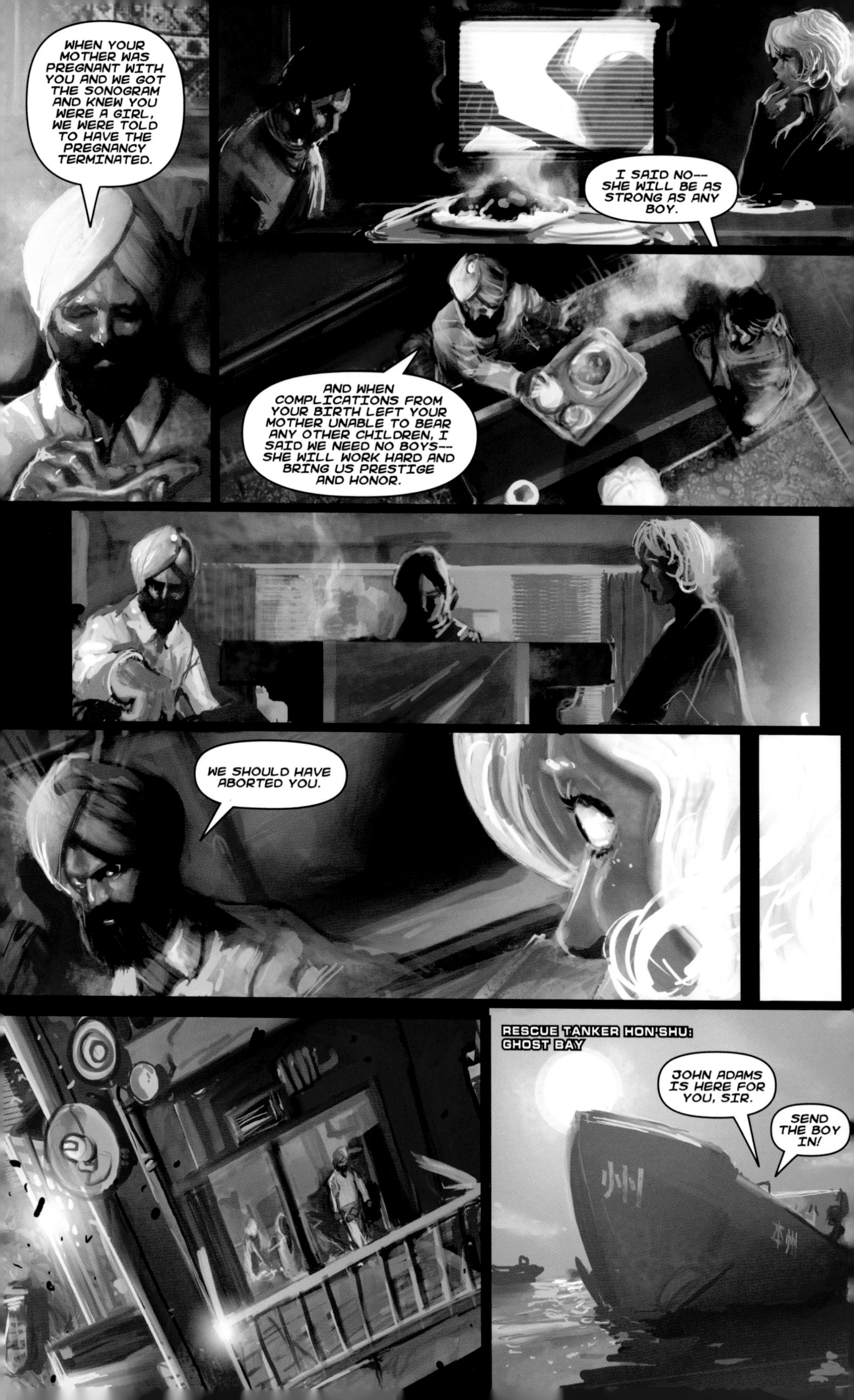
WHEN YOUR MOTHER WAS PREGNANT WITH YOU AND WE GOT THE SONOGRAM AND KNEW YOU WERE A GIRL, WE WERE TOLD TO HAVE THE PREGNANCY TERMINATED.
I SAID NO-- SHE WILL BE AS STRONG AS ANY BOY.
AND WHEN COMPLICATIONS FROM YOUR BIRTH LEFT YOUR MOTHER UNABLE TO BEAR ANY OTHER CHILDREN, I SAID WE NEED NO BOYS-- SHE WILL WORK HARD AND BRING US PRESTIGE AND HONOR.
WE SHOULD HAVE ABORTED YOU.
RESCUE TANKER HON'SHU: GHOST BAY
JOHN ADAMS IS HERE FOR YOU, SIR.
SEND THE BOY IN!

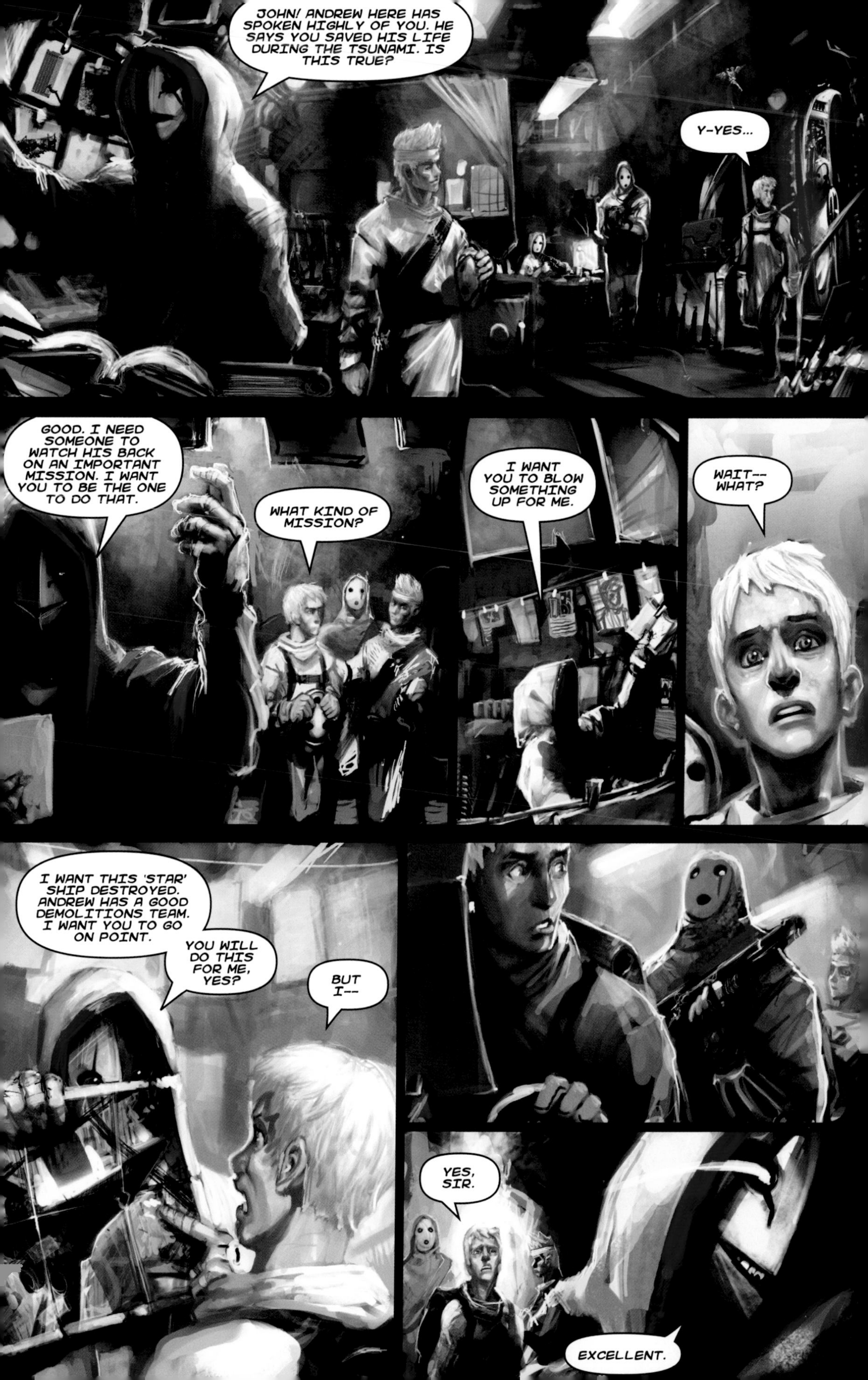
JOHN! ANDREW HERE HAS SPOKEN HIGHLY OF YOU. HE SAYS YOU SAVED HIS LIFE DURING THE TSUNAMI. IS THIS TRUE?
Y-YES...
GOOD. I NEED SOMEONE TO WATCH HIS BACK ON AN IMPORTANT MISSION. I WANT YOU TO BE THE ONE TO DO THAT.
WHAT KIND OF MISSION?
I WANT YOU TO BLOW SOMETHING UP FOR ME.
WAIT-- WHAT?
I WANT THIS 'STAR' SHIP DESTROYED. ANDREW HAS A GOOD DEMOLITIONS TEAM. I WANT YOU TO GO ON POINT.
YOU WILL DO THIS FOR ME, YES?
BUT I--
YES, SIR.
EXCELLENT.

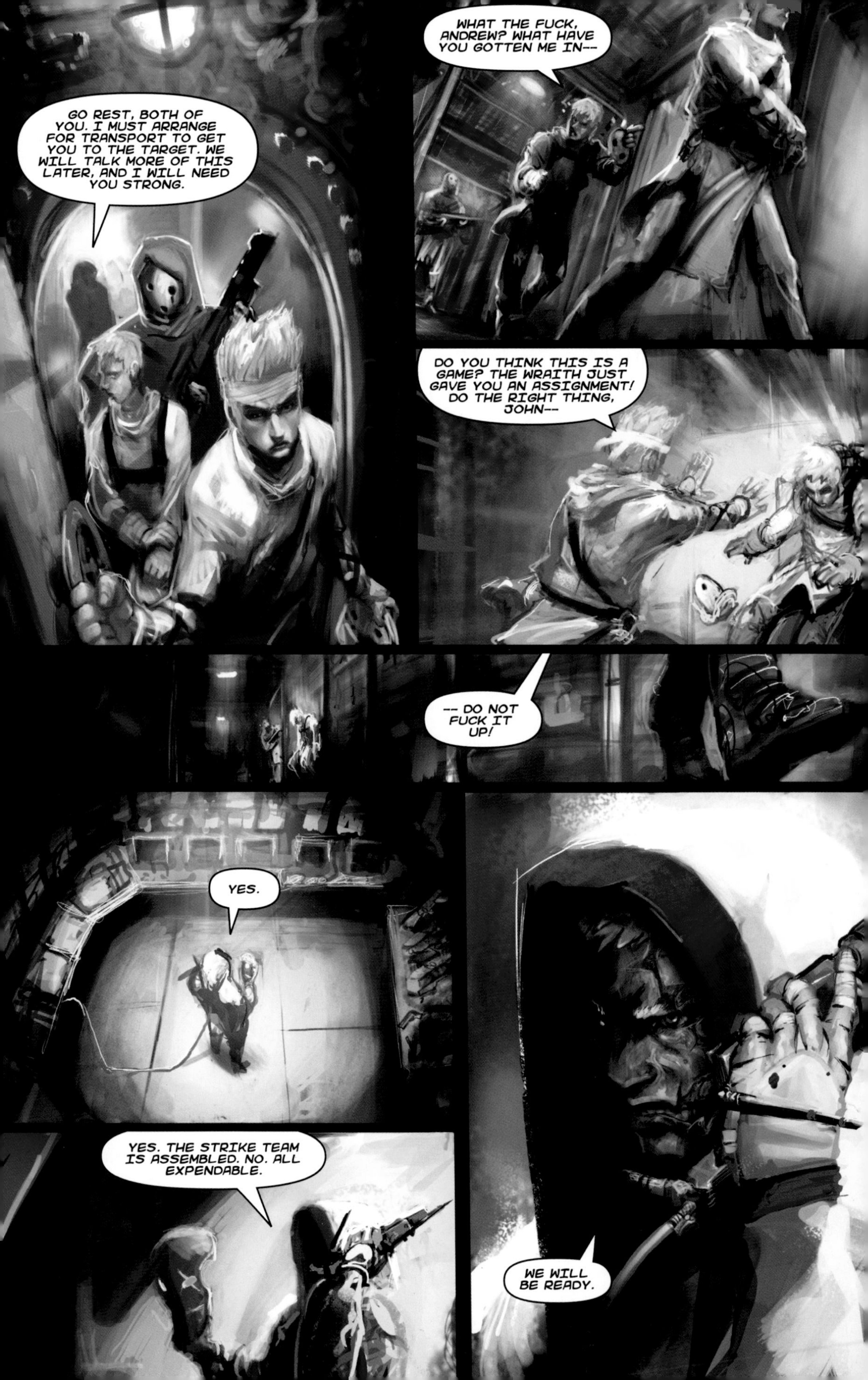
GO REST, BOTH OF YOU. I MUST ARRANGE FOR TRANSPORT TO GET YOU TO THE TARGET. WE WILL TALK MORE OF THIS LATER, AND I WILL NEED YOU STRONG.
WHAT THE FUCK, ANDREW? WHAT HAVE YOU GOTTEN ME IN--
DO YOU THINK THIS IS A GAME? THE WRAITH JUST GAVE YOU AN ASSIGNMENT! DO THE RIGHT THING, JOHN--
-- DO NOT FUCK IT UP!
YES.
YES. THE STRIKE TEAM IS ASSEMBLED. NO. ALL EXPENDABLE.
WE WILL BE READY.

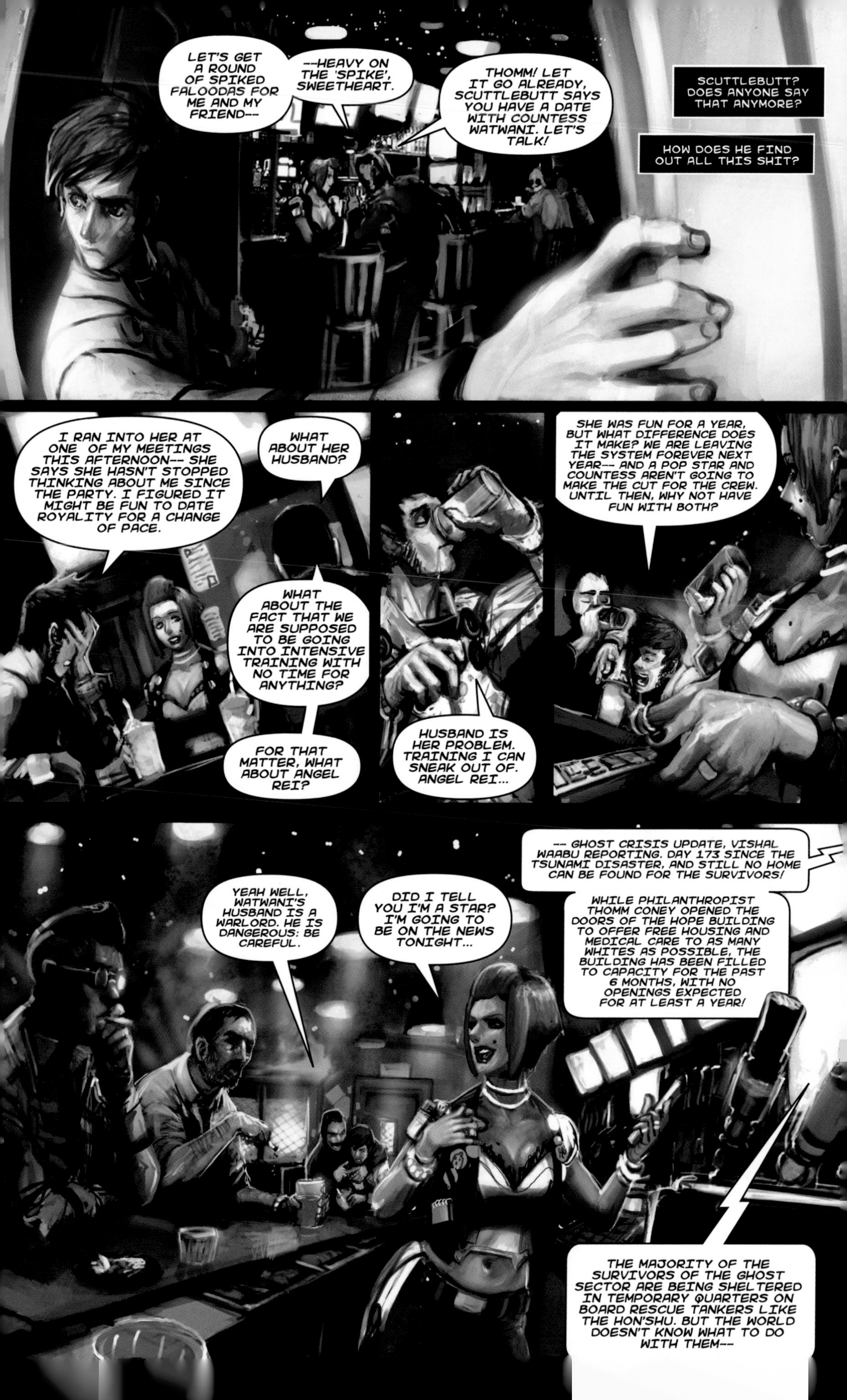
LET'S GET A ROUND OF SPIKED FALOODAS FOR ME AND MY FRIEND--
--HEAVY ON THE 'SPIKE', SWEETHEART.
THOMM! LET IT GO ALREADY, SCUTTLEBUTT SAYS YOU HAVE A DATE WITH COUNTESS WATWANI. LET'S TALK!
SCUTTLEBUTT? DOES ANYONE SAY THAT ANYMORE?
HOW DOES HE FIND OUT ALL THIS SHIT?
I RAN INTO HER AT ONE OF MY MEETINGS THIS AFTERNOON-- SHE SAYS SHE HASN'T STOPPED THINKING ABOUT ME SINCE THE PARTY. I FIGURED IT MIGHT BE FUN TO DATE ROYALITY FOR A CHANGE OF PACE.
WHAT ABOUT HER HUSBAND?
WHAT ABOUT THE FACT THAT WE ARE SUPPOSED TO BE GOING INTO INTENSIVE TRAINING WITH NO TIME FOR ANYTHING?
FOR THAT MATTER, WHAT ABOUT ANGEL REI?
HUSBAND IS HER PROBLEM. TRAINING I CAN SNEAK OUT OF. ANGEL REI...
SHE WAS FUN FOR A YEAR, BUT WHAT DIFFERENCE DOES IT MAKE? WE ARE LEAVING THE SYSTEM FOREVER NEXT YEAR-- AND A POP STAR AND COUNTESS AREN'T GOING TO MAKE THE CUT FOR THE CREW. UNTIL THEN, WHY NOT HAVE FUN WITH BOTH?
YEAH WELL, WATWANI'S HUSBAND IS A WARLORD. HE IS DANGEROUS: BE CAREFUL.
DID I TELL YOU I'M A STAR? I'M GOING TO BE ON THE NEWS TONIGHT...
-- GHOST CRISIS UPDATE, VISHAL WAABU REPORTING. DAY 173 SINCE THE TSUNAMI DISASTER, AND STILL NO HOME CAN BE FOUND FOR THE SURVIVORS!
WHILE PHILANTHROPIST THOMM CONEY OPENED THE DOORS OF THE HOPE BUILDING TO OFFER FREE HOUSING AND MEDICAL CARE TO AS MANY WHITES AS POSSIBLE, THE BUILDING HAS BEEN FILLED TO CAPACITY FOR THE PAST 6 MONTHS, WITH NO OPENINGS EXPECTED FOR AT LEAST A YEAR!
THE MAJORITY OF THE SURVIVORS OF THE GHOST SECTOR ARE BEING SHELTERED IN TEMPORARY QUARTERS ON BOARD RESCUE TANKERS LIKE THE HON'SHU. BUT THE WORLD DOESN'T KNOW WHAT TO DO WITH THEM--

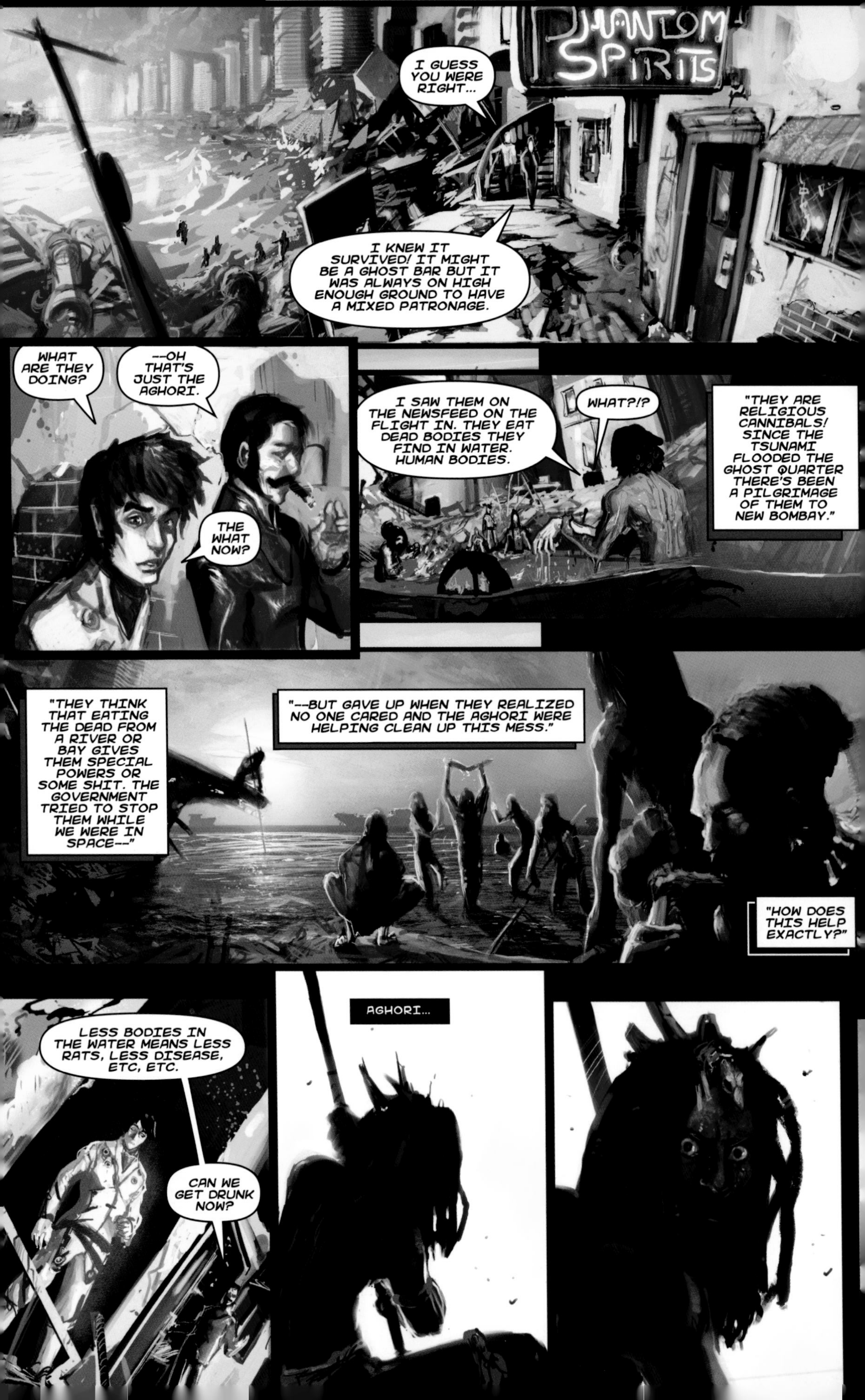

PHANTOM SPIRITS
I GUESS YOU WERE RIGHT...
I KNEW IT SURVIVED! IT MIGHT BE A GHOST BAR BUT IT WAS ALWAYS ON HIGH ENOUGH GROUND TO HAVE A MIXED PATRONAGE.
WHAT ARE THEY DOING?
--OH THAT'S JUST THE AGHORI.
THE WHAT NOW?
I SAW THEM ON THE NEWSFEED ON THE FLIGHT IN. THEY EAT DEAD BODIES THEY FIND IN WATER. HUMAN BODIES.
WHAT?!?
"THEY ARE RELIGIOUS CANNIBALS! SINCE THE TSUNAMI FLOODED THE GHOST QUARTER THERE'S BEEN A PILGRIMAGE OF THEM TO NEW BOMBAY."
"THEY THINK THAT EATING THE DEAD FROM A RIVER OR BAY GIVES THEM SPECIAL POWERS OR SOME SHIT. THE GOVERNMENT TRIED TO STOP THEM WHILE WE WERE IN SPACE--"
"--BUT GAVE UP WHEN THEY REALIZED NO ONE CARED AND THE AGHORI WERE HELPING CLEAN UP THIS MESS."
"HOW DOES THIS HELP EXACTLY?"
LESS BODIES IN THE WATER MEANS LESS RATS, LESS DISEASE, ETC, ETC.
CAN WE GET DRUNK NOW?
AGHORI...

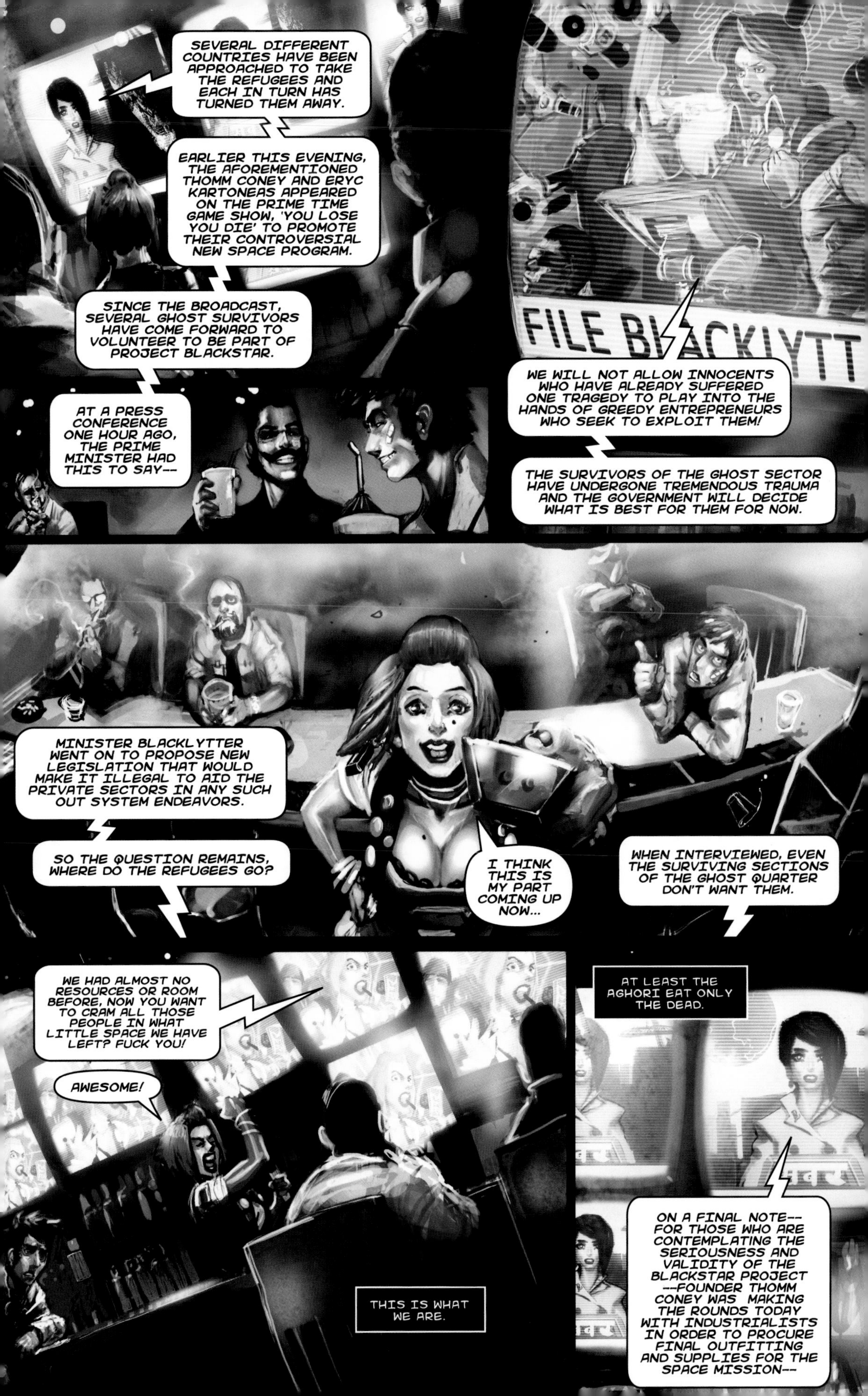
SEVERAL DIFFERENT COUNTRIES HAVE BEEN APPROACHED TO TAKE THE REFUGEES AND EACH IN TURN HAS TURNED THEM AWAY.
EARLIER THIS EVENING, THE AFOREMENTIONED THOMM CONEY AND ERYC KARTONEAS APPEARED ON THE PRIME TIME GAME SHOW, 'YOU LOSE YOU DIE' TO PROMOTE THEIR CONTROVERSIAL NEW SPACE PROGRAM.
SINCE THE BROADCAST, SEVERAL GHOST SURVIVORS HAVE COME FORWARD TO VOLUNTEER TO BE PART OF PROJECT BLACKSTAR.
AT A PRESS CONFERENCE ONE HOUR AGO, THE PRIME MINISTER HAD THIS TO SAY--
FILE BLACKLYTT
WE WILL NOT ALLOW INNOCENTS WHO HAVE ALREADY SUFFERED ONE TRAGEDY TO PLAY INTO THE HANDS OF GREEDY ENTREPRENEURS WHO SEEK TO EXPLOIT THEM!
THE SURVIVORS OF THE GHOST SECTOR HAVE UNDERGONE TREMENDOUS TRAUMA AND THE GOVERNMENT WILL DECIDE WHAT IS BEST FOR THEM FOR NOW.
MINISTER BLACKLYTTER WENT ON TO PROPOSE NEW LEGISLATION THAT WOULD MAKE IT ILLEGAL TO AID THE PRIVATE SECTORS IN ANY SUCH OUT SYSTEM ENDEAVORS.
SO THE QUESTION REMAINS, WHERE DO THE REFUGEES GO?
I THINK THIS IS MY PART COMING UP NOW...
WHEN INTERVIEWED, EVEN THE SURVIVING SECTIONS OF THE GHOST QUARTER DON'T WANT THEM.
WE HAD ALMOST NO RESOURCES OR ROOM BEFORE, NOW YOU WANT TO CRAM ALL THOSE PEOPLE IN WHAT LITTLE SPACE WE HAVE LEFT? FUCK YOU!
AWESOME!
THIS IS WHAT WE ARE.
AT LEAST THE AGHORI EAT ONLY THE DEAD.
ON A FINAL NOTE-- FOR THOSE WHO ARE CONTEMPLATING THE SERIOUSNESS AND VALIDITY OF THE BLACKSTAR PROJECT --FOUNDER THOMM CONEY WAS MAKING THE ROUNDS TODAY WITH INDUSTRIALISTS IN ORDER TO PROCURE FINAL OUTFITTING AND SUPPLIES FOR THE SPACE MISSION--

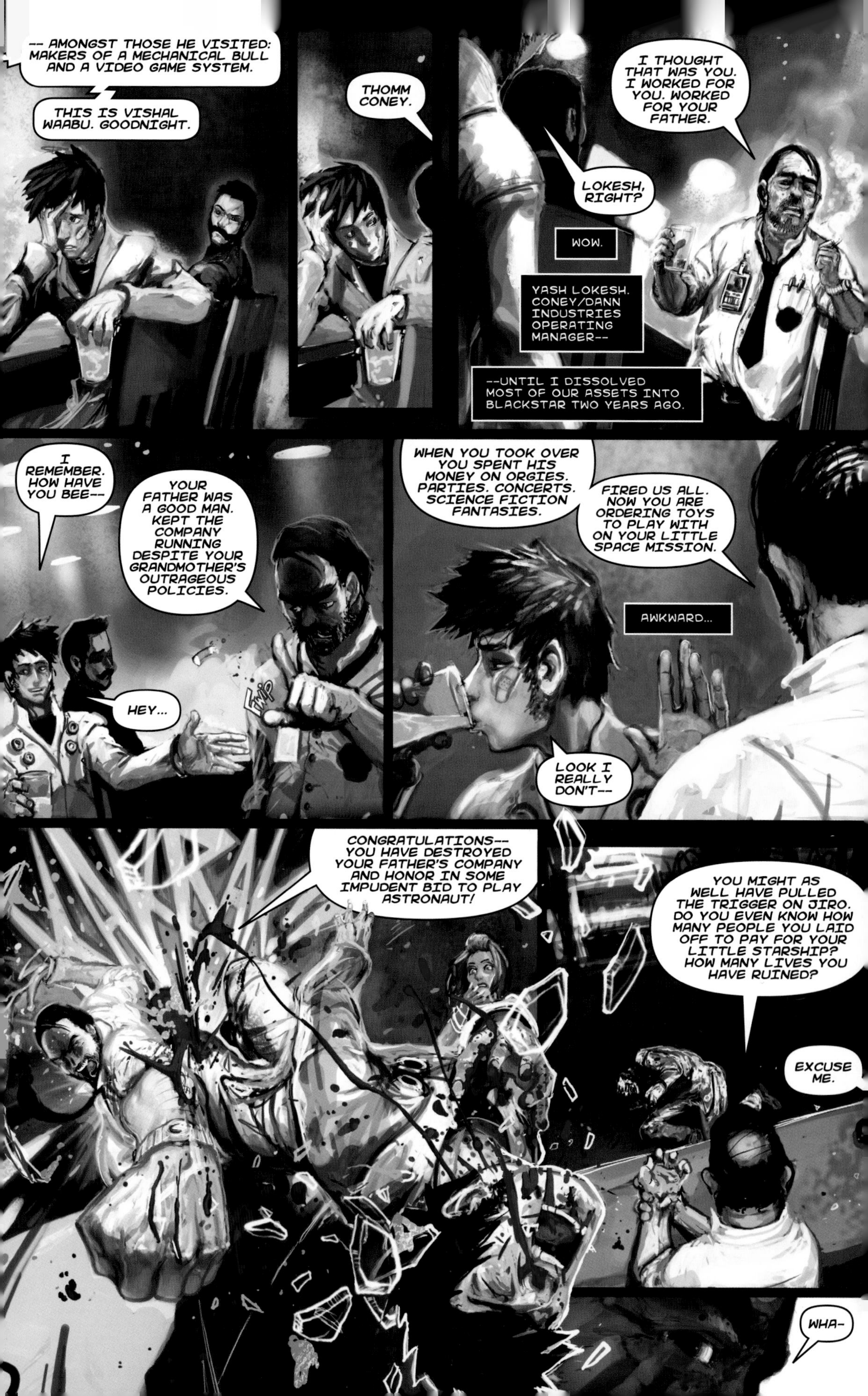
-- AMONGST THOSE HE VISITED: MAKERS OF A MECHANICAL BULL AND A VIDEO GAME SYSTEM.
THIS IS VISHAL WAABU. GOODNIGHT.
THOMM CONEY.
I THOUGHT THAT WAS YOU. I WORKED FOR YOU. WORKED FOR YOUR FATHER.
LOKESH, RIGHT?
WOW.
YASH LOKESH. CONEY/DANN INDUSTRIES OPERATING MANAGER--
--UNTIL I DISSOLVED MOST OF OUR ASSETS INTO BLACKSTAR TWO YEARS AGO.
I REMEMBER. HOW HAVE YOU BEE--
YOUR FATHER WAS A GOOD MAN. KEPT THE COMPANY RUNNING DESPITE YOUR GRANDMOTHER'S OUTRAGEOUS POLICIES.
HEY...
WHEN YOU TOOK OVER YOU SPENT HIS MONEY ON ORGIES. PARTIES. CONCERTS. SCIENCE FICTION FANTASIES.
FIRED US ALL. NOW YOU ARE ORDERING TOYS TO PLAY WITH ON YOUR LITTLE SPACE MISSION.
AWKWARD...
LOOK I REALLY DON'T--
CONGRATULATIONS-- YOU HAVE DESTROYED YOUR FATHER'S COMPANY AND HONOR IN SOME IMPUDENT BID TO PLAY ASTRONAUT!
YOU MIGHT AS WELL HAVE PULLED THE TRIGGER ON JIRO. DO YOU EVEN KNOW HOW MANY PEOPLE YOU LAID OFF TO PAY FOR YOUR LITTLE STARSHIP? HOW MANY LIVES YOU HAVE RUINED?
EXCUSE ME.
WHA-

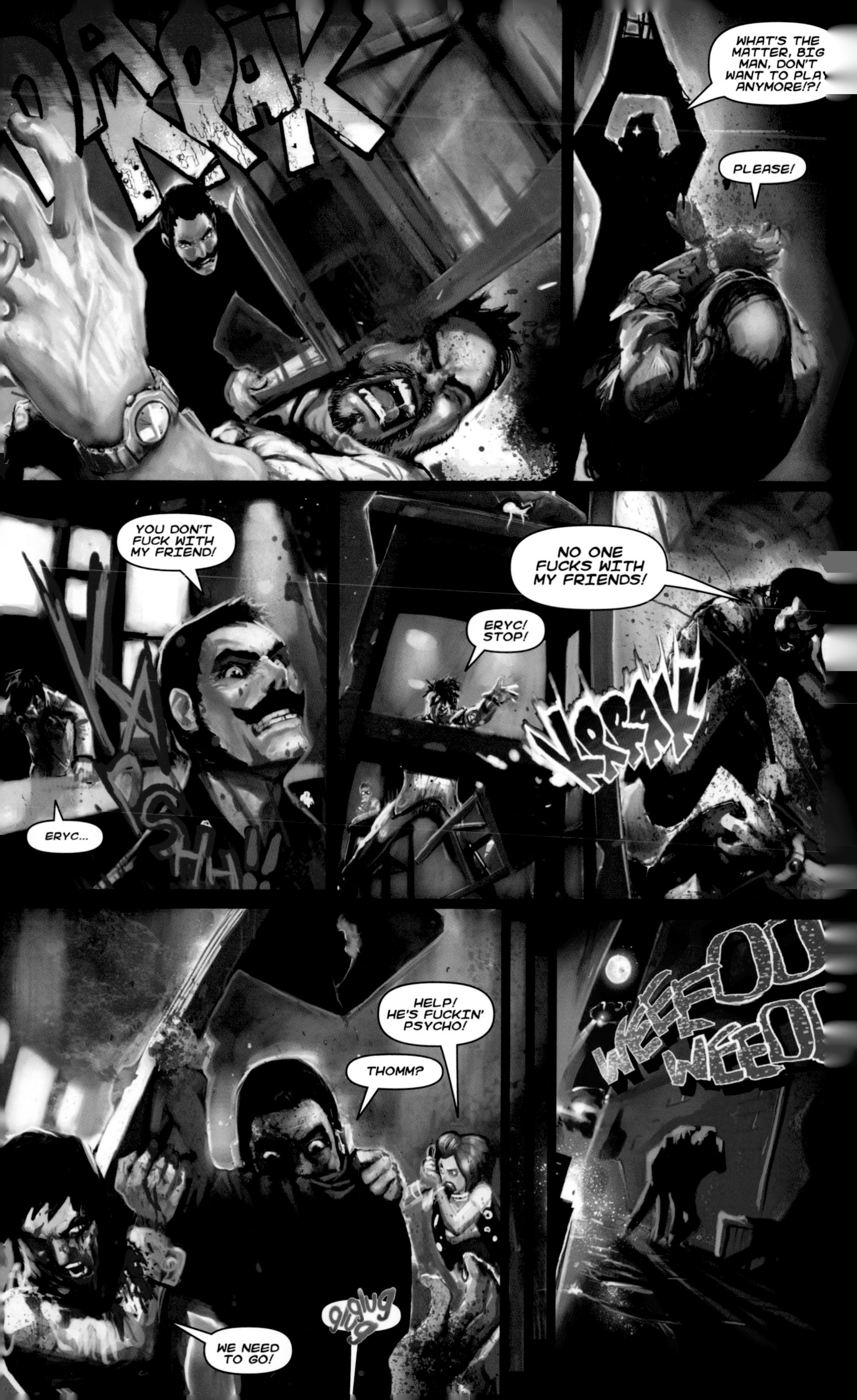
WHAT'S THE MATTER, BIG MAN, DON'T WANT TO PLAY ANYMORE!?!
PLEASE!
YOU DON'T FUCK WITH MY FRIEND!
ERYC...
ERYC! STOP!
NO ONE FUCKS WITH MY FRIENDS!
HELP! HE'S FUCKIN' PSYCHO!
THOMM?
WE NEED TO GO!
glug glug

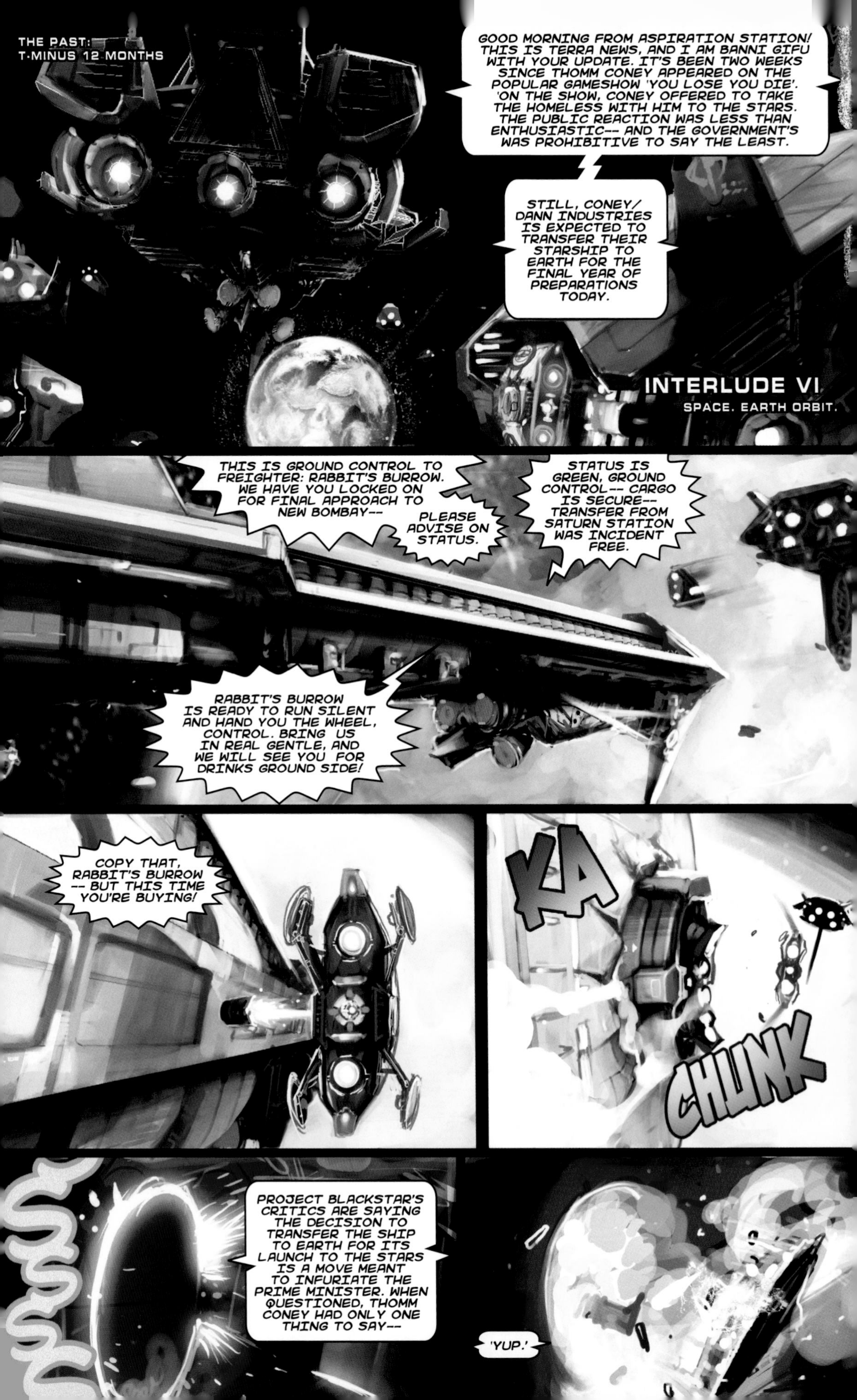
THE PAST:
T-MINUS 12 MONTHS
GOOD MORNING FROM ASPIRATION STATION! THIS IS TERRA NEWS, AND I AM BANNI GIFU WITH YOUR UPDATE. IT'S BEEN TWO WEEKS SINCE THOMM CONEY APPEARED ON THE POPULAR GAMESHOW 'YOU LOSE YOU DIE'. 'ON THE SHOW, CONEY OFFERED TO TAKE THE HOMELESS WITH HIM TO THE STARS. THE PUBLIC REACTION WAS LESS THAN ENTHUSIASTIC-- AND THE GOVERNMENT'S WAS PROHIBITIVE TO SAY THE LEAST.
STILL, CONEY/ DANN INDUSTRIES IS EXPECTED TO TRANSFER THEIR STARSHIP TO EARTH FOR THE FINAL YEAR OF PREPARATIONS TODAY.
INTERLUDE VI
SPACE. EARTH ORBIT.
THIS IS GROUND CONTROL TO FREIGHTER: RABBIT'S BURROW. WE HAVE YOU LOCKED ON FOR FINAL APPROACH TO NEW BOMBAY--
PLEASE ADVISE ON STATUS.
STATUS IS GREEN, GROUND CONTROL-- CARGO IS SECURE-- TRANSFER FROM SATURN STATION WAS INCIDENT FREE.
RABBIT'S BURROW IS READY TO RUN SILENT AND HAND YOU THE WHEEL, CONTROL. BRING US IN REAL GENTLE, AND WE WILL SEE YOU FOR DRINKS GROUND SIDE!
COPY THAT, RABBIT'S BURROW -- BUT THIS TIME YOU'RE BUYING!
KA
CHUNK
PROJECT BLACKSTAR'S CRITICS ARE SAYING THE DECISION TO TRANSFER THE SHIP TO EARTH FOR ITS LAUNCH TO THE STARS IS A MOVE MEANT TO INFURIATE THE PRIME MINISTER. WHEN QUESTIONED, THOMM CONEY HAD ONLY ONE THING TO SAY--
'YUP.'

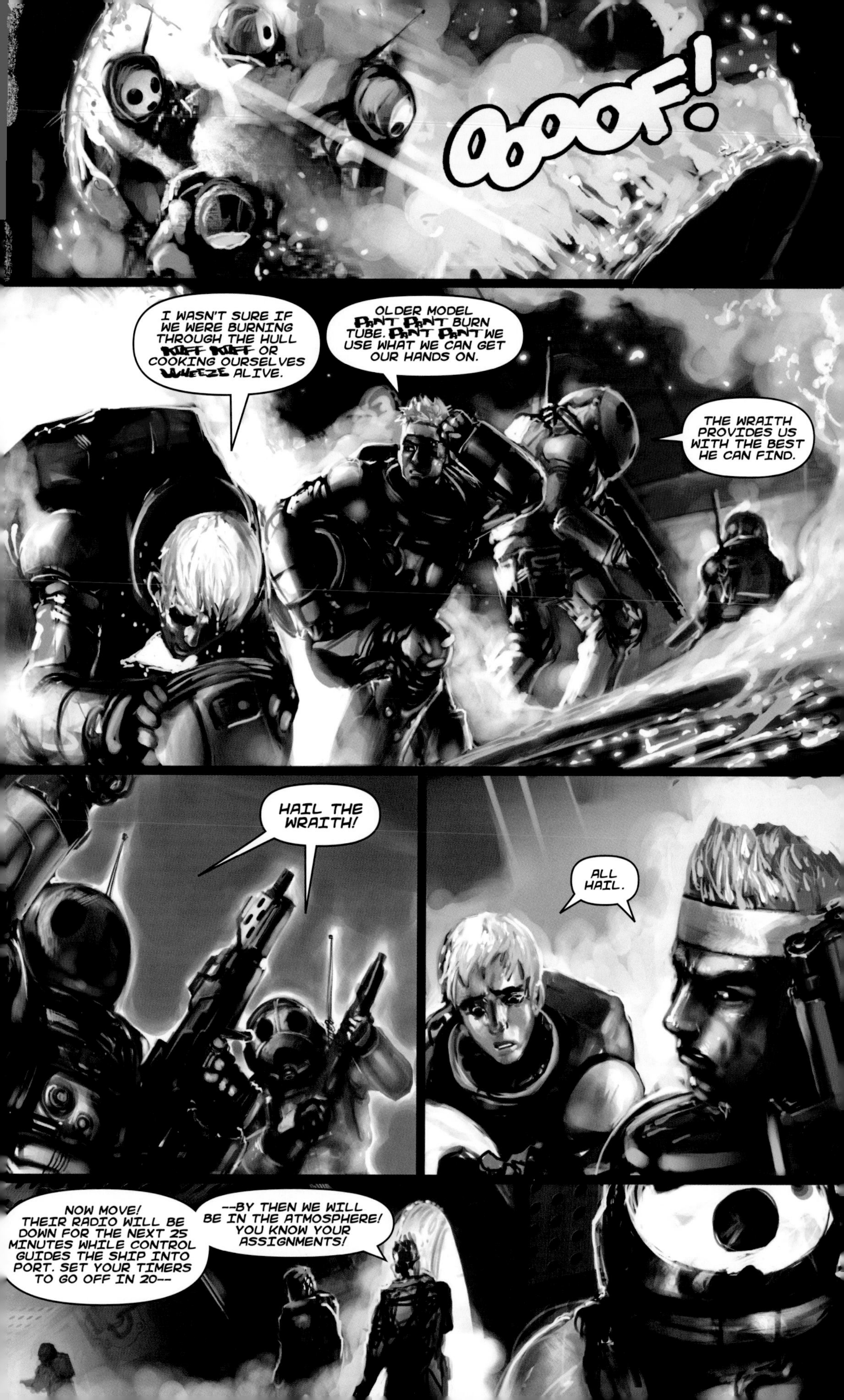
OOOOF!
I WASN'T SURE IF WE WERE BURNING THROUGH THE HULL KOFF KOFF OR COOKING OURSELVES WHEEZE ALIVE.
OLDER MODEL PANT PANT BURN TUBE. PANT PANT WE USE WHAT WE CAN GET OUR HANDS ON.
THE WRAITH PROVIDES US WITH THE BEST HE CAN FIND.
HAIL THE WRAITH!
ALL HAIL.
NOW MOVE! THEIR RADIO WILL BE DOWN FOR THE NEXT 25 MINUTES WHILE CONTROL GUIDES THE SHIP INTO PORT. SET YOUR TIMERS TO GO OFF IN 20--
--BY THEN WE WILL BE IN THE ATMOSPHERE! YOU KNOW YOUR ASSIGNMENTS!

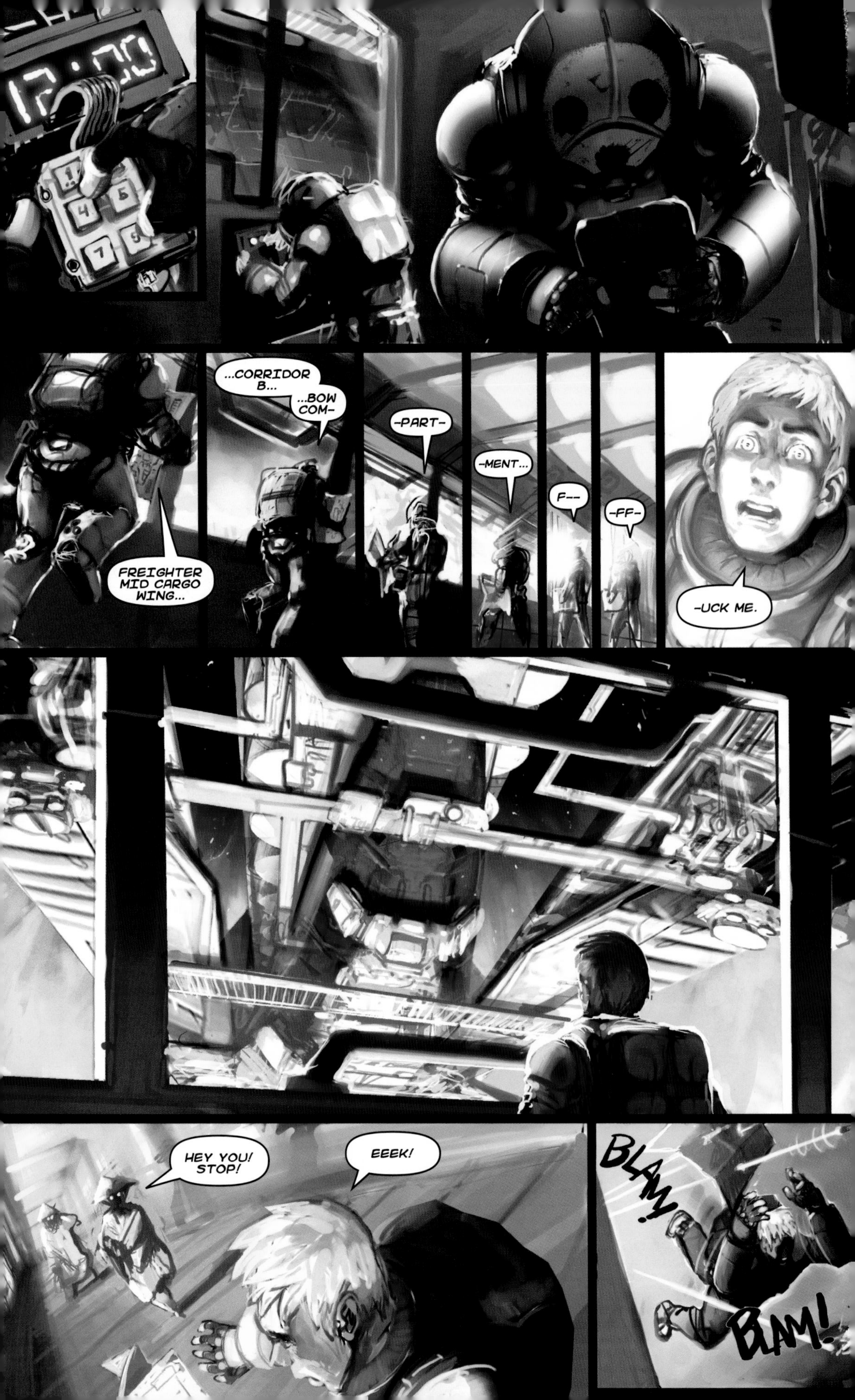
FREIGHTER MID CARGO WING...
...CORRIDOR B...
...BOW COM-
-PART-
-MENT...
F--
-FF-
-UCK ME.
HEY YOU! STOP!
EEEK!
BLAM!
BLAM!

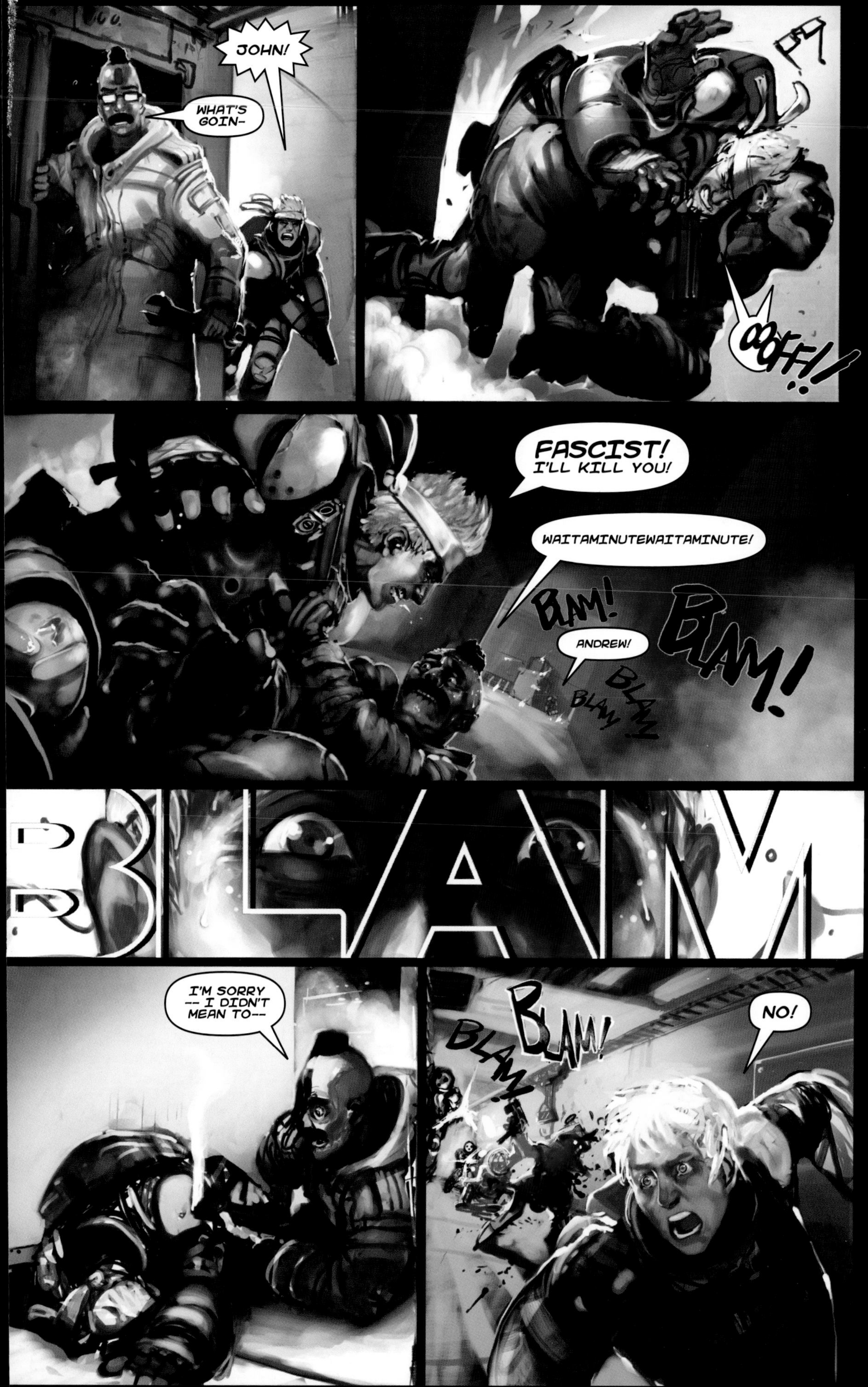
JOHN!
WHAT'S GOIN-
OOFF!!
FASCIST! I'LL KILL YOU!
WAITAMINUTEWAITAMINUTE!
BLAM!
BLAM!
ANDREW!
BLAM
BLAM
BLAM
I'M SORRY -- I DIDN'T MEAN TO--
BLAM!
BLAM!
NO!

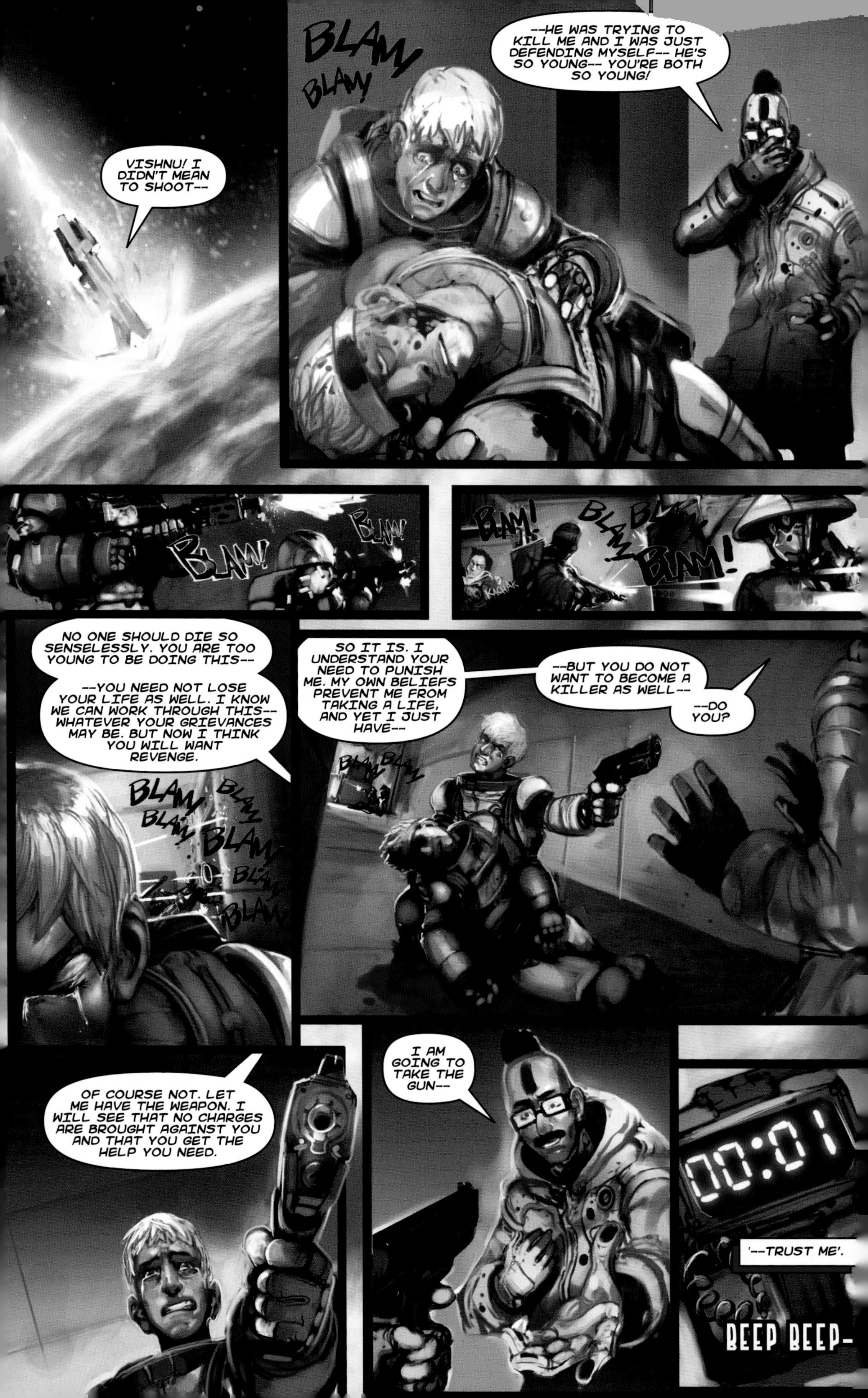

VISHNU! I DIDN'T MEAN TO SHOOT--
BLAM
BLAM!
--HE WAS TRYING TO KILL ME AND I WAS JUST DEFENDING MYSELF-- HE'S SO YOUNG-- YOU'RE BOTH SO YOUNG!
BLAM!
BLAM!
BLAM!
KACHAK
BLAM
BLAM!
NO ONE SHOULD DIE SO SENSELESSLY. YOU ARE TOO YOUNG TO BE DOING THIS--
--YOU NEED NOT LOSE YOUR LIFE AS WELL. I KNOW WE CAN WORK THROUGH THIS-- WHATEVER YOUR GRIEVANCES MAY BE. BUT NOW I THINK YOU WILL WANT REVENGE.
BLAM BLAM BLAM BLAM BLAM BLAM
SO IT IS. I UNDERSTAND YOUR NEED TO PUNISH ME. MY OWN BELIEFS PREVENT ME FROM TAKING A LIFE, AND YET I JUST HAVE--
--BUT YOU DO NOT WANT TO BECOME A KILLER AS WELL--
--DO YOU?
BLAM BLAM
OF COURSE NOT. LET ME HAVE THE WEAPON. I WILL SEE THAT NO CHARGES ARE BROUGHT AGAINST YOU AND THAT YOU GET THE HELP YOU NEED.
I AM GOING TO TAKE THE GUN--
00:01
'--TRUST ME'.
BEEP BEEP-

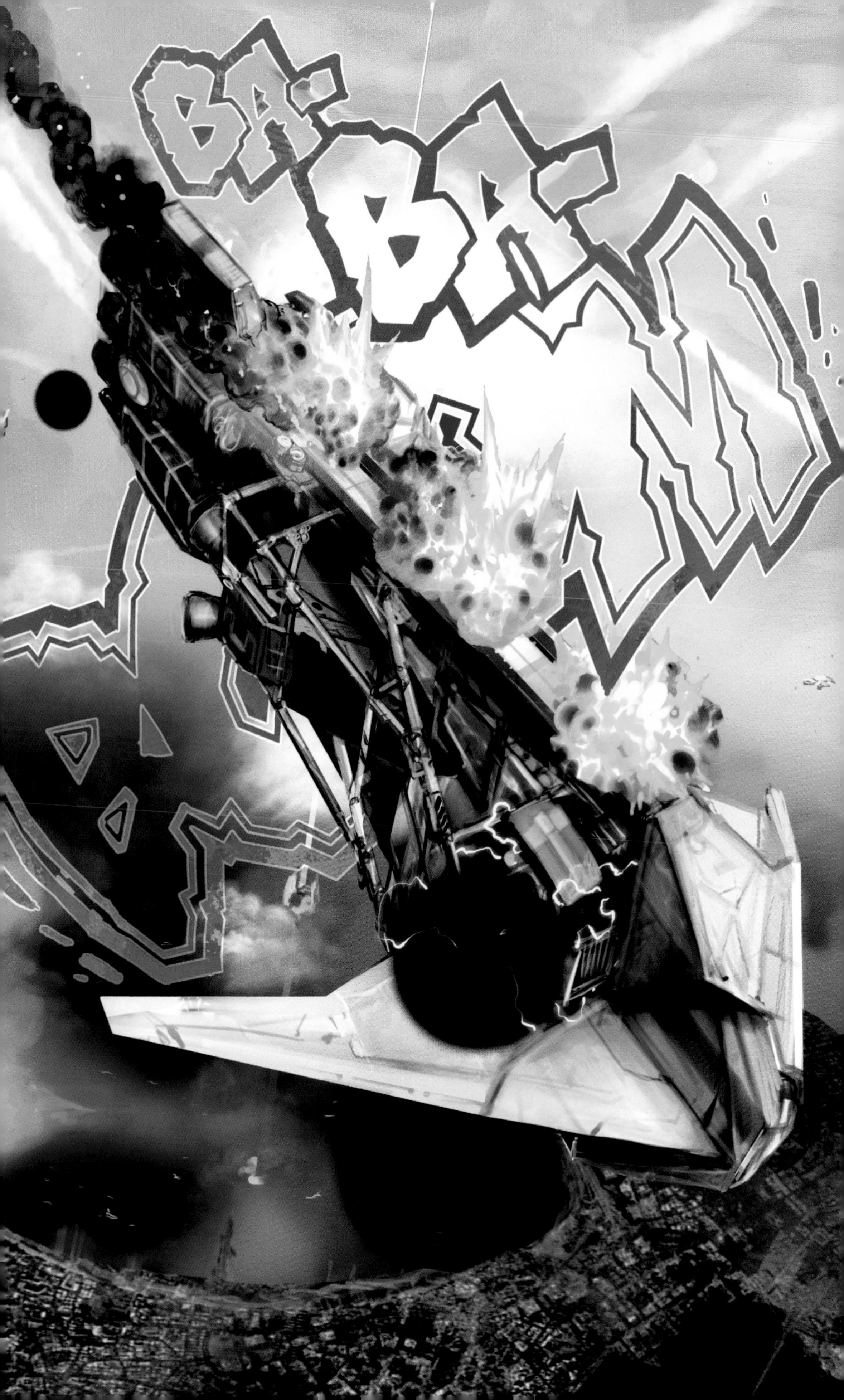
BA-
BA-

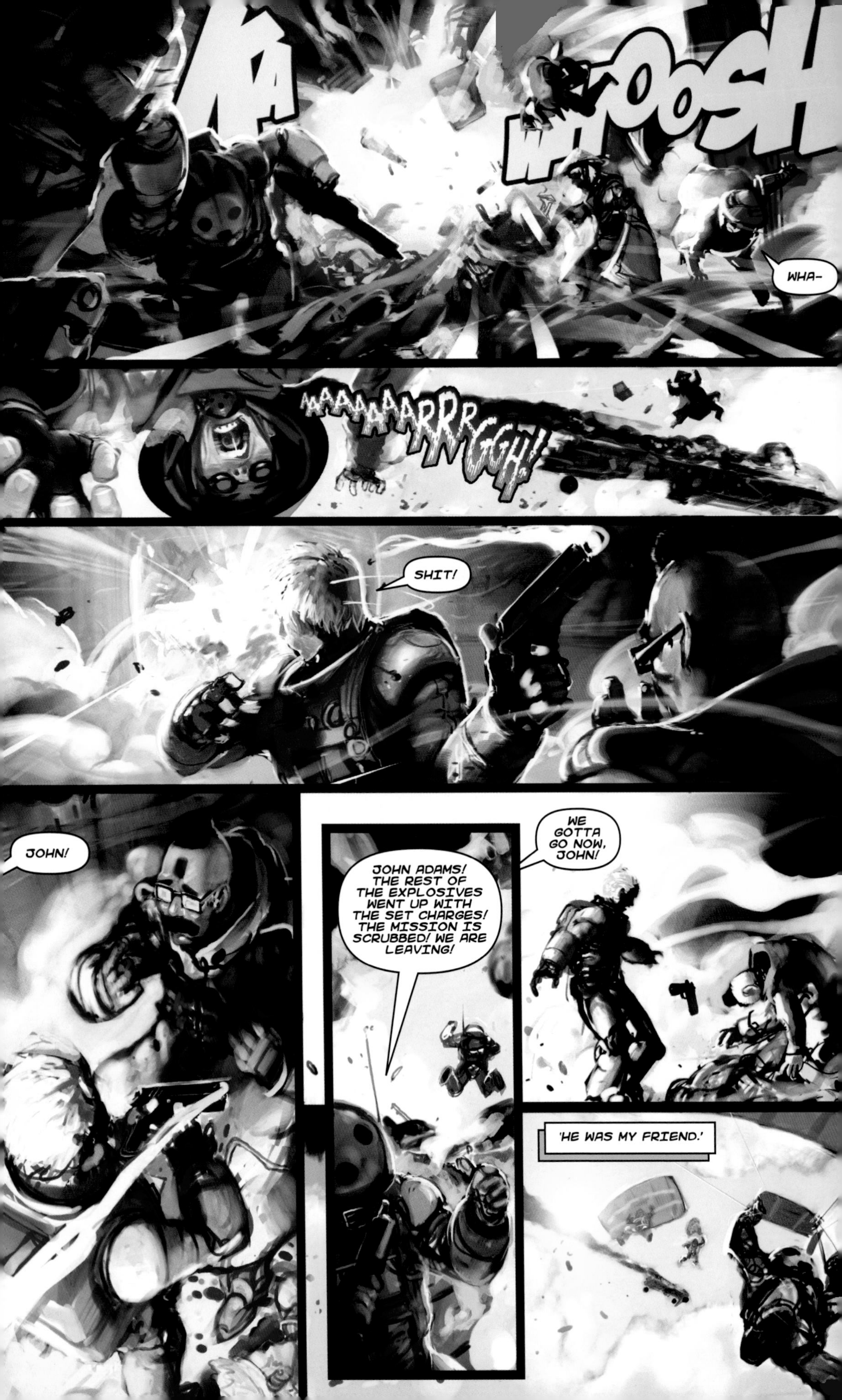
KA
WHOOSH
WHA-
AAAAAAARRRGGH!
SHIT!
JOHN!
JOHN ADAMS! THE REST OF THE EXPLOSIVES WENT UP WITH THE SET CHARGES! THE MISSION IS SCRUBBED! WE ARE LEAVING!
WE GOTTA GO NOW, JOHN!
'HE WAS MY FRIEND.'

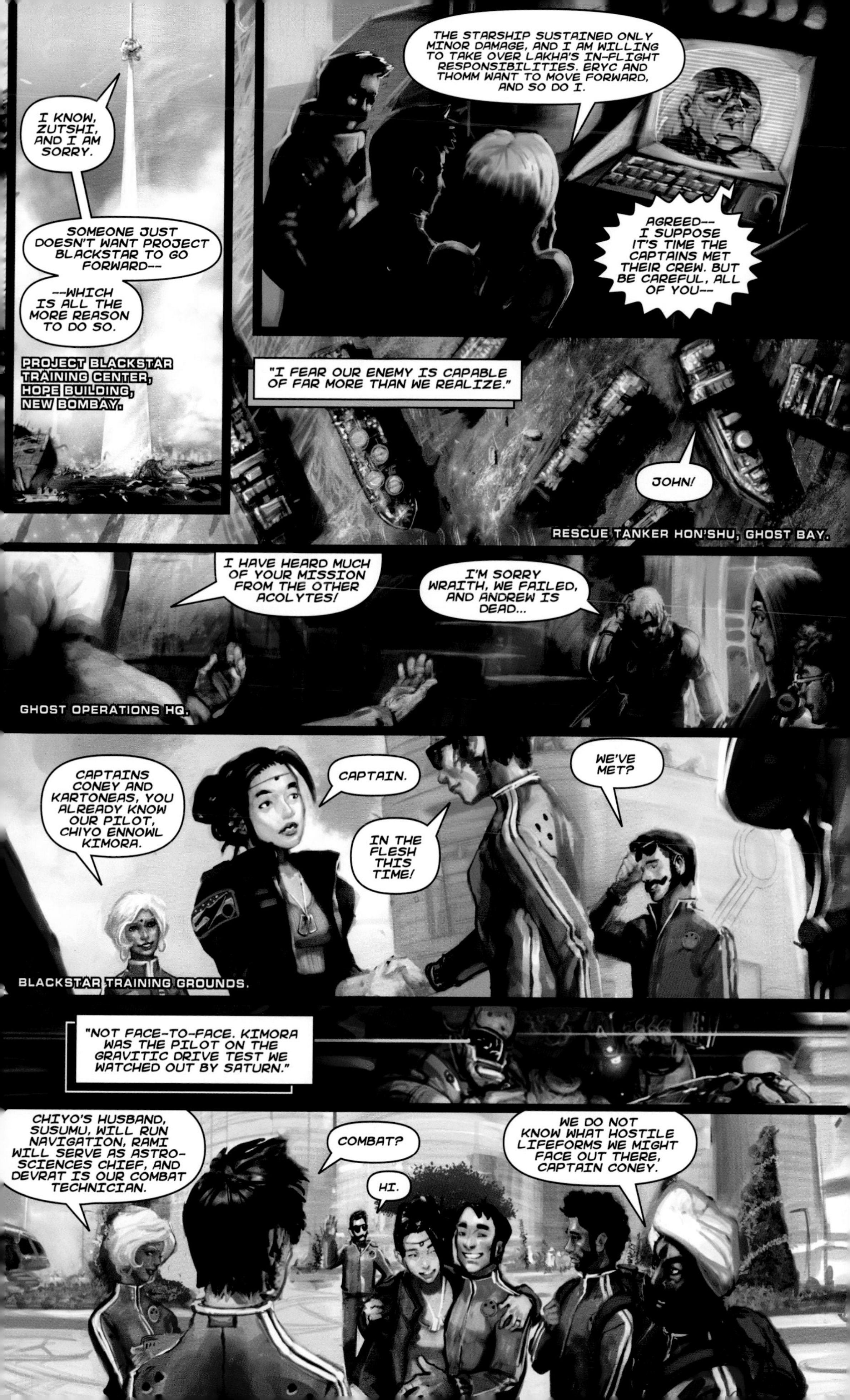
I KNOW, ZUTSHI, AND I AM SORRY.
SOMEONE JUST DOESN'T WANT PROJECT BLACKSTAR TO GO FORWARD--
--WHICH IS ALL THE MORE REASON TO DO SO.
PROJECT BLACKSTAR TRAINING CENTER, HOPE BUILDING, NEW BOMBAY.
THE STARSHIP SUSTAINED ONLY MINOR DAMAGE, AND I AM WILLING TO TAKE OVER LAKHA'S IN-FLIGHT RESPONSIBILITIES. ERYC AND THOMM WANT TO MOVE FORWARD, AND SO DO I.
AGREED-- I SUPPOSE IT'S TIME THE CAPTAINS MET THEIR CREW. BUT BE CAREFUL, ALL OF YOU--
"I FEAR OUR ENEMY IS CAPABLE OF FAR MORE THAN WE REALIZE."
JOHN!
RESCUE TANKER HON'SHU, GHOST BAY.
GHOST OPERATIONS HQ.
I HAVE HEARD MUCH OF YOUR MISSION FROM THE OTHER ACOLYTES!
I'M SORRY WRAITH, WE FAILED, AND ANDREW IS DEAD...
BLACKSTAR TRAINING GROUNDS.
CAPTAINS CONEY AND KARTONEAS, YOU ALREADY KNOW OUR PILOT, CHIYO ENNOWL KIMORA.
CAPTAIN.
WE'VE MET?
IN THE FLESH THIS TIME!
"NOT FACE-TO-FACE. KIMORA WAS THE PILOT ON THE GRAVITIC DRIVE TEST WE WATCHED OUT BY SATURN."
CHIYO'S HUSBAND, SUSUMU, WILL RUN NAVIGATION, RAMI WILL SERVE AS ASTRO-SCIENCES CHIEF, AND DEVRAT IS OUR COMBAT TECHNICIAN.
COMBAT?
HI.
WE DO NOT KNOW WHAT HOSTILE LIFEFORMS WE MIGHT FACE OUT THERE, CAPTAIN CONEY.

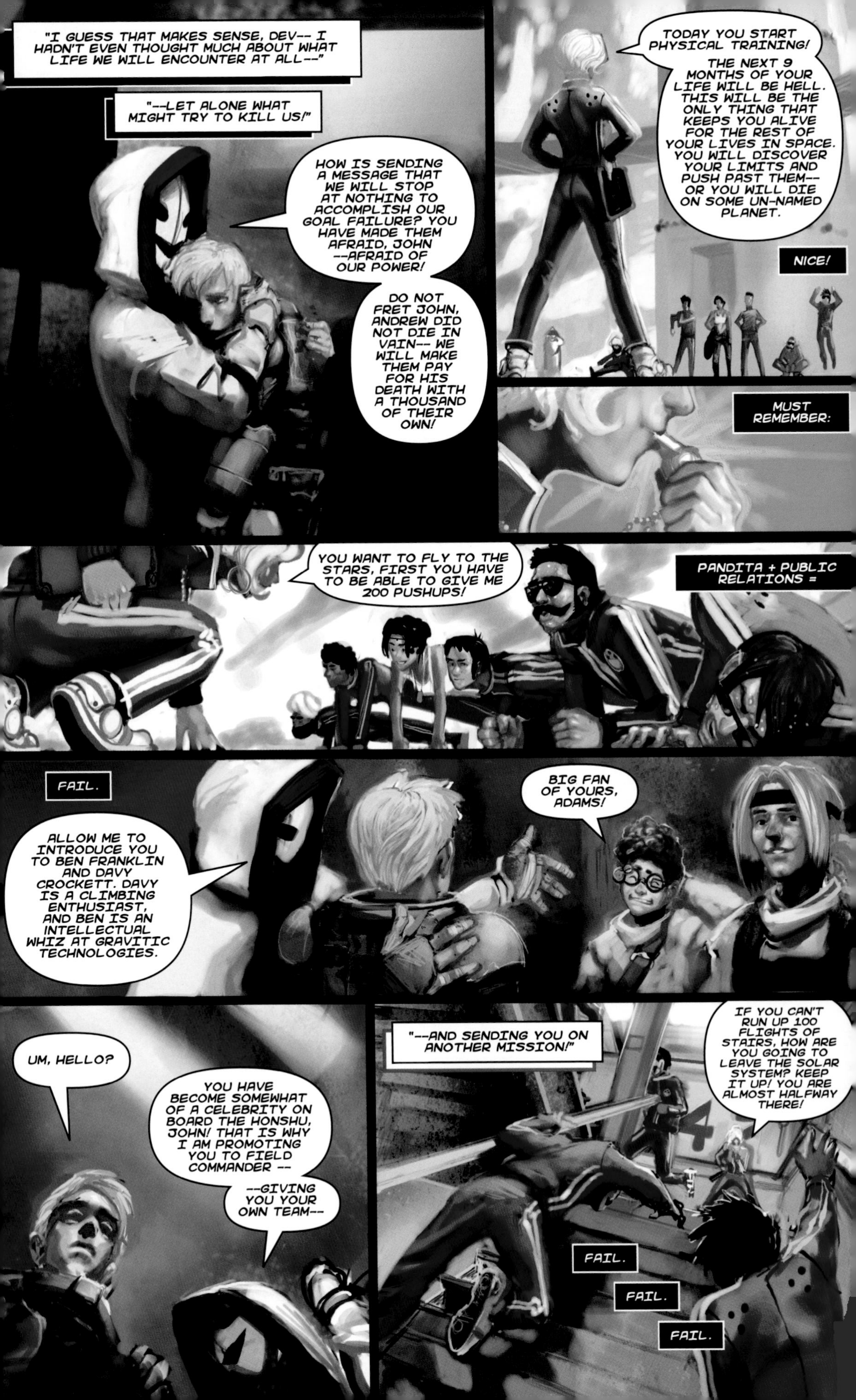

"I GUESS THAT MAKES SENSE, DEV-- I HADN'T EVEN THOUGHT MUCH ABOUT WHAT LIFE WE WILL ENCOUNTER AT ALL--"
"--LET ALONE WHAT MIGHT TRY TO KILL US!"
HOW IS SENDING A MESSAGE THAT WE WILL STOP AT NOTHING TO ACCOMPLISH OUR GOAL FAILURE? YOU HAVE MADE THEM AFRAID, JOHN --AFRAID OF OUR POWER!
DO NOT FRET JOHN, ANDREW DID NOT DIE IN VAIN-- WE WILL MAKE THEM PAY FOR HIS DEATH WITH A THOUSAND OF THEIR OWN!
TODAY YOU START PHYSICAL TRAINING!
THE NEXT 9 MONTHS OF YOUR LIFE WILL BE HELL. THIS WILL BE THE ONLY THING THAT KEEPS YOU ALIVE FOR THE REST OF YOUR LIVES IN SPACE. YOU WILL DISCOVER YOUR LIMITS AND PUSH PAST THEM-- OR YOU WILL DIE ON SOME UN-NAMED PLANET.
NICE!
MUST REMEMBER:
YOU WANT TO FLY TO THE STARS, FIRST YOU HAVE TO BE ABLE TO GIVE ME 200 PUSHUPS!
PANDITA + PUBLIC RELATIONS =
FAIL.
ALLOW ME TO INTRODUCE YOU TO BEN FRANKLIN AND DAVY CROCKETT. DAVY IS A CLIMBING ENTHUSIAST, AND BEN IS AN INTELLECTUAL WHIZ AT GRAVITIC TECHNOLOGIES.
BIG FAN OF YOURS, ADAMS!
UM, HELLO?
YOU HAVE BECOME SOMEWHAT OF A CELEBRITY ON BOARD THE HONSHU, JOHN! THAT IS WHY I AM PROMOTING YOU TO FIELD COMMANDER --
--GIVING YOU YOUR OWN TEAM--
"--AND SENDING YOU ON ANOTHER MISSION!"
IF YOU CAN'T RUN UP 100 FLIGHTS OF STAIRS, HOW ARE YOU GOING TO LEAVE THE SOLAR SYSTEM? KEEP IT UP! YOU ARE ALMOST HALFWAY THERE!
FAIL.
FAIL.
FAIL.

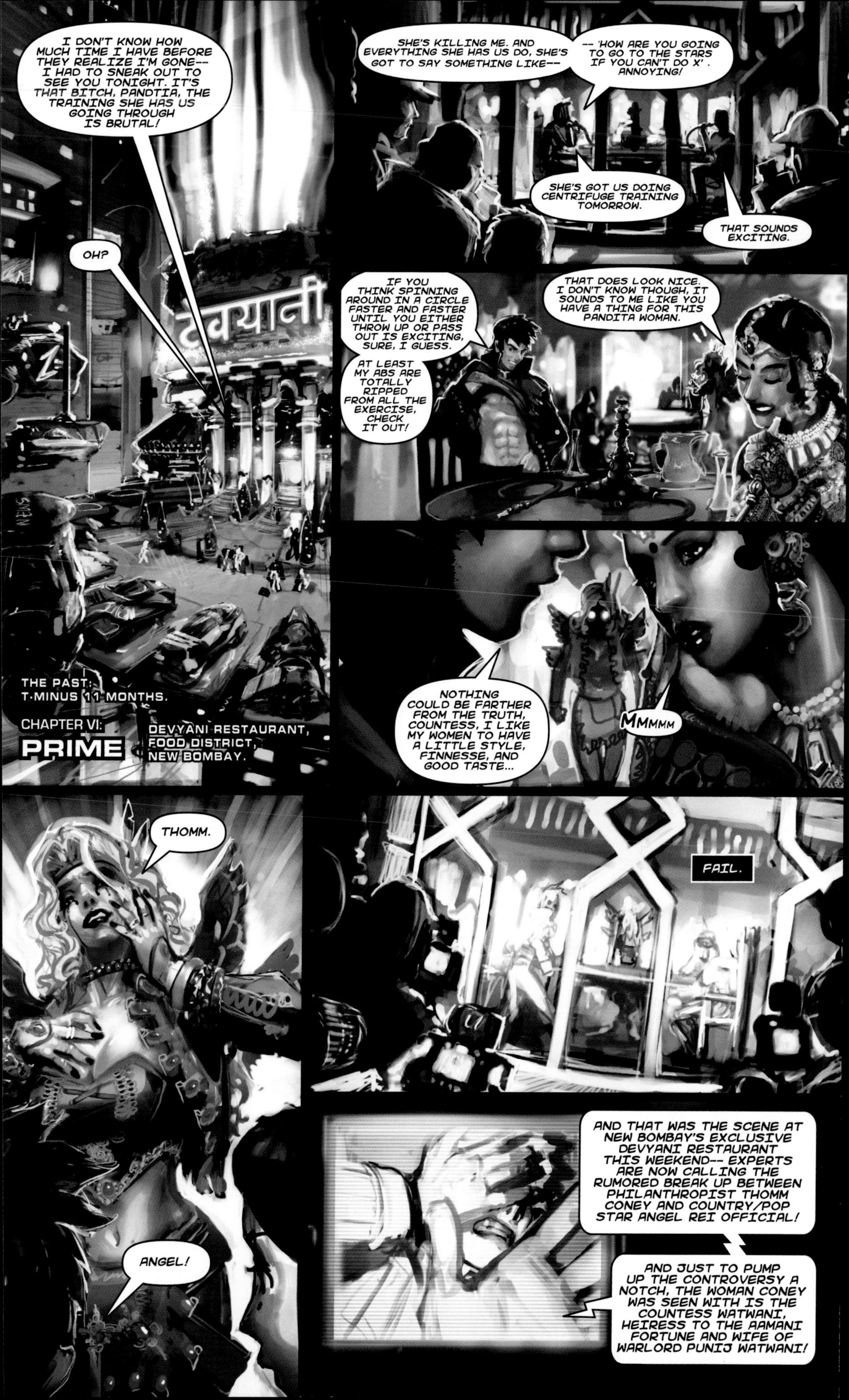

I DON'T KNOW HOW MUCH TIME I HAVE BEFORE THEY REALIZE I'M GONE-- I HAD TO SNEAK OUT TO SEE YOU TONIGHT. IT'S THAT BITCH, PANDTIA, THE TRAINING SHE HAS US GOING THROUGH IS BRUTAL!
OH?
THE PAST: T-MINUS 11 MONTHS.
CHAPTER VI:
PRIME
DEVYANI RESTAURANT, FOOD DISTRICT, NEW BOMBAY.
SHE'S KILLING ME. AND EVERYTHING SHE HAS US DO, SHE'S GOT TO SAY SOMETHING LIKE--
-- 'HOW ARE YOU GOING TO GO TO THE STARS IF YOU CAN'T DO X' . ANNOYING!
SHE'S GOT US DOING CENTRIFUGE TRAINING TOMORROW.
THAT SOUNDS EXCITING.
IF YOU THINK SPINNING AROUND IN A CIRCLE FASTER AND FASTER UNTIL YOU EITHER THROW UP OR PASS OUT IS EXCITING, SURE, I GUESS.
AT LEAST MY ABS ARE TOTALLY RIPPED FROM ALL THE EXERCISE, CHECK IT OUT!
THAT DOES LOOK NICE. I DON'T KNOW THOUGH, IT SOUNDS TO ME LIKE YOU HAVE A THING FOR THIS PANDITA WOMAN.
NOTHING COULD BE FARTHER FROM THE TRUTH, COUNTESS, I LIKE MY WOMEN TO HAVE A LITTLE STYLE, FINNESSE, AND GOOD TASTE...
MMMMM
THOMM.
ANGEL!
FAIL.
AND THAT WAS THE SCENE AT NEW BOMBAY'S EXCLUSIVE DEVYANI RESTAURANT THIS WEEKEND-- EXPERTS ARE NOW CALLING THE RUMORED BREAK UP BETWEEN PHILANTHROPIST THOMM CONEY AND COUNTRY/POP STAR ANGEL REI OFFICIAL!
AND JUST TO PUMP UP THE CONTROVERSY A NOTCH, THE WOMAN CONEY WAS SEEN WITH IS THE COUNTESS WATWANI, HEIRESS TO THE AAMANI FORTUNE AND WIFE OF WARLORD PUNIJ WATWANI!

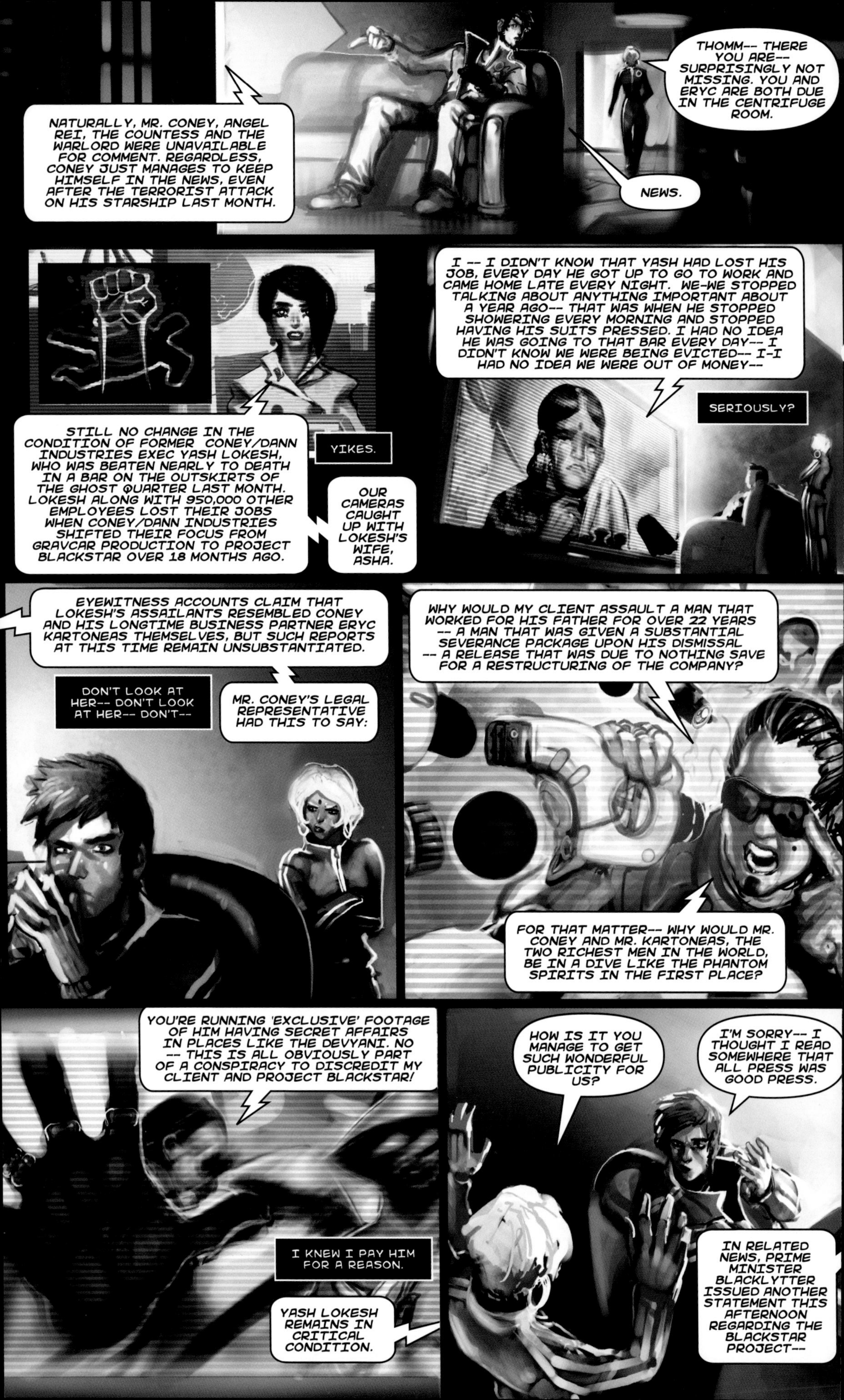
NATURALLY, MR. CONEY, ANGEL REI, THE COUNTESS AND THE WARLORD WERE UNAVAILABLE FOR COMMENT. REGARDLESS, CONEY JUST MANAGES TO KEEP HIMSELF IN THE NEWS, EVEN AFTER THE TERRORIST ATTACK ON HIS STARSHIP LAST MONTH.
THOMM-- THERE YOU ARE-- SURPRISINGLY NOT MISSING. YOU AND ERYC ARE BOTH DUE IN THE CENTRIFUGE ROOM.
NEWS.
STILL NO CHANGE IN THE CONDITION OF FORMER CONEY/DANN INDUSTRIES EXEC YASH LOKESH, WHO WAS BEATEN NEARLY TO DEATH IN A BAR ON THE OUTSKIRTS OF THE GHOST QUARTER LAST MONTH. LOKESH ALONG WITH 950,000 OTHER EMPLOYEES LOST THEIR JOBS WHEN CONEY/DANN INDUSTRIES SHIFTED THEIR FOCUS FROM GRAVCAR PRODUCTION TO PROJECT BLACKSTAR OVER 18 MONTHS AGO.
YIKES.
OUR CAMERAS CAUGHT UP WITH LOKESH'S WIFE, ASHA.
I -- I DIDN'T KNOW THAT YASH HAD LOST HIS JOB, EVERY DAY HE GOT UP TO GO TO WORK AND CAME HOME LATE EVERY NIGHT. WE-WE STOPPED TALKING ABOUT ANYTHING IMPORTANT ABOUT A YEAR AGO-- THAT WAS WHEN HE STOPPED SHOWERING EVERY MORNING AND STOPPED HAVING HIS SUITS PRESSED. I HAD NO IDEA HE WAS GOING TO THAT BAR EVERY DAY-- I DIDN'T KNOW WE WERE BEING EVICTED-- I-I HAD NO IDEA WE WERE OUT OF MONEY--
SERIOUSLY?
EYEWITNESS ACCOUNTS CLAIM THAT LOKESH'S ASSAILANTS RESEMBLED CONEY AND HIS LONGTIME BUSINESS PARTNER ERYC KARTONEAS THEMSELVES, BUT SUCH REPORTS AT THIS TIME REMAIN UNSUBSTANTIATED.
DON'T LOOK AT HER-- DON'T LOOK AT HER-- DON'T--
MR. CONEY'S LEGAL REPRESENTATIVE HAD THIS TO SAY:
WHY WOULD MY CLIENT ASSAULT A MAN THAT WORKED FOR HIS FATHER FOR OVER 22 YEARS -- A MAN THAT WAS GIVEN A SUBSTANTIAL SEVERANCE PACKAGE UPON HIS DISMISSAL -- A RELEASE THAT WAS DUE TO NOTHING SAVE FOR A RESTRUCTURING OF THE COMPANY?
FOR THAT MATTER-- WHY WOULD MR. CONEY AND MR. KARTONEAS, THE TWO RICHEST MEN IN THE WORLD, BE IN A DIVE LIKE THE PHANTOM SPIRITS IN THE FIRST PLACE?
YOU'RE RUNNING 'EXCLUSIVE' FOOTAGE OF HIM HAVING SECRET AFFAIRS IN PLACES LIKE THE DEVYANI. NO -- THIS IS ALL OBVIOUSLY PART OF A CONSPIRACY TO DISCREDIT MY CLIENT AND PROJECT BLACKSTAR!
I KNEW I PAY HIM FOR A REASON.
YASH LOKESH REMAINS IN CRITICAL CONDITION.
HOW IS IT YOU MANAGE TO GET SUCH WONDERFUL PUBLICITY FOR US?
I'M SORRY-- I THOUGHT I READ SOMEWHERE THAT ALL PRESS WAS GOOD PRESS.
IN RELATED NEWS, PRIME MINISTER BLACKLYTTER ISSUED ANOTHER STATEMENT THIS AFTERNOON REGARDING THE BLACKSTAR PROJECT--

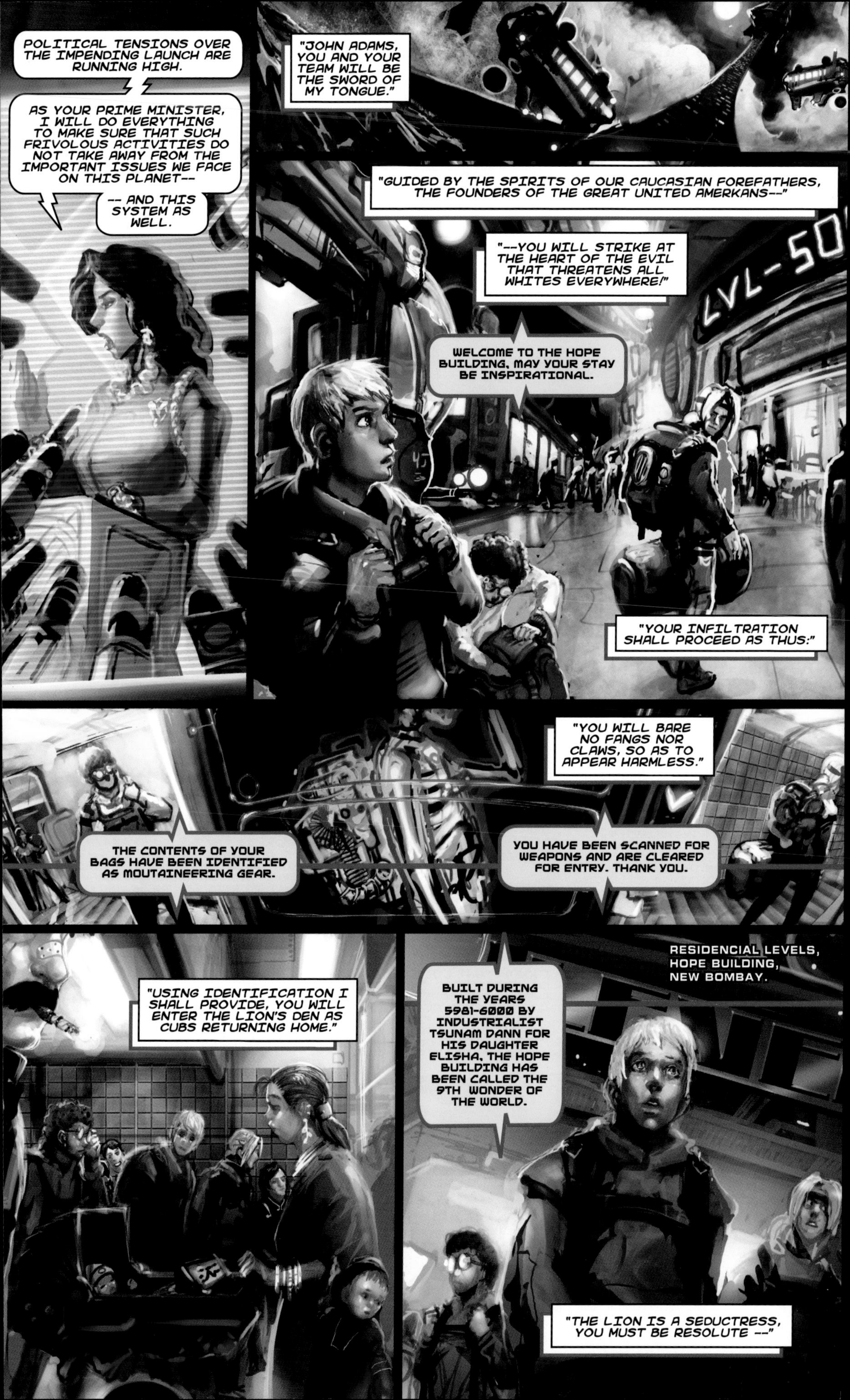
POLITICAL TENSIONS OVER THE IMPENDING LAUNCH ARE RUNNING HIGH.
AS YOUR PRIME MINISTER, I WILL DO EVERYTHING TO MAKE SURE THAT SUCH FRIVOLOUS ACTIVITIES DO NOT TAKE AWAY FROM THE IMPORTANT ISSUES WE FACE ON THIS PLANET--
-- AND THIS SYSTEM AS WELL.
"JOHN ADAMS, YOU AND YOUR TEAM WILL BE THE SWORD OF MY TONGUE."
"GUIDED BY THE SPIRITS OF OUR CAUCASIAN FOREFATHERS, THE FOUNDERS OF THE GREAT UNITED AMERKANS--"
"--YOU WILL STRIKE AT THE HEART OF THE EVIL THAT THREATENS ALL WHITES EVERYWHERE!"
LVL-50
WELCOME TO THE HOPE BUILDING, MAY YOUR STAY BE INSPIRATIONAL.
"YOUR INFILTRATION SHALL PROCEED AS THUS:"
"YOU WILL BARE NO FANGS NOR CLAWS, SO AS TO APPEAR HARMLESS."
THE CONTENTS OF YOUR BAGS HAVE BEEN IDENTIFIED AS MOUTAINEERING GEAR.
YOU HAVE BEEN SCANNED FOR WEAPONS AND ARE CLEARED FOR ENTRY. THANK YOU.
"USING IDENTIFICATION I SHALL PROVIDE, YOU WILL ENTER THE LION'S DEN AS CUBS RETURNING HOME."
RESIDENCIAL LEVELS, HOPE BUILDING, NEW BOMBAY.
BUILT DURING THE YEARS 5981-6000 BY INDUSTRIALIST TSUNAM DANN FOR HIS DAUGHTER ELISHA, THE HOPE BUILDING HAS BEEN CALLED THE 9TH WONDER OF THE WORLD.
"THE LION IS A SEDUCTRESS, YOU MUST BE RESOLUTE --"

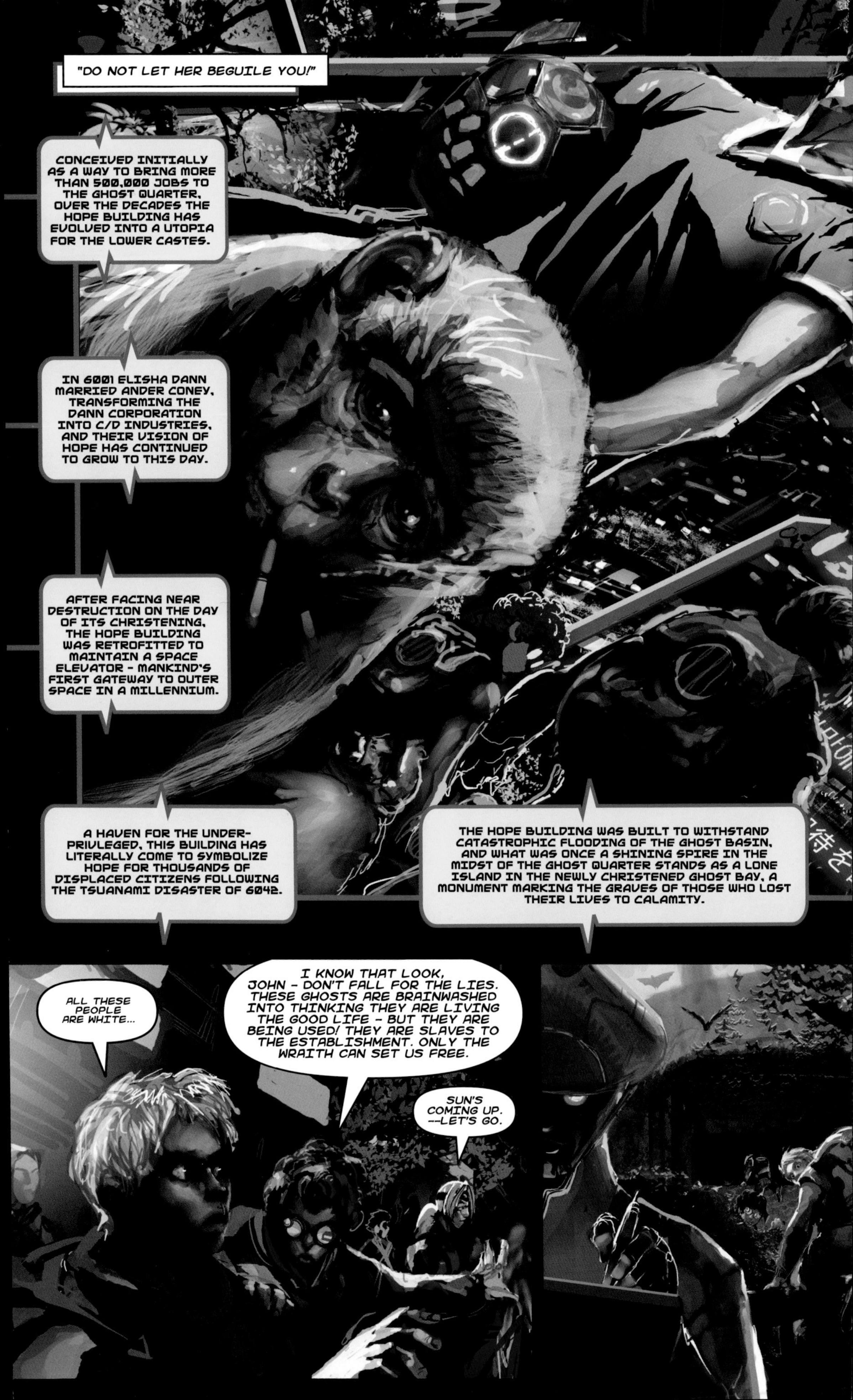
"DO NOT LET HER BEGUILE YOU!"
CONCEIVED INITIALLY AS A WAY TO BRING MORE THAN 500,000 JOBS TO THE GHOST QUARTER, OVER THE DECADES THE HOPE BUILDING HAS EVOLVED INTO A UTOPIA FOR THE LOWER CASTES.
IN 6001 ELISHA DANN MARRIED ANDER CONEY, TRANSFORMING THE DANN CORPORATION INTO C/D INDUSTRIES, AND THEIR VISION OF HOPE HAS CONTINUED TO GROW TO THIS DAY.
AFTER FACING NEAR DESTRUCTION ON THE DAY OF ITS CHRISTENING, THE HOPE BUILDING WAS RETROFITTED TO MAINTAIN A SPACE ELEVATOR - MANKIND'S FIRST GATEWAY TO OUTER SPACE IN A MILLENNIUM.
A HAVEN FOR THE UNDER-PRIVLEGED, THIS BUILDING HAS LITERALLY COME TO SYMBOLIZE HOPE FOR THOUSANDS OF DISPLACED CITIZENS FOLLOWING THE TSUANAMI DISASTER OF 6042.
THE HOPE BUILDING WAS BUILT TO WITHSTAND CATASTROPHIC FLOODING OF THE GHOST BASIN, AND WHAT WAS ONCE A SHINING SPIRE IN THE MIDST OF THE GHOST QUARTER STANDS AS A LONE ISLAND IN THE NEWLY CHRISTENED GHOST BAY, A MONUMENT MARKING THE GRAVES OF THOSE WHO LOST THEIR LIVES TO CALAMITY.
ALL THESE PEOPLE ARE WHITE...
I KNOW THAT LOOK, JOHN - DON'T FALL FOR THE LIES. THESE GHOSTS ARE BRAINWASHED INTO THINKING THEY ARE LIVING THE GOOD LIFE - BUT THEY ARE BEING USED! THEY ARE SLAVES TO THE ESTABLISHMENT. ONLY THE WRAITH CAN SET US FREE.
SUN'S COMING UP. --LET'S GO.

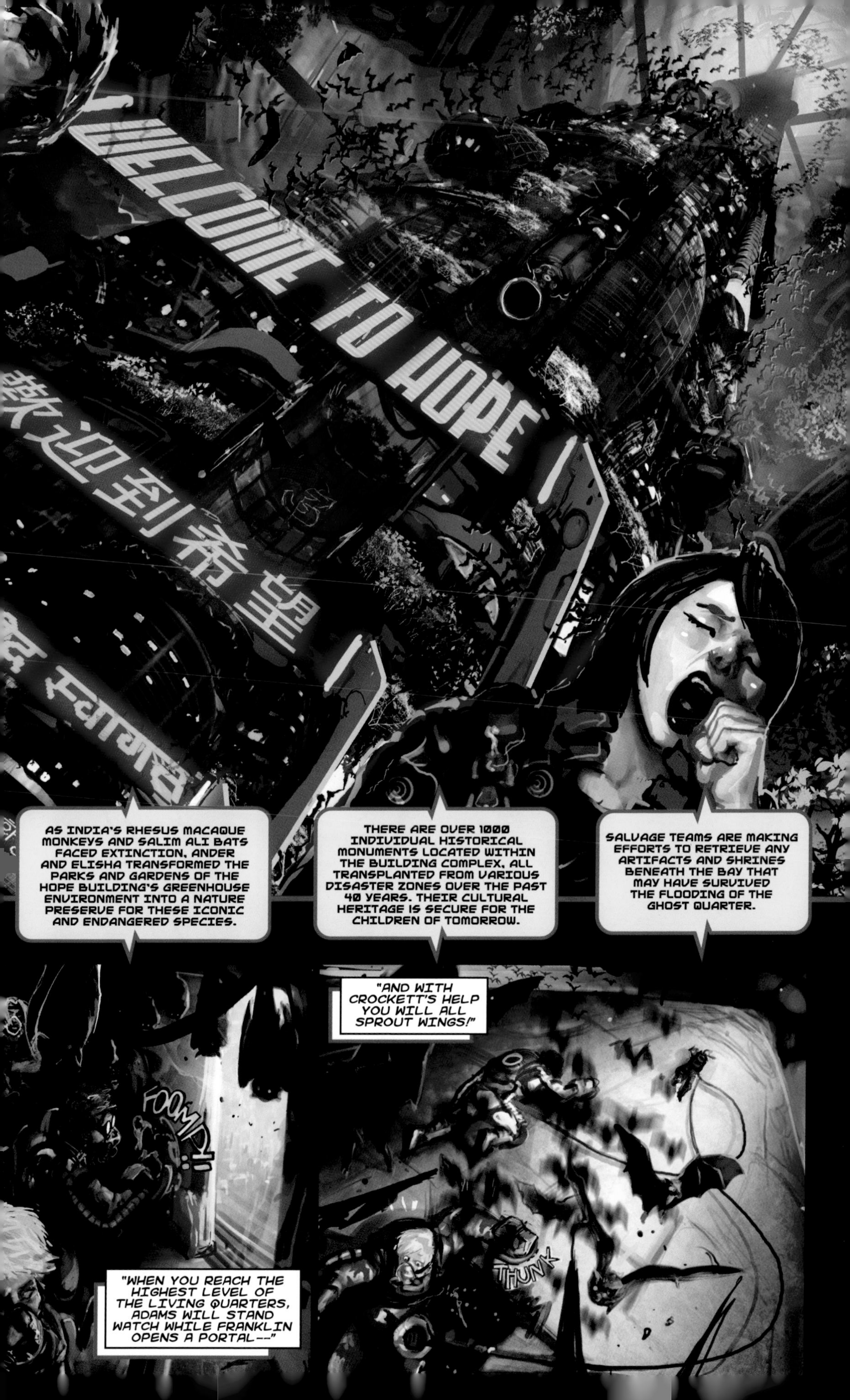
WELCOME TO HOPE
歡迎到希望
AS INDIA'S RHESUS MACAQUE MONKEYS AND SALIM ALI BATS FACED EXTINCTION, ANDER AND ELISHA TRANSFORMED THE PARKS AND GARDENS OF THE HOPE BUILDING'S GREENHOUSE ENVIRONMENT INTO A NATURE PRESERVE FOR THESE ICONIC AND ENDANGERED SPECIES.
THERE ARE OVER 1000 INDIVIDUAL HISTORICAL MONUMENTS LOCATED WITHIN THE BUILDING COMPLEX, ALL TRANSPLANTED FROM VARIOUS DISASTER ZONES OVER THE PAST 40 YEARS. THEIR CULTURAL HERITAGE IS SECURE FOR THE CHILDREN OF TOMORROW.
SALVAGE TEAMS ARE MAKING EFFORTS TO RETRIEVE ANY ARTIFACTS AND SHRINES BENEATH THE BAY THAT MAY HAVE SURVIVED THE FLOODING OF THE GHOST QUARTER.
FOOMP!!
"WHEN YOU REACH THE HIGHEST LEVEL OF THE LIVING QUARTERS, ADAMS WILL STAND WATCH WHILE FRANKLIN OPENS A PORTAL--"
"AND WITH CROCKETT'S HELP YOU WILL ALL SPROUT WINGS!"
THUNK

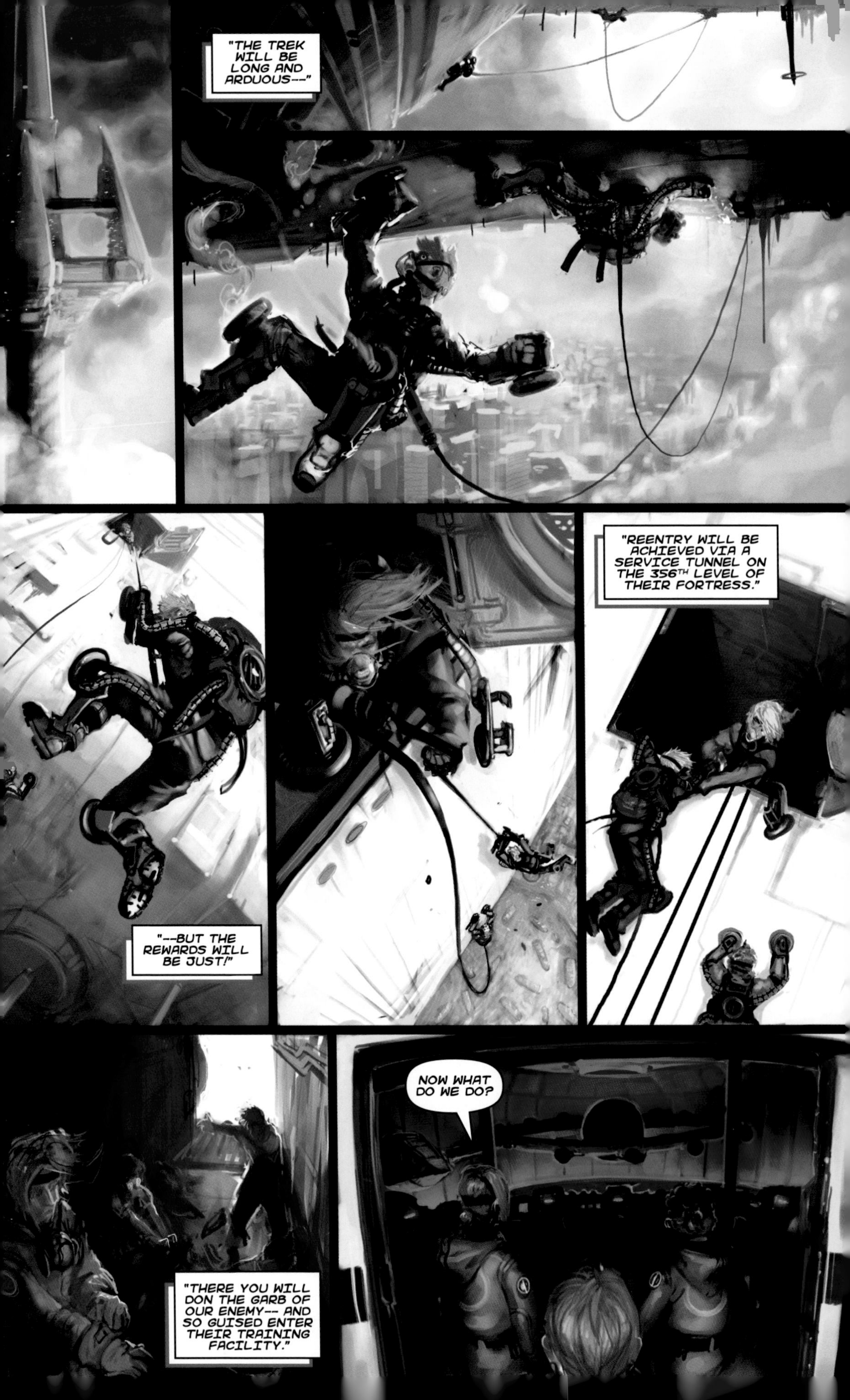
"THE TREK WILL BE LONG AND ARDUOUS--"
"--BUT THE REWARDS WILL BE JUST!"
"REENTRY WILL BE ACHIEVED VIA A SERVICE TUNNEL ON THE 356TH LEVEL OF THEIR FORTRESS."
"THERE YOU WILL DON THE GARB OF OUR ENEMY-- AND SO GUISED ENTER THEIR TRAINING FACILITY."
NOW WHAT DO WE DO?

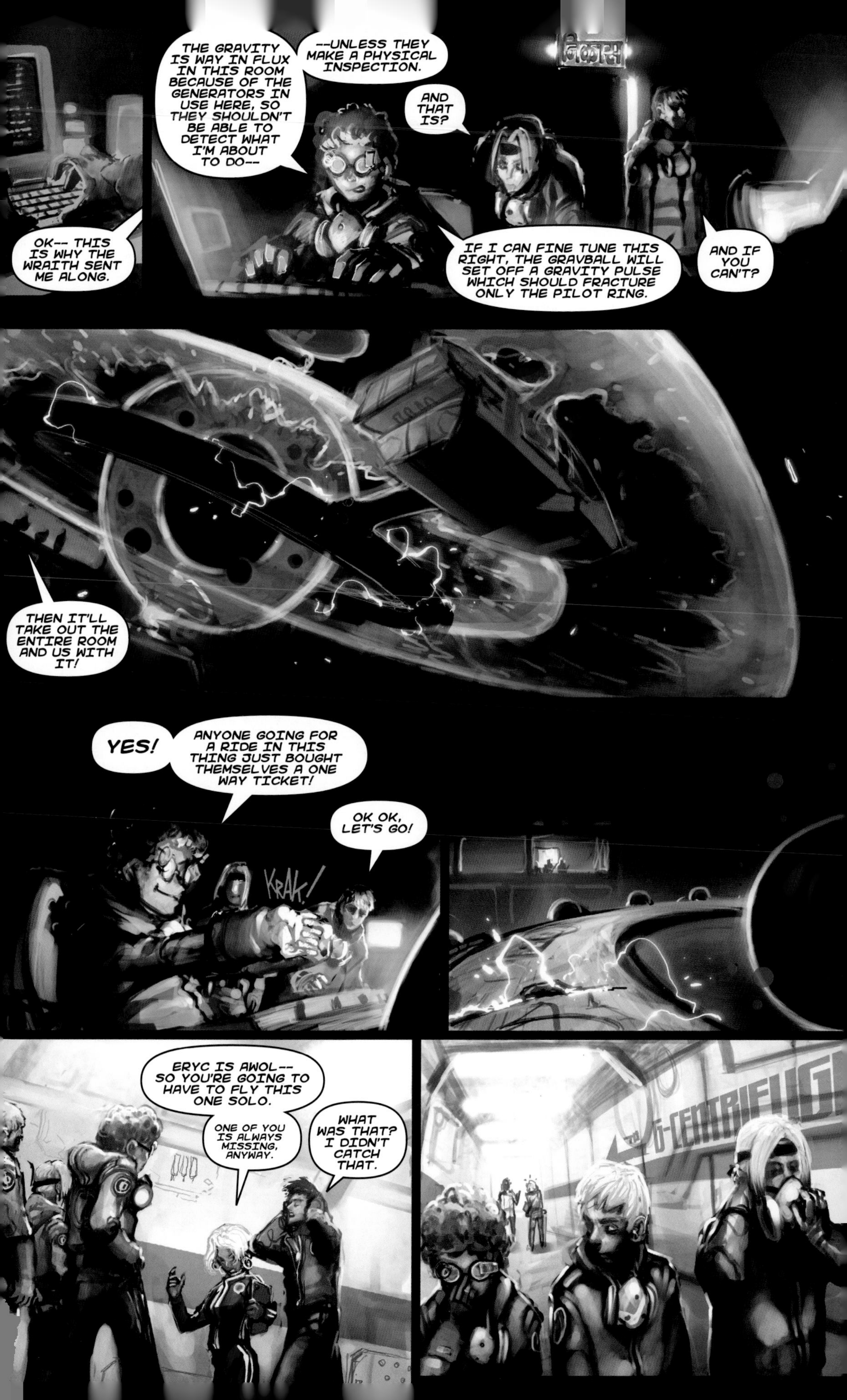
OK-- THIS IS WHY THE WRAITH SENT ME ALONG.
THE GRAVITY IS WAY IN FLUX IN THIS ROOM BECAUSE OF THE GENERATORS IN USE HERE, SO THEY SHOULDN'T BE ABLE TO DETECT WHAT I'M ABOUT TO DO--
--UNLESS THEY MAKE A PHYSICAL INSPECTION.
AND THAT IS?
IF I CAN FINE TUNE THIS RIGHT, THE GRAVBALL WILL SET OFF A GRAVITY PULSE WHICH SHOULD FRACTURE ONLY THE PILOT RING.
AND IF YOU CAN'T?
THEN IT'LL TAKE OUT THE ENTIRE ROOM AND US WITH IT!
YES!
ANYONE GOING FOR A RIDE IN THIS THING JUST BOUGHT THEMSELVES A ONE WAY TICKET!
OK OK, LET'S GO!
KRAK!
ERYC IS AWOL-- SO YOU'RE GOING TO HAVE TO FLY THIS ONE SOLO.
ONE OF YOU IS ALWAYS MISSING, ANYWAY.
WHAT WAS THAT? I DIDN'T CATCH THAT.

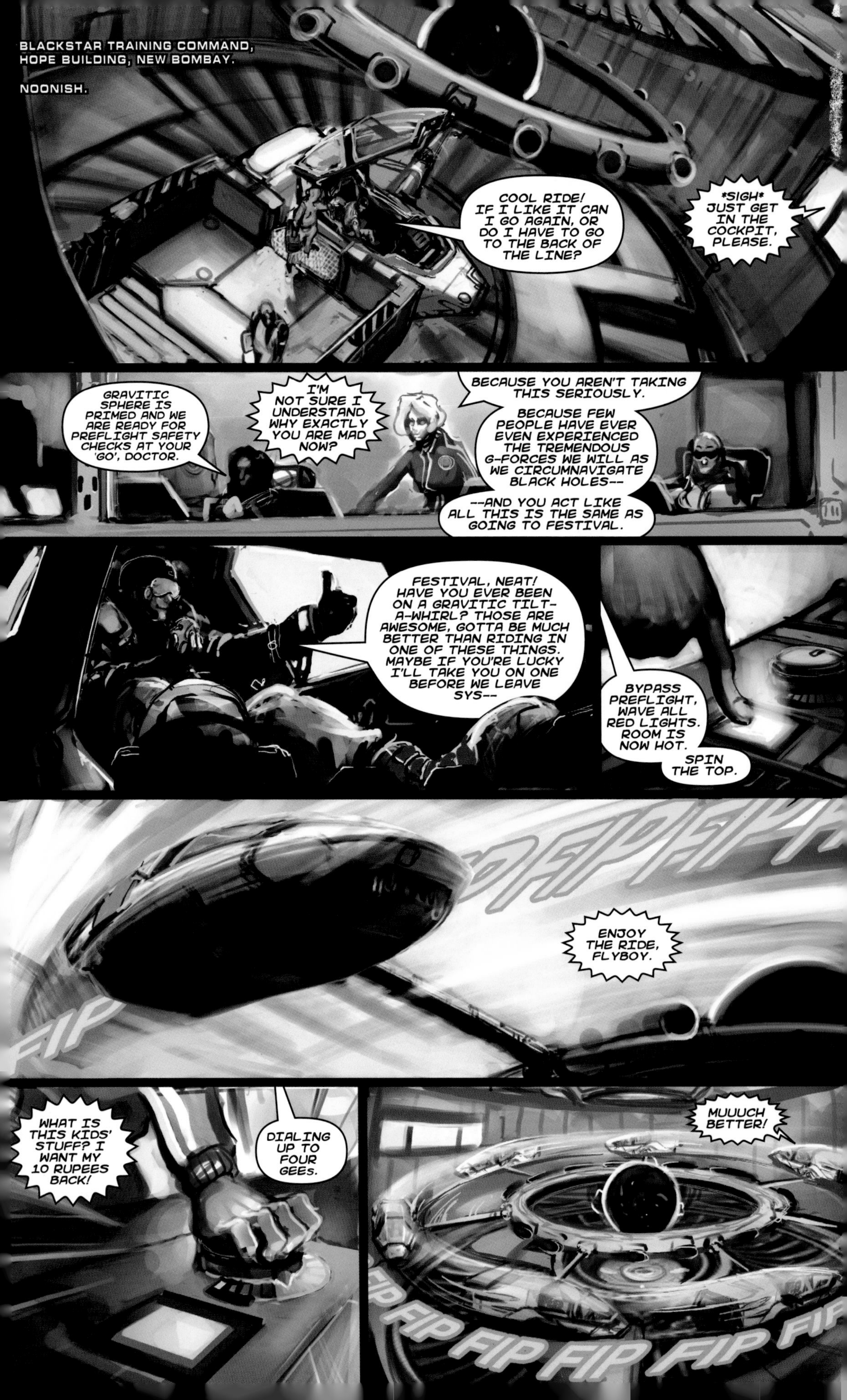
BLACKSTAR TRAINING COMMAND, HOPE BUILDING, NEW BOMBAY.
NOONISH.
COOL RIDE! IF I LIKE IT CAN I GO AGAIN, OR DO I HAVE TO GO TO THE BACK OF THE LINE?
SIGH JUST GET IN THE COCKPIT, PLEASE.
GRAVITIC SPHERE IS PRIMED AND WE ARE READY FOR PREFLIGHT SAFETY CHECKS AT YOUR 'GO', DOCTOR.
I'M NOT SURE I UNDERSTAND WHY EXACTLY YOU ARE MAD NOW?
BECAUSE YOU AREN'T TAKING THIS SERIOUSLY.
BECAUSE FEW PEOPLE HAVE EVER EVEN EXPERIENCED THE TREMENDOUS G-FORCES WE WILL AS WE CIRCUMNAVIGATE BLACK HOLES--
--AND YOU ACT LIKE ALL THIS IS THE SAME AS GOING TO FESTIVAL.
FESTIVAL, NEAT! HAVE YOU EVER BEEN ON A GRAVITIC TILT-A-WHIRL? THOSE ARE AWESOME, GOTTA BE MUCH BETTER THAN RIDING IN ONE OF THESE THINGS. MAYBE IF YOU'RE LUCKY I'LL TAKE YOU ON ONE BEFORE WE LEAVE SYS--
BYPASS PREFLIGHT, WAVE ALL RED LIGHTS. ROOM IS NOW HOT.
SPIN THE TOP.
FFAFFAFFA
ENJOY THE RIDE, FLYBOY.
FIP
WHAT IS THIS KIDS' STUFF? I WANT MY 10 RUPEES BACK!
DIALING UP TO FOUR GEES.
MUUUCH BETTER!
FIP FIP FIP FIP FIP FIP FIP

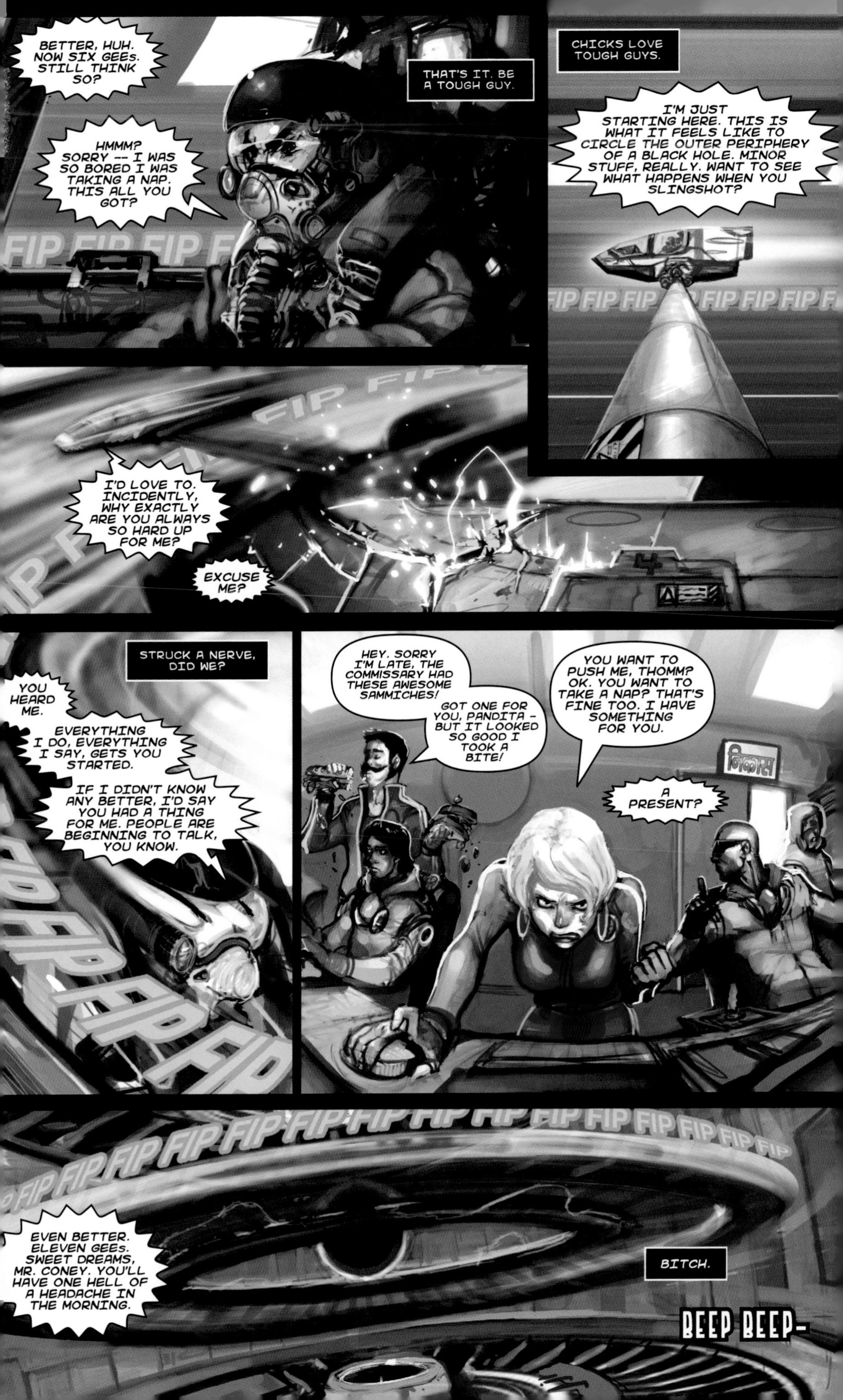
BETTER, HUH. NOW SIX GEEs. STILL THINK SO?
THAT'S IT. BE A TOUGH GUY.
HMMM? SORRY -- I WAS SO BORED I WAS TAKING A NAP. THIS ALL YOU GOT?
FIP FIP FIP
CHICKS LOVE TOUGH GUYS.
I'M JUST STARTING HERE. THIS IS WHAT IT FEELS LIKE TO CIRCLE THE OUTER PERIPHERY OF A BLACK HOLE. MINOR STUFF, REALLY. WANT TO SEE WHAT HAPPENS WHEN YOU SLINGSHOT?
FIP FIP FIP FIP FIP FIP
FIP FIP
I'D LOVE TO. INCIDENTLY, WHY EXACTLY ARE YOU ALWAYS SO HARD UP FOR ME?
EXCUSE ME?
STRUCK A NERVE, DID WE?
YOU HEARD ME.
EVERYTHING I DO, EVERYTHING I SAY, GETS YOU STARTED.
IF I DIDN'T KNOW ANY BETTER, I'D SAY YOU HAD A THING FOR ME. PEOPLE ARE BEGINNING TO TALK, YOU KNOW.
FIP FIP FIP
HEY. SORRY I'M LATE, THE COMMISSARY HAD THESE AWESOME SAMMICHES!
GOT ONE FOR YOU, PANDITA - BUT IT LOOKED SO GOOD I TOOK A BITE!
YOU WANT TO PUSH ME, THOMM? OK. YOU WANT TO TAKE A NAP? THAT'S FINE TOO. I HAVE SOMETHING FOR YOU.
A PRESENT?
FIP FIP FIP FIP FIP FIP FIP FIP FIP FIP FIP FIP FIP FIP
EVEN BETTER. ELEVEN GEEs. SWEET DREAMS, MR. CONEY. YOU'LL HAVE ONE HELL OF A HEADACHE IN THE MORNING.
BITCH.
BEEP BEEP-

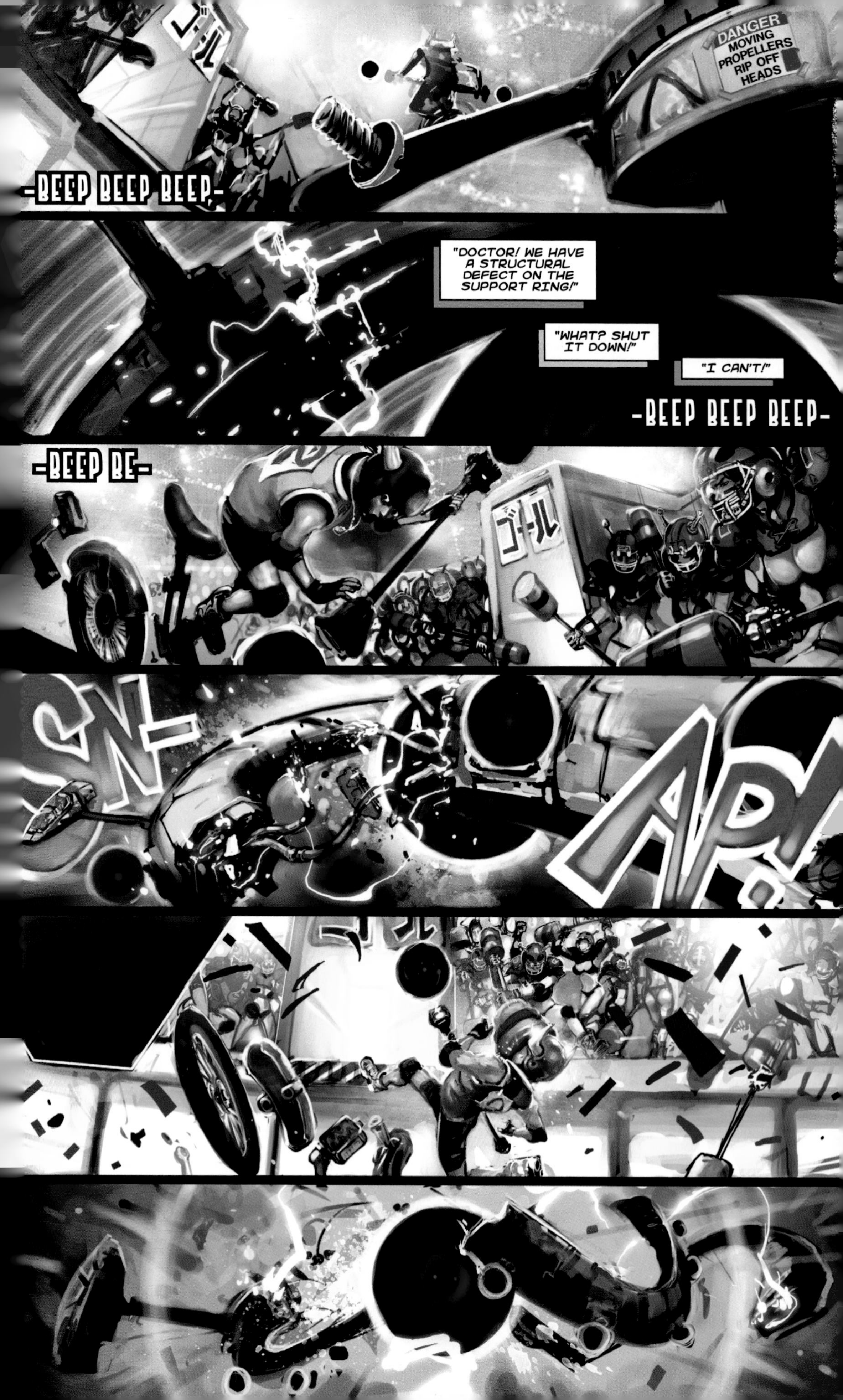

ゴール
DANGER
MOVING PROPELLERS RIP OFF HEADS
-BEEP BEEP BEEP-
"DOCTOR! WE HAVE A STRUCTURAL DEFECT ON THE SUPPORT RING!"
"WHAT? SHUT IT DOWN!"
"I CAN'T!"
-BEEP BEEP BEEP-
-BEEP BE-
ゴール
SN-
AP

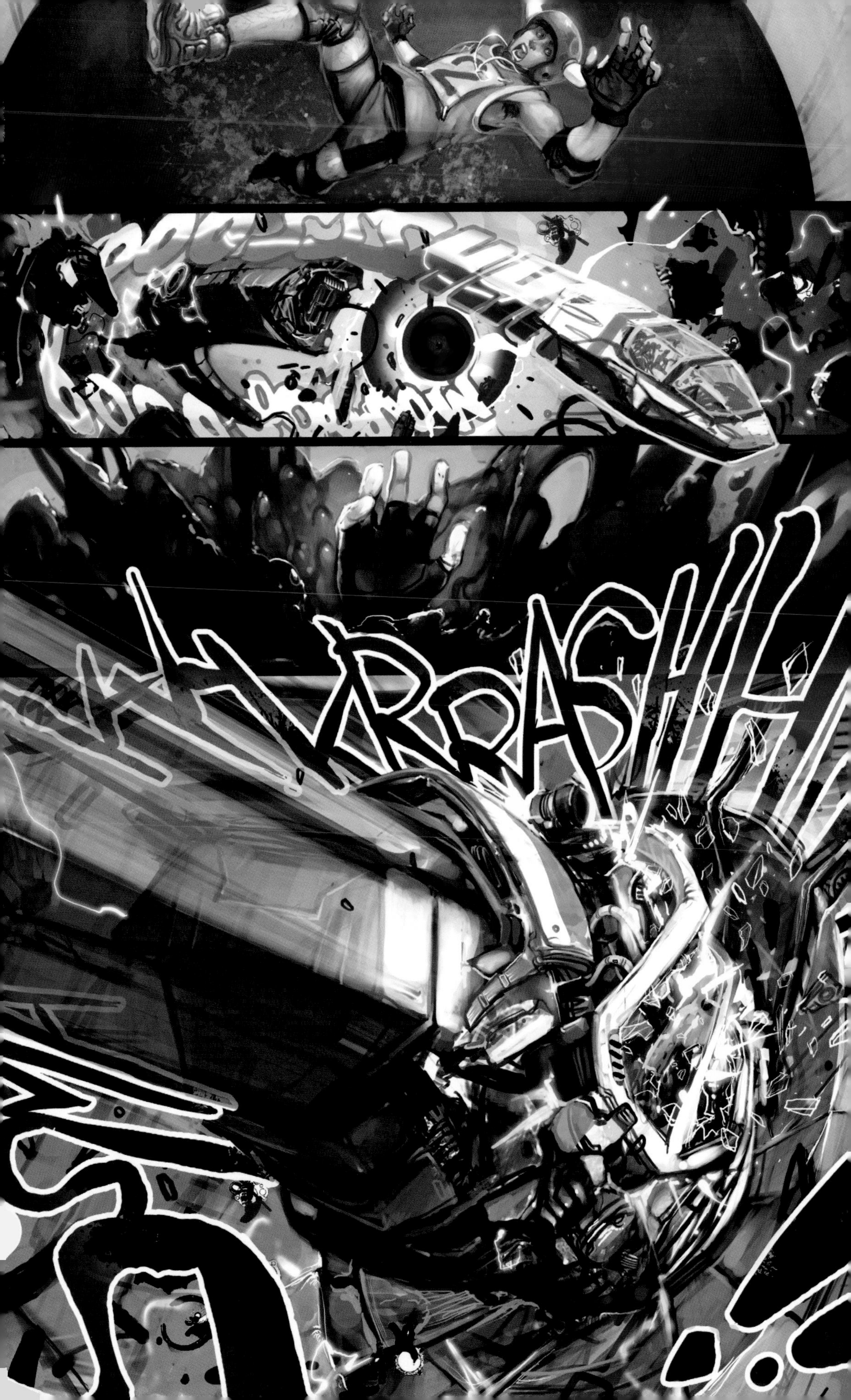
KRRASHH!!

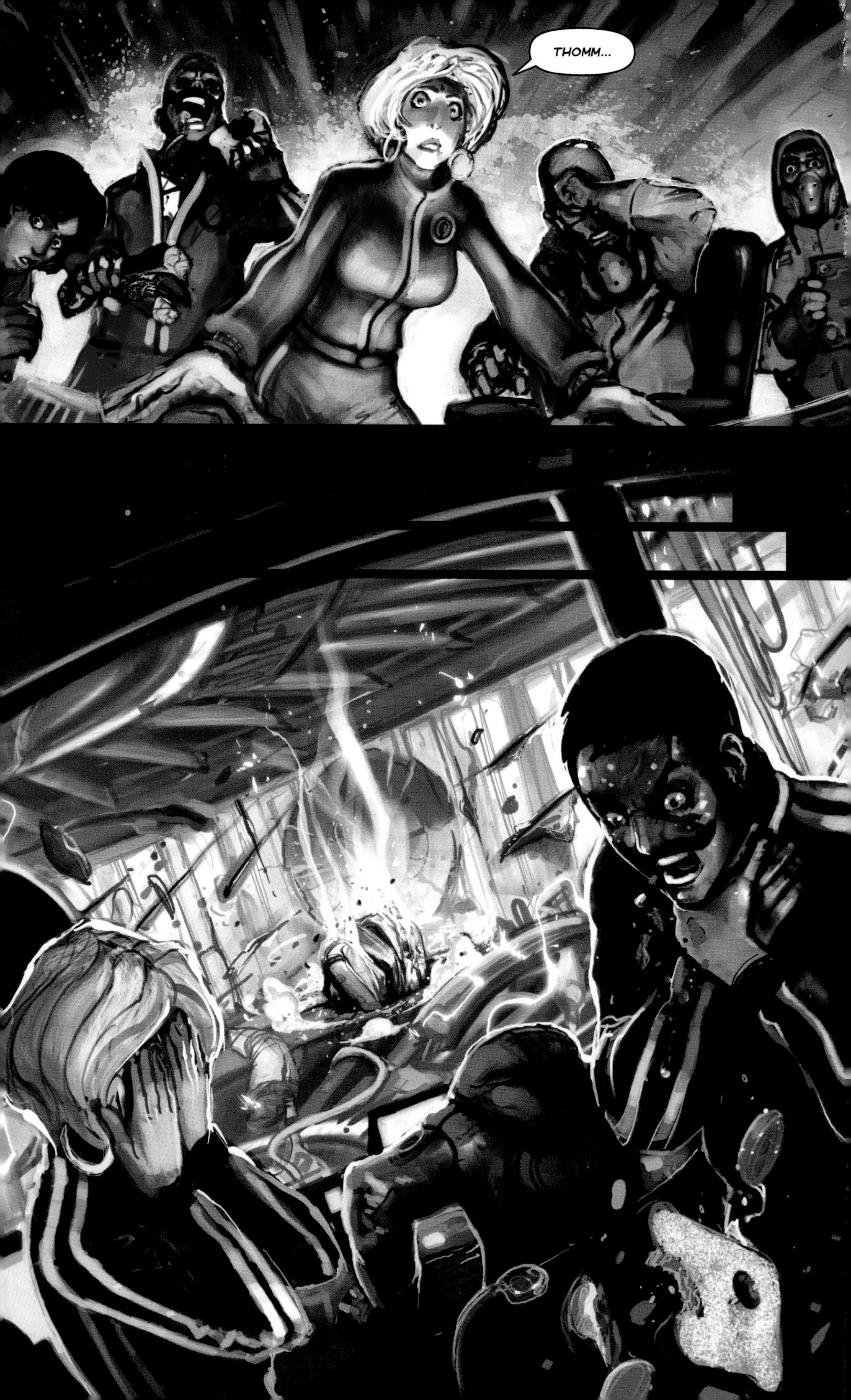
THOMM...

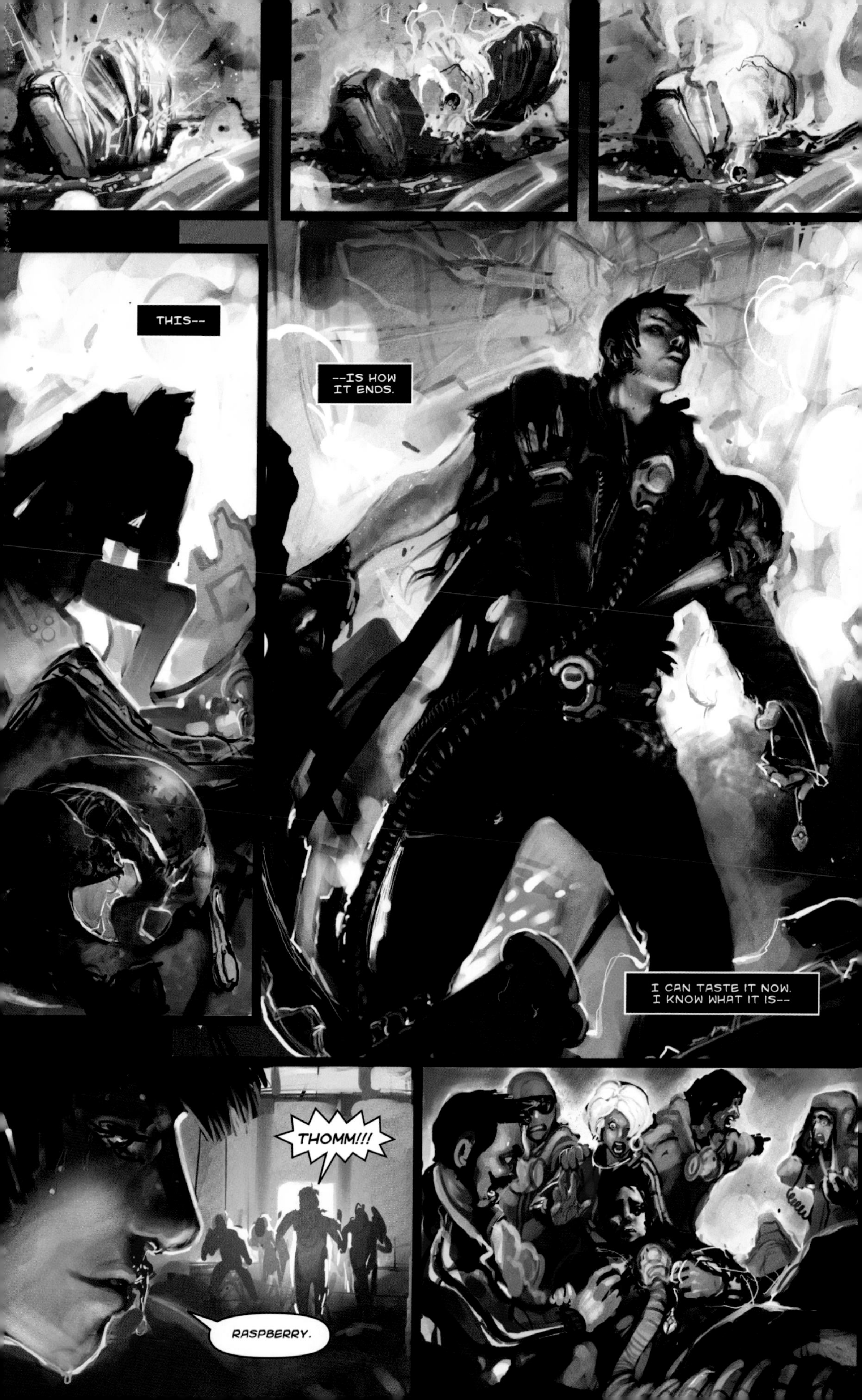
THIS--
--IS HOW IT ENDS.
I CAN TASTE IT NOW. I KNOW WHAT IT IS--
THOMM!!!
RASPBERRY.

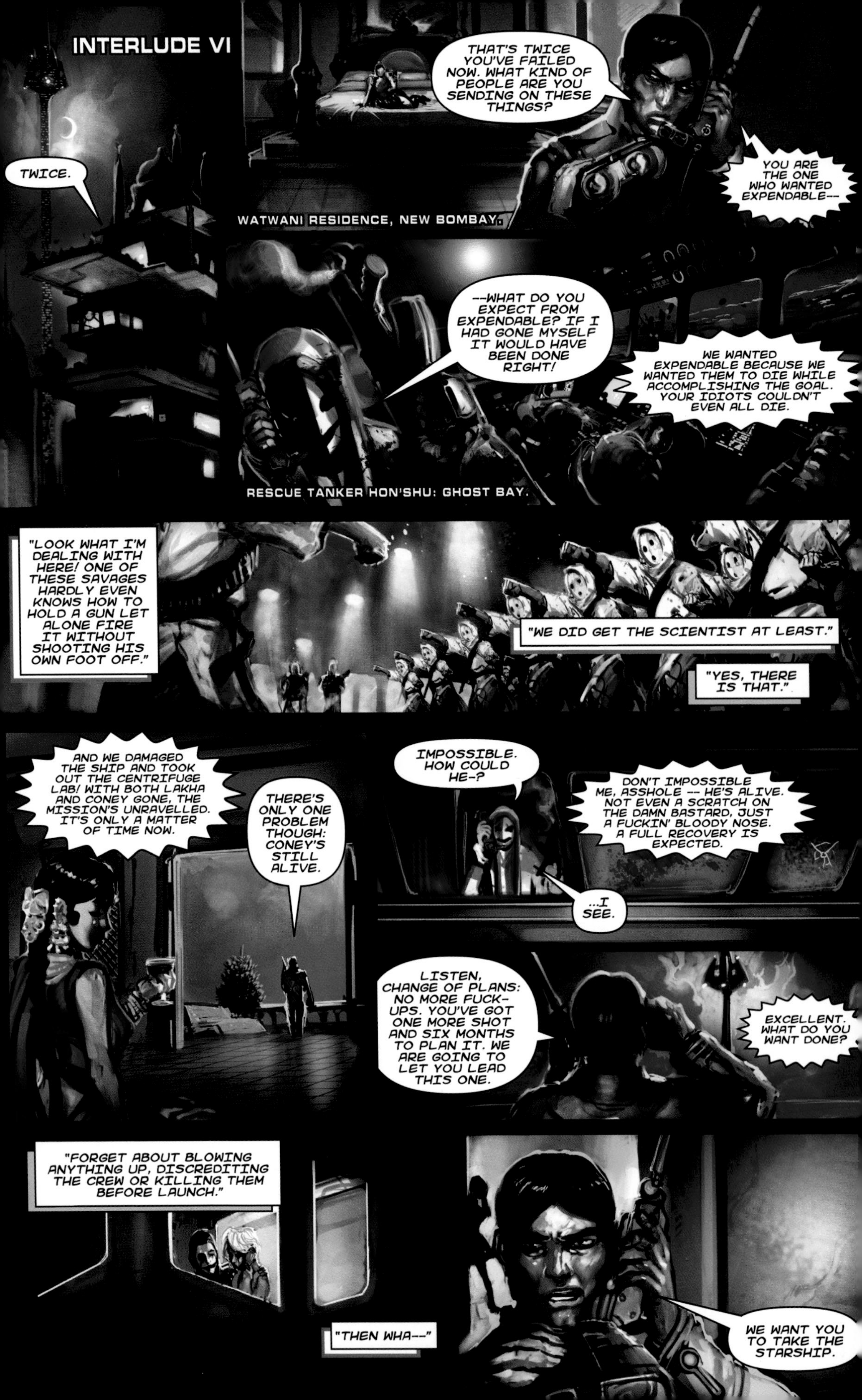
INTERLUDE VI
THAT'S TWICE YOU'VE FAILED NOW. WHAT KIND OF PEOPLE ARE YOU SENDING ON THESE THINGS?
TWICE.
YOU ARE THE ONE WHO WANTED EXPENDABLE--
WATWANI RESIDENCE, NEW BOMBAY.
--WHAT DO YOU EXPECT FROM EXPENDABLE? IF I HAD GONE MYSELF IT WOULD HAVE BEEN DONE RIGHT!
WE WANTED EXPENDABLE BECAUSE WE WANTED THEM TO DIE WHILE ACCOMPLISHING THE GOAL. YOUR IDIOTS COULDN'T EVEN ALL DIE.
RESCUE TANKER HON'SHU: GHOST BAY.
"LOOK WHAT I'M DEALING WITH HERE! ONE OF THESE SAVAGES HARDLY EVEN KNOWS HOW TO HOLD A GUN LET ALONE FIRE IT WITHOUT SHOOTING HIS OWN FOOT OFF."
"WE DID GET THE SCIENTIST AT LEAST."
"YES, THERE IS THAT."
AND WE DAMAGED THE SHIP AND TOOK OUT THE CENTRIFUGE LAB! WITH BOTH LAKHA AND CONEY GONE, THE MISSION'S UNRAVELLED. IT'S ONLY A MATTER OF TIME NOW.
THERE'S ONLY ONE PROBLEM THOUGH: CONEY'S STILL ALIVE.
IMPOSSIBLE. HOW COULD HE-?
DON'T IMPOSSIBLE ME, ASSHOLE -- HE'S ALIVE. NOT EVEN A SCRATCH ON THE DAMN BASTARD, JUST A FUCKIN' BLOODY NOSE. A FULL RECOVERY IS EXPECTED.
...I SEE.
LISTEN, CHANGE OF PLANS: NO MORE FUCK-UPS. YOU'VE GOT ONE MORE SHOT AND SIX MONTHS TO PLAN IT. WE ARE GOING TO LET YOU LEAD THIS ONE.
EXCELLENT. WHAT DO YOU WANT DONE?
"FORGET ABOUT BLOWING ANYTHING UP, DISCREDITING THE CREW OR KILLING THEM BEFORE LAUNCH."
"THEN WHA--"
WE WANT YOU TO TAKE THE STARSHIP.

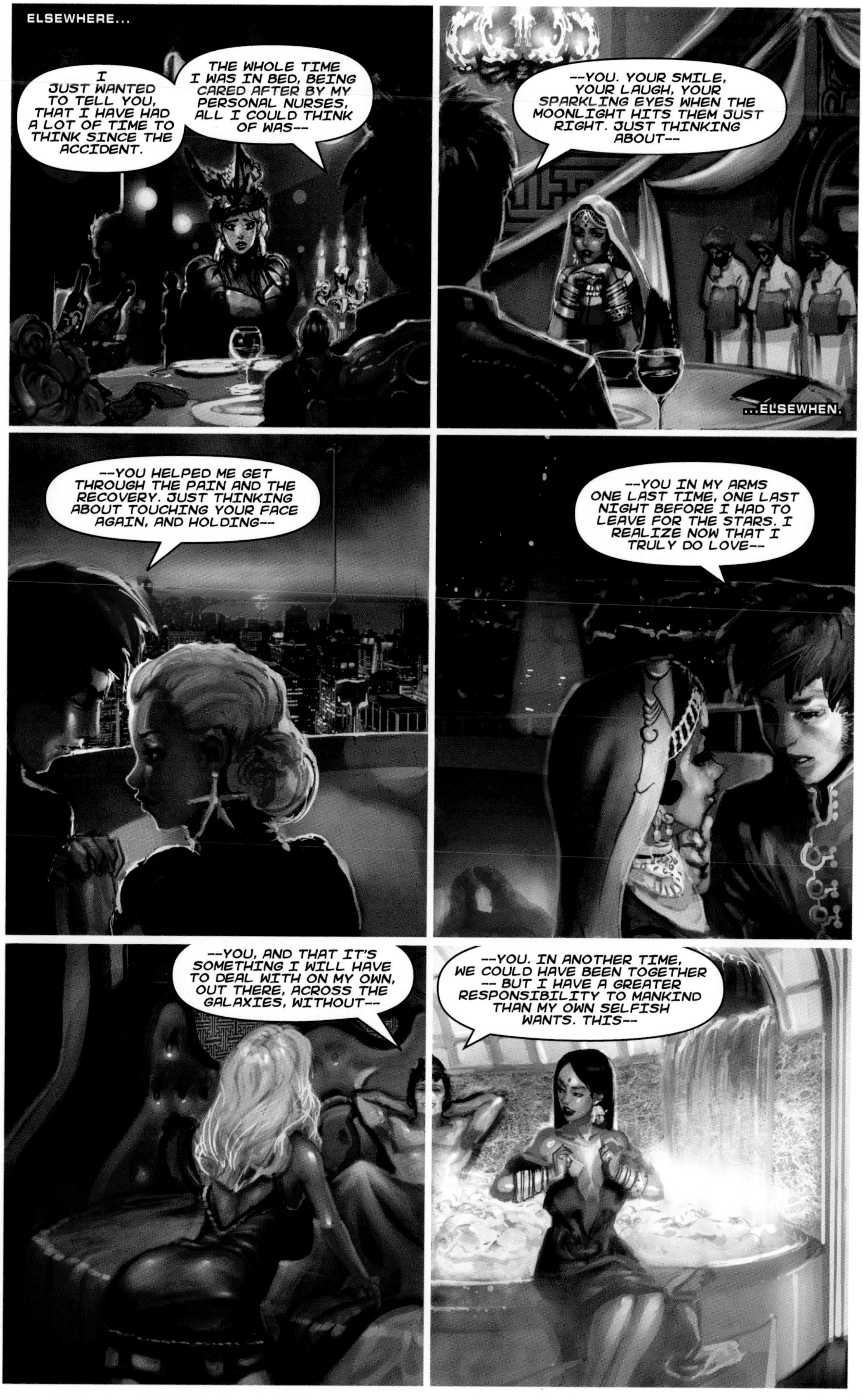
ELSEWHERE...
I JUST WANTED TO TELL YOU, THAT I HAVE HAD A LOT OF TIME TO THINK SINCE THE ACCIDENT.
THE WHOLE TIME I WAS IN BED, BEING CARED AFTER BY MY PERSONAL NURSES, ALL I COULD THINK OF WAS--
--YOU. YOUR SMILE, YOUR LAUGH, YOUR SPARKLING EYES WHEN THE MOONLIGHT HITS THEM JUST RIGHT. JUST THINKING ABOUT--
...ELSEWHEN.
--YOU HELPED ME GET THROUGH THE PAIN AND THE RECOVERY. JUST THINKING ABOUT TOUCHING YOUR FACE AGAIN, AND HOLDING--
--YOU IN MY ARMS ONE LAST TIME, ONE LAST NIGHT BEFORE I HAD TO LEAVE FOR THE STARS. I REALIZE NOW THAT I TRULY DO LOVE--
--YOU, AND THAT IT'S SOMETHING I WILL HAVE TO DEAL WITH ON MY OWN, OUT THERE, ACROSS THE GALAXIES, WITHOUT--
--YOU. IN ANOTHER TIME, WE COULD HAVE BEEN TOGETHER -- BUT I HAVE A GREATER RESPONSIBILITY TO MANKIND THAN MY OWN SELFISH WANTS. THIS--

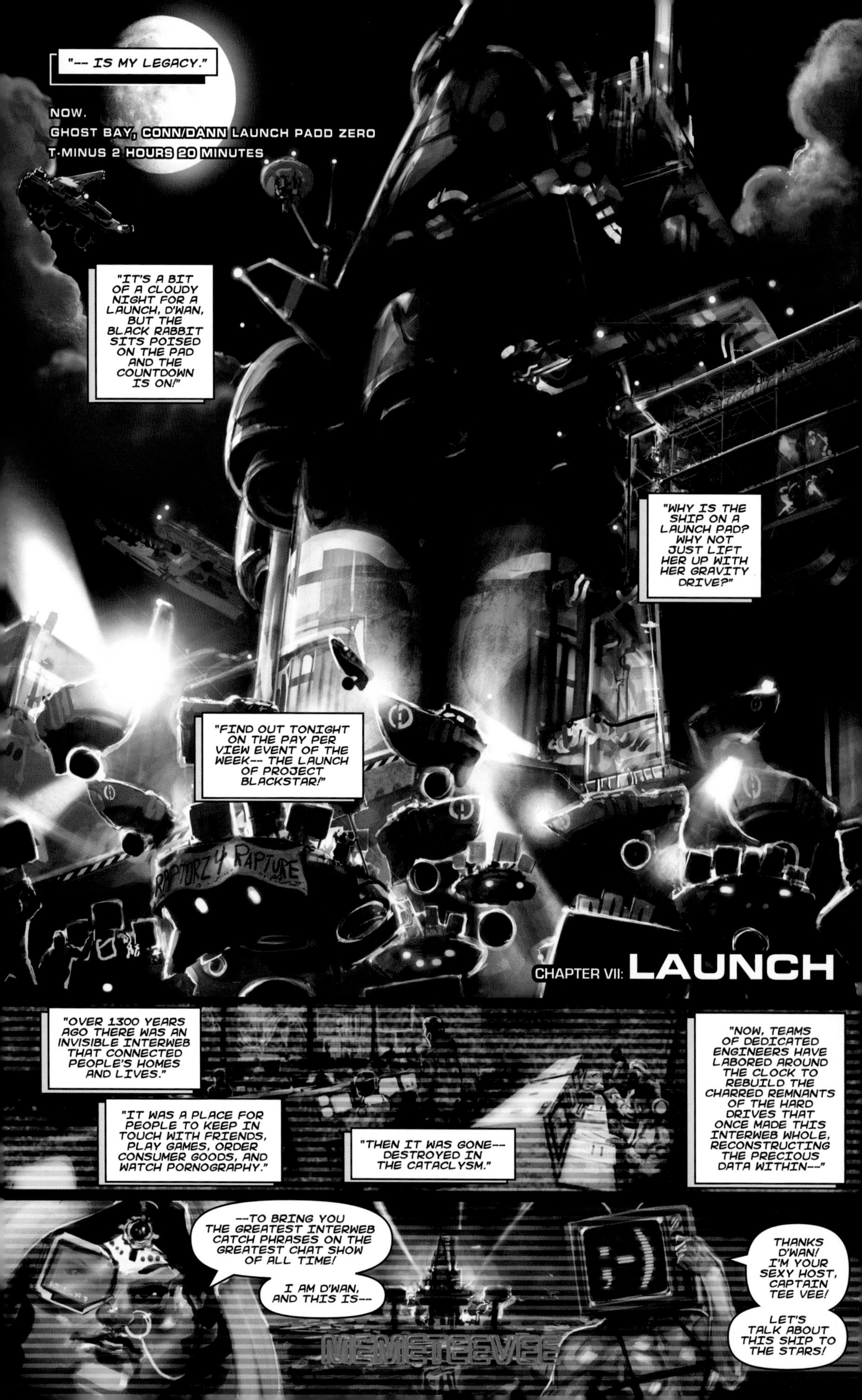

"-- IS MY LEGACY."
NOW.
GHOST BAY, CONN/DANN LAUNCH PADD ZERO
T-MINUS 2 HOURS 20 MINUTES
"IT'S A BIT OF A CLOUDY NIGHT FOR A LAUNCH, D'WAN, BUT THE BLACK RABBIT SITS POISED ON THE PAD AND THE COUNTDOWN IS ON!"
"WHY IS THE SHIP ON A LAUNCH PAD? WHY NOT JUST LIFT HER UP WITH HER GRAVITY DRIVE?"
"FIND OUT TONIGHT ON THE PAY PER VIEW EVENT OF THE WEEK-- THE LAUNCH OF PROJECT BLACKSTAR!"
RAPTURZ 4 RAPTURE
CHAPTER VII: LAUNCH
"OVER 1300 YEARS AGO THERE WAS AN INVISIBLE INTERWEB THAT CONNECTED PEOPLE'S HOMES AND LIVES."
"IT WAS A PLACE FOR PEOPLE TO KEEP IN TOUCH WITH FRIENDS, PLAY GAMES, ORDER CONSUMER GOODS, AND WATCH PORNOGRAPHY."
"THEN IT WAS GONE-- DESTROYED IN THE CATACLYSM."
"NOW, TEAMS OF DEDICATED ENGINEERS HAVE LABORED AROUND THE CLOCK TO REBUILD THE CHARRED REMNANTS OF THE HARD DRIVES THAT ONCE MADE THIS INTERWEB WHOLE, RECONSTRUCTING THE PRECIOUS DATA WITHIN--"
--TO BRING YOU THE GREATEST INTERWEB CATCH PHRASES ON THE GREATEST CHAT SHOW OF ALL TIME!
I AM D'WAN, AND THIS IS--
MEMETEEVEE
THANKS D'WAN! I'M YOUR SEXY HOST, CAPTAIN TEE VEE!
LET'S TALK ABOUT THIS SHIP TO THE STARS!

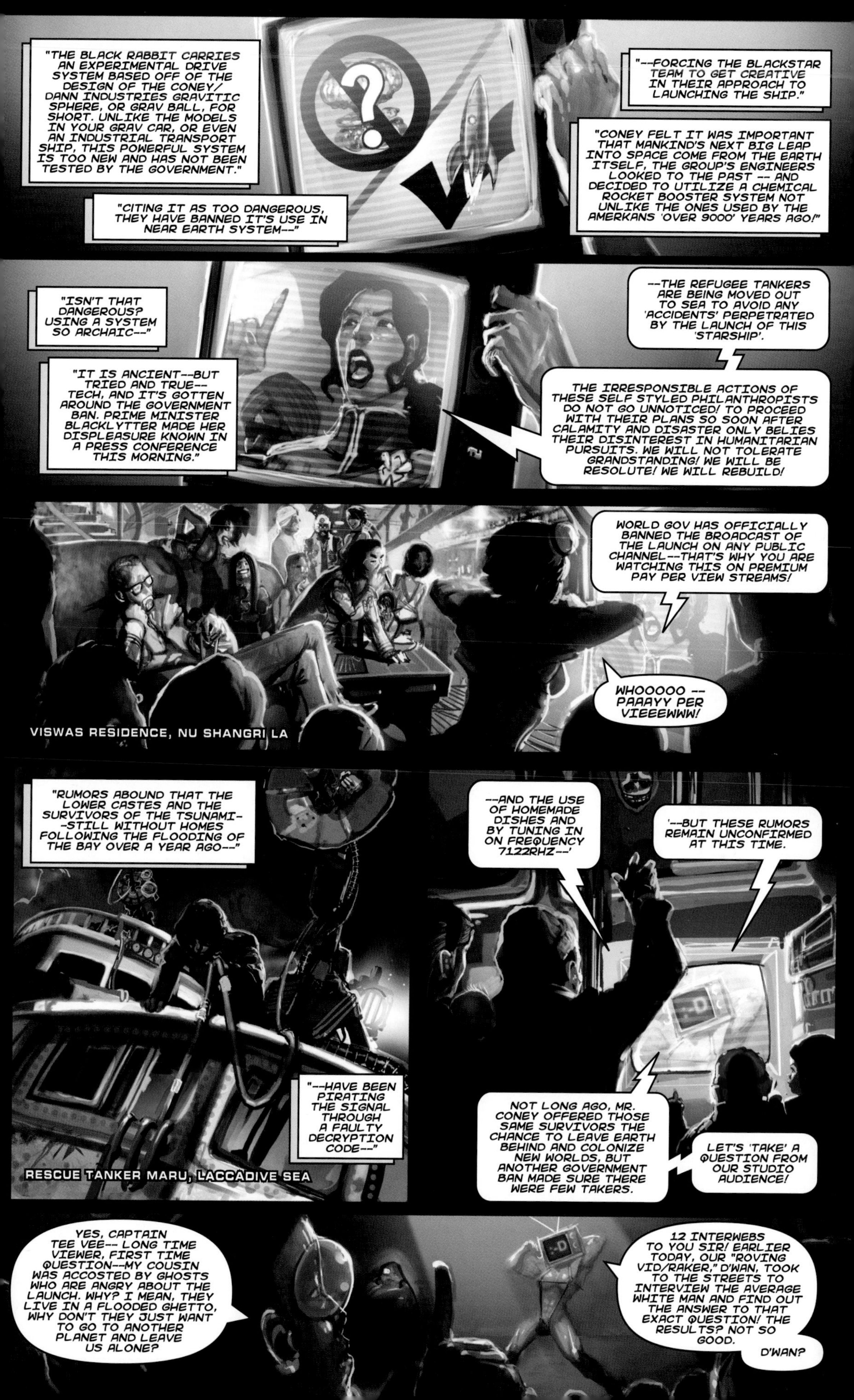
"THE BLACK RABBIT CARRIES AN EXPERIMENTAL DRIVE SYSTEM BASED OFF OF THE DESIGN OF THE CONEY/ DANN INDUSTRIES GRAVITIC SPHERE, OR GRAV BALL, FOR SHORT. UNLIKE THE MODELS IN YOUR GRAV CAR, OR EVEN AN INDUSTRIAL TRANSPORT SHIP, THIS POWERFUL SYSTEM IS TOO NEW AND HAS NOT BEEN TESTED BY THE GOVERNMENT."
"CITING IT AS TOO DANGEROUS, THEY HAVE BANNED IT'S USE IN NEAR EARTH SYSTEM--"
"--FORCING THE BLACKSTAR TEAM TO GET CREATIVE IN THEIR APPROACH TO LAUNCHING THE SHIP."
"CONEY FELT IT WAS IMPORTANT THAT MANKIND'S NEXT BIG LEAP INTO SPACE COME FROM THE EARTH ITSELF, THE GROUP'S ENGINEERS LOOKED TO THE PAST -- AND DECIDED TO UTILIZE A CHEMICAL ROCKET BOOSTER SYSTEM NOT UNLIKE THE ONES USED BY THE AMERKANS 'OVER 9000' YEARS AGO!"
"ISN'T THAT DANGEROUS? USING A SYSTEM SO ARCHAIC--"
"IT IS ANCIENT--BUT TRIED AND TRUE-- TECH, AND IT'S GOTTEN AROUND THE GOVERNMENT BAN. PRIME MINISTER BLACKLYTTER MADE HER DISPLEASURE KNOWN IN A PRESS CONFERENCE THIS MORNING."
--THE REFUGEE TANKERS ARE BEING MOVED OUT TO SEA TO AVOID ANY 'ACCIDENTS' PERPETRATED BY THE LAUNCH OF THIS 'STARSHIP'.
THE IRRESPONSIBLE ACTIONS OF THESE SELF STYLED PHILANTHROPISTS DO NOT GO UNNOTICED! TO PROCEED WITH THEIR PLANS SO SOON AFTER CALAMITY AND DISASTER ONLY BELIES THEIR DISINTEREST IN HUMANITARIAN PURSUITS. WE WILL NOT TOLERATE GRANDSTANDING! WE WILL BE RESOLUTE! WE WILL REBUILD!
WORLD GOV HAS OFFICIALLY BANNED THE BROADCAST OF THE LAUNCH ON ANY PUBLIC CHANNEL--THAT'S WHY YOU ARE WATCHING THIS ON PREMIUM PAY PER VIEW STREAMS!
WHOOOOO -- PAAAYY PER VIEEEWWW!
VISWAS RESIDENCE, NU SHANGRI LA
"RUMORS ABOUND THAT THE LOWER CASTES AND THE SURVIVORS OF THE TSUNAMI- -STILL WITHOUT HOMES FOLLOWING THE FLOODING OF THE BAY OVER A YEAR AGO--"
"--HAVE BEEN PIRATING THE SIGNAL THROUGH A FAULTY DECRYPTION CODE--"
RESCUE TANKER MARU, LACCADIVE SEA
--AND THE USE OF HOMEMADE DISHES AND BY TUNING IN ON FREQUENCY 7122RHZ--'
'--BUT THESE RUMORS REMAIN UNCONFIRMED AT THIS TIME.
NOT LONG AGO, MR. CONEY OFFERED THOSE SAME SURVIVORS THE CHANCE TO LEAVE EARTH BEHIND AND COLONIZE NEW WORLDS, BUT ANOTHER GOVERNMENT BAN MADE SURE THERE WERE FEW TAKERS.
LET'S 'TAKE' A QUESTION FROM OUR STUDIO AUDIENCE!
YES, CAPTAIN TEE VEE-- LONG TIME VIEWER, FIRST TIME QUESTION--MY COUSIN WAS ACCOSTED BY GHOSTS WHO ARE ANGRY ABOUT THE LAUNCH. WHY? I MEAN, THEY LIVE IN A FLOODED GHETTO, WHY DON'T THEY JUST WANT TO GO TO ANOTHER PLANET AND LEAVE US ALONE?
12 INTERWEBS TO YOU SIR! EARLIER TODAY, OUR "ROVING VID/RAKER," D'WAN, TOOK TO THE STREETS TO INTERVIEW THE AVERAGE WHITE MAN AND FIND OUT THE ANSWER TO THAT EXACT QUESTION! THE RESULTS? NOT SO GOOD.
D'WAN?

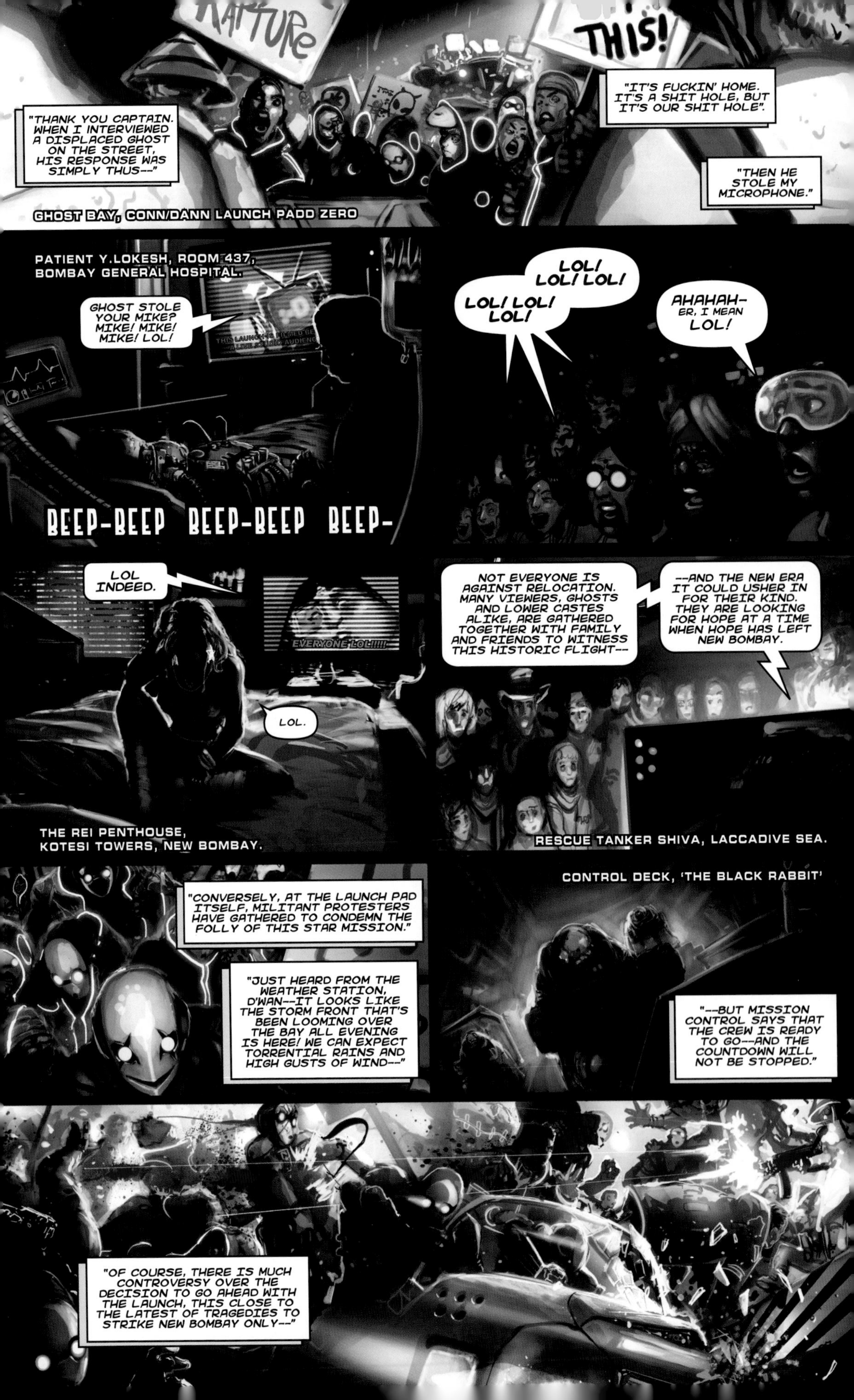

RAPTURE
THIS!
"THANK YOU CAPTAIN. WHEN I INTERVIEWED A DISPLACED GHOST ON THE STREET, HIS RESPONSE WAS SIMPLY THUS--"
"IT'S FUCKIN' HOME. IT'S A SHIT HOLE, BUT IT'S OUR SHIT HOLE".
"THEN HE STOLE MY MICROPHONE."
GHOST BAY, CONN/DANN LAUNCH PADD ZERO
PATIENT Y.LOKESH, ROOM 437, BOMBAY GENERAL HOSPITAL.
GHOST STOLE YOUR MIKE? MIKE! MIKE! MIKE! LOL!
BEEP-BEEP BEEP-BEEP BEEP-
LOL! LOL! LOL!
LOL! LOL! LOL!
AHAHAH- ER, I MEAN LOL!
LOL INDEED.
EVERYONE LOL!!!!!
LOL.
THE REI PENTHOUSE, KOTESI TOWERS, NEW BOMBAY.
NOT EVERYONE IS AGAINST RELOCATION. MANY VIEWERS, GHOSTS AND LOWER CASTES ALIKE, ARE GATHERED TOGETHER WITH FAMILY AND FRIENDS TO WITNESS THIS HISTORIC FLIGHT--
--AND THE NEW ERA IT COULD USHER IN FOR THEIR KIND. THEY ARE LOOKING FOR HOPE AT A TIME WHEN HOPE HAS LEFT NEW BOMBAY.
RESCUE TANKER SHIVA, LACCADIVE SEA.
"CONVERSELY, AT THE LAUNCH PAD ITSELF, MILITANT PROTESTERS HAVE GATHERED TO CONDEMN THE FOLLY OF THIS STAR MISSION."
"JUST HEARD FROM THE WEATHER STATION, D'WAN--IT LOOKS LIKE THE STORM FRONT THAT'S BEEN LOOMING OVER THE BAY ALL EVENING IS HERE! WE CAN EXPECT TORRENTIAL RAINS AND HIGH GUSTS OF WIND--"
CONTROL DECK, 'THE BLACK RABBIT'
"--BUT MISSION CONTROL SAYS THAT THE CREW IS READY TO GO--AND THE COUNTDOWN WILL NOT BE STOPPED."
"OF COURSE, THERE IS MUCH CONTROVERSY OVER THE DECISION TO GO AHEAD WITH THE LAUNCH, THIS CLOSE TO THE LATEST OF TRAGEDIES TO STRIKE NEW BOMBAY ONLY--"

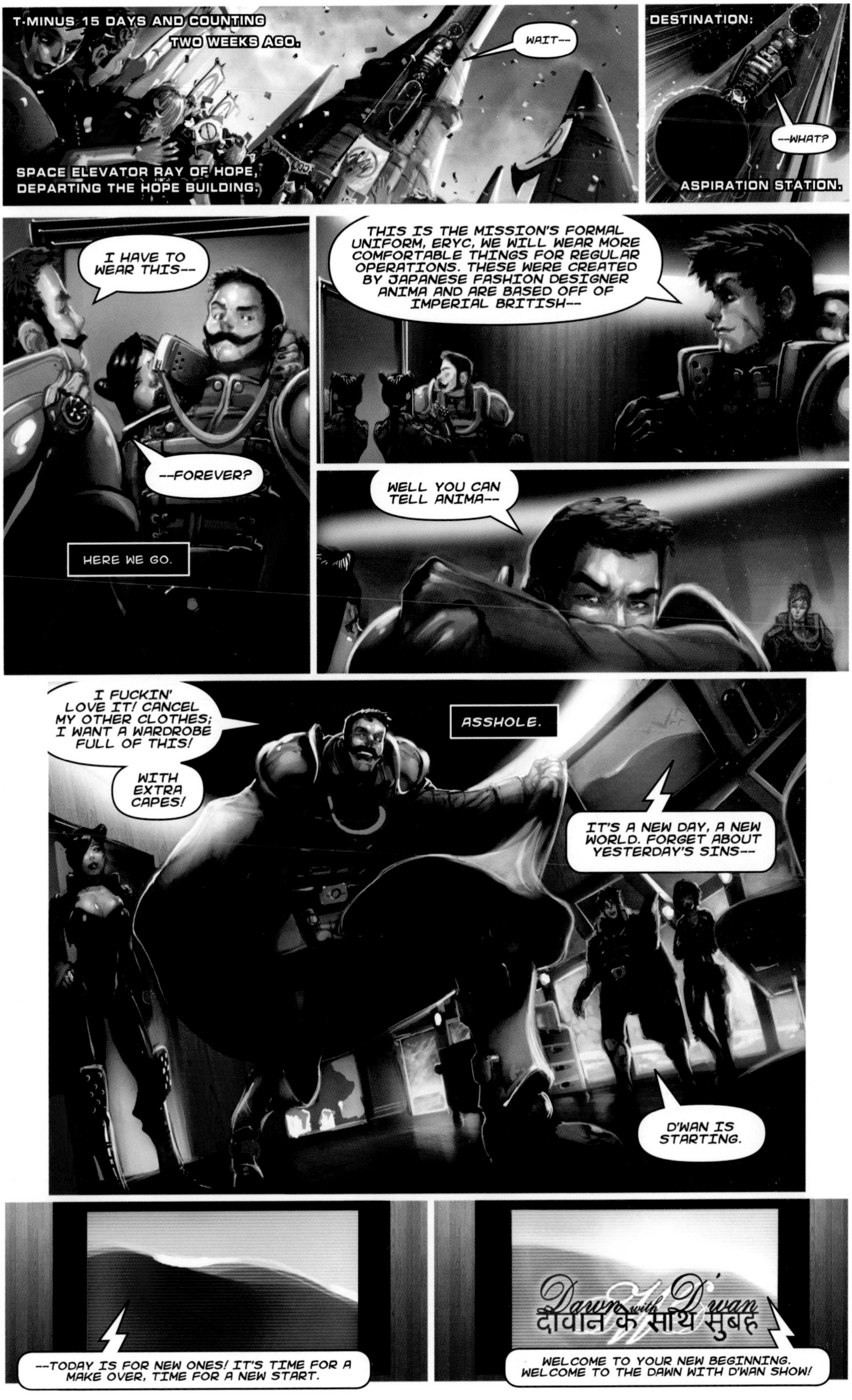
T-MINUS 15 DAYS AND COUNTING
TWO WEEKS AGO.
WAIT--
SPACE ELEVATOR RAY OF HOPE, DEPARTING THE HOPE BUILDING.
DESTINATION:
--WHAT?
ASPIRATION STATION.
I HAVE TO WEAR THIS--
--FOREVER?
HERE WE GO.
THIS IS THE MISSION'S FORMAL UNIFORM, ERYC, WE WILL WEAR MORE COMFORTABLE THINGS FOR REGULAR OPERATIONS. THESE WERE CREATED BY JAPANESE FASHION DESIGNER ANIMA AND ARE BASED OFF OF IMPERIAL BRITISH--
WELL YOU CAN TELL ANIMA--
I FUCKIN' LOVE IT! CANCEL MY OTHER CLOTHES; I WANT A WARDROBE FULL OF THIS!
WITH EXTRA CAPES!
ASSHOLE.
IT'S A NEW DAY, A NEW WORLD. FORGET ABOUT YESTERDAY'S SINS--
D'WAN IS STARTING.
--TODAY IS FOR NEW ONES! IT'S TIME FOR A MAKE OVER, TIME FOR A NEW START.
Dawn with D'wan
दीवान के साथ सुबह
WELCOME TO YOUR NEW BEGINNING. WELCOME TO THE DAWN WITH D'WAN SHOW!

FIRST, TODAY WE NEED TO TALK ABOUT A SERIOUS ISSUE THAT IS VERY SERIOUS-- THE UPCOMING ONE YEAR ANNIVERSARY OF THE FLOODING OF THE GHOST QUARTER.

ONE YEAR AGO A TSUNAMI OF UNKNOWN ORIGINS SLAMMED INTO THE WESTERN SEABOARD, OVERPOWERING THE LEVEE WHICH HAS KEPT THE GHOST QUARTER SAFE FOR THE PAST 400 YEARS. COUNTLESS WHITES WERE KILLED, AND THE SLUM WAS TRANSFORMED INTO A BAY.

WELCOME TO MY SHOW, AND MY GLORIOUS BODY-- BUT WE CAN GET INTO THAT LATER!

1178kg

LAUGH हंसो

HAHAHA

IT'S REALLY EASY TO JUST THINK BAD THINGS HAPPEN TO BAD PEOPLE-- BUT WHEN I THINK ABOUT THOSE POOR WHITE PEOPLE I GET VERY UPSET AND SAD, AND SO SHOULD YOU!

I MEAN, DESPITE THE FACT THAT GHOSTS ARE A BURDEN ON OUR SOCIETY, AND THAT THEY ARE RESPONSIBLE FOR 90% OF CRIMES IN THE COMMUNITY-- NOT ALL OF THEM ARE BAD!

MY SERVANTS ARE ALL GHOSTS, AND I EVEN HAVE A WHITE FRIEND!

"SO IT MAKES ME HAPPY TO KNOW THAT THE ONE-YEAR CEREMONY WILL SEE THOMM CONEY REVEAL THE PLANS TO HOPE ISLAND AND CABLE CITY, --AN EXPANSION OF HIS FAMILY'S HOPE BUILDING CONCEPT THAT WILL INCLUDE FREE HOUSING FOR THOSE HOMELESS, AS WELL AS PROVIDE SPACE TRAINING TO THOSE WHO WISH TO BECOME PART OF HIS OUTSYSTEM PROGRAM."

"'OUTSYSTEM' WILL FOLLOW PROJECT BLACKSTAR'S EXPLORATION OF THE STARS, SEEDING WHITE AND LOWER CASTE COLONIES ON NEW PLANETS. HOLDING A SPECIAL SERVICE IN GEOSYNCHRONOUS ORBIT OVER NEW BOMBAY AT ASPIRATION STATION."

ASPIRATION STATION

ELEVATOR CABLE

HOPE

NEW BOMBAY

"CONEY AND THE COMMAND CREW OF PROJECT BLACKSTAR ARE GOING TO DO A PRESS CONFERENCE ON THE ORBITING PLATFORM IN THEIR FULL UNIFORM REGALIA!"

ELEVATOR CABLE

HOPE BUILDING

FINANCIAL DISTRICT

FORMER LEVEE

CABLE CITY PROJECT

HOPE ISLAND PROJECT

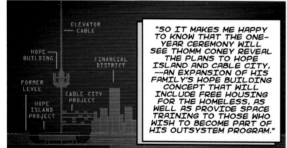

LUCKY GUESTS FROM NEW BOMBAY LEFT EARLY THIS MORNING ON A THREE DAY JOURNEY UP TO ASPIRATION VIA SPACE ELEVATOR ALONG WITH CONEY AND KARTONEAS!

THESE LUCKY LOTTERY WINNERS GET TO FIND OUT DETAILS OF BLACKSTAR MISSION, OUTSYSTEM, AND HOPE ISLAND FIRST HAND.

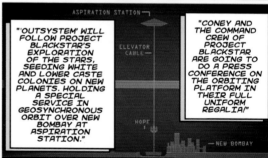

OM NOM NOM!

"WE NEED TO TALK."

BUSY. INITIATING NEW RECRUITS.

SHUT UP AND PUT ON THE NEWS.

RTE G7
JCTN 7E

WATWANI LIMOUSINE, ROUTE G7, NEW BOMBAY

"THOSE SAME GUESTS WILL BE THE FIRST TO SEE A NEWLY COMPLETED YAKSHAGANA OF OUR NATIONAL EPIC, THE MAHABHARATA, STARRING DALAJA FALGUNI AND CHAHEL GAGAN! THE FULL DRAMA IS COMPILED FROM NEWLY RECONSTRUCTED DATA FROM THE ANCIENT INTERWEBS!"

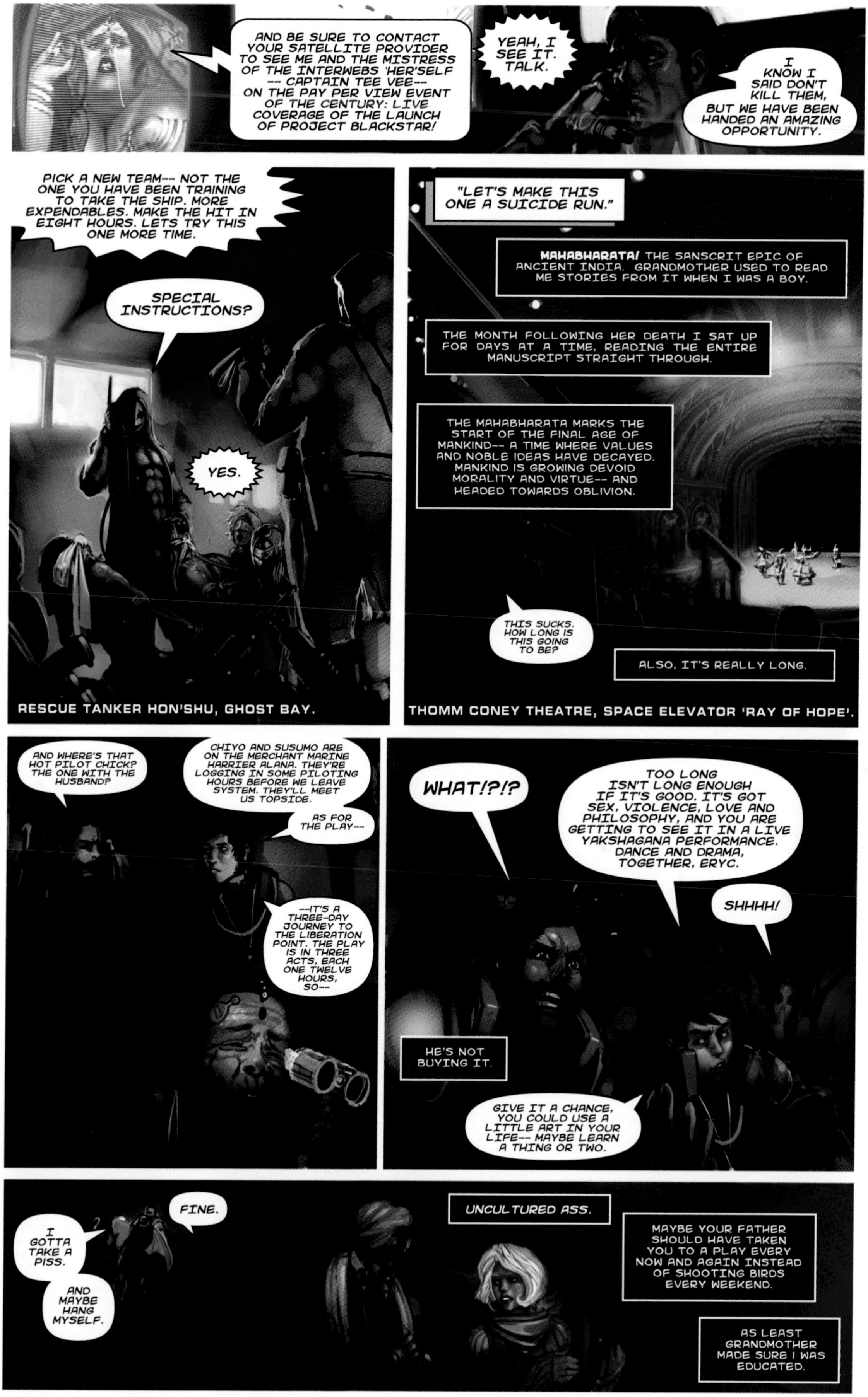

AND BE SURE TO CONTACT YOUR SATELLITE PROVIDER TO SEE ME AND THE MISTRESS OF THE INTERWEBS 'HER'SELF -- CAPTAIN TEE VEE-- ON THE PAY PER VIEW EVENT OF THE CENTURY: LIVE COVERAGE OF THE LAUNCH OF PROJECT BLACKSTAR!
YEAH, I SEE IT. TALK.
I KNOW I SAID DON'T KILL THEM, BUT WE HAVE BEEN HANDED AN AMAZING OPPORTUNITY.
PICK A NEW TEAM-- NOT THE ONE YOU HAVE BEEN TRAINING TO TAKE THE SHIP. MORE EXPENDABLES. MAKE THE HIT IN EIGHT HOURS. LETS TRY THIS ONE MORE TIME.
SPECIAL INSTRUCTIONS?
YES.
RESCUE TANKER HON'SHU, GHOST BAY.
"LET'S MAKE THIS ONE A SUICIDE RUN."
MAHABHARATA! THE SANSCRIT EPIC OF ANCIENT INDIA. GRANDMOTHER USED TO READ ME STORIES FROM IT WHEN I WAS A BOY.
THE MONTH FOLLOWING HER DEATH I SAT UP FOR DAYS AT A TIME, READING THE ENTIRE MANUSCRIPT STRAIGHT THROUGH.
THE MAHABHARATA MARKS THE START OF THE FINAL AGE OF MANKIND-- A TIME WHERE VALUES AND NOBLE IDEAS HAVE DECAYED. MANKIND IS GROWING DEVOID MORALITY AND VIRTUE-- AND HEADED TOWARDS OBLIVION.
THIS SUCKS. HOW LONG IS THIS GOING TO BE?
ALSO, IT'S REALLY LONG.
THOMM CONEY THEATRE, SPACE ELEVATOR 'RAY OF HOPE'.
AND WHERE'S THAT HOT PILOT CHICK? THE ONE WITH THE HUSBAND?
CHIYO AND SUSUMO ARE ON THE MERCHANT MARINE HARRIER ALANA. THEY'RE LOGGING IN SOME PILOTING HOURS BEFORE WE LEAVE SYSTEM. THEY'LL MEET US TOPSIDE.
AS FOR THE PLAY--
--IT'S A THREE-DAY JOURNEY TO THE LIBERATION POINT. THE PLAY IS IN THREE ACTS, EACH ONE TWELVE HOURS, SO--
WHAT!?!?
TOO LONG ISN'T LONG ENOUGH IF IT'S GOOD. IT'S GOT SEX, VIOLENCE, LOVE AND PHILOSOPHY, AND YOU ARE GETTING TO SEE IT IN A LIVE YAKSHAGANA PERFORMANCE. DANCE AND DRAMA, TOGETHER, ERYC.
SHHHH!
HE'S NOT BUYING IT.
GIVE IT A CHANCE, YOU COULD USE A LITTLE ART IN YOUR LIFE-- MAYBE LEARN A THING OR TWO.
I GOTTA TAKE A PISS.
FINE.
AND MAYBE HANG MYSELF.
UNCULTURED ASS.
MAYBE YOUR FATHER SHOULD HAVE TAKEN YOU TO A PLAY EVERY NOW AND AGAIN INSTEAD OF SHOOTING BIRDS EVERY WEEKEND.
AS LEAST GRANDMOTHER MADE SURE I WAS EDUCATED.

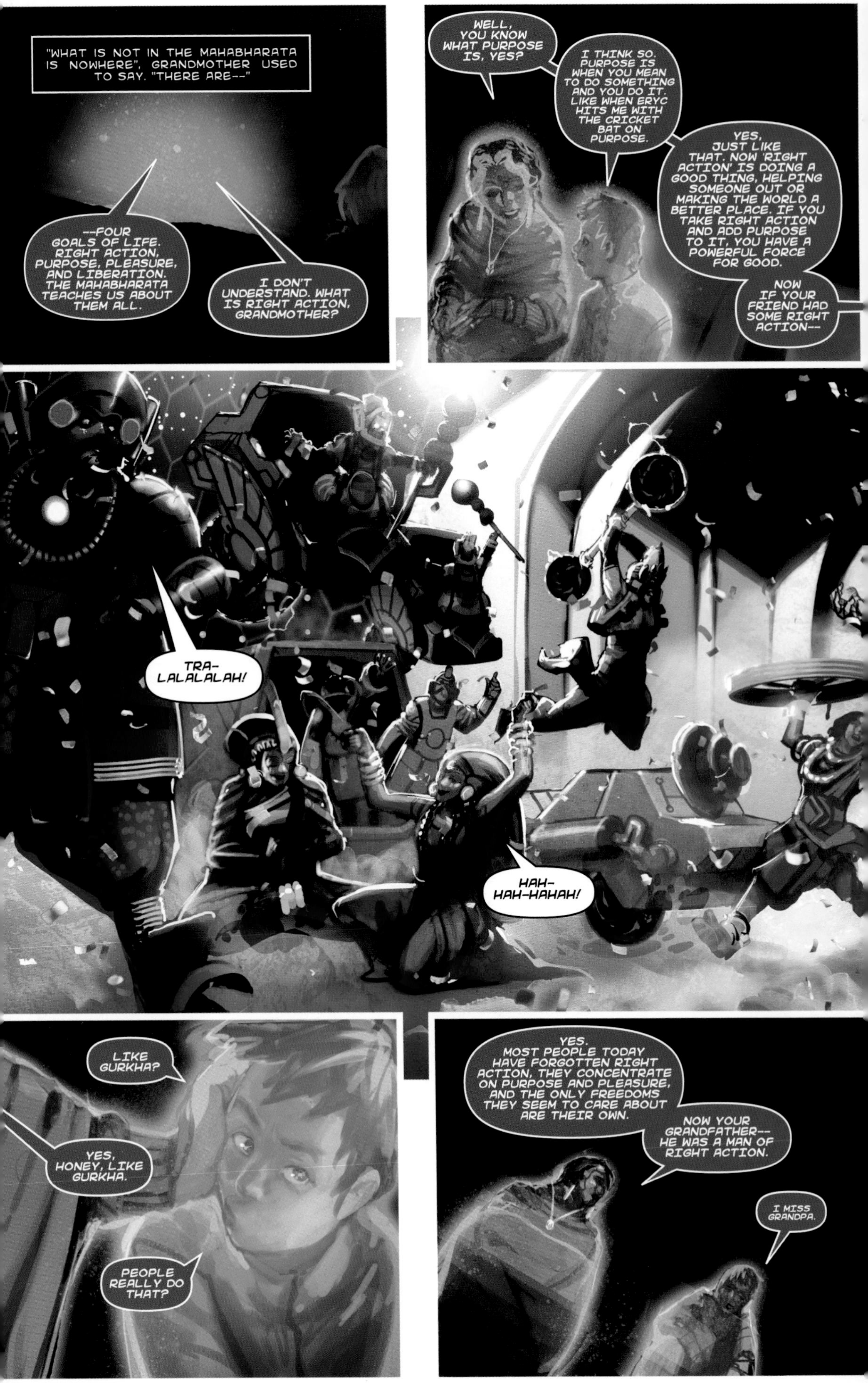
"WHAT IS NOT IN THE MAHABHARATA IS NOWHERE", GRANDMOTHER USED TO SAY. "THERE ARE--"
--FOUR GOALS OF LIFE. RIGHT ACTION, PURPOSE, PLEASURE, AND LIBERATION. THE MAHABHARATA TEACHES US ABOUT THEM ALL.
I DON'T UNDERSTAND. WHAT IS RIGHT ACTION, GRANDMOTHER?
WELL, YOU KNOW WHAT PURPOSE IS, YES?
I THINK SO. PURPOSE IS WHEN YOU MEAN TO DO SOMETHING AND YOU DO IT. LIKE WHEN ERYC HITS ME WITH THE CRICKET BAT ON PURPOSE.
YES, JUST LIKE THAT. NOW 'RIGHT ACTION' IS DOING A GOOD THING, HELPING SOMEONE OUT OR MAKING THE WORLD A BETTER PLACE. IF YOU TAKE RIGHT ACTION AND ADD PURPOSE TO IT, YOU HAVE A POWERFUL FORCE FOR GOOD.
NOW IF YOUR FRIEND HAD SOME RIGHT ACTION--
TRA-LALALALAH!
HAH-HAH-HAHAH!
LIKE GURKHA?
YES, HONEY, LIKE GURKHA.
PEOPLE REALLY DO THAT?
YES. MOST PEOPLE TODAY HAVE FORGOTTEN RIGHT ACTION, THEY CONCENTRATE ON PURPOSE AND PLEASURE, AND THE ONLY FREEDOMS THEY SEEM TO CARE ABOUT ARE THEIR OWN.
NOW YOUR GRANDFATHER--HE WAS A MAN OF RIGHT ACTION.
I MISS GRANDPA.

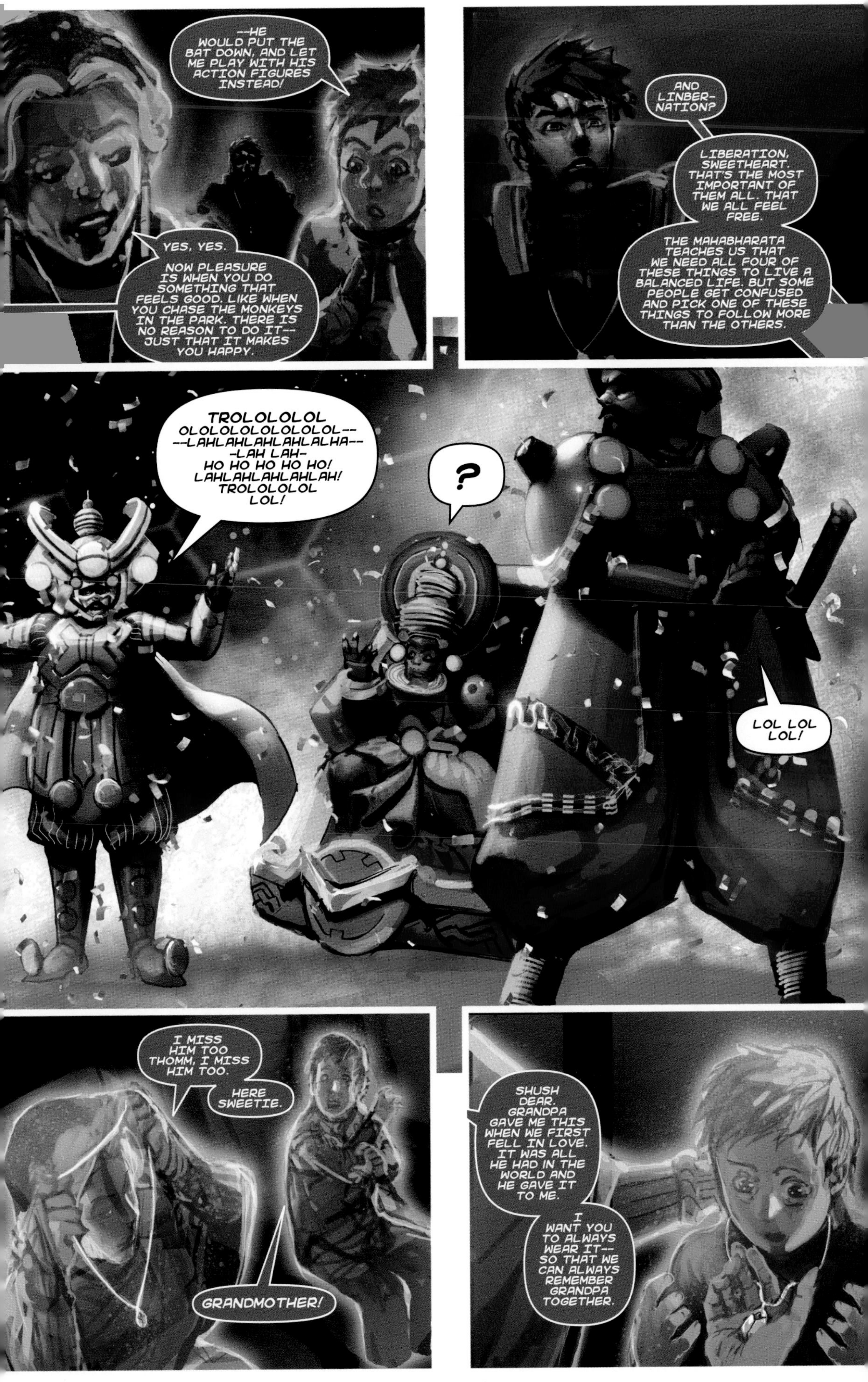
--HE WOULD PUT THE BAT DOWN, AND LET ME PLAY WITH HIS ACTION FIGURES INSTEAD!
YES, YES.
NOW PLEASURE IS WHEN YOU DO SOMETHING THAT FEELS GOOD. LIKE WHEN YOU CHASE THE MONKEYS IN THE PARK. THERE IS NO REASON TO DO IT--JUST THAT IT MAKES YOU HAPPY.
AND LINBER-NATION?
LIBERATION, SWEETHEART. THAT'S THE MOST IMPORTANT OF THEM ALL. THAT WE ALL FEEL FREE.
THE MAHABHARATA TEACHES US THAT WE NEED ALL FOUR OF THESE THINGS TO LIVE A BALANCED LIFE. BUT SOME PEOPLE GET CONFUSED AND PICK ONE OF THESE THINGS TO FOLLOW MORE THAN THE OTHERS.
TROLOLOLOL OLOLOLOLOLOLOLOL----LAHLAHLAHLAHLALHA---LAH LAH-HO HO HO HO HO! LAHLAHLAHLAHLAH! TROLOLOLOL LOL!
?
LOL LOL LOL!
I MISS HIM TOO THOMM, I MISS HIM TOO.
HERE SWEETIE.
GRANDMOTHER!
SHUSH DEAR. GRANDPA GAVE ME THIS WHEN WE FIRST FELL IN LOVE. IT WAS ALL HE HAD IN THE WORLD AND HE GAVE IT TO ME.
I WANT YOU TO ALWAYS WEAR IT--SO THAT WE CAN ALWAYS REMEMBER GRANDPA TOGETHER.

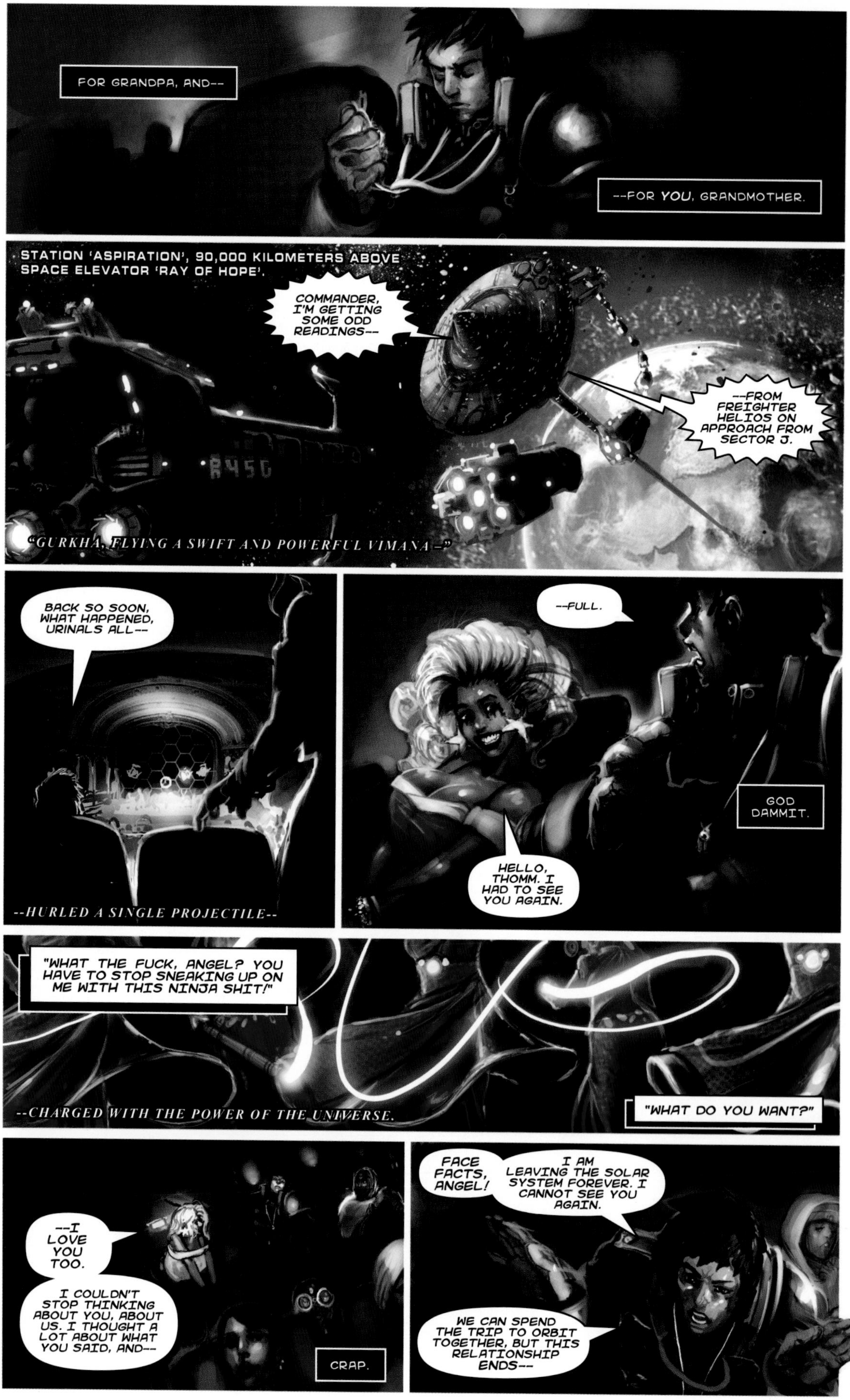
FOR GRANDPA, AND--
--FOR YOU, GRANDMOTHER.
STATION 'ASPIRATION', 90,000 KILOMETERS ABOVE SPACE ELEVATOR 'RAY OF HOPE'.
COMMANDER, I'M GETTING SOME ODD READINGS--
--FROM FREIGHTER HELIOS ON APPROACH FROM SECTOR J.
R45G
"GURKHA, FLYING A SWIFT AND POWERFUL VIMANA--"
BACK SO SOON, WHAT HAPPENED, URINALS ALL--
--HURLED A SINGLE PROJECTILE--
--FULL.
GOD DAMMIT.
HELLO, THOMM. I HAD TO SEE YOU AGAIN.
"WHAT THE FUCK, ANGEL? YOU HAVE TO STOP SNEAKING UP ON ME WITH THIS NINJA SHIT!"
--CHARGED WITH THE POWER OF THE UNIVERSE.
"WHAT DO YOU WANT?"
--I LOVE YOU TOO.
I COULDN'T STOP THINKING ABOUT YOU, ABOUT US. I THOUGHT A LOT ABOUT WHAT YOU SAID, AND--
CRAP.
FACE FACTS, ANGEL!
I AM LEAVING THE SOLAR SYSTEM FOREVER. I CANNOT SEE YOU AGAIN.
WE CAN SPEND THE TRIP TO ORBIT TOGETHER, BUT THIS RELATIONSHIP ENDS--

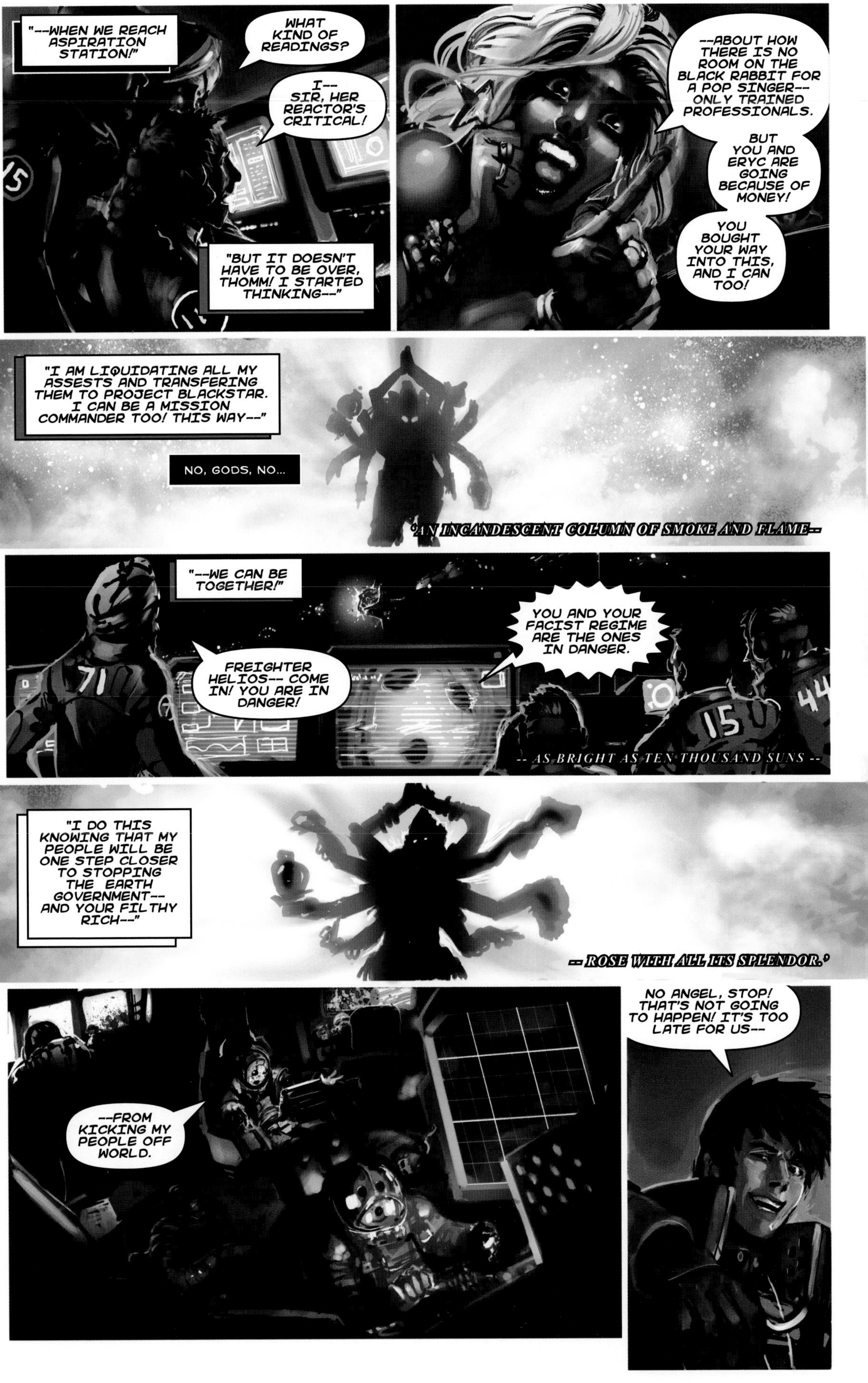
"--WHEN WE REACH ASPIRATION STATION!"
WHAT KIND OF READINGS?
I-- SIR, HER REACTOR'S CRITICAL!
"BUT IT DOESN'T HAVE TO BE OVER, THOMM! I STARTED THINKING--"
--ABOUT HOW THERE IS NO ROOM ON THE BLACK RABBIT FOR A POP SINGER-- ONLY TRAINED PROFESSIONALS.
BUT YOU AND ERYC ARE GOING BECAUSE OF MONEY!
YOU BOUGHT YOUR WAY INTO THIS, AND I CAN TOO!
"I AM LIQUIDATING ALL MY ASSESTS AND TRANSFERING THEM TO PROJECT BLACKSTAR. I CAN BE A MISSION COMMANDER TOO! THIS WAY--"
NO, GODS, NO...
'AN INCANDESCENT COLUMN OF SMOKE AND FLAME--
"--WE CAN BE TOGETHER!"
FREIGHTER HELIOS-- COME IN! YOU ARE IN DANGER!
YOU AND YOUR FACIST REGIME ARE THE ONES IN DANGER.
-- AS BRIGHT AS TEN THOUSAND SUNS --
"I DO THIS KNOWING THAT MY PEOPLE WILL BE ONE STEP CLOSER TO STOPPING THE EARTH GOVERNMENT-- AND YOUR FILTHY RICH--"
-- ROSE WITH ALL ITS SPLENDOR.'
--FROM KICKING MY PEOPLE OFF WORLD.
NO ANGEL, STOP! THAT'S NOT GOING TO HAPPEN! IT'S TOO LATE FOR US--

"--ITS TOO LATE!"

I DO THIS FOR MY FAMILY WHO DIED IN THE TSUNAMI YOU CREATED.

I DO THIS IN THE NAME OF GOD AND ALL GHOSTS--

'IT WAS AN UNKNOWN WEAPON.'

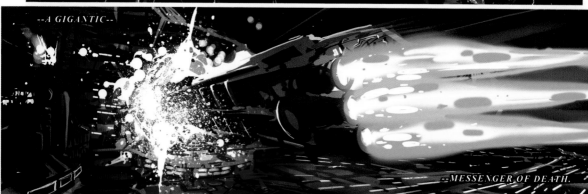

--I DO THIS FOR THE WRAITH!

TRAFFIC CONTROL, ASPIRATION STATION.

AN IRON THUNDERBOLT--

--A GIGANTIC--

--MESSENGER OF DEATH.

RRUMMBE

--HUH?

GRAND CONCERT HALL, IN PREPERATION FOR TSUNAMI RELIEF CEREMONY, ASPIRATION STATION.

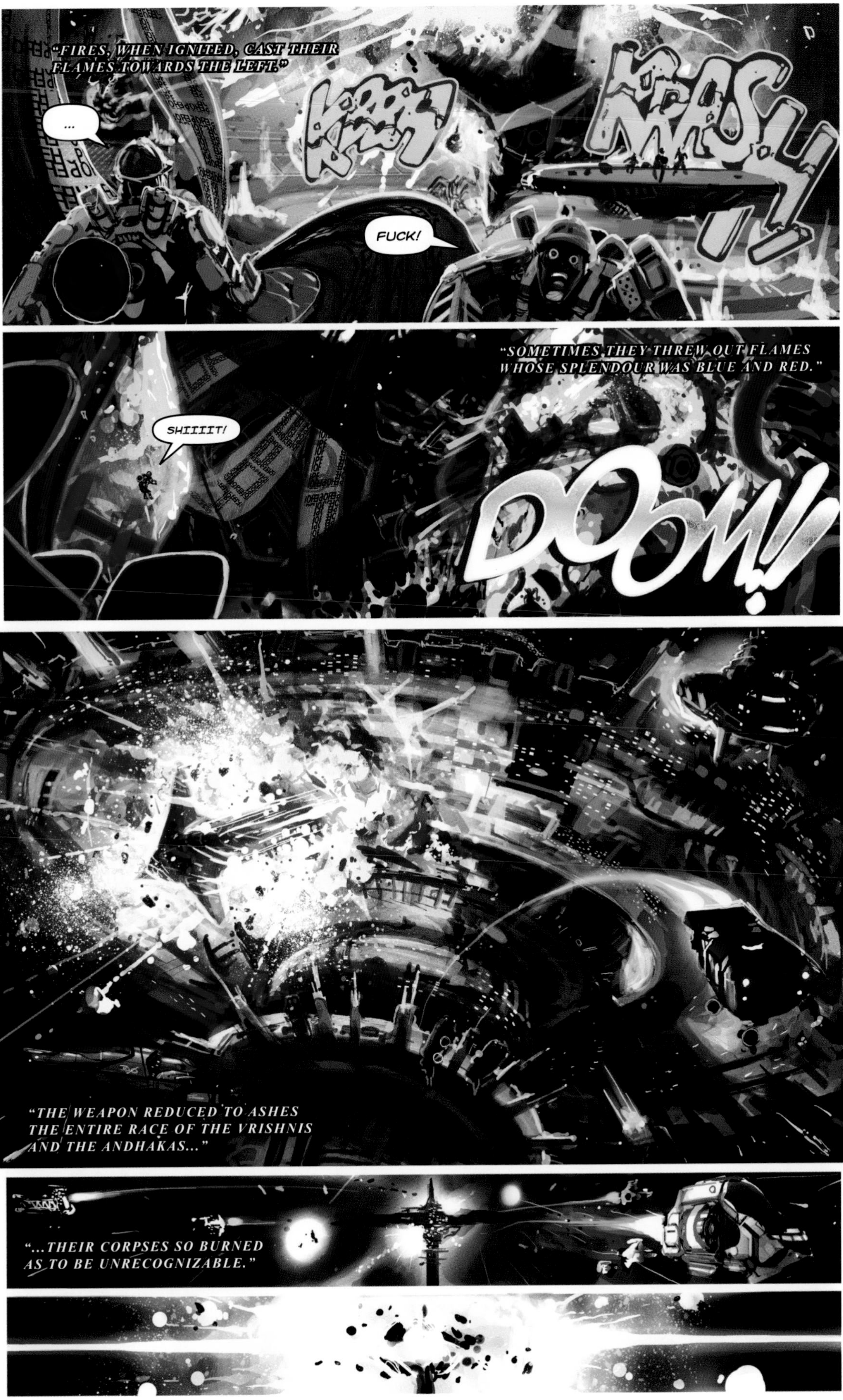
"FIRES, WHEN IGNITED, CAST THEIR FLAMES TOWARDS THE LEFT."
...
FUCK!
"SOMETIMES THEY THREW OUT FLAMES WHOSE SPLENDOUR WAS BLUE AND RED."
SHIIIIT!
DOOM!
"THE WEAPON REDUCED TO ASHES THE ENTIRE RACE OF THE VRISHNIS AND THE ANDHAKAS..."
"...THEIR CORPSES SO BURNED AS TO BE UNRECOGNIZABLE."

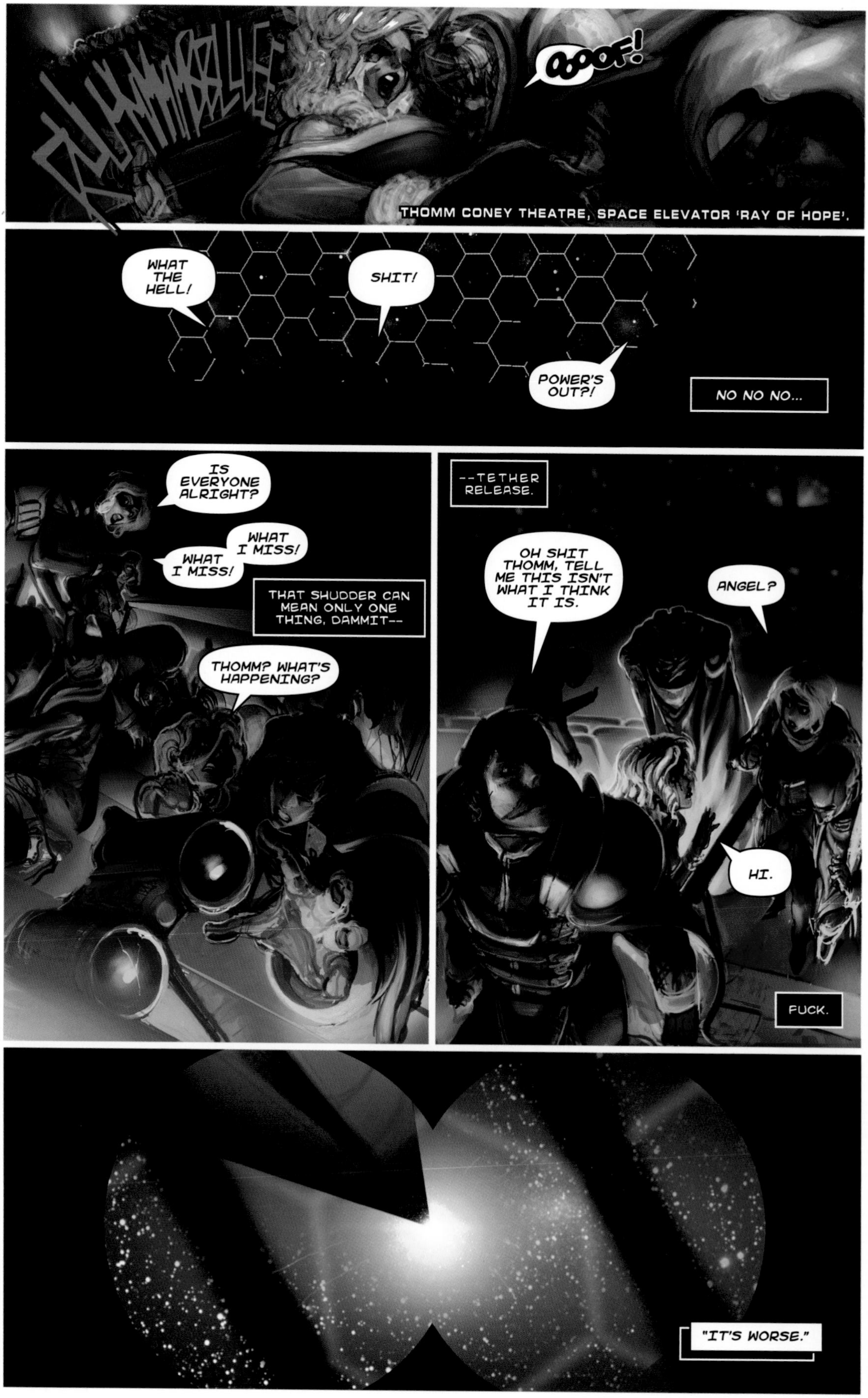
THOMM CONEY THEATRE, SPACE ELEVATOR 'RAY OF HOPE'.
WHAT THE HELL!
SHIT!
POWER'S OUT?!
NO NO NO...
IS EVERYONE ALRIGHT?
WHAT I MISS!
WHAT I MISS!
THAT SHUDDER CAN MEAN ONLY ONE THING, DAMMIT--
THOMM? WHAT'S HAPPENING?
--TETHER RELEASE.
OH SHIT THOMM, TELL ME THIS ISN'T WHAT I THINK IT IS.
ANGEL?
HI.
FUCK.
"IT'S WORSE."

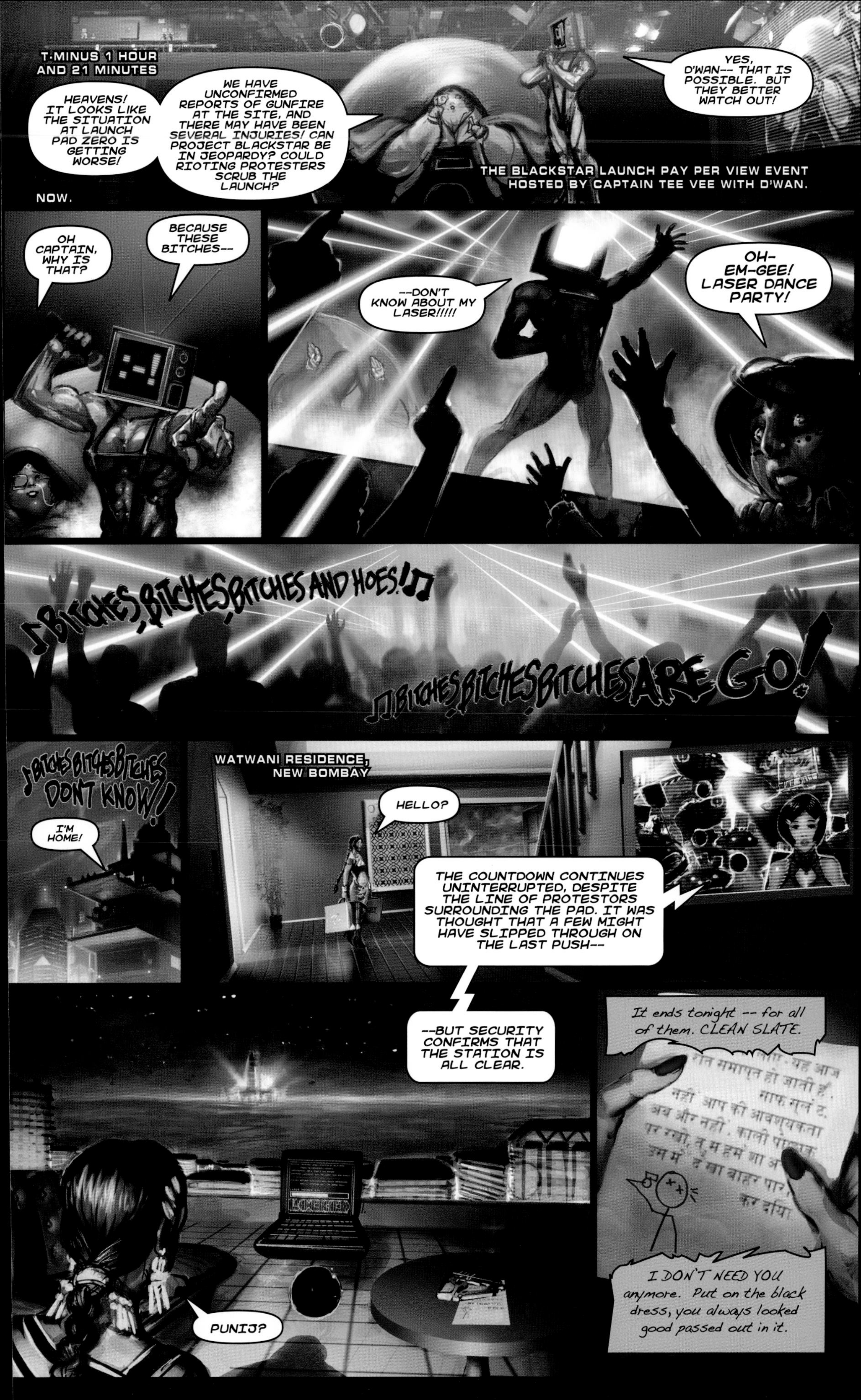

T-MINUS 1 HOUR AND 21 MINUTES
HEAVENS! IT LOOKS LIKE THE SITUATION AT LAUNCH PAD ZERO IS GETTING WORSE!
WE HAVE UNCONFIRMED REPORTS OF GUNFIRE AT THE SITE, AND THERE MAY HAVE BEEN SEVERAL INJURIES! CAN PROJECT BLACKSTAR BE IN JEOPARDY? COULD RIOTING PROTESTERS SCRUB THE LAUNCH?
YES, D'WAN-- THAT IS POSSIBLE. BUT THEY BETTER WATCH OUT!
THE BLACKSTAR LAUNCH PAY PER VIEW EVENT HOSTED BY CAPTAIN TEE VEE WITH D'WAN.
NOW.
OH CAPTAIN, WHY IS THAT?
BECAUSE THESE BITCHES--
--DON'T KNOW ABOUT MY LASER!!!!!
OH-EM-GEE! LASER DANCE PARTY!
♪BITCHES, BITCHES, BITCHES AND HOES!♪
♪BITCHES, BITCHES, BITCHES ARE GO!
♪BITCHES BITCHES BITCHES DON'T KNOW!!
I'M HOME!
WATWANI RESIDENCE, NEW BOMBAY
HELLO?
THE COUNTDOWN CONTINUES UNINTERRUPTED, DESPITE THE LINE OF PROTESTORS SURROUNDING THE PAD. IT WAS THOUGHT THAT A FEW MIGHT HAVE SLIPPED THROUGH ON THE LAST PUSH--
--BUT SECURITY CONFIRMS THAT THE STATION IS ALL CLEAR.
It ends tonight -- for all of them. CLEAN SLATE.
I DON'T NEED YOU anymore. Put on the black dress, you always looked good passed out in it.
PUNIJ?

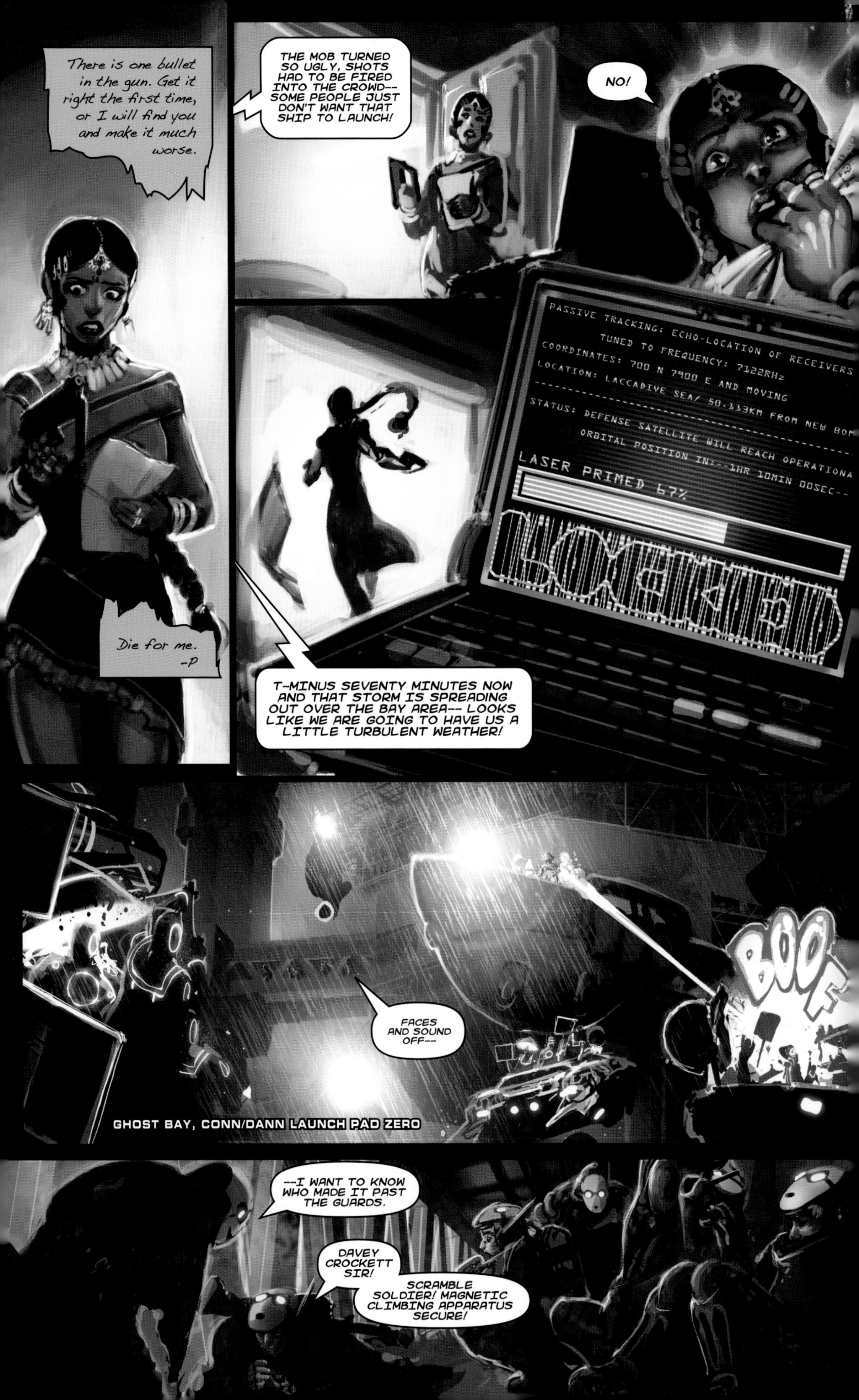

There is one bullet in the gun. Get it right the first time, or I will find you and make it much worse.
Die for me. -P
THE MOB TURNED SO UGLY, SHOTS HAD TO BE FIRED INTO THE CROWD-- SOME PEOPLE JUST DON'T WANT THAT SHIP TO LAUNCH!
NO!
PASSIVE TRACKING: ECHO-LOCATION OF RECEIVERS
TUNED TO FREQUENCY: 7122RHz
COORDINATES: 700 N 7900 E AND MOVING
LOCATION: LACCADIVE SEA/ 50.113KM FROM NEW BOM
STATUS: DEFENSE SATELLITE WILL REACH OPERATIONA
ORBITAL POSITION IN:--1HR 10MIN 00SEC--
LASER PRIMED 67%
T-MINUS SEVENTY MINUTES NOW AND THAT STORM IS SPREADING OUT OVER THE BAY AREA-- LOOKS LIKE WE ARE GOING TO HAVE US A LITTLE TURBULENT WEATHER!
GHOST BAY, CONN/DANN LAUNCH PAD ZERO
FACES AND SOUND OFF--
BOOF
--I WANT TO KNOW WHO MADE IT PAST THE GUARDS.
DAVEY CROCKETT SIR!
SCRAMBLE SOLDIER! MAGNETIC CLIMBING APPARATUS SECURE!

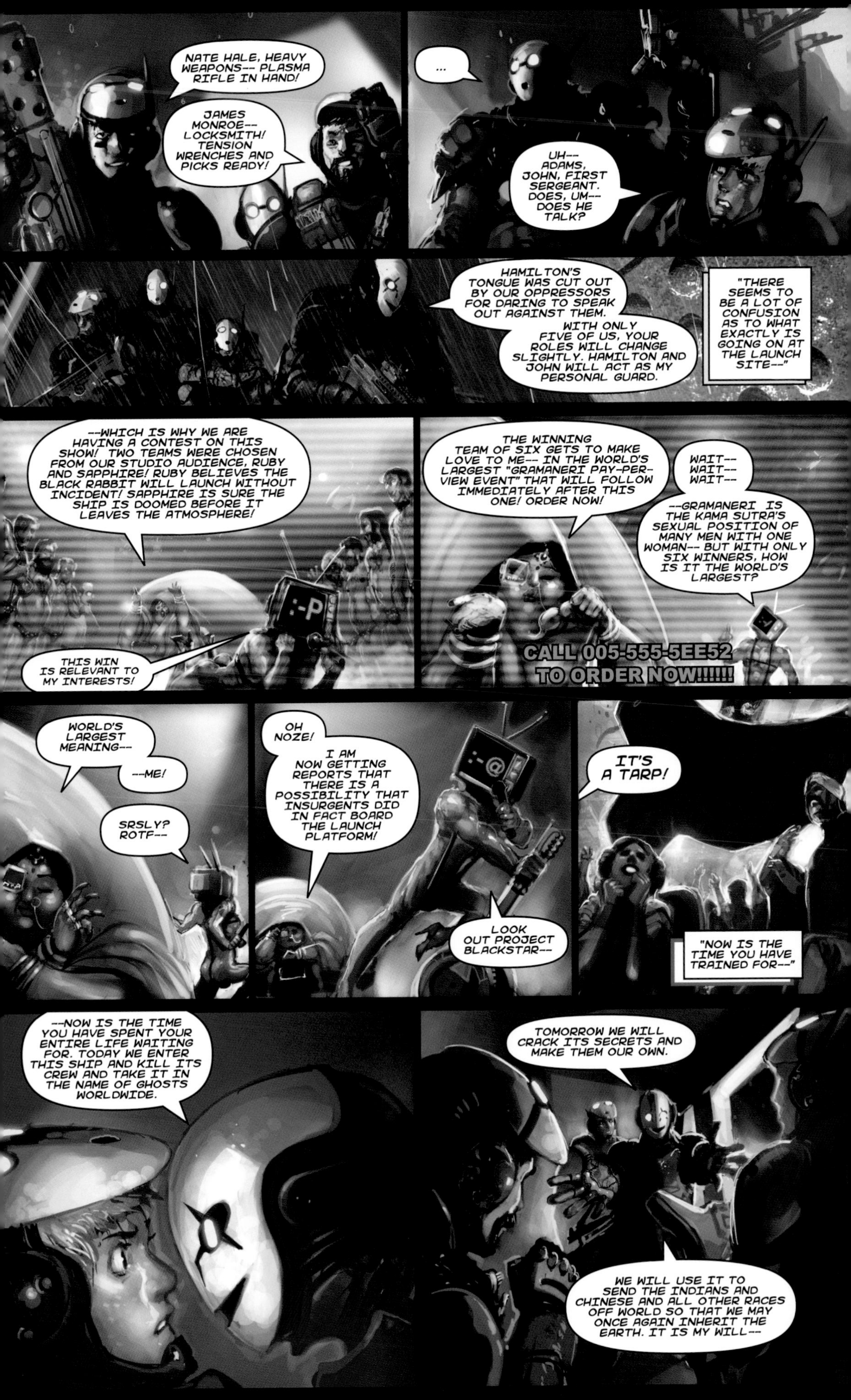
NATE HALE, HEAVY WEAPONS-- PLASMA RIFLE IN HAND!
JAMES MONROE-- LOCKSMITH! TENSION WRENCHES AND PICKS READY!
...
UH-- ADAMS, JOHN, FIRST SERGEANT. DOES, UM-- DOES HE TALK?
HAMILTON'S TONGUE WAS CUT OUT BY OUR OPPRESSORS FOR DARING TO SPEAK OUT AGAINST THEM.
WITH ONLY FIVE OF US, YOUR ROLES WILL CHANGE SLIGHTLY. HAMILTON AND JOHN WILL ACT AS MY PERSONAL GUARD.
"THERE SEEMS TO BE A LOT OF CONFUSION AS TO WHAT EXACTLY IS GOING ON AT THE LAUNCH SITE--"
--WHICH IS WHY WE ARE HAVING A CONTEST ON THIS SHOW! TWO TEAMS WERE CHOSEN FROM OUR STUDIO AUDIENCE, RUBY AND SAPPHIRE! RUBY BELIEVES THE BLACK RABBIT WILL LAUNCH WITHOUT INCIDENT! SAPPHIRE IS SURE THE SHIP IS DOOMED BEFORE IT LEAVES THE ATMOSPHERE!
:-P
THIS WIN IS RELEVANT TO MY INTERESTS!
THE WINNING TEAM OF SIX GETS TO MAKE LOVE TO ME-- IN THE WORLD'S LARGEST "GRAMANERI PAY-PER-VIEW EVENT" THAT WILL FOLLOW IMMEDIATELY AFTER THIS ONE! ORDER NOW!
WAIT-- WAIT-- WAIT--
--GRAMANERI IS THE KAMA SUTRA'S SEXUAL POSITION OF MANY MEN WITH ONE WOMAN-- BUT WITH ONLY SIX WINNERS, HOW IS IT THE WORLD'S LARGEST?
CALL 005-555-5EE52 TO ORDER NOW!!!!!!
WORLD'S LARGEST MEANING--
--ME!
SRSLY? ROTF--
OH NOZE!
I AM NOW GETTING REPORTS THAT THERE IS A POSSIBILITY THAT INSURGENTS DID IN FACT BOARD THE LAUNCH PLATFORM!
:-@
LOOK OUT PROJECT BLACKSTAR--
IT'S A TARP!
"NOW IS THE TIME YOU HAVE TRAINED FOR--"
--NOW IS THE TIME YOU HAVE SPENT YOUR ENTIRE LIFE WAITING FOR. TODAY WE ENTER THIS SHIP AND KILL ITS CREW AND TAKE IT IN THE NAME OF GHOSTS WORLDWIDE.
TOMORROW WE WILL CRACK ITS SECRETS AND MAKE THEM OUR OWN.
WE WILL USE IT TO SEND THE INDIANS AND CHINESE AND ALL OTHER RACES OFF WORLD SO THAT WE MAY ONCE AGAIN INHERIT THE EARTH. IT IS MY WILL--

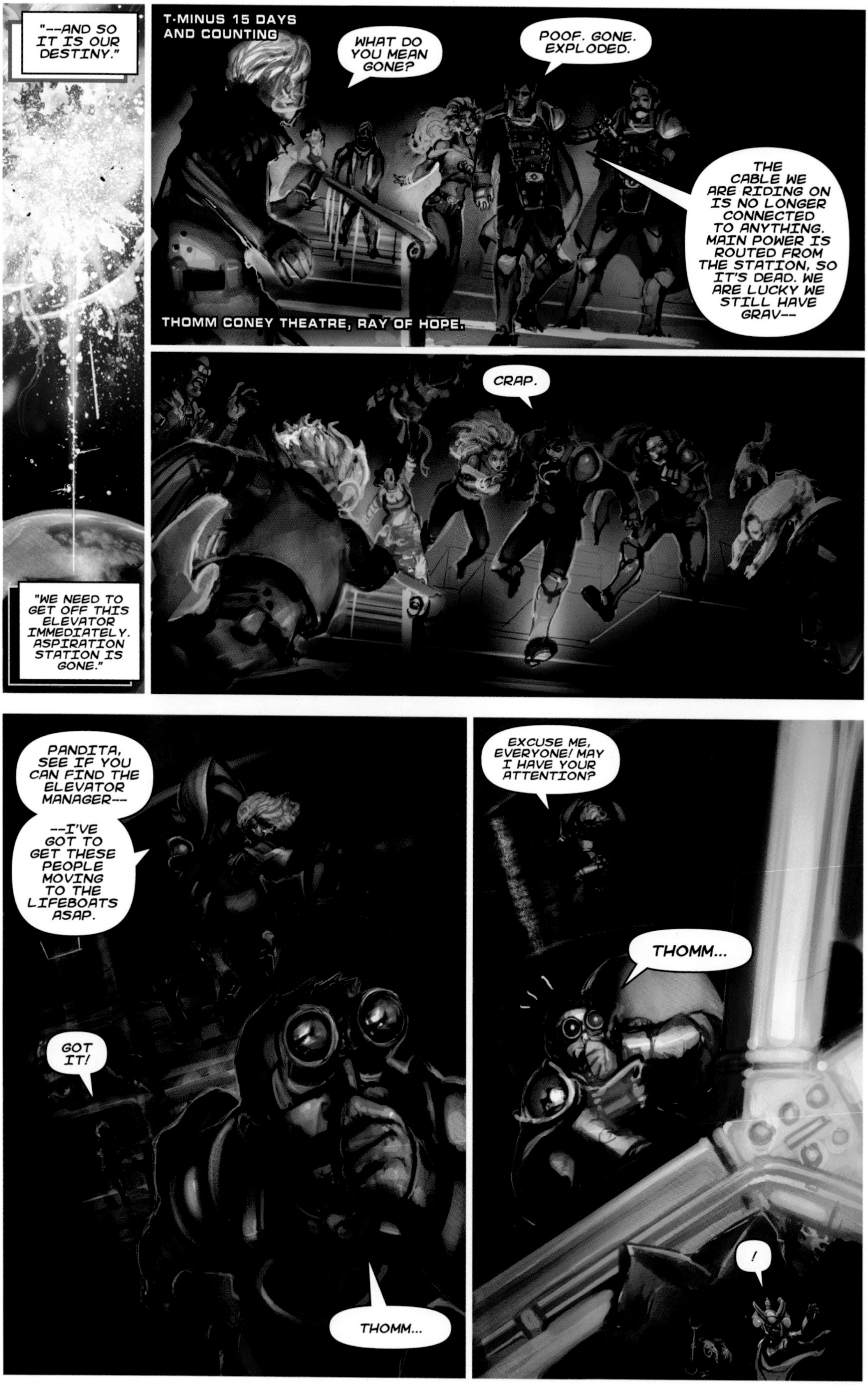
"--AND SO IT IS OUR DESTINY."
"WE NEED TO GET OFF THIS ELEVATOR IMMEDIATELY. ASPIRATION STATION IS GONE."
T-MINUS 15 DAYS AND COUNTING
WHAT DO YOU MEAN GONE?
POOF. GONE. EXPLODED.
THE CABLE WE ARE RIDING ON IS NO LONGER CONNECTED TO ANYTHING. MAIN POWER IS ROUTED FROM THE STATION, SO IT'S DEAD. WE ARE LUCKY WE STILL HAVE GRAV--
THOMM CONEY THEATRE, RAY OF HOPE.
CRAP.
PANDITA, SEE IF YOU CAN FIND THE ELEVATOR MANAGER--
--I'VE GOT TO GET THESE PEOPLE MOVING TO THE LIFEBOATS ASAP.
GOT IT!
THOMM...
EXCUSE ME, EVERYONE! MAY I HAVE YOUR ATTENTION?
THOMM...
!

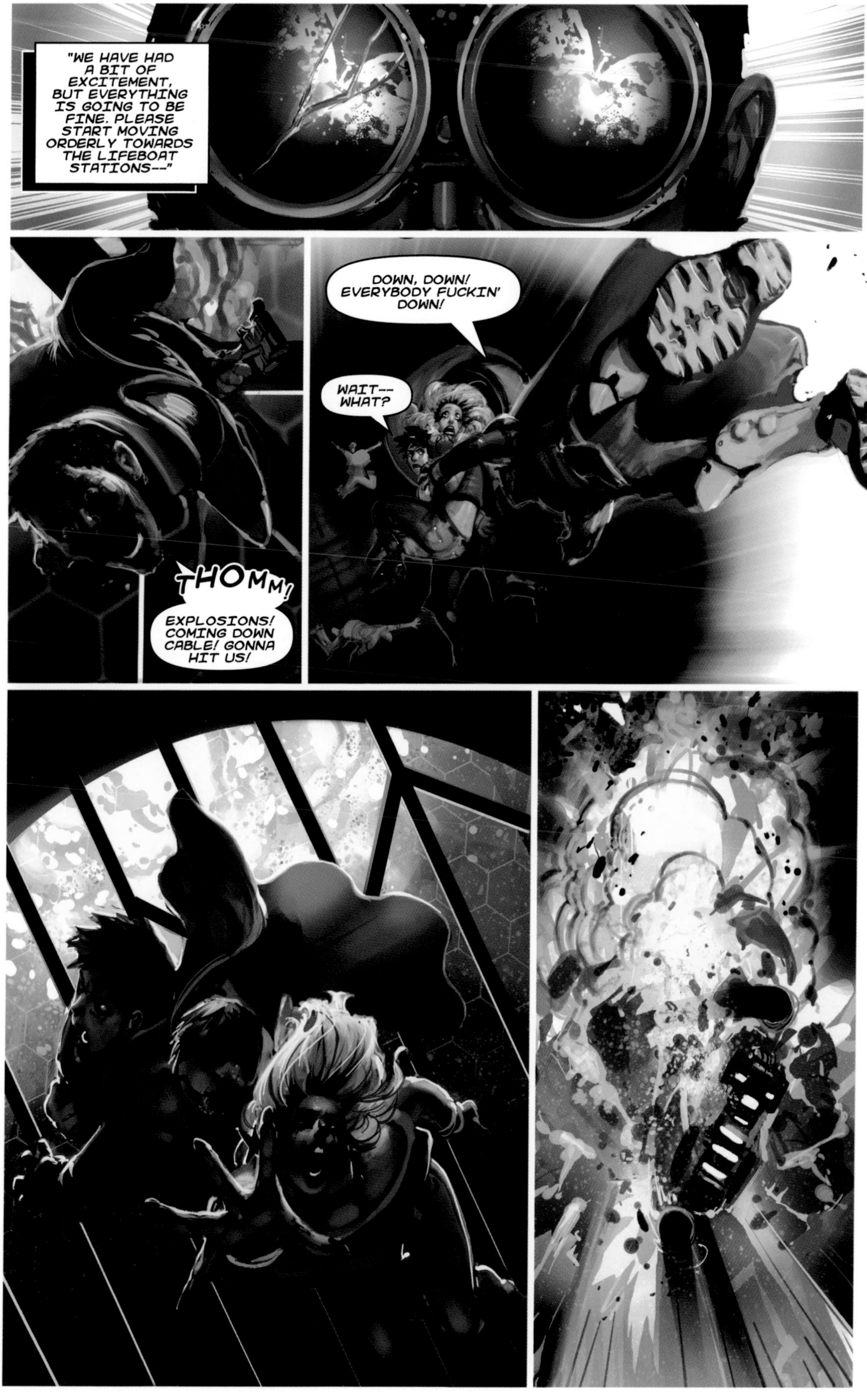
"WE HAVE HAD A BIT OF EXCITEMENT, BUT EVERYTHING IS GOING TO BE FINE. PLEASE START MOVING ORDERLY TOWARDS THE LIFEBOAT STATIONS--"
THOMM!
EXPLOSIONS! COMING DOWN CABLE! GONNA HIT US!
DOWN, DOWN! EVERYBODY FUCKIN' DOWN!
WAIT-- WHAT?

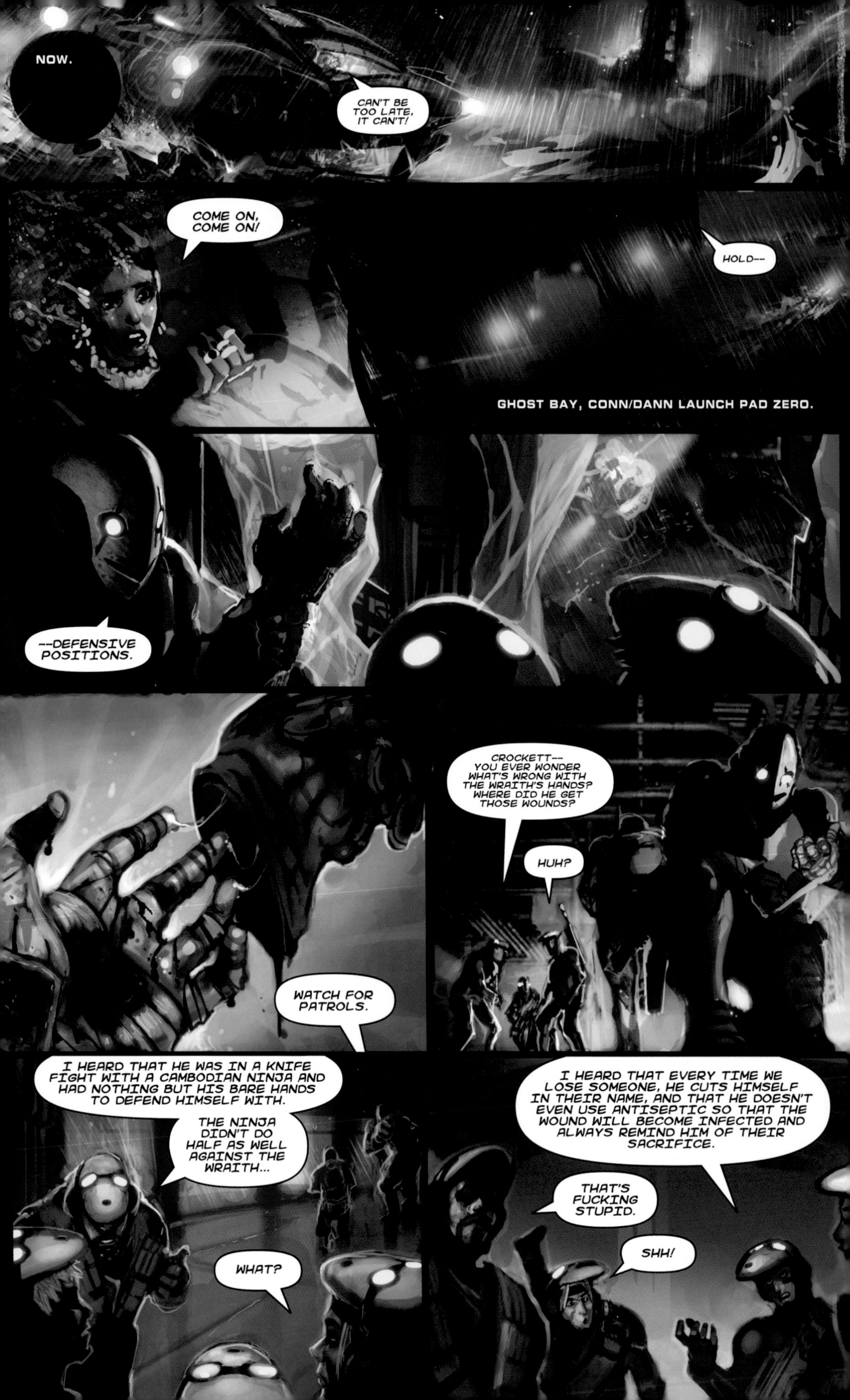
NOW.
CAN'T BE TOO LATE, IT CAN'T!
COME ON, COME ON!
HOLD--
GHOST BAY, CONN/DANN LAUNCH PAD ZERO.
--DEFENSIVE POSITIONS.
WATCH FOR PATROLS.
CROCKETT-- YOU EVER WONDER WHAT'S WRONG WITH THE WRAITH'S HANDS? WHERE DID HE GET THOSE WOUNDS?
HUH?
I HEARD THAT HE WAS IN A KNIFE FIGHT WITH A CAMBODIAN NINJA AND HAD NOTHING BUT HIS BARE HANDS TO DEFEND HIMSELF WITH.
THE NINJA DIDN'T DO HALF AS WELL AGAINST THE WRAITH...
WHAT?
I HEARD THAT EVERY TIME WE LOSE SOMEONE, HE CUTS HIMSELF IN THEIR NAME, AND THAT HE DOESN'T EVEN USE ANTISEPTIC SO THAT THE WOUND WILL BECOME INFECTED AND ALWAYS REMIND HIM OF THEIR SACRIFICE.
THAT'S FUCKING STUPID.
SHH!

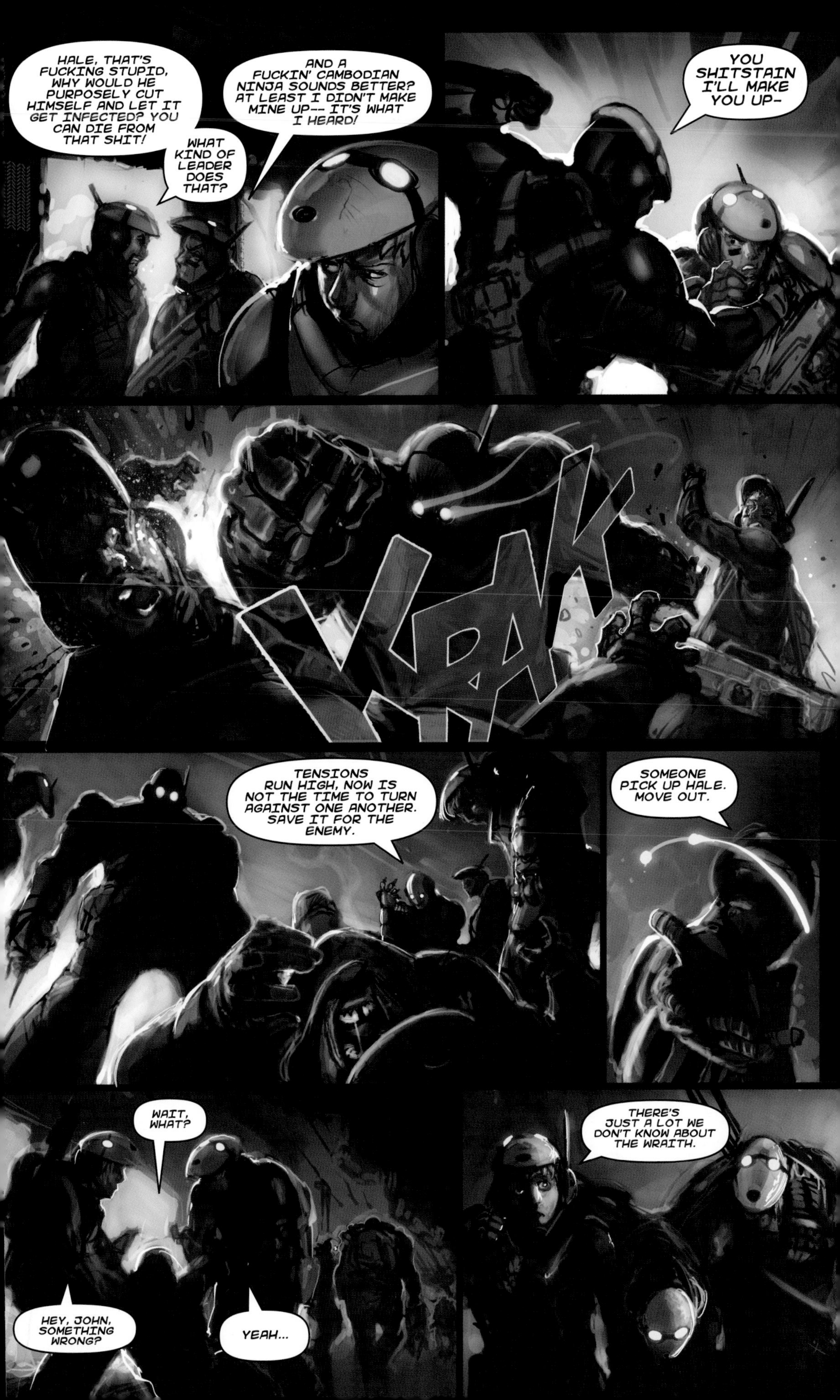
HALE, THAT'S FUCKING STUPID, WHY WOULD HE PURPOSELY CUT HIMSELF AND LET IT GET INFECTED? YOU CAN DIE FROM THAT SHIT!
WHAT KIND OF LEADER DOES THAT?
AND A FUCKIN' CAMBODIAN NINJA SOUNDS BETTER? AT LEAST I DIDN'T MAKE MINE UP-- IT'S WHAT I HEARD!
YOU SHITSTAIN I'LL MAKE YOU UP-
KRAK
TENSIONS RUN HIGH, NOW IS NOT THE TIME TO TURN AGAINST ONE ANOTHER. SAVE IT FOR THE ENEMY.
SOMEONE PICK UP HALE. MOVE OUT.
WAIT, WHAT?
HEY, JOHN, SOMETHING WRONG?
YEAH...
THERE'S JUST A LOT WE DON'T KNOW ABOUT THE WRAITH.

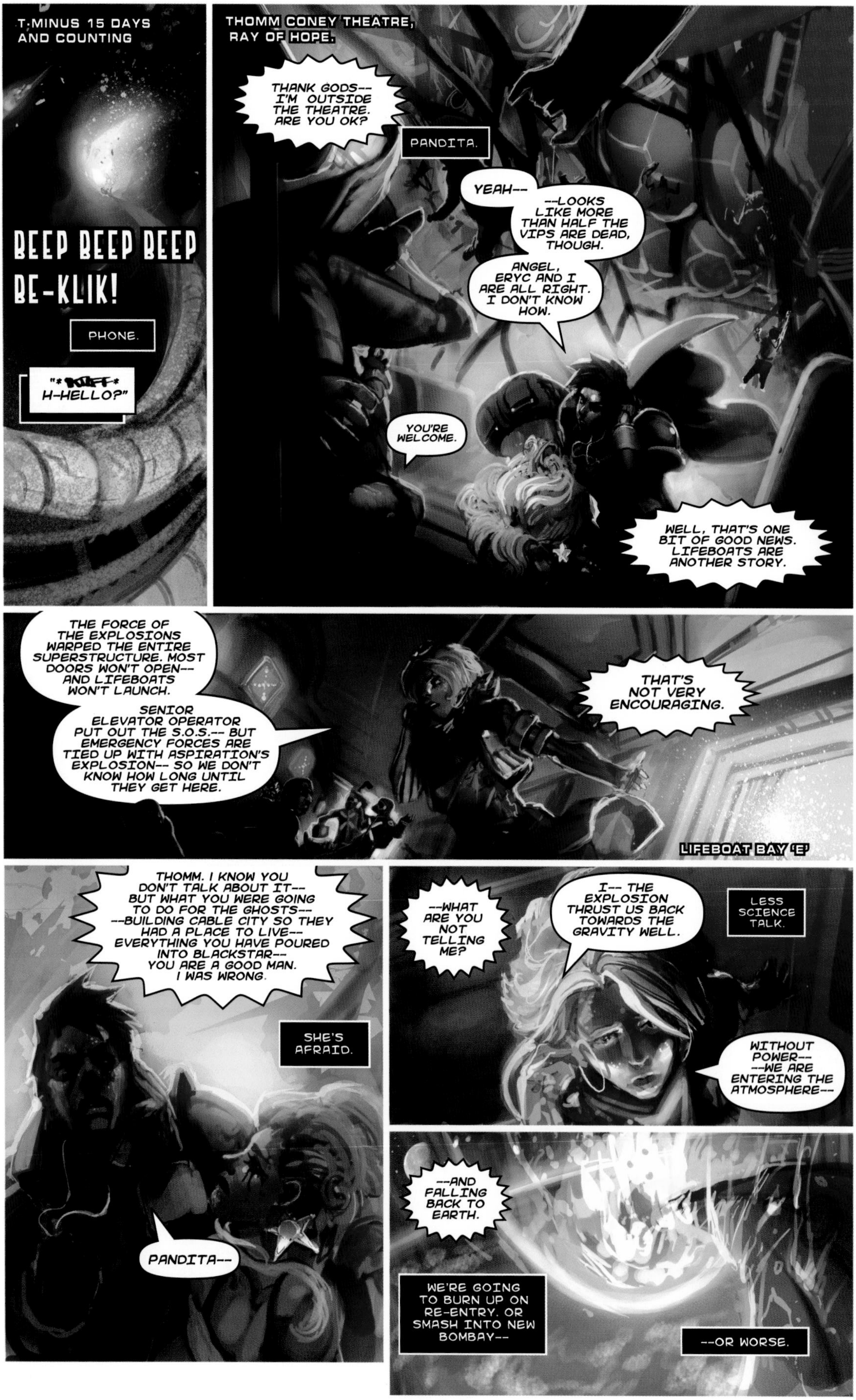

T-MINUS 15 DAYS AND COUNTING
BEEP BEEP BEEP BE-KLIK!
PHONE.
H-HELLO?"
THOMM CONEY THEATRE, RAY OF HOPE.
THANK GODS-- I'M OUTSIDE THE THEATRE. ARE YOU OK?
PANDITA.
YEAH--
--LOOKS LIKE MORE THAN HALF THE VIPS ARE DEAD, THOUGH.
ANGEL, ERYC AND I ARE ALL RIGHT. I DON'T KNOW HOW.
YOU'RE WELCOME.
WELL, THAT'S ONE BIT OF GOOD NEWS. LIFEBOATS ARE ANOTHER STORY.
THE FORCE OF THE EXPLOSIONS WARPED THE ENTIRE SUPERSTRUCTURE. MOST DOORS WON'T OPEN-- AND LIFEBOATS WON'T LAUNCH.
SENIOR ELEVATOR OPERATOR PUT OUT THE S.O.S.-- BUT EMERGENCY FORCES ARE TIED UP WITH ASPIRATION'S EXPLOSION-- SO WE DON'T KNOW HOW LONG UNTIL THEY GET HERE.
THAT'S NOT VERY ENCOURAGING.
LIFEBOAT BAY 'E'
THOMM. I KNOW YOU DON'T TALK ABOUT IT-- BUT WHAT YOU WERE GOING TO DO FOR THE GHOSTS-- --BUILDING CABLE CITY SO THEY HAD A PLACE TO LIVE-- EVERYTHING YOU HAVE POURED INTO BLACKSTAR-- YOU ARE A GOOD MAN. I WAS WRONG.
SHE'S AFRAID.
PANDITA--
--WHAT ARE YOU NOT TELLING ME?
I-- THE EXPLOSION THRUST US BACK TOWARDS THE GRAVITY WELL.
LESS SCIENCE TALK.
WITHOUT POWER-- --WE ARE ENTERING THE ATMOSPHERE--
--AND FALLING BACK TO EARTH.
WE'RE GOING TO BURN UP ON RE-ENTRY. OR SMASH INTO NEW BOMBAY--
--OR WORSE.

I'M COMING TO YOU.

THOMM, IT'S BETTER THIS WAY.

WHAT?

IT'S IRONIC, REALLY-- SPACE WAS GOING TO RUIN OUR LOVE--

--BUT NOW WE WILL DIE HERE TOGETHER-- AND BE IN SPACE FOREVER.

ANGEL--

--ARE YOU OUT OF YOUR FUCKIN' MIND!?!

DID YOU THINK I WAS REALLY IN LOVE WITH YOU? ARE YOU REALLY THAT STUPID?

I DIDN'T FUCKIN' PUT UP ALL MY MONEY AND DO ALL THIS WORK FOR NOTHING!

I HAVE MUCH MORE IMPORTANT THINGS TO DO! I'M GOING TO FIGHT TO GET US THE FUCK OUT OF THIS SHIT, NOT CURL UP AND DIE WITH YOU!

I...

IT'S FUCKIN' OVER, DO YOU UNDERSTAND ME?

THOMM.

RESCUE CRAFT IS HERE, LOOKS LIKE THE ALANA--

--WE'RE SAVED.

OH.

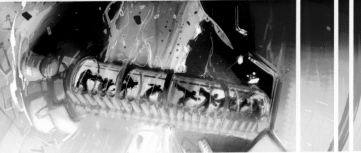

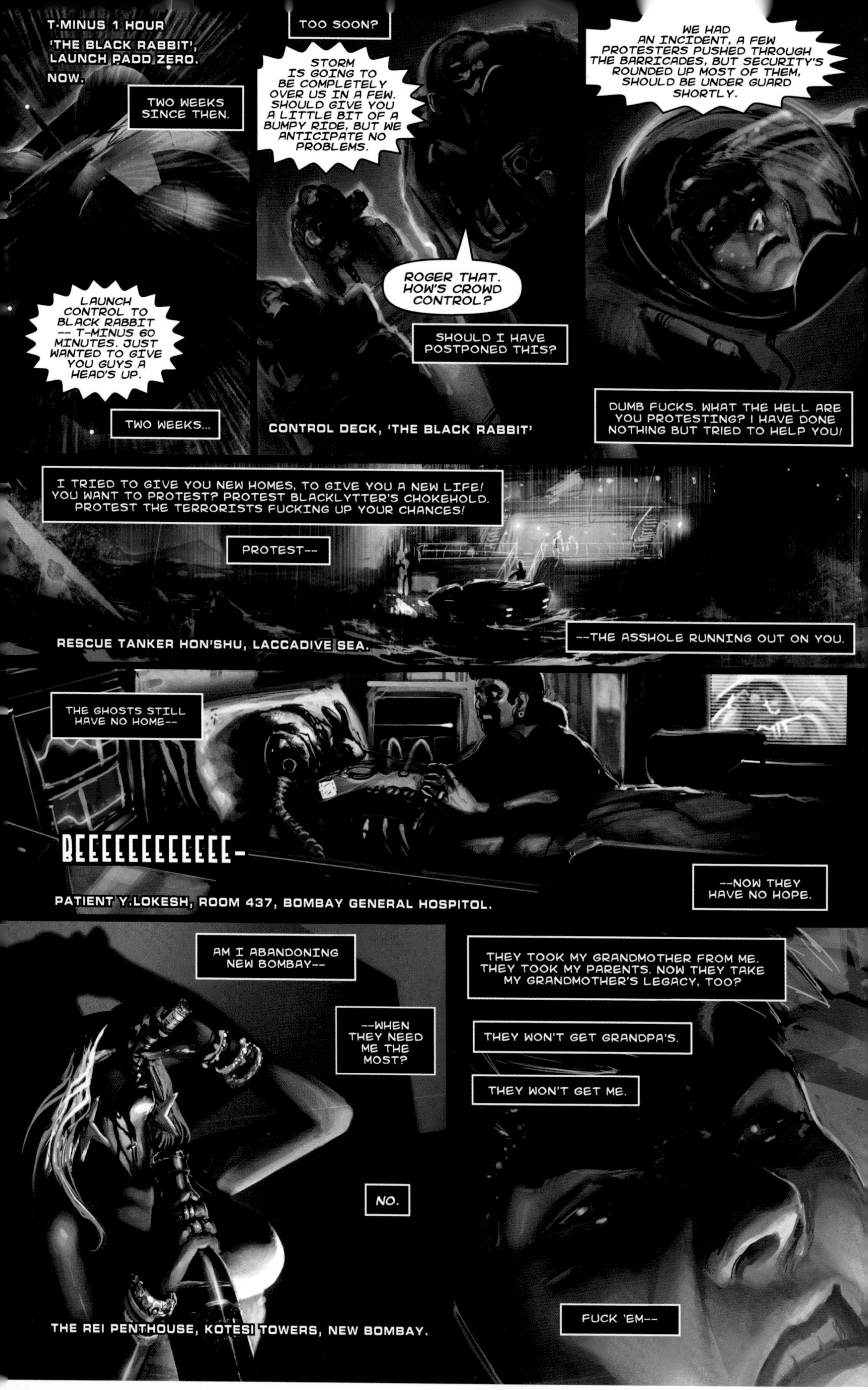
T-MINUS 1 HOUR
'THE BLACK RABBIT', LAUNCH PADD ZERO.
NOW.
TWO WEEKS SINCE THEN.
LAUNCH CONTROL TO BLACK RABBIT -- T-MINUS 60 MINUTES. JUST WANTED TO GIVE YOU GUYS A HEAD'S UP.
TWO WEEKS...
TOO SOON?
STORM IS GOING TO BE COMPLETELY OVER US IN A FEW. SHOULD GIVE YOU A LITTLE BIT OF A BUMPY RIDE, BUT WE ANTICIPATE NO PROBLEMS.
ROGER THAT. HOW'S CROWD CONTROL?
SHOULD I HAVE POSTPONED THIS?
CONTROL DECK, 'THE BLACK RABBIT'
WE HAD AN INCIDENT, A FEW PROTESTERS PUSHED THROUGH THE BARRICADES, BUT SECURITY'S ROUNDED UP MOST OF THEM, SHOULD BE UNDER GUARD SHORTLY.
DUMB FUCKS. WHAT THE HELL ARE YOU PROTESTING? I HAVE DONE NOTHING BUT TRIED TO HELP YOU!
I TRIED TO GIVE YOU NEW HOMES, TO GIVE YOU A NEW LIFE! YOU WANT TO PROTEST? PROTEST BLACKLYTTER'S CHOKEHOLD. PROTEST THE TERRORISTS FUCKING UP YOUR CHANCES!
PROTEST--
RESCUE TANKER HON'SHU, LACCADIVE SEA.
--THE ASSHOLE RUNNING OUT ON YOU.
THE GHOSTS STILL HAVE NO HOME--
BEEEEEEEEEEE-
PATIENT Y.LOKESH, ROOM 437, BOMBAY GENERAL HOSPITOL.
--NOW THEY HAVE NO HOPE.
AM I ABANDONING NEW BOMBAY--
--WHEN THEY NEED ME THE MOST?
NO.
THE REI PENTHOUSE, KOTESI TOWERS, NEW BOMBAY.
THEY TOOK MY GRANDMOTHER FROM ME. THEY TOOK MY PARENTS. NOW THEY TAKE MY GRANDMOTHER'S LEGACY, TOO?
THEY WON'T GET GRANDPA'S.
THEY WON'T GET ME.
FUCK 'EM--

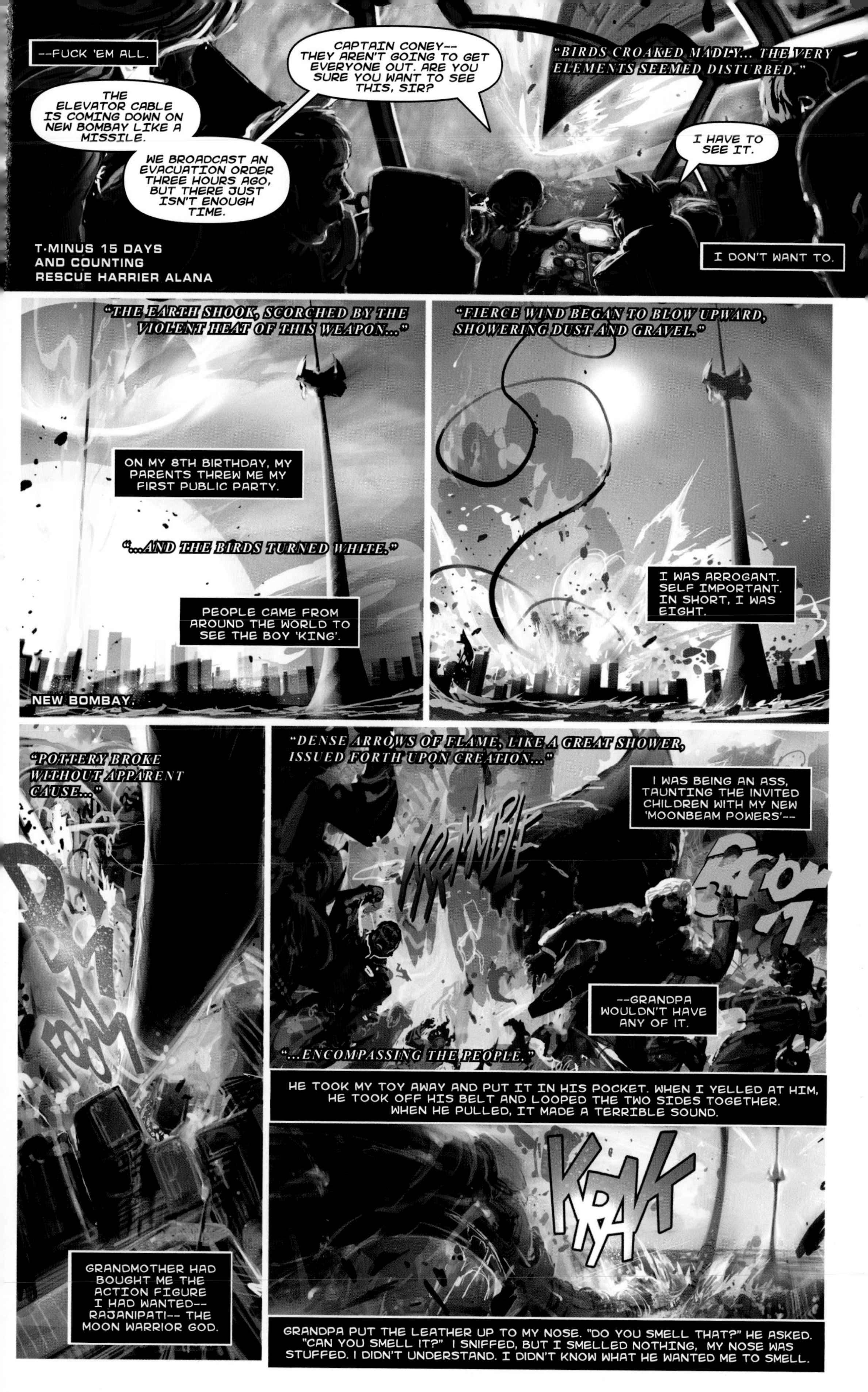
--FUCK 'EM ALL.
“BIRDS CROAKED MADLY... THE VERY ELEMENTS SEEMED DISTURBED.”
THE ELEVATOR CABLE IS COMING DOWN ON NEW BOMBAY LIKE A MISSILE.
WE BROADCAST AN EVACUATION ORDER THREE HOURS AGO, BUT THERE JUST ISN'T ENOUGH TIME.
CAPTAIN CONEY-- THEY AREN'T GOING TO GET EVERYONE OUT. ARE YOU SURE YOU WANT TO SEE THIS, SIR?
I HAVE TO SEE IT.
T-MINUS 15 DAYS AND COUNTING
RESCUE HARRIER ALANA
I DON'T WANT TO.
“THE EARTH SHOOK, SCORCHED BY THE VIOLENT HEAT OF THIS WEAPON...”
ON MY 8TH BIRTHDAY, MY PARENTS THREW ME MY FIRST PUBLIC PARTY.
“...AND THE BIRDS TURNED WHITE.”
PEOPLE CAME FROM AROUND THE WORLD TO SEE THE BOY 'KING'.
NEW BOMBAY.
“FIERCE WIND BEGAN TO BLOW UPWARD, SHOWERING DUST AND GRAVEL.”
I WAS ARROGANT. SELF IMPORTANT. IN SHORT, I WAS EIGHT.
“POTTERY BROKE WITHOUT APPARENT CAUSE...”
GRANDMOTHER HAD BOUGHT ME THE ACTION FIGURE I HAD WANTED-- RAJANIPATI-- THE MOON WARRIOR GOD.
“DENSE ARROWS OF FLAME, LIKE A GREAT SHOWER, ISSUED FORTH UPON CREATION...”
I WAS BEING AN ASS, TAUNTING THE INVITED CHILDREN WITH MY NEW 'MOONBEAM POWERS'--
--GRANDPA WOULDN'T HAVE ANY OF IT.
“...ENCOMPASSING THE PEOPLE.”
HE TOOK MY TOY AWAY AND PUT IT IN HIS POCKET. WHEN I YELLED AT HIM, HE TOOK OFF HIS BELT AND LOOPED THE TWO SIDES TOGETHER. WHEN HE PULLED, IT MADE A TERRIBLE SOUND.
KRAK
GRANDPA PUT THE LEATHER UP TO MY NOSE. “DO YOU SMELL THAT?” HE ASKED. “CAN YOU SMELL IT?” I SNIFFED, BUT I SMELLED NOTHING, MY NOSE WAS STUFFED. I DIDN'T UNDERSTAND. I DIDN'T KNOW WHAT HE WANTED ME TO SMELL.

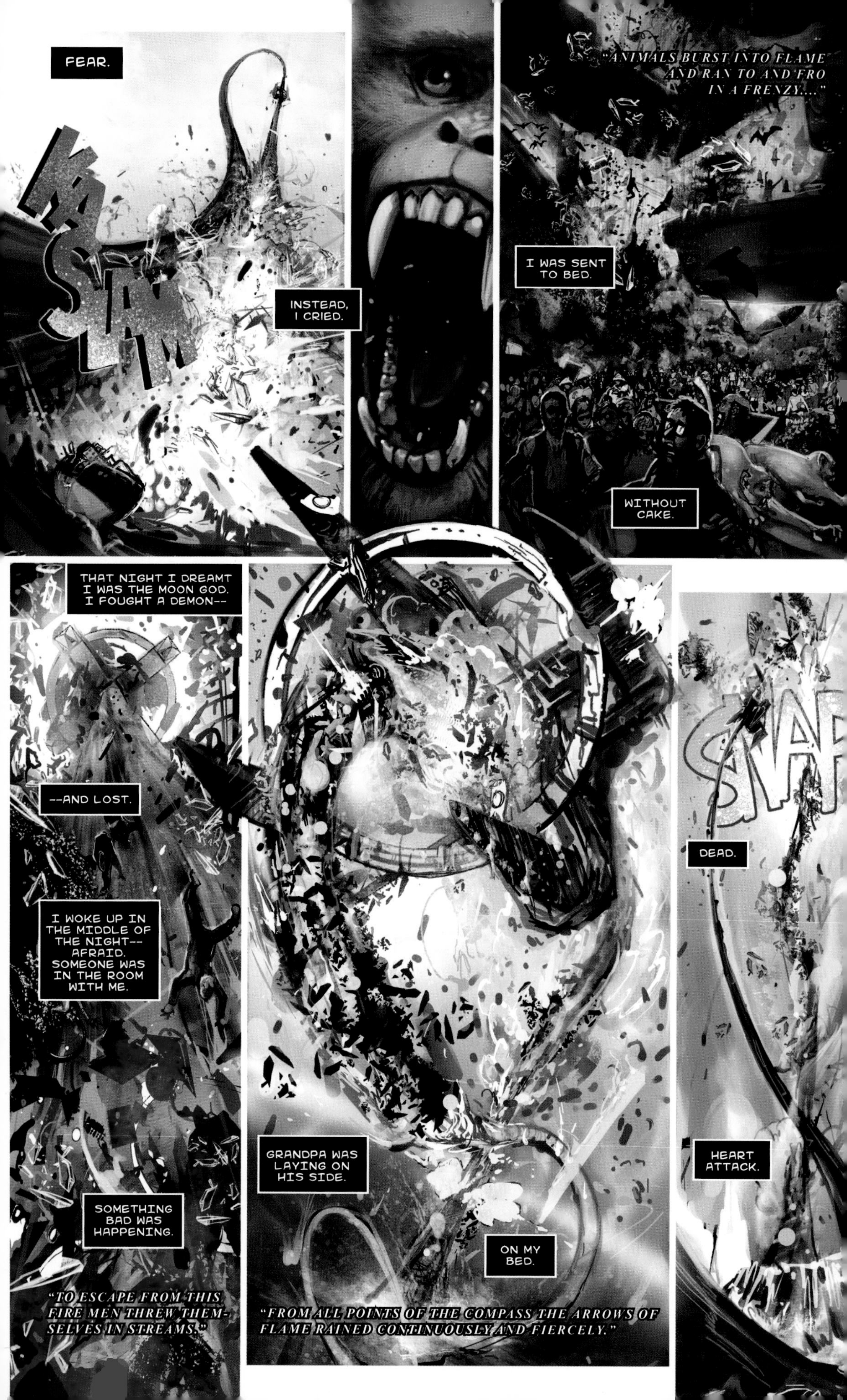
FEAR.
KASLAM
INSTEAD, I CRIED.
"ANIMALS BURST INTO FLAME AND RAN TO AND FRO IN A FRENZY...."
I WAS SENT TO BED.
WITHOUT CAKE.
THAT NIGHT I DREAMT I WAS THE MOON GOD. I FOUGHT A DEMON--
--AND LOST.
I WOKE UP IN THE MIDDLE OF THE NIGHT--AFRAID. SOMEONE WAS IN THE ROOM WITH ME.
SOMETHING BAD WAS HAPPENING.
"TO ESCAPE FROM THIS FIRE MEN THREW THEMSELVES IN STREAMS."
GRANDPA WAS LAYING ON HIS SIDE.
ON MY BED.
"FROM ALL POINTS OF THE COMPASS THE ARROWS OF FLAME RAINED CONTINUOUSLY AND FIERCELY."
DEAD.
HEART ATTACK.

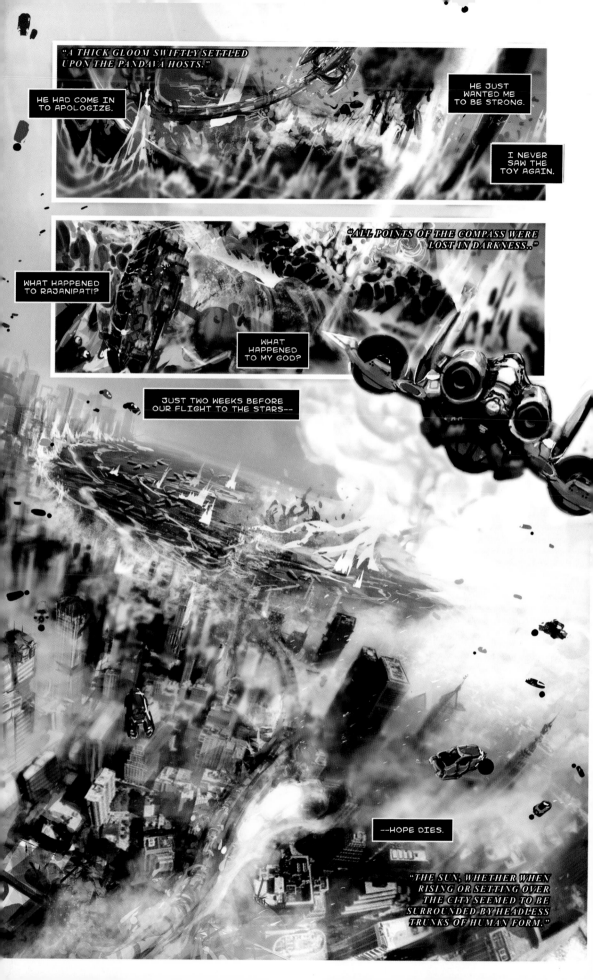

"A THICK GLOOM SWIFTLY SETTLED UPON THE PANDAVA HOSTS."

HE HAD COME IN TO APOLOGIZE.

HE JUST WANTED ME TO BE STRONG.

I NEVER SAW THE TOY AGAIN.

"ALL POINTS OF THE COMPASS WERE LOST IN DARKNESS.."

WHAT HAPPENED TO RAJANIPATI?

WHAT HAPPENED TO MY GOD?

JUST TWO WEEKS BEFORE OUR FLIGHT TO THE STARS--

--HOPE DIES.

"THE SUN, WHETHER WHEN RISING OR SETTING OVER THE CITY SEEMED TO BE SURROUNDED BY HEADLESS TRUNKS OF HUMAN FORM."

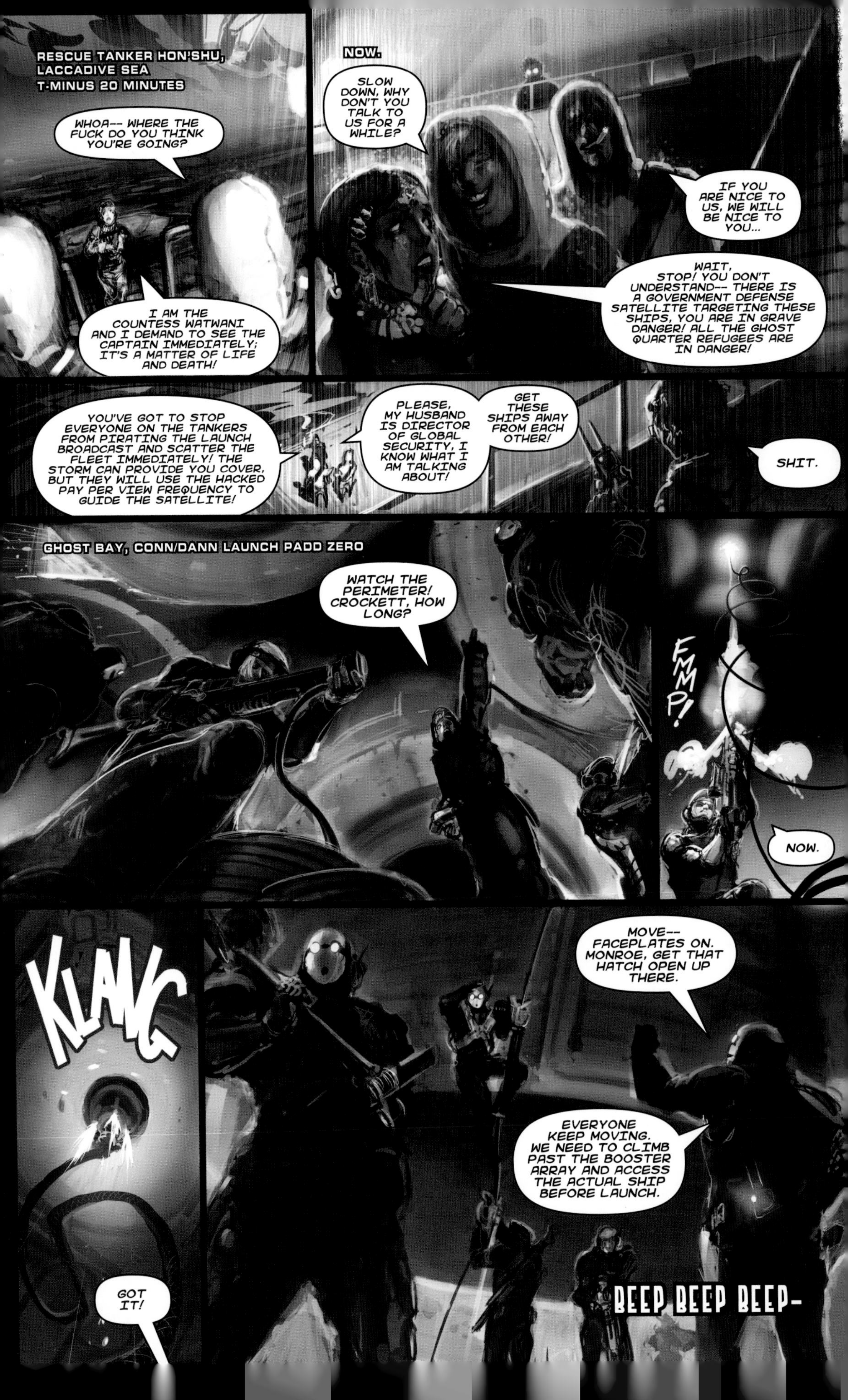

RESCUE TANKER HON'SHU, LACCADIVE SEA
T-MINUS 20 MINUTES
WHOA-- WHERE THE FUCK DO YOU THINK YOU'RE GOING?
I AM THE COUNTESS WATWANI AND I DEMAND TO SEE THE CAPTAIN IMMEDIATELY; IT'S A MATTER OF LIFE AND DEATH!
NOW.
SLOW DOWN, WHY DON'T YOU TALK TO US FOR A WHILE?
IF YOU ARE NICE TO US, WE WILL BE NICE TO YOU...
WAIT, STOP! YOU DON'T UNDERSTAND-- THERE IS A GOVERNMENT DEFENSE SATELLITE TARGETING THESE SHIPS, YOU ARE IN GRAVE DANGER! ALL THE GHOST QUARTER REFUGEES ARE IN DANGER!
YOU'VE GOT TO STOP EVERYONE ON THE TANKERS FROM PIRATING THE LAUNCH BROADCAST AND SCATTER THE FLEET IMMEDIATELY! THE STORM CAN PROVIDE YOU COVER, BUT THEY WILL USE THE HACKED PAY PER VIEW FREQUENCY TO GUIDE THE SATELLITE!
PLEASE, MY HUSBAND IS DIRECTOR OF GLOBAL SECURITY, I KNOW WHAT I AM TALKING ABOUT!
GET THESE SHIPS AWAY FROM EACH OTHER!
SHIT.
GHOST BAY, CONN/DANN LAUNCH PADD ZERO
WATCH THE PERIMETER! CROCKETT, HOW LONG?
FMMP!
NOW.
KLANG
GOT IT!
MOVE-- FACEPLATES ON. MONROE, GET THAT HATCH OPEN UP THERE.
EVERYONE KEEP MOVING. WE NEED TO CLIMB PAST THE BOOSTER ARRAY AND ACCESS THE ACTUAL SHIP BEFORE LAUNCH.
BEEP BEEP BEEP-

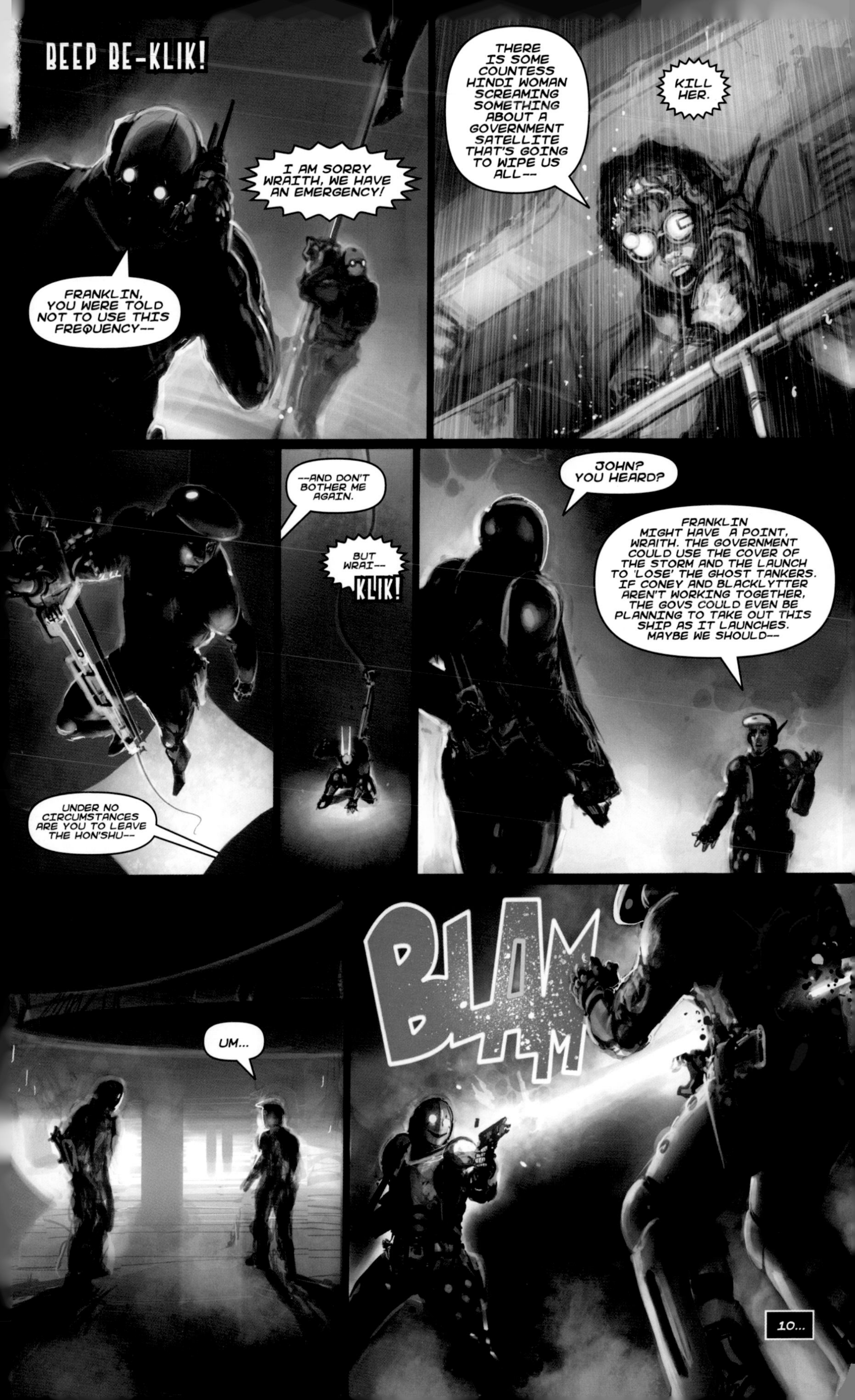
BEEP BE-KLIK!
I AM SORRY WRAITH, WE HAVE AN EMERGENCY!
FRANKLIN, YOU WERE TOLD NOT TO USE THIS FREQUENCY--
THERE IS SOME COUNTESS HINDI WOMAN SCREAMING SOMETHING ABOUT A GOVERNMENT SATELLITE THAT'S GOING TO WIPE US ALL--
KILL HER.
UNDER NO CIRCUMSTANCES ARE YOU TO LEAVE THE HON'SHU--
--AND DON'T BOTHER ME AGAIN.
BUT WRAI--
KLIK!
JOHN? YOU HEARD?
FRANKLIN MIGHT HAVE A POINT, WRAITH. THE GOVERNMENT COULD USE THE COVER OF THE STORM AND THE LAUNCH TO 'LOSE' THE GHOST TANKERS. IF CONEY AND BLACKLYTTER AREN'T WORKING TOGETHER, THE GOVS COULD EVEN BE PLANNING TO TAKE OUT THIS SHIP AS IT LAUNCHES. MAYBE WE SHOULD--
UM...
BLAM
10...

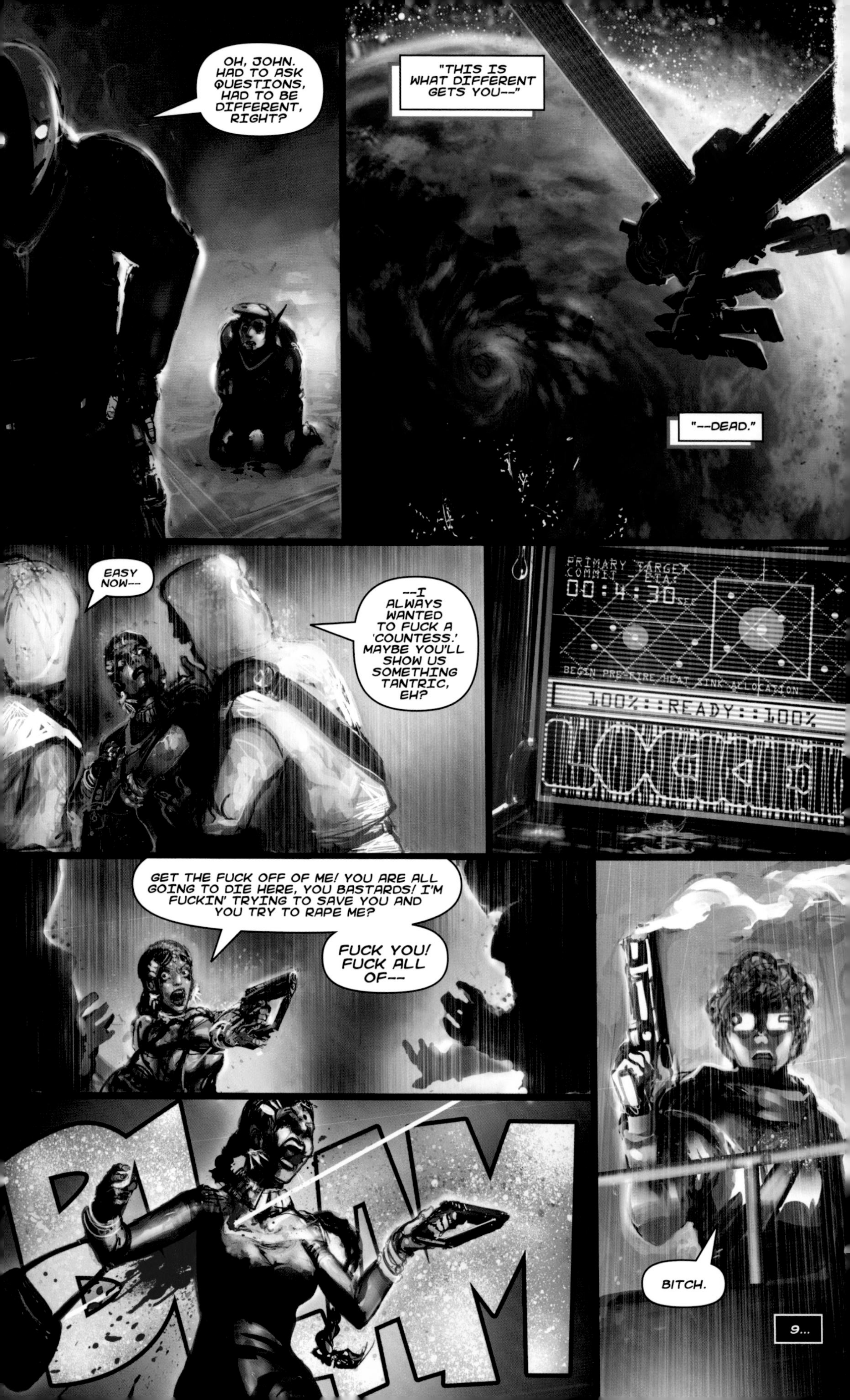
OH, JOHN. HAD TO ASK QUESTIONS, HAD TO BE DIFFERENT, RIGHT?
"THIS IS WHAT DIFFERENT GETS YOU--"
"--DEAD."
EASY NOW--
--I ALWAYS WANTED TO FUCK A 'COUNTESS.' MAYBE YOU'LL SHOW US SOMETHING TANTRIC, EH?
PRIMARY TARGET COMMIT - ETA:
00:4:30SEC
BEGIN PRE-FIRE HEAT SINK ALLOCATION
100%::READY::100%
GET THE FUCK OFF OF ME! YOU ARE ALL GOING TO DIE HERE, YOU BASTARDS! I'M FUCKIN' TRYING TO SAVE YOU AND YOU TRY TO RAPE ME?
FUCK YOU! FUCK ALL OF--
BITCH.

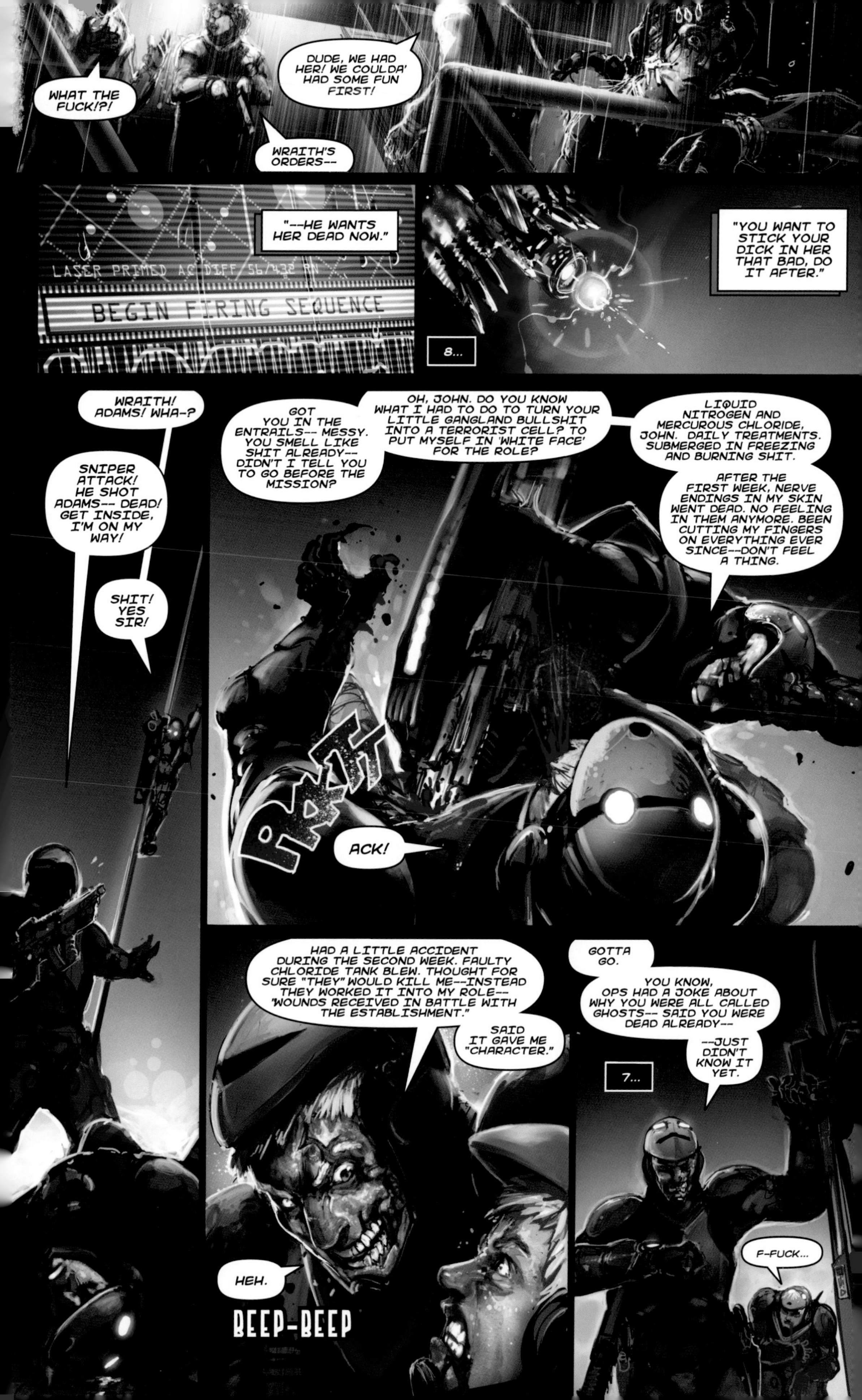
WHAT THE FUCK!?!
DUDE, WE HAD HER! WE COULDA' HAD SOME FUN FIRST!
WRAITH'S ORDERS--
LASER PRIMED AC DIFF 56/432 RN
BEGIN FIRING SEQUENCE
"--HE WANTS HER DEAD NOW."
"YOU WANT TO STICK YOUR DICK IN HER THAT BAD, DO IT AFTER."
8...
WRAITH! ADAMS! WHA-?
SNIPER ATTACK! HE SHOT ADAMS-- DEAD! GET INSIDE, I'M ON MY WAY!
SHIT! YES SIR!
GOT YOU IN THE ENTRAILS-- MESSY. YOU SMELL LIKE SHIT ALREADY--DIDN'T I TELL YOU TO GO BEFORE THE MISSION?
OH, JOHN. DO YOU KNOW WHAT I HAD TO DO TO TURN YOUR LITTLE GANGLAND BULLSHIT INTO A TERRORIST CELL? TO PUT MYSELF IN 'WHITE FACE' FOR THE ROLE?
LIQUID NITROGEN AND MERCUROUS CHLORIDE, JOHN. DAILY TREATMENTS. SUBMERGED IN FREEZING AND BURNING SHIT.
AFTER THE FIRST WEEK, NERVE ENDINGS IN MY SKIN WENT DEAD. NO FEELING IN THEM ANYMORE. BEEN CUTTING MY FINGERS ON EVERYTHING EVER SINCE--DON'T FEEL A THING.
RAKIT
ACK!
HAD A LITTLE ACCIDENT DURING THE SECOND WEEK. FAULTY CHLORIDE TANK BLEW. THOUGHT FOR SURE "THEY" WOULD KILL ME--INSTEAD THEY WORKED IT INTO MY ROLE--"WOUNDS RECEIVED IN BATTLE WITH THE ESTABLISHMENT."
SAID IT GAVE ME "CHARACTER."
HEH.
BEEP-BEEP
GOTTA GO.
YOU KNOW, OPS HAD A JOKE ABOUT WHY YOU WERE ALL CALLED GHOSTS-- SAID YOU WERE DEAD ALREADY--
--JUST DIDN'T KNOW IT YET.
7...
F-FUCK...

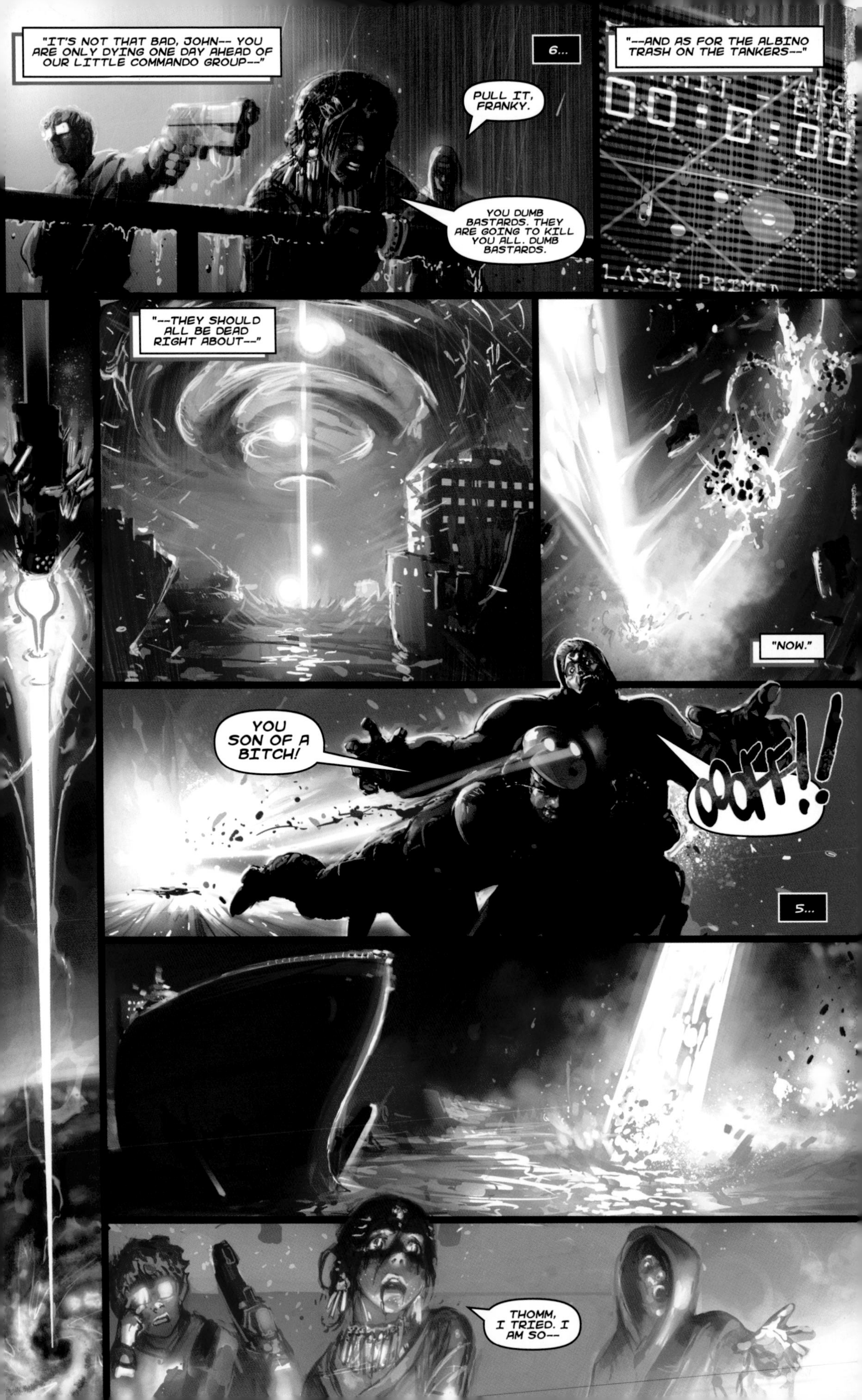
"IT'S NOT THAT BAD, JOHN-- YOU ARE ONLY DYING ONE DAY AHEAD OF OUR LITTLE COMMANDO GROUP--"
6...
PULL IT, FRANKY.
YOU DUMB BASTARDS. THEY ARE GOING TO KILL YOU ALL. DUMB BASTARDS.
"--AND AS FOR THE ALBINO TRASH ON THE TANKERS--"
00:0:00
LASER PRIMED
"--THEY SHOULD ALL BE DEAD RIGHT ABOUT--"
"NOW."
YOU SON OF A BITCH!
OOOFF!!
5...
THOMM, I TRIED. I AM SO--

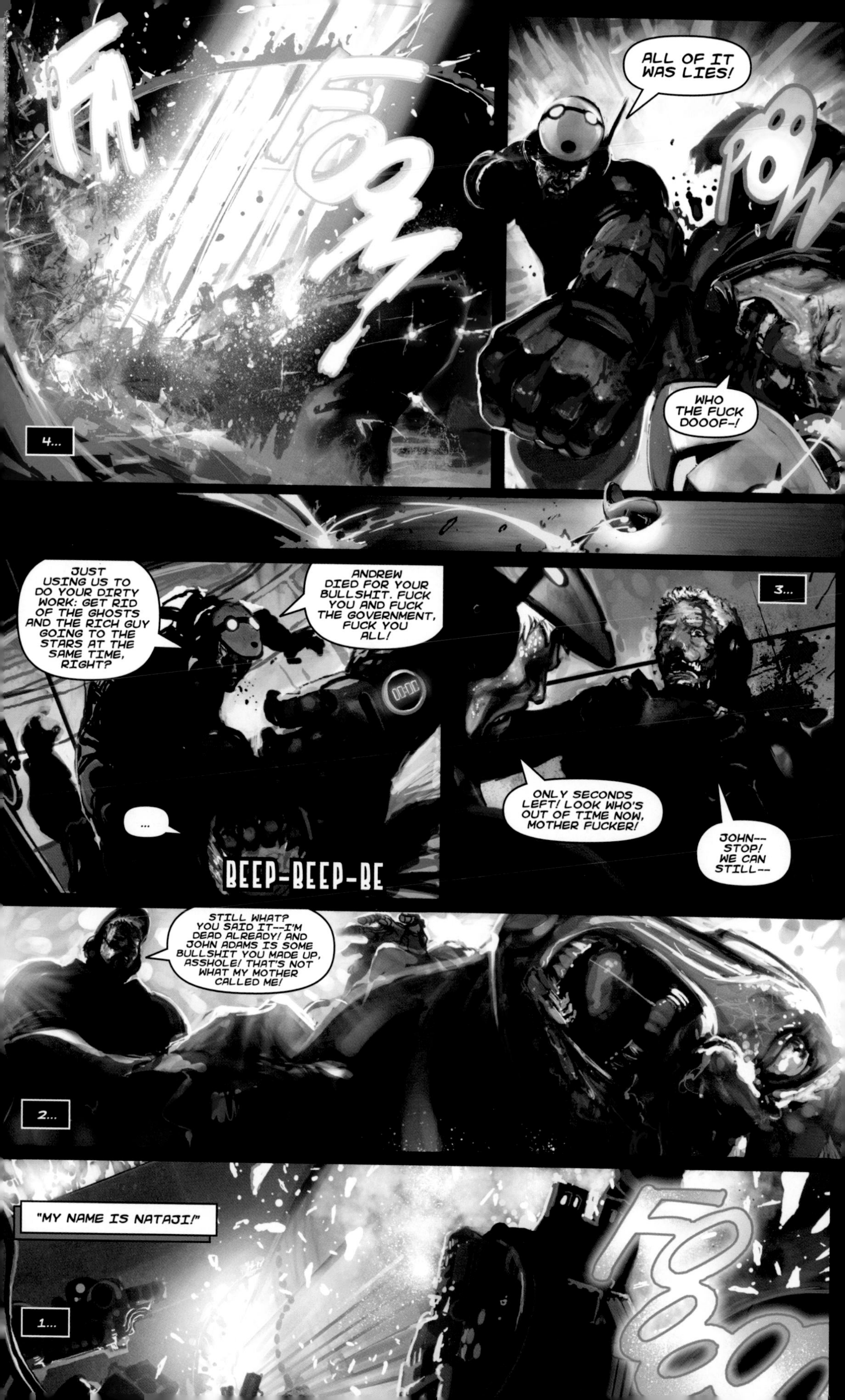

FA-WHOOM
4...
ALL OF IT WAS LIES!
POW
WHO THE FUCK DOOOF-!
JUST USING US TO DO YOUR DIRTY WORK: GET RID OF THE GHOSTS AND THE RICH GUY GOING TO THE STARS AT THE SAME TIME, RIGHT?
ANDREW DIED FOR YOUR BULLSHIT. FUCK YOU AND FUCK THE GOVERNMENT, FUCK YOU ALL!
...
BEEP-BEEP-BE
3...
ONLY SECONDS LEFT! LOOK WHO'S OUT OF TIME NOW, MOTHER FUCKER!
JOHN-- STOP! WE CAN STILL--
STILL WHAT? YOU SAID IT--I'M DEAD ALREADY! AND JOHN ADAMS IS SOME BULLSHIT YOU MADE UP, ASSHOLE! THAT'S NOT WHAT MY MOTHER CALLED ME!
2...
"MY NAME IS NATAJI!"
1...
FOOO

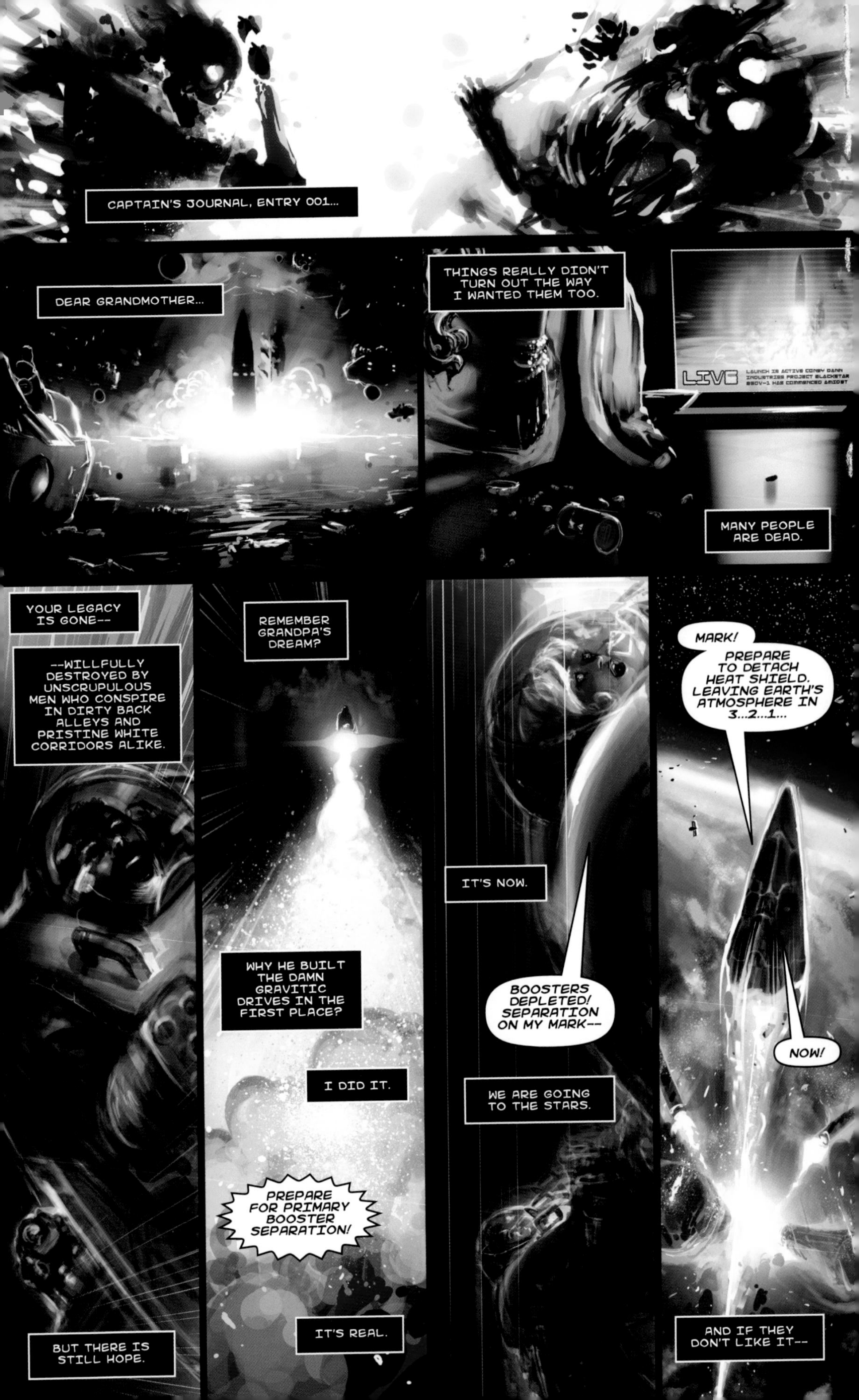
CAPTAIN'S JOURNAL, ENTRY 001...
DEAR GRANDMOTHER...
THINGS REALLY DIDN'T TURN OUT THE WAY I WANTED THEM TOO.
LIVE
LAUNCH IS ACTIVE CONEY DANN INDUSTRIES PROJECT BLACKSTAR SSDV-1 HAS COMMENCED AMIDST
MANY PEOPLE ARE DEAD.
YOUR LEGACY IS GONE--
--WILLFULLY DESTROYED BY UNSCRUPULOUS MEN WHO CONSPIRE IN DIRTY BACK ALLEYS AND PRISTINE WHITE CORRIDORS ALIKE.
BUT THERE IS STILL HOPE.
REMEMBER GRANDPA'S DREAM?
WHY HE BUILT THE DAMN GRAVITIC DRIVES IN THE FIRST PLACE?
I DID IT.
PREPARE FOR PRIMARY BOOSTER SEPARATION!
IT'S REAL.
IT'S NOW.
BOOSTERS DEPLETED! SEPARATION ON MY MARK--
WE ARE GOING TO THE STARS.
MARK!
PREPARE TO DETACH HEAT SHIELD. LEAVING EARTH'S ATMOSPHERE IN 3...2...1...
NOW!
AND IF THEY DON'T LIKE IT--

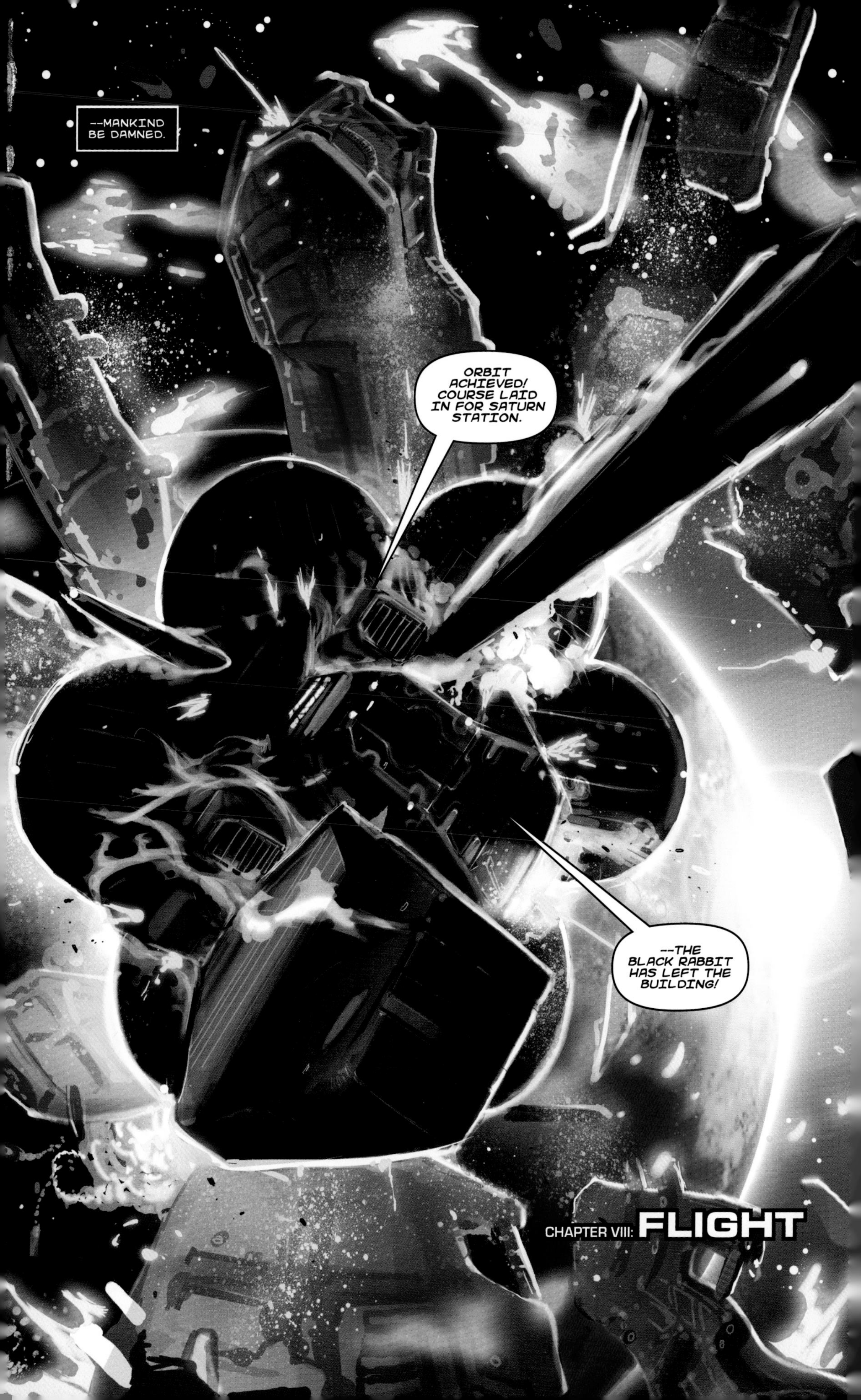
--MANKIND BE DAMNED.
ORBIT ACHIEVED! COURSE LAID IN FOR SATURN STATION.
--THE BLACK RABBIT HAS LEFT THE BUILDING!
CHAPTER VIII: FLIGHT

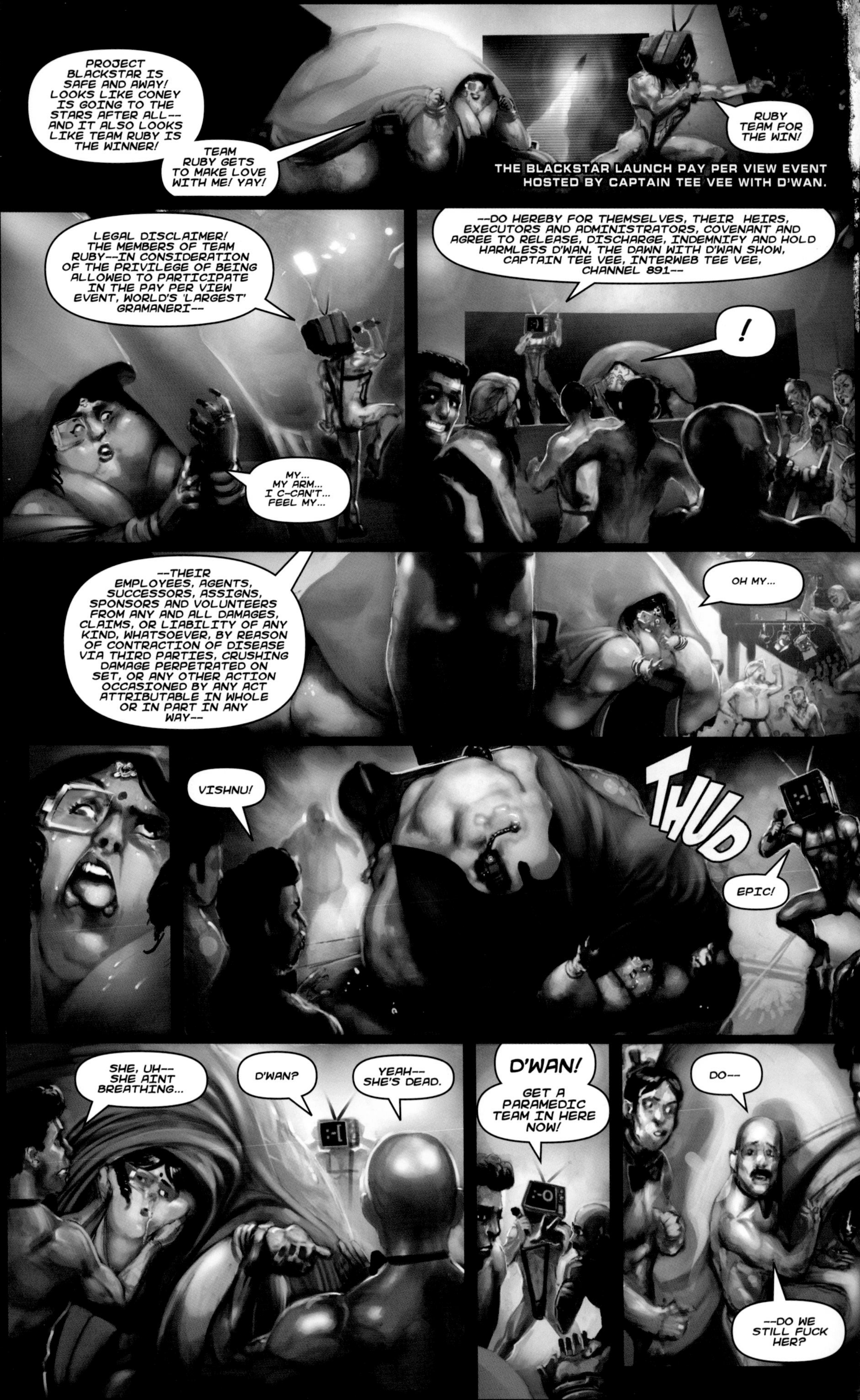
PROJECT BLACKSTAR IS SAFE AND AWAY! LOOKS LIKE CONEY IS GOING TO THE STARS AFTER ALL-- AND IT ALSO LOOKS LIKE TEAM RUBY IS THE WINNER!
TEAM RUBY GETS TO MAKE LOVE WITH ME! YAY!
RUBY TEAM FOR THE WIN!
THE BLACKSTAR LAUNCH PAY PER VIEW EVENT HOSTED BY CAPTAIN TEE VEE WITH D'WAN.
LEGAL DISCLAIMER! THE MEMBERS OF TEAM RUBY--IN CONSIDERATION OF THE PRIVILEGE OF BEING ALLOWED TO PARTICIPATE IN THE PAY PER VIEW EVENT, WORLD'S 'LARGEST' GRAMANERI--
MY... MY ARM... I C-CAN'T... FEEL MY...
--DO HEREBY FOR THEMSELVES, THEIR HEIRS, EXECUTORS AND ADMINISTRATORS, COVENANT AND AGREE TO RELEASE, DISCHARGE, INDEMNIFY AND HOLD HARMLESS D'WAN, THE DAWN WITH D'WAN SHOW, CAPTAIN TEE VEE, INTERWEB TEE VEE, CHANNEL 891--
!
--THEIR EMPLOYEES, AGENTS, SUCCESSORS, ASSIGNS, SPONSORS AND VOLUNTEERS FROM ANY AND ALL DAMAGES, CLAIMS, OR LIABILITY OF ANY KIND, WHATSOEVER, BY REASON OF CONTRACTION OF DISEASE VIA THIRD PARTIES, CRUSHING DAMAGE PERPETRATED ON SET, OR ANY OTHER ACTION OCCASIONED BY ANY ACT ATTRIBUTABLE IN WHOLE OR IN PART IN ANY WAY--
OH MY...
VISHNU!
THUD
EPIC!
SHE, UH-- SHE AINT BREATHING...
D'WAN?
YEAH-- SHE'S DEAD.
D'WAN!
GET A PARAMEDIC TEAM IN HERE NOW!
DO--
--DO WE STILL FUCK HER?

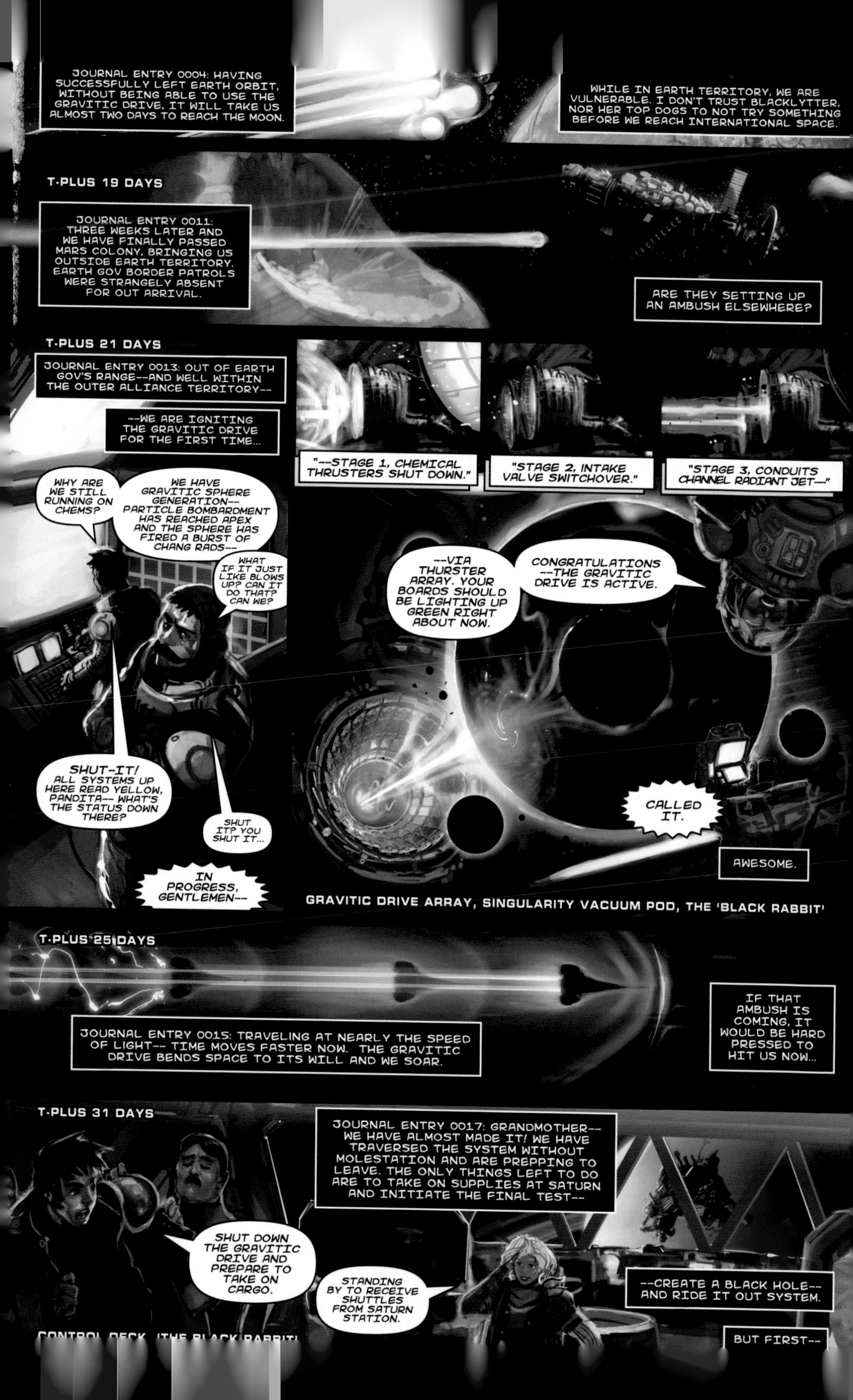
JOURNAL ENTRY 0004: HAVING SUCCESSFULLY LEFT EARTH ORBIT, WITHOUT BEING ABLE TO USE THE GRAVITIC DRIVE, IT WILL TAKE US ALMOST TWO DAYS TO REACH THE MOON.
WHILE IN EARTH TERRITORY, WE ARE VULNERABLE. I DON'T TRUST BLACKLYTTER, NOR HER TOP DOGS TO NOT TRY SOMETHING BEFORE WE REACH INTERNATIONAL SPACE.
T-PLUS 19 DAYS
JOURNAL ENTRY 0011: THREE WEEKS LATER AND WE HAVE FINALLY PASSED MARS COLONY, BRINGING US OUTSIDE EARTH TERRITORY. EARTH GOV BORDER PATROLS WERE STRANGELY ABSENT FOR OUT ARRIVAL.
ARE THEY SETTING UP AN AMBUSH ELSEWHERE?
T-PLUS 21 DAYS
JOURNAL ENTRY 0013: OUT OF EARTH GOV'S RANGE--AND WELL WITHIN THE OUTER ALLIANCE TERRITORY--
--WE ARE IGNITING THE GRAVITIC DRIVE FOR THE FIRST TIME...
"--STAGE 1, CHEMICAL THRUSTERS SHUT DOWN."
"STAGE 2, INTAKE VALVE SWITCHOVER."
"STAGE 3, CONDUITS CHANNEL RADIANT JET--"
WHY ARE WE STILL RUNNING ON CHEMS?
WE HAVE GRAVITIC SPHERE GENERATION-- PARTICLE BOMBARDMENT HAS REACHED APEX AND THE SPHERE HAS FIRED A BURST OF CHANG RADS--
WHAT IF IT JUST LIKE BLOWS UP? CAN IT DO THAT? CAN WE?
--VIA THURSTER ARRAY. YOUR BOARDS SHOULD BE LIGHTING UP GREEN RIGHT ABOUT NOW.
CONGRATULATIONS --THE GRAVITIC DRIVE IS ACTIVE.
SHUT-IT! ALL SYSTEMS UP HERE READ YELLOW, PANDITA-- WHAT'S THE STATUS DOWN THERE?
SHUT IT? YOU SHUT IT...
IN PROGRESS, GENTLEMEN--
CALLED IT.
AWESOME.
GRAVITIC DRIVE ARRAY, SINGULARITY VACUUM POD, THE 'BLACK RABBIT'
T-PLUS 25 DAYS
JOURNAL ENTRY 0015: TRAVELING AT NEARLY THE SPEED OF LIGHT-- TIME MOVES FASTER NOW. THE GRAVITIC DRIVE BENDS SPACE TO ITS WILL AND WE SOAR.
IF THAT AMBUSH IS COMING, IT WOULD BE HARD PRESSED TO HIT US NOW...
T-PLUS 31 DAYS
JOURNAL ENTRY 0017: GRANDMOTHER-- WE HAVE ALMOST MADE IT! WE HAVE TRAVERSED THE SYSTEM WITHOUT MOLESTATION AND ARE PREPPING TO LEAVE. THE ONLY THINGS LEFT TO DO ARE TO TAKE ON SUPPLIES AT SATURN AND INITIATE THE FINAL TEST--
SHUT DOWN THE GRAVITIC DRIVE AND PREPARE TO TAKE ON CARGO.
STANDING BY TO RECEIVE SHUTTLES FROM SATURN STATION.
--CREATE A BLACK HOLE-- AND RIDE IT OUT SYSTEM.
BUT FIRST--

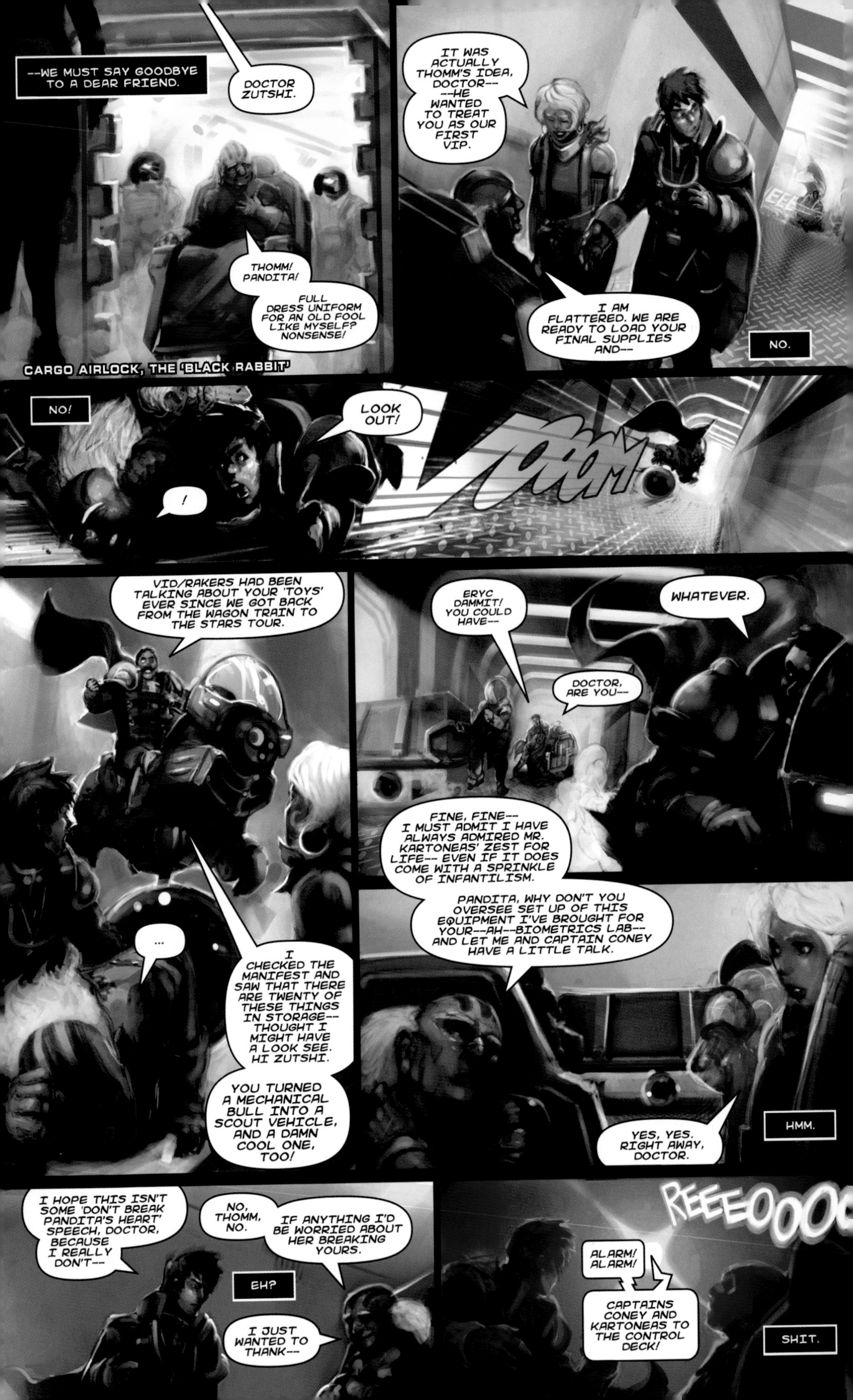
--WE MUST SAY GOODBYE TO A DEAR FRIEND.
DOCTOR ZUTSHI.
THOMM! PANDITA!
FULL DRESS UNIFORM FOR AN OLD FOOL LIKE MYSELF? NONSENSE!
CARGO AIRLOCK, THE 'BLACK RABBIT'
IT WAS ACTUALLY THOMM'S IDEA, DOCTOR-- --HE WANTED TO TREAT YOU AS OUR FIRST VIP.
I AM FLATTERED. WE ARE READY TO LOAD YOUR FINAL SUPPLIES AND--
NO.
NO!
LOOK OUT!
!
VOOM
VID/RAKERS HAD BEEN TALKING ABOUT YOUR 'TOYS' EVER SINCE WE GOT BACK FROM THE WAGON TRAIN TO THE STARS TOUR.
...
I CHECKED THE MANIFEST AND SAW THAT THERE ARE TWENTY OF THESE THINGS IN STORAGE-- THOUGHT I MIGHT HAVE A LOOK SEE. HI ZUTSHI.
YOU TURNED A MECHANICAL BULL INTO A SCOUT VEHICLE, AND A DAMN COOL ONE, TOO!
ERYC DAMMIT! YOU COULD HAVE--
WHATEVER.
DOCTOR, ARE YOU--
FINE, FINE-- I MUST ADMIT I HAVE ALWAYS ADMIRED MR. KARTONEAS' ZEST FOR LIFE-- EVEN IF IT DOES COME WITH A SPRINKLE OF INFANTILISM.
PANDITA, WHY DON'T YOU OVERSEE SET UP OF THIS EQUIPMENT I'VE BROUGHT FOR YOUR--AH--BIOMETRICS LAB-- AND LET ME AND CAPTAIN CONEY HAVE A LITTLE TALK.
YES, YES. RIGHT AWAY, DOCTOR.
HMM.
I HOPE THIS ISN'T SOME 'DON'T BREAK PANDITA'S HEART' SPEECH, DOCTOR, BECAUSE I REALLY DON'T--
NO, THOMM, NO.
IF ANYTHING I'D BE WORRIED ABOUT HER BREAKING YOURS.
EH?
I JUST WANTED TO THANK--
REEEOOOO
ALARM! ALARM!
CAPTAINS CONEY AND KARTONEAS TO THE CONTROL DECK!
SHIT.

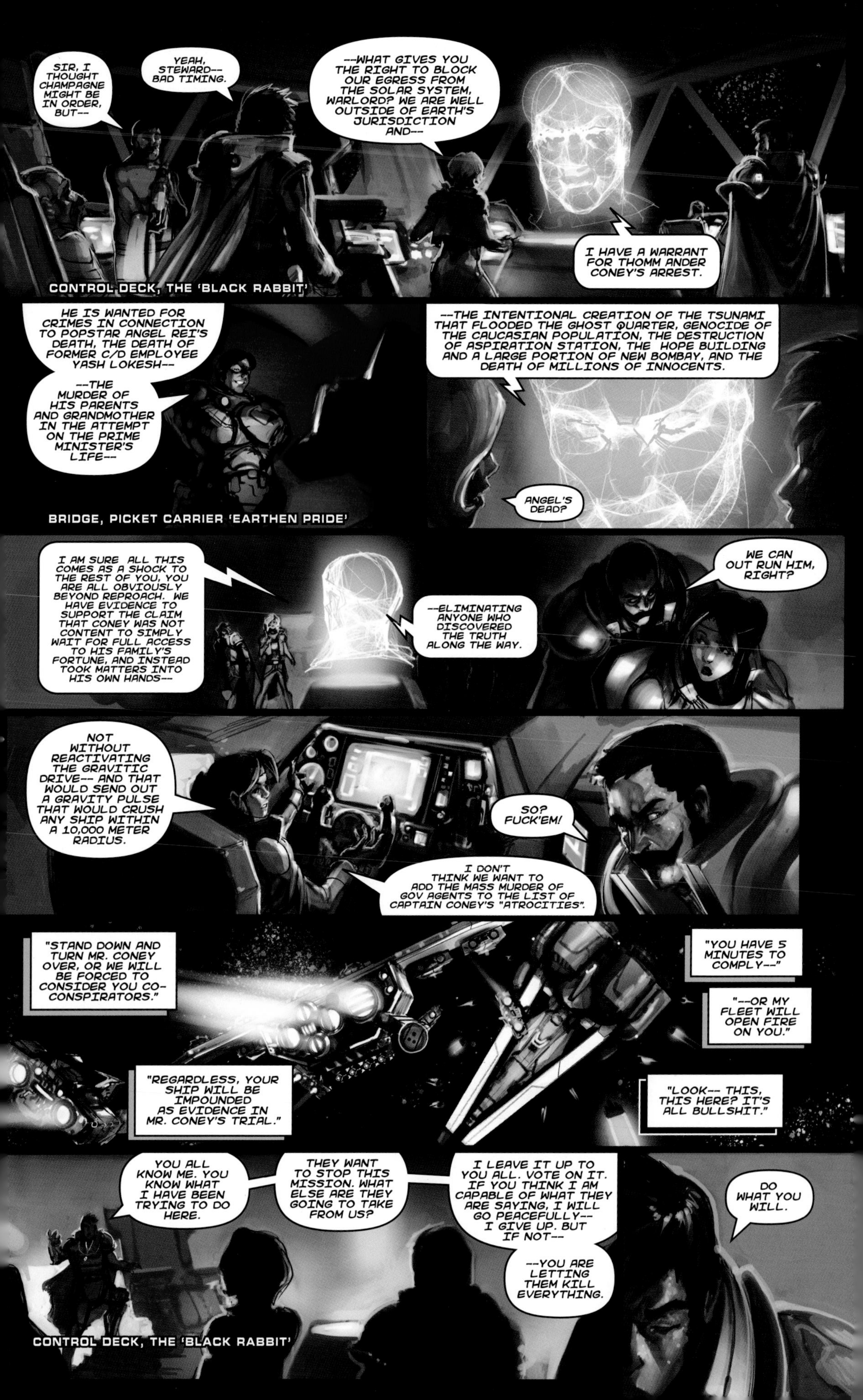
SIR, I THOUGHT CHAMPAGNE MIGHT BE IN ORDER, BUT--
YEAH, STEWARD-- BAD TIMING.
--WHAT GIVES YOU THE RIGHT TO BLOCK OUR EGRESS FROM THE SOLAR SYSTEM, WARLORD? WE ARE WELL OUTSIDE OF EARTH'S JURISDICTION AND--
I HAVE A WARRANT FOR THOMM ANDER CONEY'S ARREST.
CONTROL DECK, THE 'BLACK RABBIT'
HE IS WANTED FOR CRIMES IN CONNECTION TO POPSTAR ANGEL REI'S DEATH, THE DEATH OF FORMER C/D EMPLOYEE YASH LOKESH--
--THE MURDER OF HIS PARENTS AND GRANDMOTHER IN THE ATTEMPT ON THE PRIME MINISTER'S LIFE--
BRIDGE, PICKET CARRIER 'EARTHEN PRIDE'
--THE INTENTIONAL CREATION OF THE TSUNAMI THAT FLOODED THE GHOST QUARTER, GENOCIDE OF THE CAUCASIAN POPULATION, THE DESTRUCTION OF ASPIRATION STATION, THE HOPE BUILDING AND A LARGE PORTION OF NEW BOMBAY, AND THE DEATH OF MILLIONS OF INNOCENTS.
ANGEL'S DEAD?
I AM SURE ALL THIS COMES AS A SHOCK TO THE REST OF YOU, YOU ARE ALL OBVIOUSLY BEYOND REPROACH. WE HAVE EVIDENCE TO SUPPORT THE CLAIM THAT CONEY WAS NOT CONTENT TO SIMPLY WAIT FOR FULL ACCESS TO HIS FAMILY'S FORTUNE, AND INSTEAD TOOK MATTERS INTO HIS OWN HANDS--
--ELIMINATING ANYONE WHO DISCOVERED THE TRUTH ALONG THE WAY.
WE CAN OUT RUN HIM, RIGHT?
NOT WITHOUT REACTIVATING THE GRAVITIC DRIVE-- AND THAT WOULD SEND OUT A GRAVITY PULSE THAT WOULD CRUSH ANY SHIP WITHIN A 10,000 METER RADIUS.
SO? FUCK'EM!
I DON'T THINK WE WANT TO ADD THE MASS MURDER OF GOV AGENTS TO THE LIST OF CAPTAIN CONEY'S "ATROCITIES".
"STAND DOWN AND TURN MR. CONEY OVER, OR WE WILL BE FORCED TO CONSIDER YOU CO-CONSPIRATORS."
"YOU HAVE 5 MINUTES TO COMPLY--"
"--OR MY FLEET WILL OPEN FIRE ON YOU."
"REGARDLESS, YOUR SHIP WILL BE IMPOUNDED AS EVIDENCE IN MR. CONEY'S TRIAL."
"LOOK-- THIS, THIS HERE? IT'S ALL BULLSHIT."
YOU ALL KNOW ME. YOU KNOW WHAT I HAVE BEEN TRYING TO DO HERE.
THEY WANT TO STOP THIS MISSION. WHAT ELSE ARE THEY GOING TO TAKE FROM US?
I LEAVE IT UP TO YOU ALL. VOTE ON IT. IF YOU THINK I AM CAPABLE OF WHAT THEY ARE SAYING, I WILL GO PEACEFULLY-- I GIVE UP. BUT IF NOT--
--YOU ARE LETTING THEM KILL EVERYTHING.
DO WHAT YOU WILL.
CONTROL DECK, THE 'BLACK RABBIT'

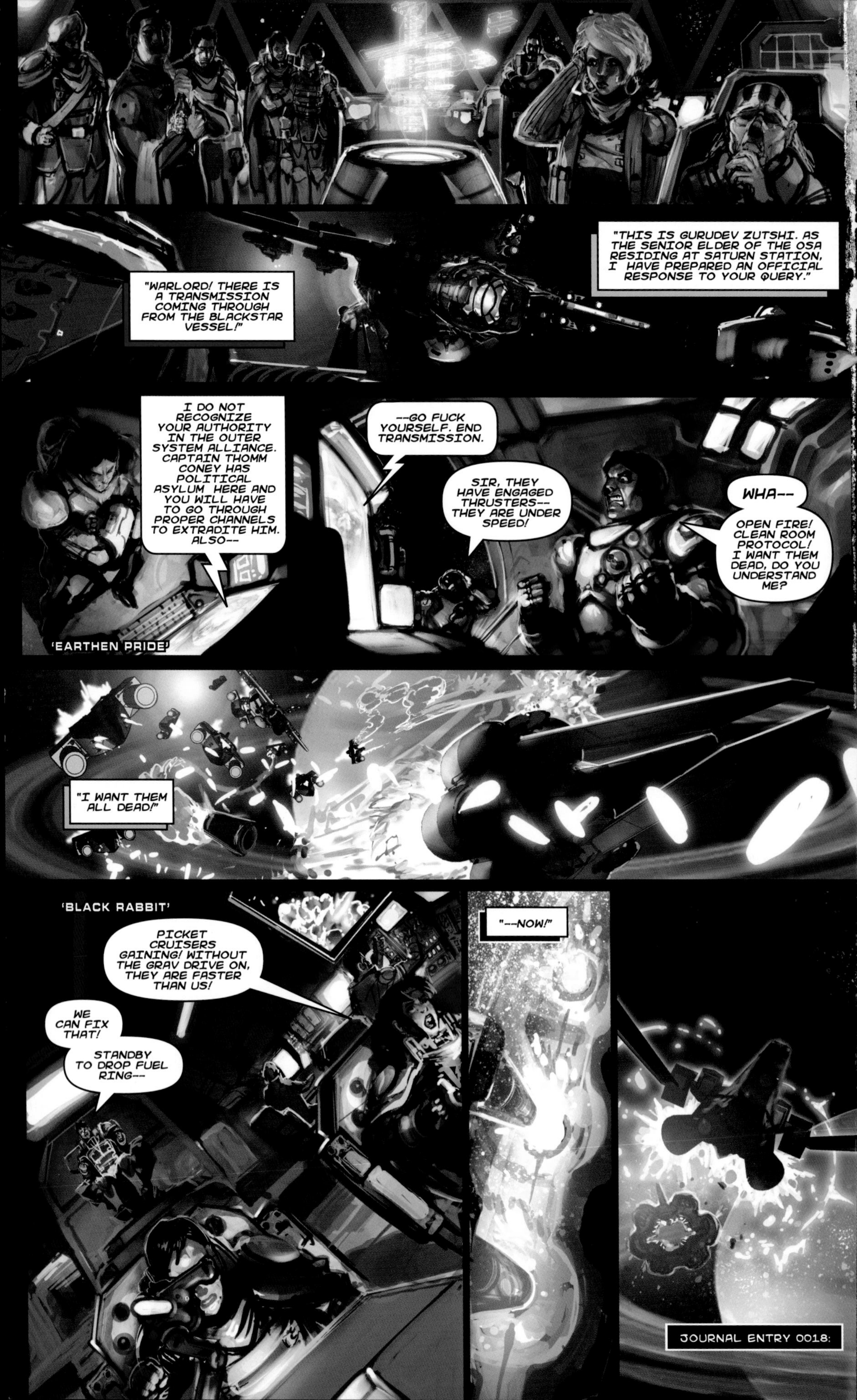
"WARLORD! THERE IS A TRANSMISSION COMING THROUGH FROM THE BLACKSTAR VESSEL!"
"THIS IS GURUDEV ZUTSHI. AS THE SENIOR ELDER OF THE OSA RESIDING AT SATURN STATION, I HAVE PREPARED AN OFFICIAL RESPONSE TO YOUR QUERY."
I DO NOT RECOGNIZE YOUR AUTHORITY IN THE OUTER SYSTEM ALLIANCE. CAPTAIN THOMM CONEY HAS POLITICAL ASYLUM HERE AND YOU WILL HAVE TO GO THROUGH PROPER CHANNELS TO EXTRADITE HIM. ALSO--
'EARTHEN PRIDE'
--GO FUCK YOURSELF. END TRANSMISSION.
SIR, THEY HAVE ENGAGED THRUSTERS-- THEY ARE UNDER SPEED!
WHA--
OPEN FIRE! CLEAN ROOM PROTOCOL! I WANT THEM DEAD, DO YOU UNDERSTAND ME?
"I WANT THEM ALL DEAD!"
'BLACK RABBIT'
PICKET CRUISERS GAINING! WITHOUT THE GRAV DRIVE ON, THEY ARE FASTER THAN US!
WE CAN FIX THAT!
STANDBY TO DROP FUEL RING--
"--NOW!"
JOURNAL ENTRY 0018:

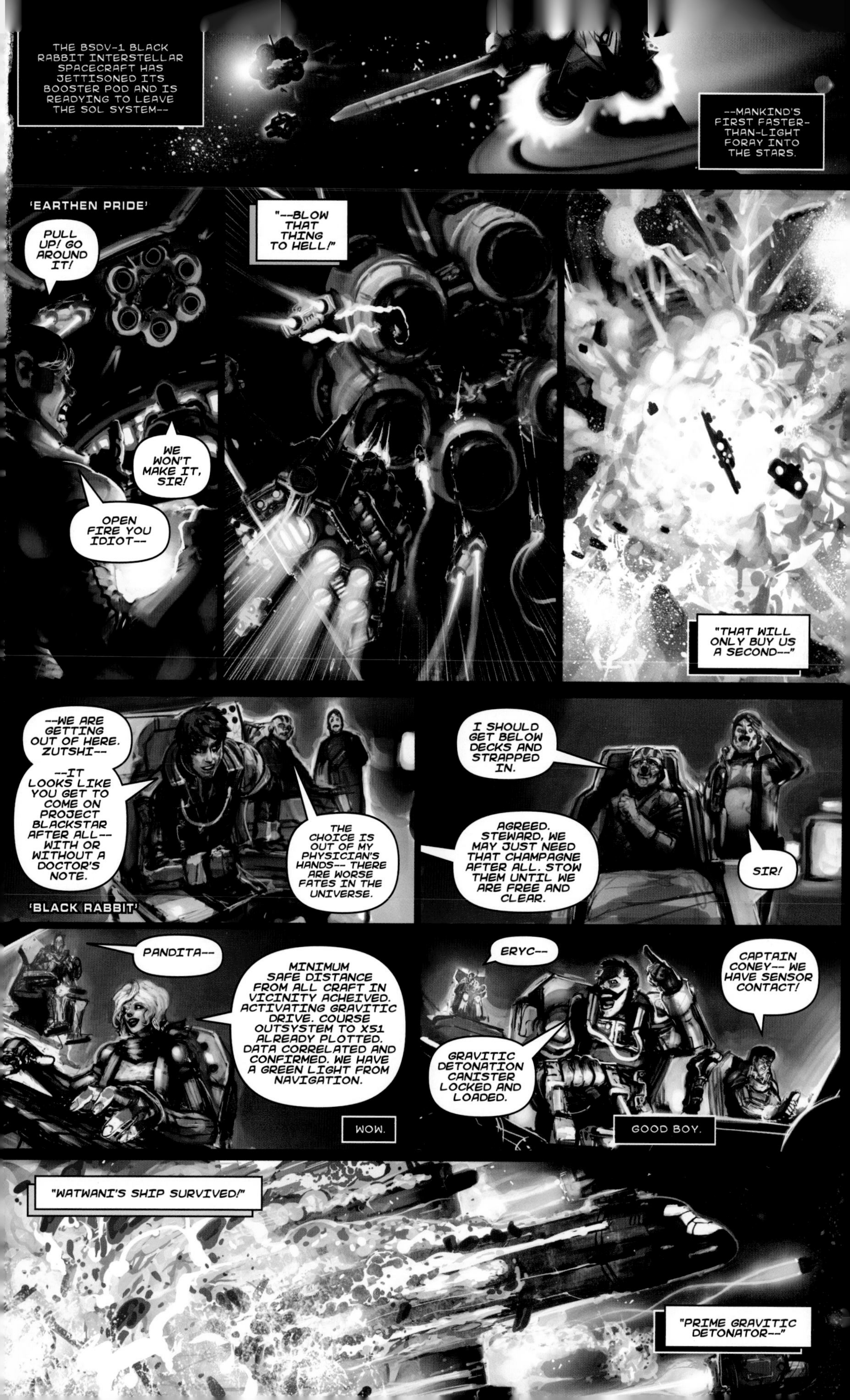
THE BSDV-1 BLACK RABBIT INTERSTELLAR SPACECRAFT HAS JETTISONED ITS BOOSTER POD AND IS READYING TO LEAVE THE SOL SYSTEM--
--MANKIND'S FIRST FASTER-THAN-LIGHT FORAY INTO THE STARS.
'EARTHEN PRIDE'
PULL UP! GO AROUND IT!
WE WON'T MAKE IT, SIR!
OPEN FIRE YOU IDIOT--
"--BLOW THAT THING TO HELL!"
"THAT WILL ONLY BUY US A SECOND--"
--WE ARE GETTING OUT OF HERE. ZUTSHI--
--IT LOOKS LIKE YOU GET TO COME ON PROJECT BLACKSTAR AFTER ALL--WITH OR WITHOUT A DOCTOR'S NOTE.
THE CHOICE IS OUT OF MY PHYSICIAN'S HANDS-- THERE ARE WORSE FATES IN THE UNIVERSE.
'BLACK RABBIT'
I SHOULD GET BELOW DECKS AND STRAPPED IN.
AGREED. STEWARD, WE MAY JUST NEED THAT CHAMPAGNE AFTER ALL. STOW THEM UNTIL WE ARE FREE AND CLEAR.
SIR!
PANDITA--
MINIMUM SAFE DISTANCE FROM ALL CRAFT IN VICINITY ACHEIVED. ACTIVATING GRAVITIC DRIVE. COURSE OUTSYSTEM TO X51 ALREADY PLOTTED. DATA CORRELATED AND CONFIRMED. WE HAVE A GREEN LIGHT FROM NAVIGATION.
WOW.
ERYC--
GRAVITIC DETONATION CANISTER LOCKED AND LOADED.
CAPTAIN CONEY-- WE HAVE SENSOR CONTACT!
GOOD BOY.
"WATWANI'S SHIP SURVIVED!"
"PRIME GRAVITIC DETONATOR--"

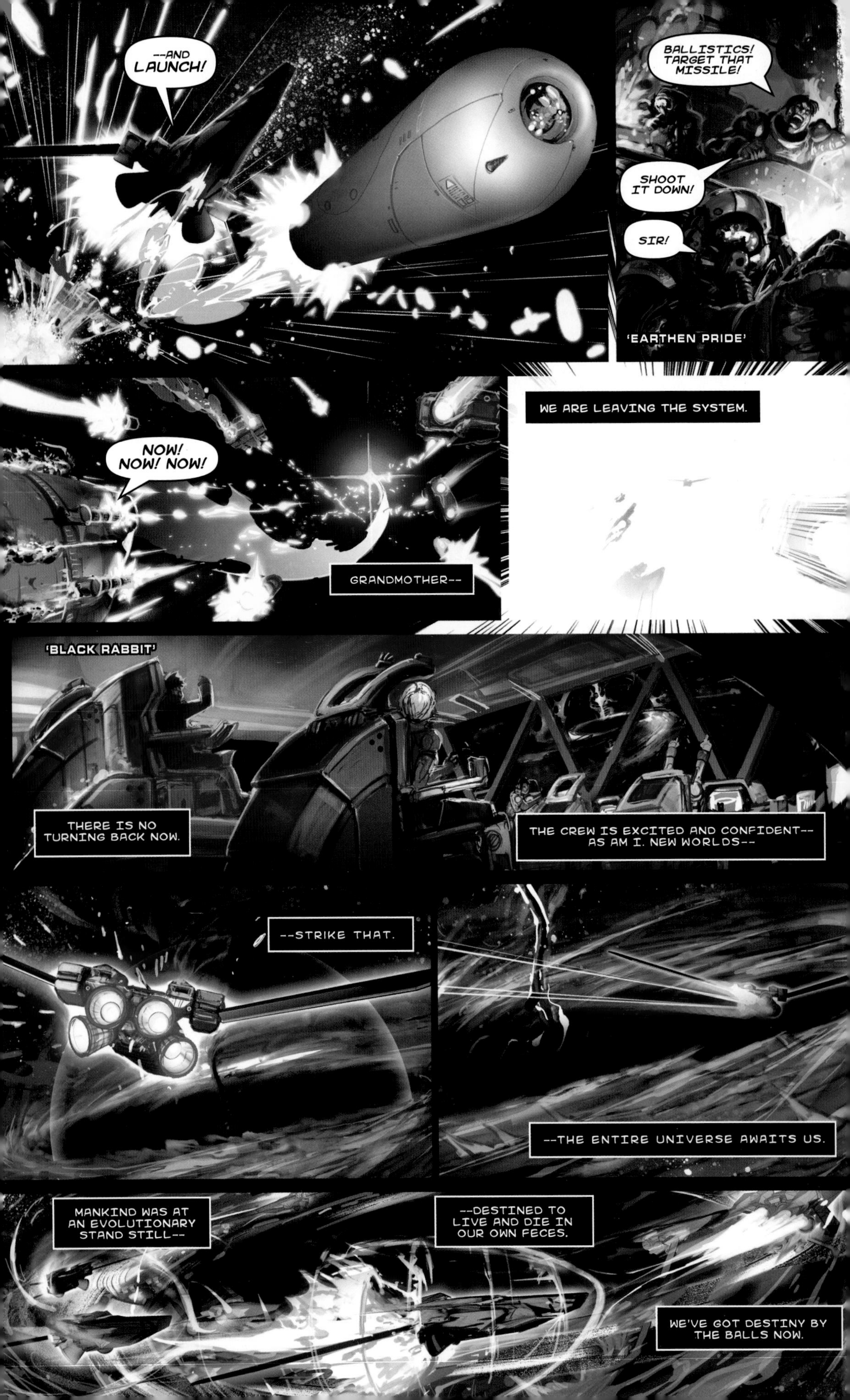
--AND
LAUNCH!
BALLISTICS! TARGET THAT MISSILE!
SHOOT IT DOWN!
SIR!
'EARTHEN PRIDE'
NOW! NOW! NOW!
GRANDMOTHER--
WE ARE LEAVING THE SYSTEM.
'BLACK RABBIT'
THERE IS NO TURNING BACK NOW.
THE CREW IS EXCITED AND CONFIDENT-- AS AM I. NEW WORLDS--
--STRIKE THAT.
--THE ENTIRE UNIVERSE AWAITS US.
MANKIND WAS AT AN EVOLUTIONARY STAND STILL--
--DESTINED TO LIVE AND DIE IN OUR OWN FECES.
WE'VE GOT DESTINY BY THE BALLS NOW.

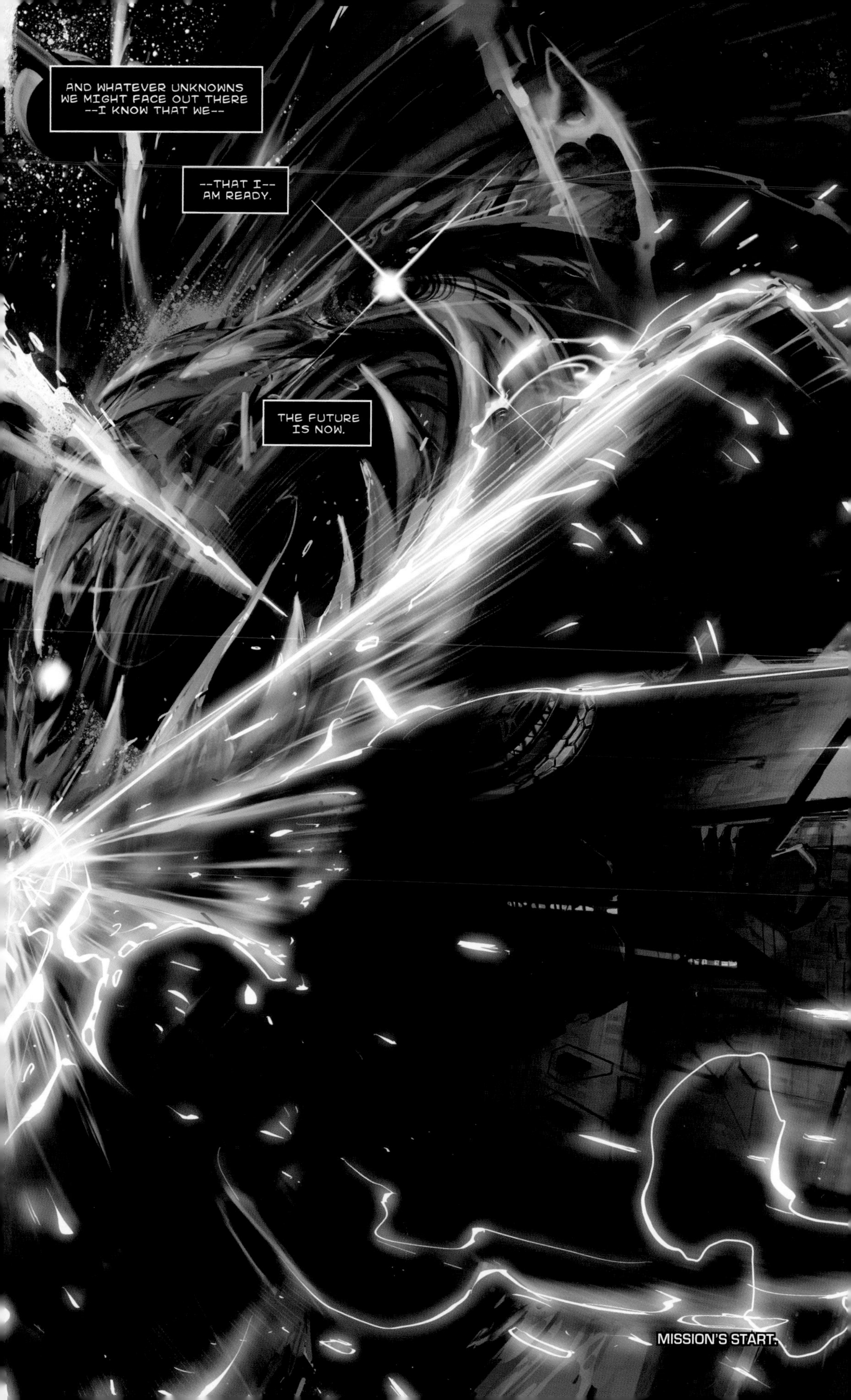
AND WHATEVER UNKNOWNS WE MIGHT FACE OUT THERE --I KNOW THAT WE--
--THAT I-- AM READY.
THE FUTURE IS NOW.
MISSION'S START.

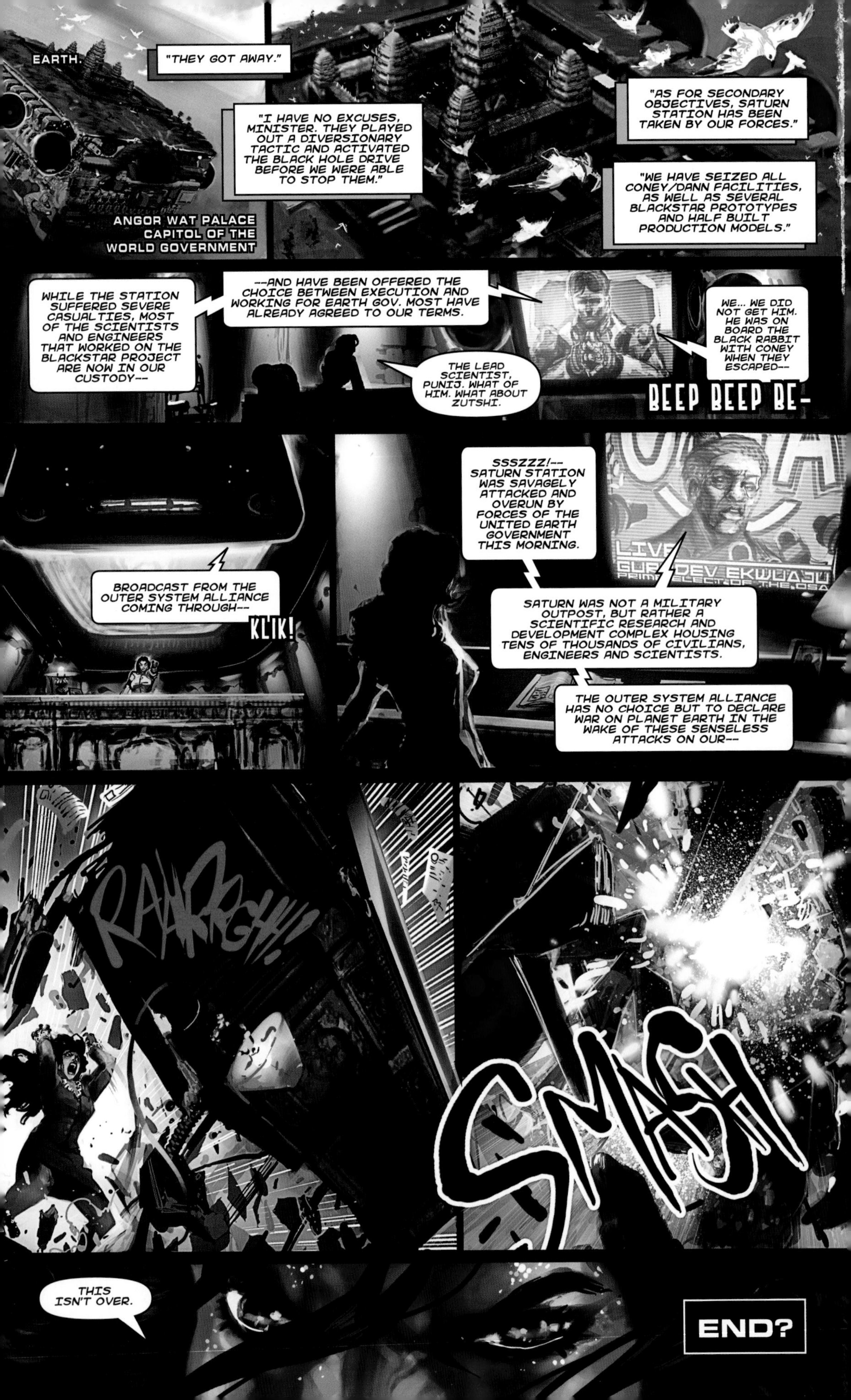
EARTH.
"THEY GOT AWAY."
ANGOR WAT PALACE CAPITOL OF THE WORLD GOVERNMENT
"I HAVE NO EXCUSES, MINISTER. THEY PLAYED OUT A DIVERSIONARY TACTIC AND ACTIVATED THE BLACK HOLE DRIVE BEFORE WE WERE ABLE TO STOP THEM."
"AS FOR SECONDARY OBJECTIVES, SATURN STATION HAS BEEN TAKEN BY OUR FORCES."
"WE HAVE SEIZED ALL CONEY/DANN FACILITIES, AS WELL AS SEVERAL BLACKSTAR PROTOTYPES AND HALF BUILT PRODUCTION MODELS."
WHILE THE STATION SUFFERED SEVERE CASUALTIES, MOST OF THE SCIENTISTS AND ENGINEERS THAT WORKED ON THE BLACKSTAR PROJECT ARE NOW IN OUR CUSTODY--
--AND HAVE BEEN OFFERED THE CHOICE BETWEEN EXECUTION AND WORKING FOR EARTH GOV. MOST HAVE ALREADY AGREED TO OUR TERMS.
THE LEAD SCIENTIST, PUNIJ. WHAT OF HIM. WHAT ABOUT ZUTSHI.
WE... WE DID NOT GET HIM. HE WAS ON BOARD THE BLACK RABBIT WITH CONEY WHEN THEY ESCAPED--
BEEP BEEP BE-
BROADCAST FROM THE OUTER SYSTEM ALLIANCE COMING THROUGH--
KLIK!
SSSZZZ!-- SATURN STATION WAS SAVAGELY ATTACKED AND OVERUN BY FORCES OF THE UNITED EARTH GOVERNMENT THIS MORNING.
LIVE
GURDEV EKWUAJU
SATURN WAS NOT A MILITARY OUTPOST, BUT RATHER A SCIENTIFIC RESEARCH AND DEVELOPMENT COMPLEX HOUSING TENS OF THOUSANDS OF CIVILIANS, ENGINEERS AND SCIENTISTS.
THE OUTER SYSTEM ALLIANCE HAS NO CHOICE BUT TO DECLARE WAR ON PLANET EARTH IN THE WAKE OF THESE SENSELESS ATTACKS ON OUR--
RAAARRGH!!
SMASH
THIS ISN'T OVER.
END?

Created and Written by
Andrew E. C. Gaska

Illustrated by
Dan Dussault

Letters by
Nina Kester

Frontispiece and Afterword by
Chandra Free

Proofs by
Duncan McLachlan

Design by
Yumi Nakamura

NASA Consultant
BJ Young

Concept
Critical Millennium uniform and Black Rabbit concepts,
CDI Freighter and logo design by
Andrew E. C. Gaska

Final starship, architectural, and character design by
Dan Dussault

Initial Critical Millennium concept by
Andrew E. C. Gaska
and Christian Berntsen

Thomm Coney and the crew of the Black Rabbit
will return in the graphic novel event:

CRITICAL MILLENNIUM:
THE DARK FRONTIER
BEACON

Paul Morrissey, *Editor*
Scott Newman, *Production Manager*

Archaia Entertainment LLC

PJ Bickett, *CEO*
Mark Smylie, *CCO*
Mike Kennedy, *Publisher*
Stephen Christy, *Editor-in-Chief*

Published by **Archaia**

Archaia Entertainment LLC
1680 Vine Street, Suite 912
Los Angeles, California, 90028, USA
www.archaia.com

ARCHAIA™
NEW STORIES. NEW WORLDS.

CRITICAL MILLENNIUM: THE DARK FRONTIER. September 2011. FIRST PRINTING

10 9 8 7 6 5 4 3 2 1

ISBN: 1-932386-98-X

ISBN 13: 978-1-932386-98-1

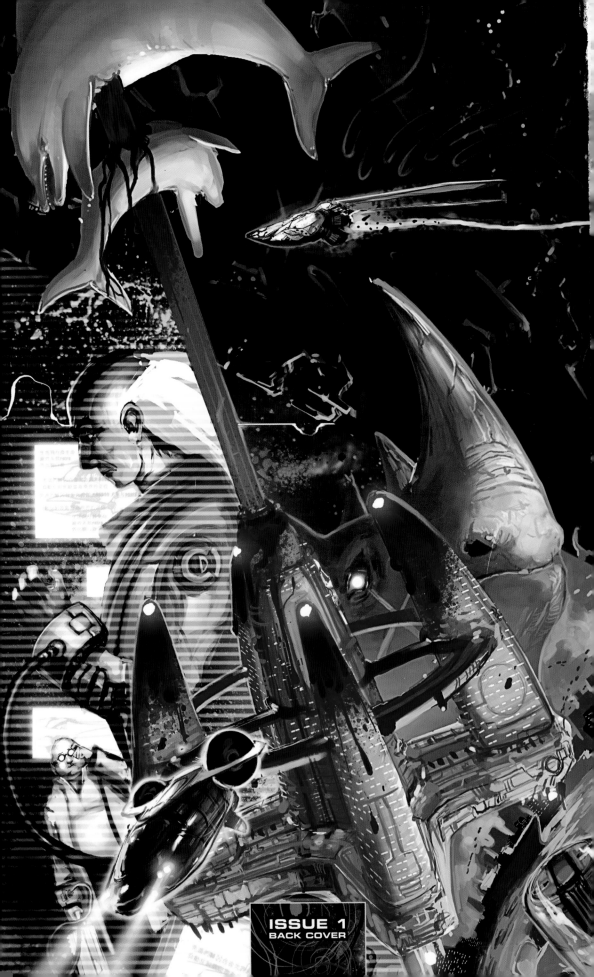

ISSUE 1
BACK COVER

ISSUE 1
FRONT COVER

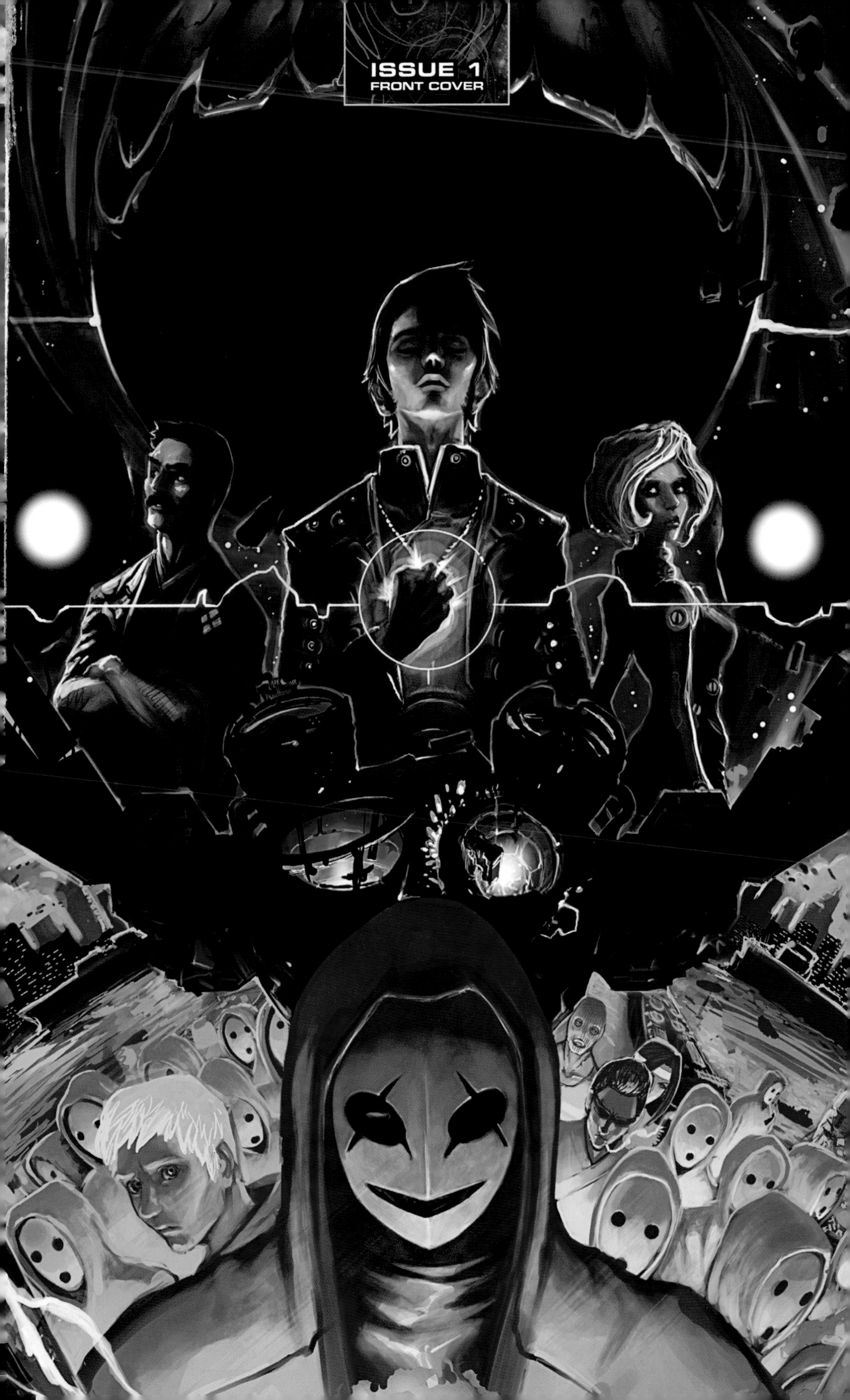

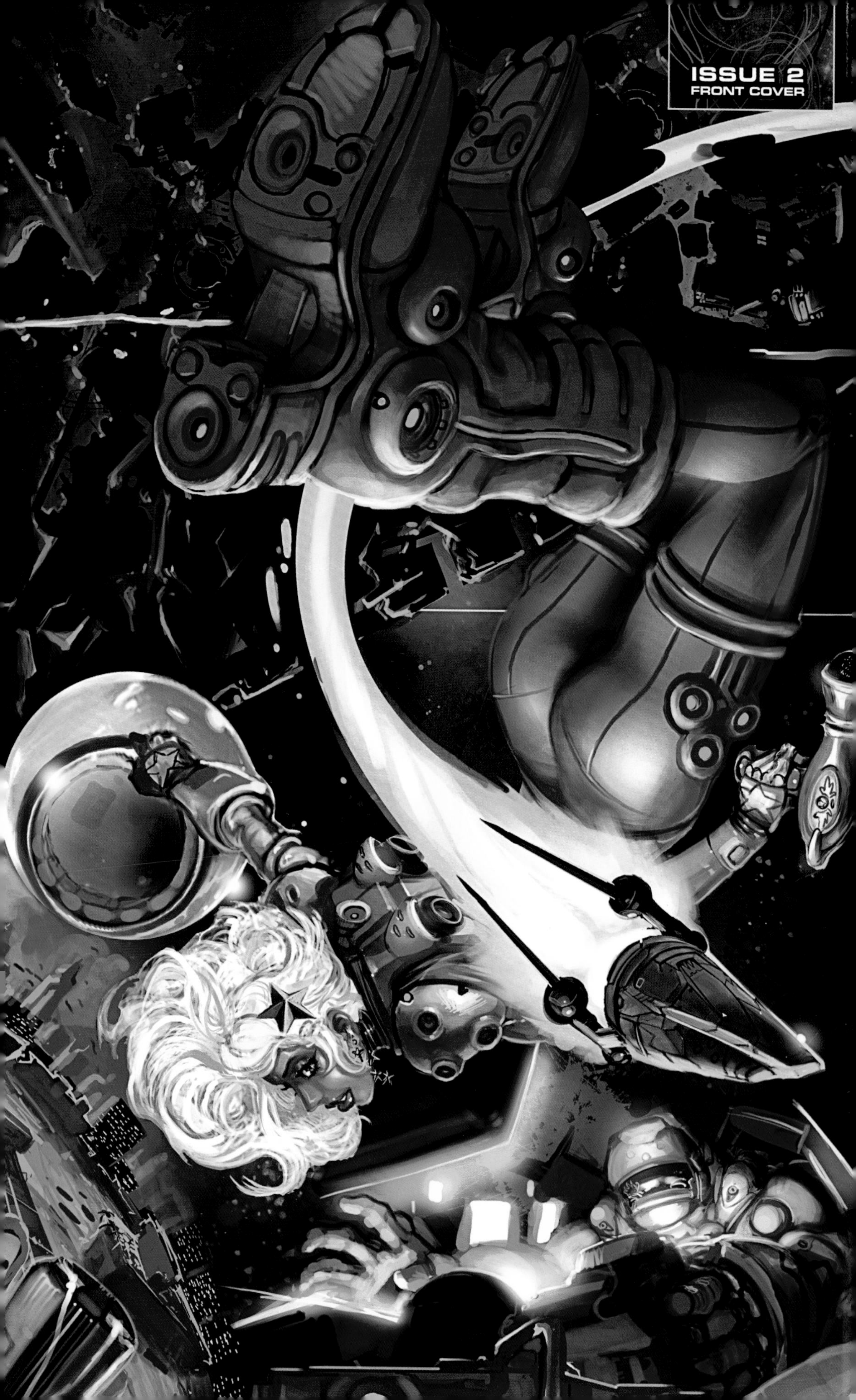

ISSUE 2
FRONT COVER

ISSUE 3
FRONT COVER

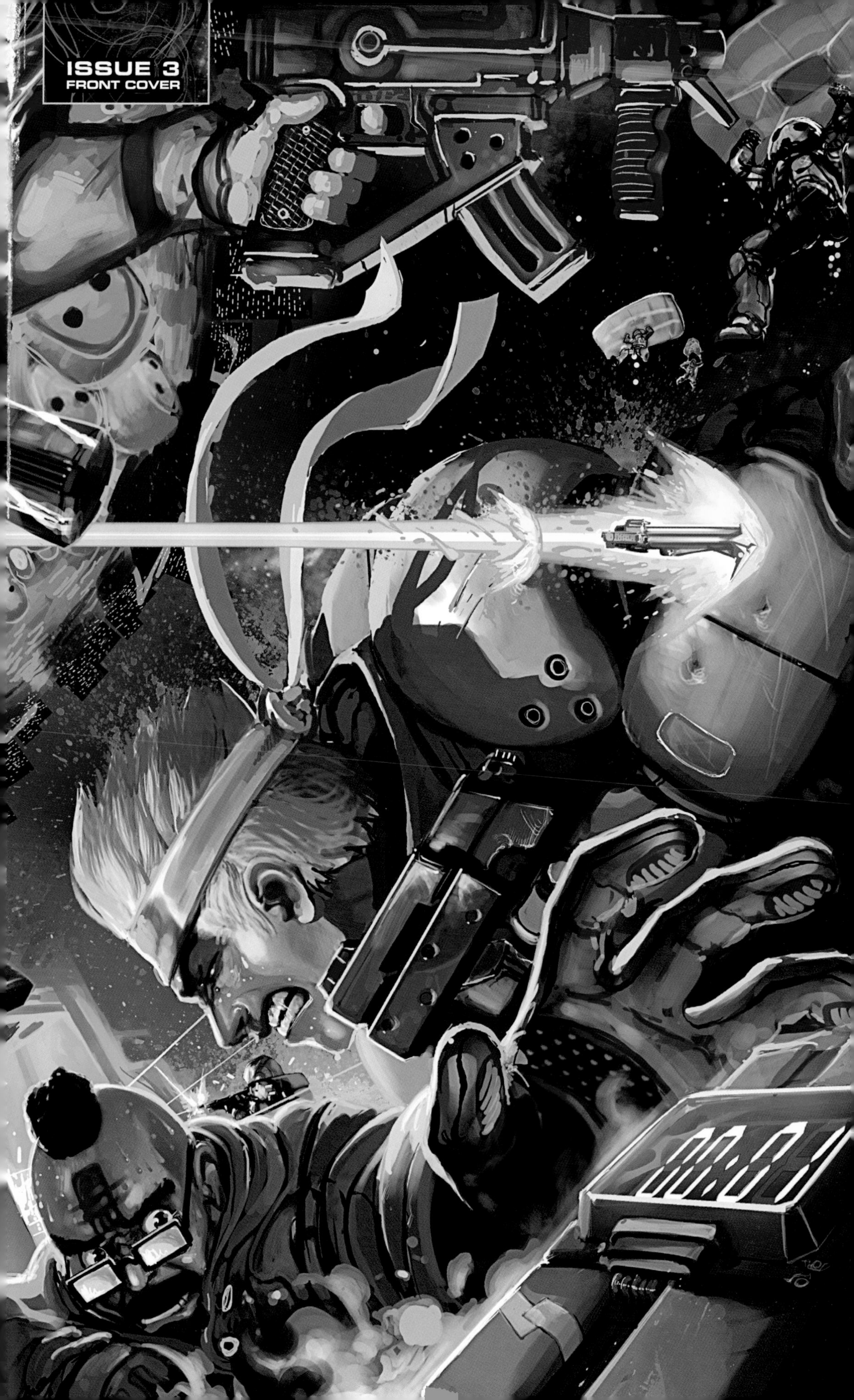

ISSUE 4
BACK COVER

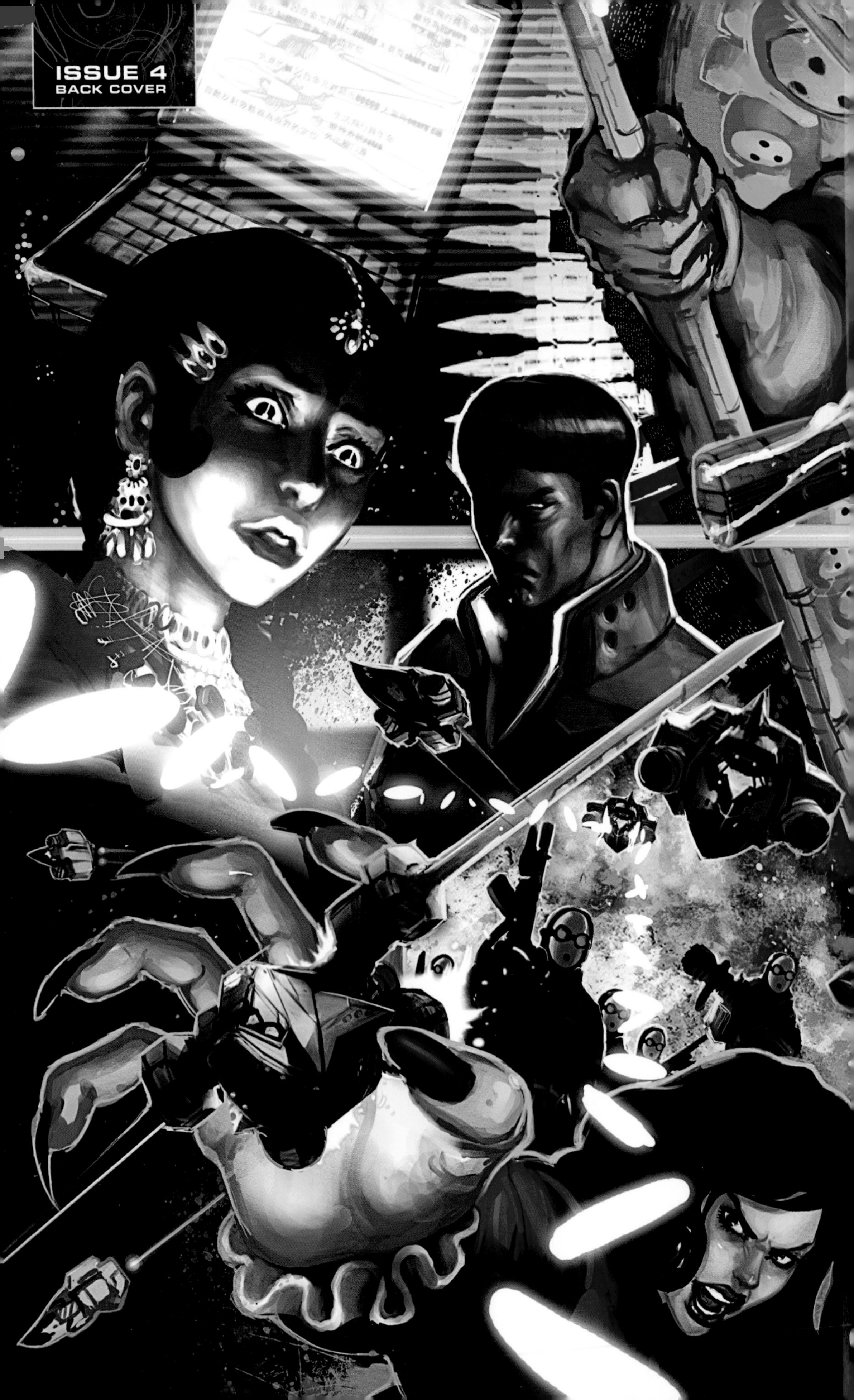

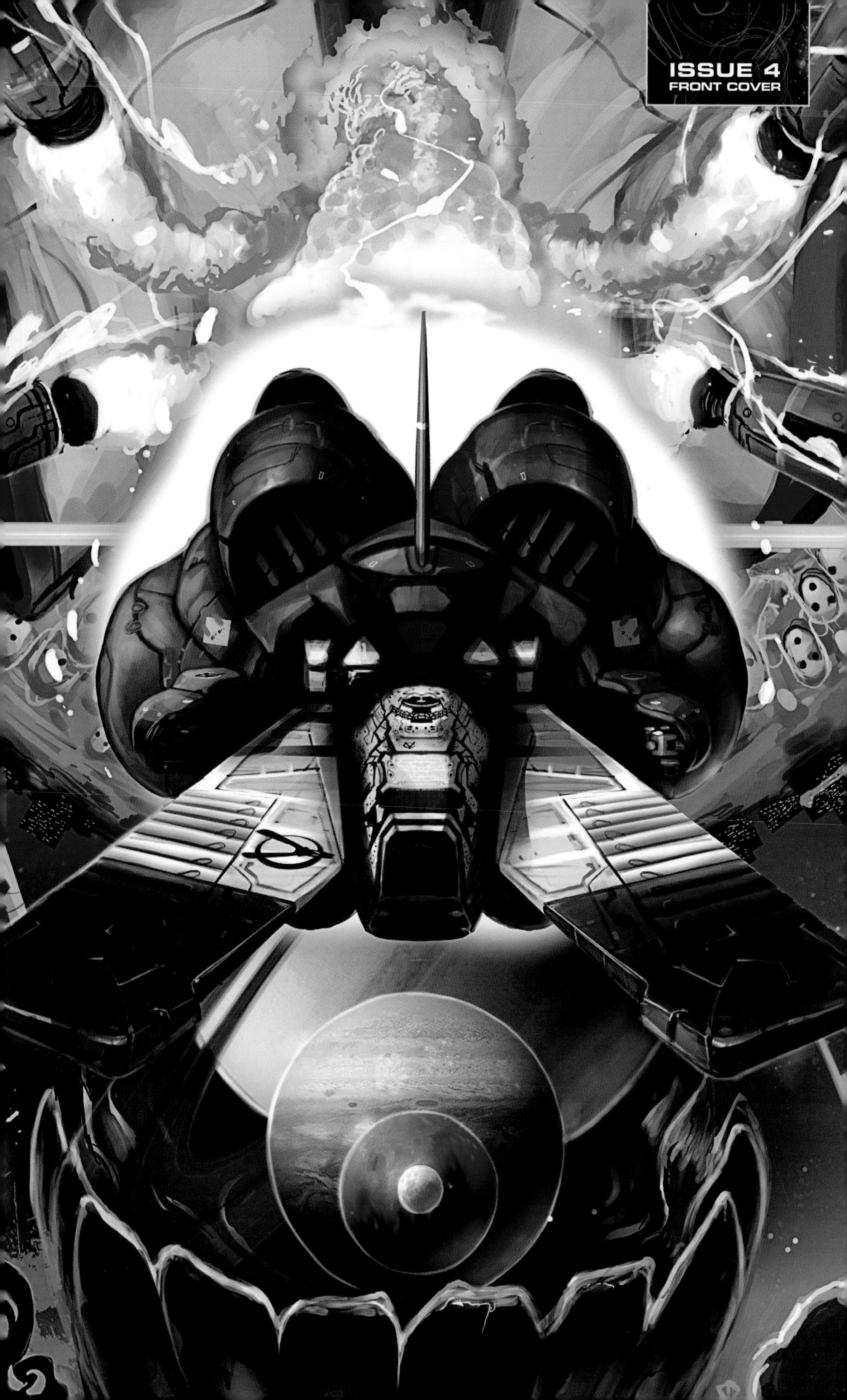

ISSUE 4
FRONT COVER

AFTERWORD

"Time isn't holding us, time doesn't hold you back…"

NEW YORK, New York, November 2010. 4:40 am, I sit in a very different place than where I was a year ago. I'm writing an afterword for a book I've grown accustom to feeling a certain amount of pride for. Just fifteen feet away from me, **Critical Millennium's** script is being tweaked with newly formed last minute touches that shake the soul. In another state away, the visuals are being concocted at a labored pace, continuing the energy that the first chapter started.

I was not a part of the birth or the creation of **Critical Millennium**, but I feel as if I always was. Something deep inside of **Critical Millennium** connects with a part of my unconscious brain, giving me that sort of "deja vu" feeling. Like I've danced with Coney once before in another time. But I've never traveled this road with Mr. Coney. Not yet…

But that's silly, isn't it?

BEEP – BEEP – BEEP –

CALIFORNIA, San Diego, Comic-Con July 2008. Among the bustle and buzz of my first San Diego Comic-con, I met a young talented upstart named Dan Dussault. He came to this convention armed and ready with a stapled sample comic, fifteen pages dancing in mostly hot greens and blacks. It was an impressive looking sci-fi book called **Critical Millennium**. The artist was so enthusiastic about how Archaia was going to publish the new creation that he was in whirlwind of words. –Speaking of words, where was his wordsmith? It seems that his counter-part, Andrew "Drew" Gaska, was roaming the con never to make an appearance at the Archaia booth. Our meeting would not happen until…

BEEP – BEEP – BEEP –

CALIFORNIA, San Diego, Comic-Con July 2010. Another Comic-con. It was one of the worst conventions I've ever had, with very few exceptions. I was uncertain about many things in my life and I had just completed my first graphic novel a week before I left for California. Train wreck doesn't even begin to describe the events of this con. On a rare night of this nightmare-con, me and my fellow Archaia friends went to an industry party. It was a very nice shindig with complimentary top shelf "helpers." I was in line to get ye' old con drink of choice (a gin and tonic) that's when a familiar face I'd seen around that weekend came to talk to me while I was in line. I wasn't aware of the gravity of our meeting. "You are joining us, aren't you?" I said instantly to him. It was then that Drew had become a part of our group. It wouldn't be until we headed out of the party that me and Drew would be laughing, skipping around San Diego like we were on the fucking yellow brick road, and chatting it up while the Godfather watched over us.

With the end of the con, I had an advance copy of **Critical Millennium** in my hands. I was excited but albeit frightened to read it. What if the writing was atrocious? The art was exceptional, but if the writing failed, my newly formed friendship with Drew would be compromised!

Compromises be damned! Ahead of me a six-hour red eye journey back to Florida with **Critical Millennium** in my hot little hands and a complimentary orange juice on my fold out tray. The next hour or so I'd be consumed with an amazing book that I had no idea would change my life.

BEEP – BEEP – BEEP –

NEW YORK, BLAM! Ventures, June 5th 2011. I came into the world of **Critical Millennium** in its 15th year of it being fused inside Drew's brain matter. It is finally leaping out of his unconscious and into the collective on a larger scale. I had the pleasure to watch it be constructed from issue 3 and to see all the labour that's gone into this project. You don't have to hear Drew ever say how much he cares about this project, it shows. From the moment on that flight where I started reading, I just knew that Gaska was infused with his work. There's a solid voice coming through and Dan's illustrious sequentials solidify the illusion of a living a breathing world.

From its innovative use of time as a structure and interwoven subplots, to its all too human characters-- you have rich and invigorating world that leaves with us with mystery and intrigue. We're on a journey for the stars filled with excitement---with the grim human experience of greed, power, excess, prejudice, consumerism, the dumbing down of culture (internet memes anyone?), a dying planet, and everything else in-between. This certainly isn't Gene Roddenberry's ideal future, but a hard look at where our culture is leading us now.

This is what good sci-fi does.

This is only the beginning. This book you hold in your hands is just a start, a glimpse into a vast universe and a story much larger in scope that will span the ages. It only took the first few pages to draw me in. Anytime you are given such an intense ending to a beginning, you just have me.

Perhaps that's all it took…

—Chandra Free

*Chandra Free is the artist/writer of **The God Machine**, published by Archaia. Chandra has also worked as an illustrator on **Fraggle Rock** (Archaia), a digital painter on **Sullengrey** (Ape Entertainment), and other freelance projects. Chandra currently lives in New York.*

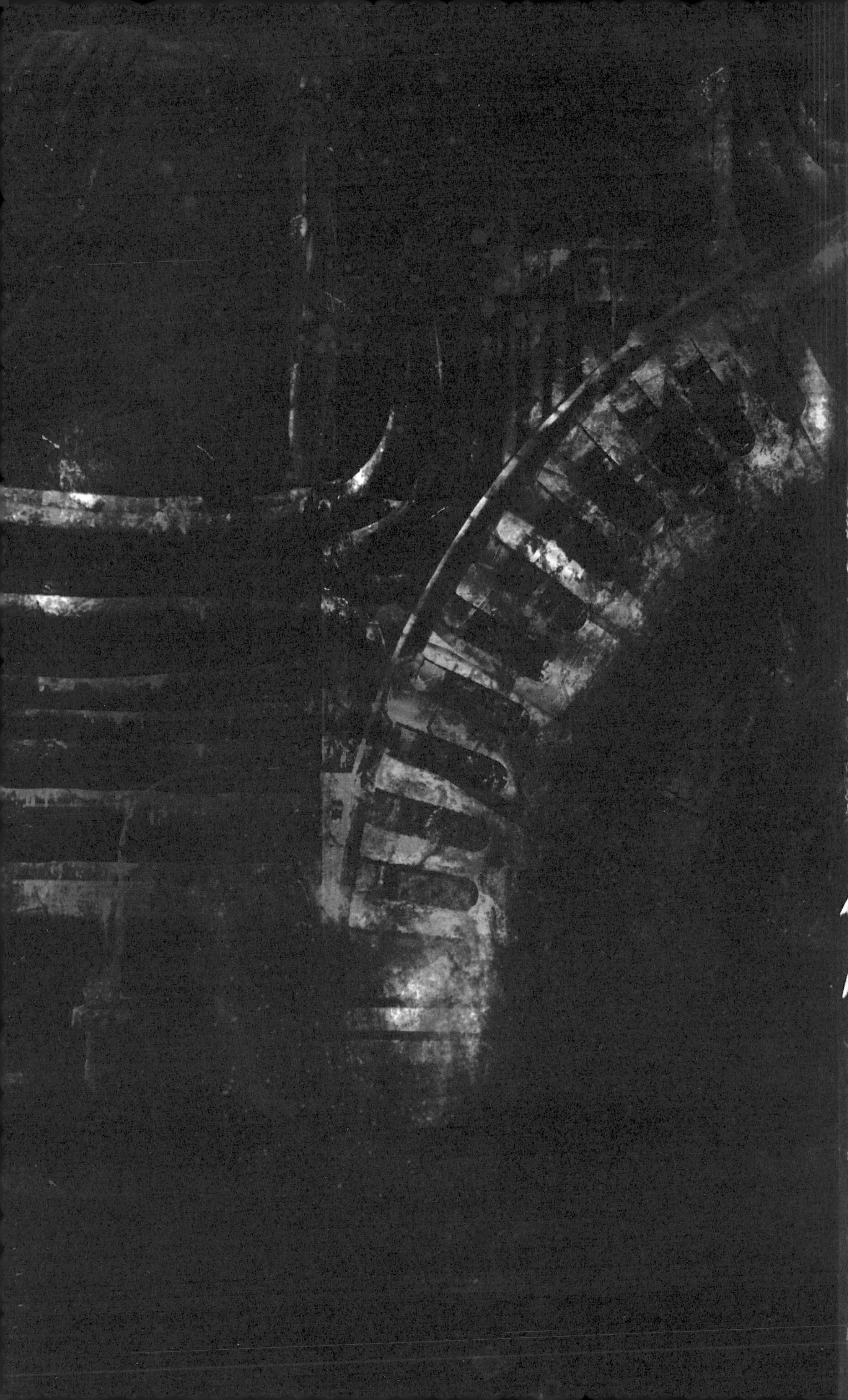